# The Renewal of Australian Schools

# The Renewal of Australian Schools:
## A Changing Perspective in Educational Planning

Edited by

**J.V. D'Cruz and P.J. Sheehan**

Second and Enlarged Edition

Published by The Australian Council for Educational Research Limited,
Frederick Street, Hawthorn, Victoria 3122.
November 1978.

Typeset in Photon Bembo by
ABB Typesetting Pty Ltd,
Collingwood, Victoria 3066.

Printed and bound by
Brown Prior Anderson Pty Ltd,
Burwood, Victoria 3125.

National Library of Australia Cataloguing-in-Publication data.

The renewal of Australian schools.

  2nd enlarged ed.
  First edition published as The renewal of Australian schools: essays on educational planning
  in Australia after the Karmel report.
  Bibliography
  ISBN 0 85563 185 6

  1. Australia. Schools Commission. 2. Educational planning — Australia — Addresses,
  essays, lectures. 3. Education — Aims and objectives — Addresses, essays, lectures. I.
  D'Cruz, J.V., ed. II. Sheehan, P.J., joint ed. III. Australian Council for Educational Research.

379.15'0994

Cover design by R. Clutterbuck.

*For the first time a young teacher enters a class independently, no longer sent by the training college to prove his efficiency. The class before him is like a mirror of mankind, so multiform, so full of contradictions, so inaccessible. He feels: 'These boys — I have not sought them out; I have been put here and have to accept them as they are — but not as they now are in this moment, no, as they really are, as they can become. But how can I find out what is in them and what can I do to make it take shape?' And the boys do not make things easy for him. They are noisy, they cause trouble, they stare at him with impudent curiosity. He is at once tempted to check this or that trouble-maker, to issue orders, to make compulsory the rules of decent behaviour, to say No, to say No to everything rising against him from beneath: he is at once tempted to start from beneath. And if one starts from beneath one perhaps never arrives above, but everything comes down. But then his eyes meet a face which strikes him. It is not a beautiful face nor particularly intelligent; but it is a real face, or rather, the chaos preceding the cosmos of a real face. On it he reads a question which is something different from the general curiosity: 'Who are you? Do you know something that concerns me? Do you bring me something? What do you bring?'*

Martin Buber

To our children

Sarah, Loretta, Mark and John

who must learn during their lives
to discern continuities and cope with change.

# Contents

## Contributors

**G.W. Bassett**          Professor of Education, Faculty of Education, University of Queensland

**Brian Crittenden**     Professor of Education, School of Education, La Trobe University

**J.V. D'Cruz**          Lecturer, School of Education, La Trobe University

**Denise Jepson**        Research Assistant, School of Education, La Trobe University

**J.P. Keeves**          Director, Australian Council for Educational Research, Melbourne

**J.K. Matthews**        Former Research Officer, Australian Council for Educational Research, Melbourne

**K.G. Mortensen**       Christian Brothers, Treacy College, Parkville

**P.W. Musgrave**        Professor of Education, Faculty of Education, Monash University

**C. Selby Smith**       Secretary, Committee of Inquiry into Education and Training, Department of the Prime Minister and Cabinet, Canberra, ACT

**P.J. Sheehan**         Senior Research Fellow, Institute of Applied Economic and Social Research, University of Melbourne

**Merv Turner**          Reader, School of Education, La Trobe University

**W.G. Walker**          Professor of Education, Faculty of Education, University of New England

**Doug White**           Senior Lecturer, School of Education, La Trobe University

# Introduction

# Culture and The Schools Commission in Educational Renewal

## J. V. D'Cruz and P. J. Sheehan

The five years 1973–78 have been years of amazingly rapid change on the Australian educational scene. Although there were some substantial developments in the years prior to 1972, our story starts with the election of the Labor Government on 2 December 1972 and the appointment of the Interim Committee for the Australian Schools Commission 10 days later. This committee reported in May 1973, the Schools Commission was established in December 1973 and large sums of additional commonwealth money flowed into Australian schools from 1 January 1974.[1] The program was initially directed at bringing about a sharp increase in resources available to schools, especially those with low resource use, although there were a number of other educational programs. As this program continued during 1974–76, many other developments were occurring concurrently. For example, there was increasing devolution of responsibility to individual schools in most state systems, while most Catholic schools were becoming more and more linked in centralized systems, and debate intensified about teaching methods, curriculum content and other matters. With the continuing movement into higher education, partly motivated by the individual's pursuit of higher occupational status, the educational credentials required for any particular job continued to increase. Most importantly, from mid-1974, the economic situation deteriorated rapidly, leading to rising unemployment, particularly among early school-leavers, and to a tendency on the part of potential school-leavers to use the schools as a refuge from unemployment. By the 1975–76 Budget, the Government was anxious to contain expenditure and this concern increased with the election of a Liberal-Country Party Government in late 1975. As a consequence, the volume of commonwealth expenditure on schools will be only marginally higher in 1979 than in 1975. But even so, the Schools Commission will disburse over $700 million in 1979 (by comparison with commonwealth spending on schools of $99 million in 1971–72) and has various programs designed to bring about change in Australian schools.

This volume aims to present an evaluation of the many facets of this ambitious renewal program and is a considerably enlarged edition of a volume published with the same title, under our editorship, in 1975. The current volume has four sections. Part I provides an analysis and assessment of the report of the Interim Committee for the Australian Schools Commission (the Karmel report) and nine of the 11 essays are reproduced unchanged from the first edition. To complete the assessment of the Karmel report, we have included in this section two important articles by Professor P. W. Musgrave

3

and by Mr Doug White, which are reprinted with permission from the *Australian Journal of Education* and *Arena* respectively. Part II considers developments subsequent to the establishment of the Australian Schools Commission and evaluates some of the programs implemented by the Commission over the 1973–78 period. Of the five essays included in this section, three are entirely new, while those by Dr Merv Turner and by Professor Brian Crittenden are expanded versions of articles appearing in *Arena* and the *Australian Journal of Education* respectively and are published with permission. We are grateful to the editors of *Arena* and to the publishers of the *Australian Journal of Education*, the Australian Council for Educational Research, for permission to publish material appearing in these journals. Part III contains an attempt by the editors to survey some of the main issues facing Australian schools five years after the initiation of the renewal program, while Part IV contains an extensive bibliography of writings relating to the Australian Schools Commission, prepared by Ms Denise Jepson of La Trobe University. We would also like to express our appreciation, for the editorial assistance given to us in the preparation of this volume, to Mr Don Maguire, Ms Jenny Lord and Mrs Jean Noel from the Australian Council for Educational Research and to Ms Lyn Yates of the School of Education, La Trobe University.

## A TURNING POINT IN EDUCATIONAL STRATEGY

Five years after the beginning of the renewal program, a multitude of issues remain unsettled. Many of these are discussed throughout this volume and some of the ones we see as most important are surveyed in the final chapter. In this introduction we would like to make some comments on two related issues of overriding significance — firstly, the state of the debate about educational renewal in Australia and of the renewal process itself, and secondly, problems and possibilities in the role of the Schools Commission in the changing pattern of educational policy.

Two facts dominate any consideration of the state of the educational renewal process in Australia in 1978. One is that, after dramatic increases in commonwealth funds provided to schools in 1974 and 1975 and large increases in state government finance for schools in the three years to 1976–77, the indications are that the volume of funds available for schools from both levels of government had stabilized by 1978 and 1979. For 1976 the Commonwealth Government allocated the same level of real recurrent resources to schools as in 1975 and reduced the volume of capital expenditure, for 1977 the Government provided total funds two per cent higher in real terms than in 1976, while in 1978 there was no change in the volume of expenditure but provision for a one per cent increase has been made in the guidelines for 1979 announced by the Minister for Education on 9 June 1978. Between 1973–74 and 1976–77 total expenditure by the State Governments on schools (excluding spending of Commonwealth Special Purpose Grants) increased by 87 per cent, implying an increase in real terms of about 20 per cent. But at the Premiers Conference on 22 June 1978, the States were severely squeezed, total commonwealth payments to the States for 1978–79 increasing by only some five per cent, in spite of an expected rate of inflation of seven to eight per cent. Thus the period of substantial increases in the volume of state government resources being devoted to schools must have come to an end and, given the policies of the present Commonwealth Government towards expenditure and towards the budget deficit, continued financial frugality by all levels of government seems inevitable. In short, the financial aspect of the renewal program, in the shape of rapid increases in the volume of resou: ces devoted to schools, is over.

The second relevant fact is that, after five years of intense activity in the educational field, there remains considerable unease about the health and direction of Australian education. Indeed, in its April 1978 report, the Schools Commission goes so far as to speak of 'uncertainty and ambiguity about authority, goals and processes' which 'none, whether administrators of systems and schools, teachers, parents or the Commission itself, can stand aside and allow . . . to continue'.[2] This continuing sense of unease reflects many factors of course — the re-thinking prompted by the fundamental change in the past five years in Australia's economic circumstances and the rise in youth unemployment, changing social attitudes and the continuing clash between progressive and traditionalist models of society and of education, and so on. But as we argue below, some major part of it would seem to be ascribable to the nature of the renewal program which has been attempted in Australian education over the past five years.

## CHANGING EMPHASES IN THE RENEWAL PROGRAM

It is evident that any assessment of the orientations of the Schools Commission cannot be divorced from those of its predecessor, the Interim Committee. In 1978, the Commission is still attempting to carry out the basic strategy for the renewal of Australian schools which was initially sketched by the Interim Committee in 1973, although emphases are changing with changing circumstances. In the main, the Interim Committee's strategy involved a concern in three general areas — firstly, a concern over inadequate levels of resources in most schools and over equity in resource standards between schools; secondly, a concern over processes of decision-making; thirdly, a concern over the purpose and content of schooling. These concerns have become the three successive major thrusts of the Schools Commission's own strategy for renewal. From 1973 to 1977, the Commission's efforts were concentrated in trying to increase the resource standards of schools in general, with positive discrimination in favour of those in most need. In 1978, the Commission reports that, with some qualification, these resource targets have been reached and, as argued above, the era of significant increases in overall resource levels in schools is over. A second, and current, phase of the

Commission's work is evident in a new emphasis in the 1978 report; the second thrust is directed towards facilitating participatory decision-making processes in identifying directions of needed change and improvement and in proposing appropriate action.[3] This participatory model had in fact originally surfaced in Chapter 2 of the Interim Committee's report.[4] And just as the participatory element had budded in the earlier reports[5], before blossoming in the 1978 report, one sees another, and third, thrust in the strategy which budded in the earlier report[6] and was alluded to in the 1978 report.[7] This third phase, which looks like blossoming at some future time, is curriculum development and, in particular, the development of a core curriculum. Indeed in the 1978 report, the Commission says that 'curriculum development and interpretations of meaningful learning will become a major focus at the national level in the coming period'.[8]

This general pattern of three successive thrusts in the renewal strategy — the concern initially being mainly with resource levels, moving gradually to more emphasis on the nature of decision-making processes in schools and school systems and only very recently to more emphasis on aspects of content and quality in education — raises obvious questions about the logical coherence of the whole strategy. Faced with discontent in the community about the quality of education in Australian schools, it is sensible to rapidly increase the resources available to schools only if one has reason to believe that the additional resources will be devoted to achieving certain specified and quality-oriented goals in schools. It is hard to see how the Commission could have had such reasons without attempting to articulate, and obtain some community consensus about, the educational goals to which the program was directed. And in its latest report, when the stress is substantially on participatory decision-making processes, the Commission regularly retreats from substantive issues about the content and practice of education to the form of the decision-making process.

Examples of this retreat from substantive issues about the content and practice of education can be drawn from the key Chapter 1 of the Commission's April 1978 report. In paragraph 1.1, the Commission mentions some of the social and cultural changes which have taken place in recent decades and argues that this raises questions such as 'What is knowledge for?' and about the traditional justification for selection of the content of the curriculum. In paragraph 1.2, the Commission mentions some of the questions posed by the change in the economic situation, by the rise in youth unemployment and by increasing credentialism. It comments that 'what useful response the schools might make to this situation or indeed its relevance for education in general is by no means clear'. These are certainly fundamental sets of issues, but after being raised they are not discussed at all, in either this chapter or in the report as a whole. The chapter in fact is devoted to the movement towards greater devolution of decision-making. However desirable this maximizing of the democratic process of decision-making may be, there is surely no reason for thinking that adequate national approaches to either of these sets of issues will emerge from a move to more participatory processes alone. In respect of such issues, it is hard to escape the conviction that the Commission has abdicated from a vital leadership role.

The Report of the Interim Committee had argued for a common curriculum that would promote basic skills for participation in society, an introduction to 'a variety of leisure pursuits' and a core element in the curriculum geared to 'the acquisition of skills and knowledge, initiation into the cultural heritage, the valuing of rationality and the broadening of opportunities to respond to and participate in artistic endeavours'.[9] The 1978 report of the Commission now serves notice that 'Curriculum development and interpretations of meaningful learning will become a major focus at national level in the coming period with the Curriculum Development Centre'.[10] This report also indicates that over time the Commission hopes to move the balance of its funding away from the simple provision of resources towards the support of projects which attempt to adapt schools to individual and social needs 'within a framework which accepts the importance of knowledge, skills and understandings in enabling people into controlling their own futures'.[11] These are only the barest hints of what it means to work up an educational framework within a cultural perspective and what such a framework might include, but it is to be hoped that they indicate that the Commission is now prepared to seriously approach the many substantive issues of the goals and content of education and of the quality of educational processes which cry out for attention in the Australian context. After five years of concentration on resource levels and on the form of decision-making processes, we believe that Australian education urgently needs leadership on issues of quality and content. The next section of this introduction makes some suggestions about the direction that leadership might take.

## CULTURE AND CONTENT IN EDUCATION

As indicated above, the history of the renewal process shows a disturbing tendency to veer towards the externals of the educational situation, whether in terms of a concentration on resource provision or on the character of decision-making processes or in some other way. Given this tendency, some recent signs suggesting that the third phase, which focuses on curriculum development, could be also diluted by a concentration on matters of form rather than of substance are disconcerting. For example, in relation to the question of a core curriculum, there is a danger that this may be reduced to the specification of a basic grid of skills which education should seek to provide. To take another example, in the 1978 report, the Commission raises the issue of how secondary schools should adjust to changed economic circumstances, and give two alternatives: we might revert to early selection so as to move some students into special work programs for the poorly qualified or we might put greater emphasis in schools on knowledge of job options and actual work conditions.[12] Both of these examples — the skills approach to core curriculum and the alternatives about the response to a new labour market situation — seem to us to be disastrously superficial responses to fundamental issues.

A new emphasis on quality and content in the renewal program must go back to basic issues about the goals we seek in schools. While there are clearly differences within the community in this area, at an appropriate level of generality and comprehensiveness the differences may be less destructive than often feared. All human societies possess as a matter of necessity a cultural basis, including some shared ideas and patterns of thought, a set of social relationships and functional social structures involving both work and communication between individual and groups, and some value systems, which impose patterns of relative importance and acceptability on thought and action. All societies also possess some means of introducing each new generation into their culture, be it a simple combination of informal instruction and learning by living in a communal situation or the relatively complex processes used in contemporary industrial society, ranging from learning in the nuclear family situation, from the media and in communities such as churches and clubs to many years of attendance at formal education institutions. Education as initiation into the living culture of a community has many important aspects, of which we would stress five here.

1 In this discussion, the culture of the human community is to be defined as the patterns of shared ideas, feelings, values, relationships and meanings which are common to that human community. In any community some such patterns must have continuity; it is necessary for the existence of a society or a culture that some patterns extend beyond the present moment and have some extension in time. These ideas, goals and meanings are also logically more fundamental than the institutions and structures in a society, for structures exist to serve certain purposes or to express a given perceived meaning and the structures which best serve that purpose or express that meaning may change at any time. Culture in this sense must be transmitted through education, while it is also the source of critical ideas about education. From this perspective our objections to an entirely school-based curriculum would be twofold: firstly, those who have the responsibility in the school to autonomously determine curriculum may not accept this conception of education, so that for this reason the school will fail to initiate the students into the culture; secondly, given that there is no proclaimed consensus within the society, shared in common by all the schools, about the crucial elements of culture, then even if schools share this view of education, they may fail to initiate their students into a *common* culture. That is, given the lack of explicit consensus about the central elements of a common culture, the 'cultures' into which schools initiate their students may touch only at random, if at all.

2 The forms of understanding which *any* individual needs are as wide as life itself; they include that which is necessary to know and to some extent control the world (work, etc.), that which is necessary to know and live with other human beings and to recognize the tension between the needs

of self and of society, that which is necessary to enjoy oneself in a satisfying way and above all that which is necessary to give some meaning to life. These types of understanding will be developed and systematized to various degrees in various cultures, but they will inevitably play some role in each person's life.

3 Work, in the sense of regular activity contributing to the society's functioning, would seem to be integral to any society. Hence, preparation for work is part of any initiation into a culture and work is, or ought to be, the individual's personal commitment to the productive endeavours of that culture. This perspective implies that preparation for work can neither be left out of nor dominate education and that work itself is one of the things to be understood in relation to the whole society. It also implies that there need be no basic conflict between education and the promotion of skills of literacy, numeracy and rational analysis, although these must be seen as instrumental to achieving the wider purpose of initiation into culturally shared meanings. Further, this view implies that labour should not be separated from an understanding of its personal and social purposes.

4 No culture can treat every activity as of equal importance, nor regard every possible action as equally acceptable. Inevitably, priorities are set up and preferences are established between different actions, in terms of the perceived meanings of, and goals for, life in the culture. Thus initiation into value systems and into moral judgments is an essential feature of education.

5 One of the fundamental commitments of our culture is to enhancing the individual's ability to assess reasons for competing claims and to developing alternative moral and cognitive perspectives. Consequently, an important feature of education as initiation into *our* culture is learning the ability to distance oneself from any given aspect of the culture, to step back to assess and pass judgment on that aspect of the culture. This act of distancing is based on the normative framework one seeks, on the possession of relevant knowledge and on developed skills of reasoning.

Crises in a society put pressure on such a conception of education, for example by leading to a potentially unbalanced heightening of emphasis on one aspect or another. At the present time in Australia, the problems generated by the economic situation and by high levels of unemployment of youth are leading to demands for direct work training to have a greater role in the schools or for schools to place greater emphasis on job education. It is undoubtedly true that recent economic trends necessitate a fundamental re-thinking of the position of preparation for work in Australian education but it is crucial that such a *re-thinking* take place instead of a simple automatic reaction in favour of greater emphasis on work-oriented programs. For example, with appropriate planning it may be possible to develop work experience programs which, as well as providing students with information about jobs, are also educative in a broader socio-cultural sense, which lead students to reflect on the world of work and drive them back into the reflective educational process in search of further understanding and skills.

Similarly, the growing cultural diversity of Australia and the breakdown of many of the sources of unity within Western culture are leading to growing emphasis on content-neutral skills. One expression of this is the view that a core curriculum can be defined and developed in terms of a grid of necessary skills alone, without any reference to forms of knowledge or the value systems in which these skills might be imbedded. Again, this move to dominant emphasis on skills seems to us to be a way of dodging the central issues, by raising up one aspect of education to a central position. Initiation into a culture is inevitably initiation into at least some of the thoughts, attitudes, values, feelings and behaviour of that culture and the acquiring of abilities involved in thought, feeling and action must be mainly developed through grappling with some of the content of that culture. To talk only of skills does not resolve problems arising from uncertainty or differences in the community about what content should be taught; it involves a substitution of a technical arrangement for that direction and coherence which in other times would flow from shared cultural meanings; and it simply involves ignoring the fact that some content will be taught and learnt in each educational situation.

The approach to education hinted at here may not be acceptable to all Australians. Our central point, however, is that the Schools Commission can no longer avoid

1 thinking seriously about general issues concerning the nature and quality of education in Australia;

2 seeking the views of various sections of the Australian community on these issues, tempered by an analysis of the major streams of continuity in Australian culture; and

3 basing its renewal program on an explicitly formulated view of what it seeks to achieve in terms of the quality and content of Australian schooling.

This need not be a recipe for mere abstract theorizing. Thus, the project to develop a core curriculum, if founded on an analysis of the intellectual, practical and value aspects of our common culture rather than on the search for a grid of skills, could, in our view, make a major contribution to improving the quality of Australian education. Many of the Schools Commission programs, such as the Disadvantaged Schools Program, the Innovations Program and the move to greater devolution of authority to the school could be usefully included and expanded in the context of a content-based strategy. And the problem of youth unemployment cries out for a general re-thinking of the relationship of education and work in Australia and for specific programs based on the results of that re-thinking.

## THE FUTURE OF THE SCHOOLS COMMISSION

With the end of the period of dramatic increases in the volume of finance available for education, the role of a Schools Commission which based its renewal program mainly on such financial increments is far from clear. And as the Commission does not have administrative responsibility in relation to any school systems, there is a limit to what it can do to promote greater devolution of decision-making in education. When one adds the point that some of its recent financing proposals have not met with widespread acceptance either in the community or in the Government, it is clear that the future of the Schools Commission, as a body seeking renewal in Australian schools, is in doubt. While we argue (as above) for significant changes in the approaches and emphases of the Commission, we would regard any major truncation of the Commission as a most retrograde step for Australian education. In the late 1970s concern about the quality and direction of Australian schooling is even more widespread in the community than it was in 1972, in spite of the big increases in expenditure which have taken place in the intervening period. Governments would be seriously in error, in our view, if they used this fact together with financial stringency as reasons for killing the renewal program, perhaps by reducing the Commission to a purely financial body. Rather, what this fact shows is that there is an urgent need in Australia for a body to think and consult about the nature and quality of education in Australia and to develop policies based on the results of this thought and consultation. The Schools Commission, in conjunction with the Curriculum Development Centre, could fulfil such a role.

## Notes

1 The major reports of the Schools Commission referred to in this introduction are:
Australia. (1973). *Schools in Australia. Report of the Interim Committee for the Australian Schools Commission.* (Chairman, P. Karmel). Canberra: AGPS.
Australia. Schools Commission. (1975). *Report for the Triennium 1976–78.* (Chairman, K. McKinnon). Canberra: AGPS.
Australia. Schools Commission. (1978). *Report for the Triennium 1978–81.* (Chairman, K. McKinnon). Canberra: AGPS.
For a comprehensive guide to references relating to the Schools Commission, see below, Denise Jepson, 'The Australian Schools Commission — A Bibliography', Chapter 17 of this volume.
2 Australia. Schools Commission. (1978). op. cit., para. 1.27.
3 ibid., para. 1.24.
4 Australia. (1973). op. cit., Chapter 2.
5 loc. cit. See also Australia. Schools Commission. (1975). op. cit., Chapter 11.
6 Australia. (1973). op. cit., paras 2.21, 3.23.
7 Australia. Schools Commission. (1978). op. cit., paras 7.17, 9.9.
8 loc. cit.
9 Australia. (1973). op. cit., para. 2.21.
10 Australia. Schools Commission. (1978). op. cit., para. 7.17. The Curriculum Development Centre (CDC) was formally established by a separate Act of Parliament in 1975, *inter alia*, to devise and develop school curricula and other educational material. Since its foundation, the CDC has initiated various curriculum projects, including the Core Curriculum and Values Education Project. Inquiries about the CDC may be directed to — The Director (Dr Malcolm Skilbeck), Curriculum Development Centre, P.O. Box 632, Manuka, ACT, 2603.
11 ibid., para. 2.76.
12 ibid., para. 1.3.

# I.  The Karmel Report

Overall Evaluation

# 1. Arguments and Assumptions of the Karmel Report: A Critique

## Brian Crittenden

It would be unfair to treat the Karmel report as though it were a rigorously argued philosophical account of educational theory. In a remarkably short time, the members of the committee responsible for the report prepared a broad range of detailed proposals for a new and large-scale initiative by the Federal Government in the financing of primary and secondary schools in Australia. As the terms of reference show, this was the precise scope of their task. However, as the members of the Committee themselves realized, they could hardly proceed intelligently to this task without some reflection on the nature of education and what the role of the primary and secondary schools should be.[1] They acknowledged that policy on the allocation of resources would inevitably have repercussions for future educational practice.[2] But, quite correctly, they did not want the current of influence to run in this direction; they agreed that issues of educational value should shape the financial decisions. As a consequence, the report does show sensitivity to the underlying conceptual and normative questions of educational theory.

However, due perhaps to the exigent political circumstances, the report does not make any contribution of its own to the understanding of these questions. For the most part, its theoretical views on education are derived from a variety of familiar sources (for example, the Plowden Report) and are usually expressed in a very compressed fashion without being drawn together into a carefully developed synthesis. Although the members of the Committee deserve praise for stating explicitly the educational assumptions that underlie their financial proposals, the fact remains that the educational theory embodied in the report hardly goes beyond the statement of assumptions. I do not intend to suggest that, in the circumstances, the Committee should have been expected to go much further — although, given the tendency for financial policies to call the educational tune, it is regrettable that there was not more time for a critical examination of the assumptions. What I wish to stress in the present context is that, while there are significant philosophical assumptions and implications in the Karmel report, the document itself does not engage in any sustained theoretical argument. The comments that follow are made in awareness of the report's immediate concern with financial proposals and the piecemeal character of its educational theory.

## THE NATURE OF EDUCATION

Although the report gives considerable attention to the socio-economic consequences of schooling, it is also clearly interested in the quality of what schools do in the name of education. In fact, at a number of points in the report, an appeal is made to a minimum acceptable level of educational attainment in our society as a criterion of differential financial grants. While there is no systematic account of what education is thought to be about, at least part of the picture can be constructed from elements scattered throughout the report.

Following its terms of reference, the report is, of course, focused on the systematic process of education that is conducted in the primary and secondary schools. In the generality of its comments, it seems to be assuming that most people have a fairly clear and commonly shared idea of what education includes in the context of these institutions.

Without attempting to work out the many internal tensions that are involved, the report tries to find a place for most of the conflicting interpretations of the role of the school at the present time. The school is to be an instrument of socialization and a crucial agent in promoting social and economic equality. At the same time, schooling should be an enjoyable experience for its own sake, the values dictated by the marketplace should be resisted, and the activities of education should be regarded as constituents in the quality of human life. The school must be responsive to the needs and interests of the individual and the group (both the local community and the nation). But it also has certain special functions: 'the acquisition of skills and knowledge, initiation into the cultural heritage, the valuing of rationality and the broadening of opportunities to respond to and participate in artistic endeavours'.[3] In performing these functions, the school must not, however, ignore 'the importance of confident, self-initiated learning and of creative response'.[4]

While all these elements may have a legitimate place in a theory of education, the question is how they are to be inter-related, what priorities are to shape the overall pattern. Despite an ample sprinkling of progressive, and even radical, educational rhetoric, it seems that the report really wants to interpret the role of the school primarily in terms of those 'special functions' quoted above. It claims, for example, that a distinct institution is required for the transmission of 'more abstract sophisticated skills'[5], and that this is the unique and specific function of the school.[6] I believe that the report is correct in interpreting the *main* purpose of the school in this way. However, given this interpretation, it would then be necessary to examine several other questions. For example, one would have to consider various practices and institutional arrangements that claim to be alternatives to the school, in which the specific functions of the school might have some place but would not be the main interest. It would also be important to explore the relationship between means and ends in the practice of education, and to examine in particular how proposals for educational reform or innovation relate to each. For instance, the claim that schools should respond to the felt needs and interests of children has subtly changed in the recent history of education from being a prescription for the manner and means of schooling to being interpreted as the determinant of its ends.

The distinction and connection between the means and ends of schooling is of special importance for the argument of the report because it strongly encourages a diversity of practices aimed at achieving a common outcome. In the present context, I wish to refer specifically to the report's emphasis on a common curriculum and educational achievement. This is a crucial element in the general structure of the argument developed through the report; although, as we shall see later, when the report comes to the point of deciding the criteria for differential grants, it shifts to other ground. Here, again, the report lacks specificity. It claims that for the period of compulsory attendance all schools should aim at the same educational outcome.[7] It seems to have in mind three main aspects: (1) basic skills for participation in society and for later re-entry, if desired, to further formal education; (2) a comprehensive core curriculum (presumably including the range of learning activities already referred to as 'the special function' of the school); and (3) an introduction to 'a variety of leisure pursuits' (see paragraphs 3.23 and 9.7). But there is no concrete illustration of what these aspects include. To suggest such criteria as what is necessary for 'full participation in our society' or what is appropriate to 'the social and individual needs of Australians at this point in time' is not very helpful.[8] Not only must we decide what the needs really are, but which ones the school should be expected to satisfy.

In addition to its references to a *common* curriculum and educational outcome, the report also emphasizes the objective of *equality* in this common outcome. I shall return to the report's policy on equality of opportunity later. Here, the point is that the report envisages a 'more equal basic achievement'[9] or at least a 'common minimum standard'.[10] But there is no clear indication in the report of just what the standard of basic achievement, to which everyone in the society should be enabled more or less equally to attain, is supposed to be. At one point, the report mentions 'capacity for independent thinking' as something everyone should acquire.[11] This leaves unanswered the question at what level the capacity for independent thought constitutes a 'common minimum standard'.[12] In summary, the report's view is that 'up to a certain level of performance' there should be no difference in the educational ends to be achieved.[13] It specifies no criteria for identifying or elaborating this level of performance.

In this first section, on the general nature of education, I have been commenting on aspects of the topic that are addressed in the report itself. I shall close by drawing attention briefly to some significant omissions.

  1 The report uses 'school', 'schooling', and 'education' without attempting to map out the differences and connections among these concepts. In referring to the school as a social institution (or physical place), we should distinguish what counts as schooling from among the many activities that the school does or can engage in (as we have seen, the report in fact applies this distinction). The task of determining what belongs to

schooling involves normative as well as descriptive criteria. It is also necessary to mark out schooling as an educational process from activities that belong to education in a much broader sense, and to take account of the dual use of 'education' in referring to both a process and an outcome.

2 The report takes for granted the present practice of compulsory school attendance. Although it supports the development of opportunities for education at any stage in life, it sees the practice of continuous schooling of children and adolescents for 12 years (or longer with the growing popularity of pre-schools) as being desirable. It believes that 'schools should offer a sufficiently relevant and attractive program to encourage students to stay to the end of the secondary schooling'.[14] The report favours a break from schooling at the end of the secondary stage, but does not consider the arguments of Paul Goodman and others for a radical reduction in the years of compulsory school attendance and the development of a variety of alternatives to continuous schooling during adolescence.

3 While the report discounts the feasibility of providing adequately for education without a distinct institution for this purpose, it does not give attention to another and quite different sense of 'deschooling', namely, the disestablishment of the school in the general social and economic order of our society. The analogy, which Illich has made popular, is, of course, between the role of the school system in contemporary industrial society and the established church in the Middle Ages. The failure to discuss this issue is significant in view of the report's endorsement of the part played by the school in promoting social and economic equality. The authors of the report could reply that their task was to make recommendations for immediate action, taking account of the actual situation. While this is so, and while there may perhaps be good reasons why the school should continue to be one of the main avenues of socio-economic advancement, the fact remains that the policy of funding suggested by the report reinforces the 'establishment' role of the school.

## SCHOOL AND COMMUNITY

Although the report provides a blueprint for a massive expansion of the Commonwealth Government's activities in relation to primary and secondary schools, its authors warmly support decentralized administration, local initiative and decision-making, and a close mutual involvement of each school and its immediate community. It is not impossible, of course, to work out a satisfactory balance between central and local authorities. The procedure of the report itself provides one illustration. It has decided what the major priority areas are to be, but has left the detailed decisions of allocation within each area to 'people actively associated with planning and operating the schools'.[15] How close this brings the decision to the local schools depends on whether the schools are already part of an administrative system, and on the size of such a system.

A confusing, and perhaps inconsistent, aspect of what the report says about responsibility for decision-making is that in certain places it seems to adopt a contemporary radical view on the virtual autonomy of each local community to determine the appropriate form of education for its members (see, for example, pp. 10-11, 112). I do not believe the report as a whole gives grounds for the suspicion that it is knowingly promoting this ideal of local autonomy in order to provoke the breakdown of intermediate levels of school organizations in Australia and thus make the local school and its community the more easy victim of manipulation by the central government.[16] However, I believe that the report is uncritical and misleading in employing the language of grass-roots community control of education. It is uncritical because it fails to examine the relativist consequences there may be for the interpretation of knowledge and education if local group autonomy is taken seriously, or the largely illusory character of independent, self-contained local committees in the highly industrial and urban Australian society, or the tyranny and cultural narrowness that a genuinely independent community can impose on its members through its own form of education.

The report is misleading because it clearly does not believe in the educational autonomy of local communities. In the first place, as we have already seen, it favours a fairly substantial core curriculum for all schools. In the second place, it explicitly refers to aspects of centralized administration even in the context of talking about local control. Thus, it claims that with the devolving of authority, 'overall planning of the scale and distribution of resources becomes more necessary' in order to avoid 'gross inequalities between regions, whether they be States or smaller areas'.[17] It also suggests that certain services, such as facilities for the continuing education of teachers, 'will need to be organized centrally to serve all schools'.[18]

Whatever the original intentions of the report, it would be a dangerous situation, both from a political and educational point of view, if the dimensions of decision-making in education were reduced to the Commonwealth Government on the one hand and a vast multitude of local communities on the other. No doubt, the state educational bureaucracies need to be dismantled. But individual schools themselves and the large number of groups in the society that have a legitimate interest in their conduct would probably best be served if schools were organized in relatively independent regional groups. In this way, schools would at least have some protection against both the whims of local communities and the power of State and Federal Governments.

## DIVERSITY

The report expresses strong approval of diversity and experimentation in the forms of schooling. However, it also builds in a number of important qualifications. Firstly, as we have seen, the report restricts diversity during the period of compulsory school attendance to the means of schooling. It expects that, for the most part, all schools will be trying to realize the same educational outcomes. I believe that the report is correct in stressing a common range of distinctively educational objectives and in encouraging a diversity of teaching and learning procedures for achieving these objectives. It is deficient, however, in that it does not reflect a careful examination of this policy of diverse means for a common end. In the first paragraph on diversity (2.10), for example, the report seems to be saying that the purpose of schools is to satisfy present social and individual needs (an end that could vary substantially from one individual or group in Australia to another), and that for this reason a diversity of procedures is desirable. This line of argument is clearly not consistent with the report's emphasis on common educational outcomes. If we believe that there are certain educational attainments that are desirable for all members of our society, then clearly the point of procedural diversity is to take account of differences in abilities, initial interests, attitudes, social conditions and so on that affect a person's chances for such attainments. Once diversity in the practices of schooling is tied to common educational objectives, there are obvious limitations on the range of practices that can be justified. Given the report's interest in equality of educational achievement, the restraints on diversity must be even greater.

On this question of means and ends in education, the basic problem in the report is that it seems to treat the relationship as a purely contingent one. In fact, however, educational methods are, to a significant degree, logically continuous with the educational outcomes. If a person is to reach an adequate level of competence in thinking critically about art or politics or the scientific explanations of natural phenomena, the processes of teaching and learning by which he comes to this stage must also be informed by the relevant criteria of critical thought.

A second front on which the report hedges its policy of diversity is in relation to the development of non-government schools. While, in general, it encourages the co-existence of a variety of alternatives to the government system, it gives precedence to the principle of equality over diversity in dealing with what it describes as 'high standard non-government schools'.[19] I shall consider this decision in the context of the final section. But it is also clear that the proliferation of alternative schools that receive government grants will be constrained for the sake of economic efficiency and in order to ensure that 'the strength and representativeness' of the public system is not diluted.[20] The arguments (educational as well as economic) for certain standards that must be met by any group wishing to establish a publicly funded school are well known. However, it is by no means obvious why the report adopts the condition that the present 'strength and representativeness' of the government schools should be maintained. It is difficult to see how it can consistently hold this view and at the same time encourage the development of a wide variety of government and non-government schools. For if the freedom to diversify is genuine, then any expansion of alternatives to the public system must diminish the strength, and probably the representativeness, of that system.

## EQUALITY AND EQUAL OPPORTUNITY

The conceptual and moral questions about equality and equal opportunity are touched on very lightly by the report. As often happens in the discussion of these themes, the report mixes together elements of liberal and egalitarian interpretations of equality as a social value. It gives a generally accurate summary of the liberal view[21], which in effect treats the issue of human equality in terms of equal opportunity. Incidentally, I do not think this view necessarily assumes, as the report claims, that there is roughly the same proportion of academically gifted individuals in each social group. Allowing that the report itself makes this assumption, it seems to incorporate much of the liberal interpretation of equality as equality of opportunity, at least as far as individuals are concerned. In relation to higher education, for example, its objective seems to be that, through the school and other social agencies, environmental differences that affect an individual's chance of scholastic success would be counter-balanced so that each one's level of attainment would depend predominantly on native capacity. In this ideal scheme of things, given the assumption about the distribution of academic ability among social groups, such groups would come to be represented among university students in the same proportion as in the total population, and the average achievement in each group would be equal. Although equality is in this sense a consequence of applying the principle of equal opportunity, it should be noticed that it is strictly statistical and depends on the truth of the above assumption.

But the report also seems to lean towards a distinctly egalitarian interpretation of equality. It speaks in terms of equality among individuals in their actual educational achievement rather than simply in their opportunities for education. The position which the report itself finally takes is not entirely clear. It points out (in paragraph 3.22) the dangers of a simple-minded effort to achieve equal average outcomes among all social groups. But, as we saw in the first section, it does envisage a common range of educational objectives for the period of compulsory schooling which presumably would be attained in a roughly equal way by everyone. It seems, therefore, to favour a policy of unequal treatment, both in the allocation of funds and the methods of teaching and learning, in order to achieve an equal outcome — a favoured egalitarian approach. However, in various statements of the report itself, and in what it actually proposes, it comes finally to endorse a somewhat different policy. In the first place, it treats equality of outcome in schooling as the way of promoting equal opportunity for all children 'to participate more fully in the society as valued and respected members of it'.[22] As the report itself notes, it is 'to this limited extent' that the committee accepts the goal of equal outcomes.[23] But, of course, it has now subordinated equal outcome at the end of schooling to equality of opportunity in the life of the adult society. Secondly, the differential grants recommended by the report are intended to bring about overall *equality* in the conditions of schooling at least in relation to

23

the aspects included by the report in its formula. The egalitarian ideal of equal outcomes would require systematic inequality in the conditions of schooling.

Despite its references to equality of achievement over a range of common educational objectives, I believe that the report is really more intent on ensuring that, as far as possible, everyone in our society would attain by the end of the period of compulsory schooling a minimum desirable level of education in relation to the common objectives. The realization of this ideal, which seems to me a thoroughly defensible one, in no way implies equality of outcome among individuals. If I have interpreted the real intent of the report correctly, it is misleading for it to talk about the schools promoting 'a more equal basic achievement between children'.[24] The objective would be more accurately stated as an *adequate*, not an equal, educational outcome for everybody.

Apart from not knowing what the report would take to be a minimum desirable standard of education, I have lingering doubts about how broadly it interprets the educational ends that are to be common to all. In a last word on common educational objectives, the report refers to the difficulty of striking a balance between achieving them and at the same time paying due regard to the uniqueness of each child. It believes the balance can be effected if each child's achievement 'is related to a previous level of mastery, and if the range of educational activities open is wide'.[25] Given these conditions, the extent of the common curriculum is likely to be very restricted. Despite the report's earlier emphasis on a substantial range of common educational ends (to be achieved in many different ways), it finally seems to leave the door open for a narrow interpretation of the 'fundamental skills' for participating in society and sharing its culture.

## DISADVANTAGE

Closely related to this issue of common educational objectives is the question of how the report understands the concept of disadvantage. In the course of a few paragraphs, it alludes to what has become a complex and controversial area of social theory. The main passages are in paragraphs 13.7(c), 9.4–9.5, and 9.12–9.13. In the first of these paragraphs, the report refers to the claim that the failure of certain social groups to do well at school is due to the bias of schools and teachers in favour of middle-class cultural values. In relation to this and other claims (for example, stereotyped teacher expectations), the report enigmatically concludes: 'some of these allegations are both contentious and difficult to test; others are more firmly established'. One cannot tell from the context whether or to what extent the authors of the report believe that the schools are instruments of middle-class values. In any case, it seems that the only indication of what precisely these values are is given in the final sentence of the paragraph: 'emphasizing verbal and abstract skills and down-grading action and experience as ways of knowing'. This particular charge against the schools is ascribed by the report to 'more radical critics'. Are we correct in assuming that the report does not agree?

Whatever view the authors of the report may in fact hold, there are dangers in talking loosely about middle-class values and applying this class label to the practice of schooling. At the very least, it is important to distinguish values that are unique to a group in society (in the sense that they constitute defining characteristics of the group) and values that have general human currency but that happen at a given time to be highly prized by only one section of a society or the members of one culture. Without this distinction we are on the slippery relativist slope and it is difficult to see where the landslide would end. We would have to extend the language of class and cultural bias to the value of critical inquiry, political freedom, science, mathematics, the sanitation measures that have dramatically reduced disease in this century, and so on. The position of the 'radical critics' referred to above would be nothing more than an expression of feeling for one set of class biases rather than another.

In the later sections of the report, the authors point out that they are interpreting 'disadvantage' strictly in terms of material poverty.[26] While the children of the poor, for various reasons, suffer serious educational deficiencies, the report emphasizes that this does not imply that poor families are 'culturally or socially deprived in any general sense'.[27] What they lack are power, the material resources to combat adversity, and 'the kind of experience which is helpful to success in school and society'.[28] What this implies is that the culture of the school and the kind of education that is valued there reflect, or are compatible with, the values of the socio-economically advantaged groups in our society, while being alien to the cultural values of the poor. The report seems unwilling to suggest that the poor, as well as other classes in the society, lack humanly desirable knowledge and skills which under suitable conditions they might acquire through schooling. Hence, in order to be consistent, the report can defend its policy of additional resources for the schooling of the poor only on the pragmatic ground that the way to socio-economic advancement in our society depends on success in the kind of education that is rewarded in our society and typically valued in our schools. This view is stated explicitly at the end of paragraph 9.12. But then, this does not seem to be consistent with what the report has said about the distinctive role of the school in transmitting the 'more abstract sophisticated skills' and the desirability of a common curriculum that embraces the main forms of knowledge and art. Certainly it is not consistent with the report's emphasis on the lifetime opportunities for engaging in the process of education, not simply as a means to socio-economic advantage, but as worthwhile in itself and for the dimensions of quality it contributes to one's life.

The general policy advocated by the report in relation to the school and socio-economic disadvantage reflects a position on a number of largely empirical questions, about which there has been much debate. Some of these questions will no doubt be discussed by other authors in this volume. One of the most important relates to the effectiveness of the school, acting mainly on its own initiative, to offset the educationally hostile influences that may exist in a child's home and neighbourhood. Perhaps schools could be more effective than they have in fact been. But the majority of evidence is fairly pessimistic, and the report goes along with this view. On several occasions, it stresses the limited potential of the school as an instrument of social reform unless it works in close co-operation with other agencies (see, for example, paragraphs 2.17, 3.19, 5.2, 9.8, 9.10). The authors of the report agree that the problems of disadvantage (i.e. poverty) require a comprehensive plan of social action in which the school would simply have a part. Yet they feel that, until such a plan is effected, it is worthwhile to provide additional financial resources for schools in areas of poverty.

A curious feature of the report's argument at this point is that it seems prepared to grant, in the face of substantial evidence, that a compensatory schooling program will make no appreciable difference to the conditions of social and economic disadvantage.[29] Yet it feels that the policy can be justified on two other grounds: firstly, granted that children have to spend 10 or more years of their lives at school, they should have the opportunity to do what they find interesting in surroundings that are as pleasant as possible; and secondly, there is the chance that with additional funds schools may be able to break down the alienation with the local community that usually exists in disadvantaged areas.[30] While these objectives *may* justify special funds for disadvantaged schools, the fact remains that most of the report's case for differential treatment is argued in terms of the contribution that schooling can make to breaking the cycle of social and economic disadvantage.

There is an irony in the report's preoccupation with disadvantage identified as material poverty. On the one hand, while poverty and educational disadvantage are no doubt closely related, there is good reason to suppose that many children of the more affluent groups in our society also suffer from educational, as distinct from socio-economic, disadvantage, both in their home environments and in their schools. On the other hand, if the main objective is to remedy poverty rather than the deficiencies of our education, the weight of evidence tends to show that the school is not a very effective instrument. Perhaps the report should have examined the evidence for the view that simple income transfers are more effective in alleviating poverty than additional expenditure on education. In any case, before a decision can be made on the effectiveness of schooling in combatting poverty in Australia, it is necessary to know in some detail what the local causes of poverty are.

## NEEDS AND PRIORITIES

It is understandable that the report does not discuss the concept of need in a general way. However, it would have been useful for it to note the main senses in which 'need' may be used. In some contexts, it is equivalent to 'want', in others it has the sense of a moral 'ought', in others it refers to a condition or means without which something that is desired or desirable cannot be achieved. The report is largely concerned with 'need' in the third of these senses. As it points out, we cannot determine the needs of a school without reference to the purposes that schools are supposed to serve. The report also notes that what counts in practice as necessary rather than merely desirable is likely to reflect the level of a society's wealth.

A primary task of the committee was to make proposals for financial assistance to schools according to their needs. Hence, the report gives its main attention to determining the most appropriate criteria on which the varying needs of schools can be assessed. The method finally adopted by the report is to take as the standard the average cost of resources used in government school systems of Australia. The relative need of a school or system is then assessed by comparing the cost of its resources with the standard. Without attempting to debate the justification of this procedure, I wish to point out that it does not seem to flow on from the general argument developed in the report to this stage. As we have seen, the report argues that everyone in our society should be enabled to achieve a minimum desirable standard in a common range of educational activities. To this end, it urges a variety of procedures and proposes a program of differential financial assistance from the Common- wealth Government. However, the formula that is adopted does not reflect criteria of a minimum educational achievement or the condition that there should be certain common outcomes, nor does it contain any reference to purposes that the school is supposed to serve (which, according to the report itself, we must know if we are to assess what various schools need)..

Assuming that all and only those items included in the catalogue of resources are significantly related to the quality of education in the school, we still do not know, as the report acknowledges, that the quality of the resources is the same from one school to another or the relative bearing of each item on the quality of education. But we also do not know that the educational achievement of most students in the average government school reaches the minimum desirable standard, whatever it may be. If their achievement happens to be more or less, the report's formula, while it might be defended on a principle of fairness, does not accurately express the report's own stated intentions.

Although the report entitles one of its sections 'concept of priority', the main question it deals with is who decides on the priorities when there are many needs competing for limited resources. As we saw in an earlier section, the committee has designated a number of general priority areas, leaving the detailed application of funds to those who are more directly involved. In general, the areas chosen by the report reflect accurately its terms of reference and its basic objective of removing sharp disparities in resources available to schools.

In its justification of the priority areas, it seems to me that the report somewhat arbitrarily balances its concern for equality and quality. The dominant tendency of its argument is for a differential allocation of public funds in order to ensure, as far as possible, a minimum desirable quality of education for every member of our society. One would expect that issues of equality would be instrumental to achieving this minimum level of educational quality. It is not clear also why the report discards the criteria of relative need in relation to the priority areas it calls teacher development and innovation. At this point, it shifts from a concern for an improvement of educational quality on an individual basis to an improvement in the society as a whole. The report obscures the matter further by suggesting that innovation is the priority area that is justified primarily for the sake of quality[31], the main purpose of the others, presumably, being to promote equality. But if the report does in fact accept this simplistic division of labour between the interests of quality and equality, it should at least place teacher development, particularly in the absence of any criteria of relative need, as a contribution to quality in education. Whether the objective is the overall quality of education in the society or the enlargement of individual opportunities for a higher quality of education, the continual upgrading of the teachers' own general and professional education is probably the most crucial priority area.[32]

Insofar as innovation (the report's own candidate for advancing the quality of education) refers to systematic large-scale research projects, there is some chance that a significant contribution might be made. However, much more would need to be said than the report could reasonably be expected to say about the nature of educational research, the involvement of teachers in the process, the machinery for relating research to policy-making and to practice, and so on.[33]

I am less optimistic about the chances of the small-scale projects making much difference to the quality of education. The report uses the currently fashionable word 'innovation'. It defines it as 'the creation of change by the introduction of something new'.[34] As it stands, this account is inadequate. If we are talking about innovation that is educationally worthwhile, it is obvious that not any novelty will do. It must satisfy criteria of epistemic and moral value and of educational significance. The report refers to the evaluation of innovatory projects in paragraph 12.7. However, it is not clear what kind of assessment is to be made of proposals or of the progress reports that authors are to submit from time to time.[35] In terms of a person's own criteria, he may correctly claim that his project is succeeding, yet the success may not be of much educational significance. At the very least, the practical difficulties of accountability in the report's scheme must be severe. If the use of public funds in this way to encourage people to 'try things out' leads to no substantial gains in the quality of education, it may nevertheless help to promote other worthwhile outcomes of the kind mentioned by the report in paragraph 12.9. But, given the competition among various needs both within education and elsewhere in the society, the question remains whether our society has the financial resources for such largesse.

## PARENTS AND THE RIGHT OF CHOICE IN EDUCATION

The policy adopted by the report on the relationship between parents' choice in education and the allocation of public funds reflects several key aspects of its general argument. The report states that the committee 'values the right of parents to educate their children outside government schools'.[36] However, it claims that, if parents choose a school whose educational standard is at present clearly above the minimum desirable level, they should not be provided with public assistance to help them make their choice. The report argues for this view in the following way. Because the amount of resources is limited, there must be priorities in the spending of public funds on education. There are many schools (both government and non-government) below the desirable standard. Until these schools have been raised to this standard, they should receive all the funds available for public expenditure on education.

In the Australian context, it seems to me that this conclusion is not justified. It would perhaps be a different matter if all parents contributed directly to the cost of their children's education and all public funds spent on schools or as subsidies to parents took account of relative needs and differences in family incomes. But in our society, free schooling is provided from public funds for any parents who, regardless of their capacity to pay, choose the government school system. In this situation, one cannot consistently grant that all parents have a right of choice in the schooling of their children, yet deny that they are entitled to expect that a fair estimate of the cost of educating a child in the government system should be applied to the education of their own children, if they choose an alternative to that system. There are several factors that seem to be ignored in the report's argument.

1 There are government schools — fully supported by public funds — that are now above the minimum desirable standard of education. A particular anomaly of this situation is that there can be wealthy parents who happily send their children to a high quality government school at public expense, while parents of average income who choose a non-government school of comparable quality have no right, in the words of the report, 'to public assistance to facilitate this choice'.[37]

2 The report links the achievement of a desirable level of education for everyone to the period of compulsory schooling. But in arguing for priorities because of the shortage of financial resources, it does not consider whether the final non-compulsory years of secondary schooling in the government system should be fully supported from public funds. In this respect, an interesting development since the writing of the report was the introduction by the Commonwealth Government of free tuition in all public institutions of tertiary education.

3 The report itself claims that 'every member of the society has an entitlement to a period of education at public expense'.[38] It is not clear how it can then consistently argue that there should be no public funds spent on certain schools.

I think it would have been fairer and more compatible with the policy of diversity and freedom of choice that the report seems to encourage if it had supported some form of a voucher system.[39] Of course, as we saw earlier, the report's enthusiasm for diversity is tempered by its commitment to maintaining the 'strength and representativeness' of the government schools.

In focusing attention on what I take to be weaknesses in the educational and social theory of the report, I am not necessarily questioning the value of its practical proposals. Although they may not achieve just what the authors of the report intend, I believe that in general their implementation will substantially improve the material conditions of schooling for a large number of Australian children. In the exposition of its theory, the report is subject to a hazard that is common to documents of its kind. When a group of people try to speak as one voice on such a controversial and complex topic as education, there is bound to be curious compromise and ambiguity. At several crucial points in the report, one is reminded of the predicament of a distinguished person during the politico-religious controversy in Australia a few years ago: 'I am not on one side or the other, and I am not sitting on the fence'.

It might be claimed that what really counts is not the stated theory but the theory that is in fact implicit in the practical recommendations of the report. From one point of view, this claim is obviously true. However, I have taken the authors at their word when they say that financial decisions in education should be guided by criteria of educational theory and value, and I have tried to draw attention to important aspects of the report in which its statement of theory is vague or ambiguous or inconsistent, either within itself or with its practical conclusions. If there are these deficiencies, they will inevitably affect the administration of the economic program and the kind of influence it exercises on the practice of education. I do not wish to imply that it is possible to unite the conflicting claims of equality, diversity, and quality, for example, in a perfectly harmonious system. However, I believe a more satisfactory synthesis than we find in the report can be achieved. This might be one of the research priorities that the Australian Schools Commission should encourage. As the Karmel report itself acknowledges, 'in the longer run, consideration of the purposes and values of Australian education is of greater importance than any short-term accretion of resources'.[40]

## Notes

1 Australia. (1973). *Schools in Australia. Report of the Interim Committee for the Australian Schools Commission.* (Chairman, P. Karmel). Canberra: AGPS. p.4.
2 ibid.: 10.
3 ibid.: 14.
4 loc. cit.
5 ibid.: 13.
6 ibid.: 14.
7 ibid.: 12.
8 ibid.: 11.
9 loc. cit.
10 ibid.: 50.
11 loc. cit.
12 loc. cit.
13 ibid.: 93.
14 ibid.: 15.
15 ibid.: 52.

16 This seems to be the charge that Doug White makes against the report. (See Chapter 3 of this volume.) He is clearly opposed to the version of progressive education based on group solipsism and believes that the report supports this version because it leads to a fragmented and easily manipulated society.

17 Australia. (1973). op. cit.: 10.

18 ibid.: 11.

19 ibid.: 12.

20 loc. cit.

21 ibid.: 16–17.

22 ibid.: 23.

23 loc. cit.

24 ibid.: 11.

25 ibid.: 93–94.

26 This move simply shifts the question of meaning to the concept of poverty. Even when poverty is interpreted in purely economic terms, it may be measured in various ways: for example, in relation to the actual pattern of incomes in the society (such as incomes falling below a certain proportion of the national average), or on the basis of what is thought to constitute a minimum desirable standard of living. If one takes the first approach (a version of which seems to be adopted by the report), many of the poor in Australia would be among the reasonably well-to-do in many other countries. The second approach is also relative, to some extent, to the general material conditions of a society. However, in a country such as Australia it could give a quite different view of poverty from that of the first method.

27 ibid.: 93.

28 loc. cit.

29 ibid.: 95.

30 ibid.: 94.

31 ibid.: 126.

32 If this claim is correct, it raises serious questions about the possibility of improving the quality of education in a society bent on encouraging everyone to spend more and more time engaged in *formal* education (i.e., systematic learning in a more or less structured course of studies, under the guidance of teachers, in a distinct institution). How will the State of Victoria, for example, with its three and a half million people, find enough *competent* teachers over the next few years to staff its centres of early childhood education, its primary and secondary schools, its four universities, and its multitude of colleges and institutes now busily turning themselves into mini-universities? We need to take a much more parsimonious view of the kind of education that depends on schooling (especially in distinct institutions), and enlarge the opportunities for on-the-job training and continuing informal self-education.

At one point, the report suggests that the school might be the nucleus of a community centre (paragraph 2.20). If we are to break away from the tendency to school- and juvenile-fixation in our society, we need a more inclusive, more flexible, concept of a cultural centre. The school might well be associated, but given the cultural needs and interests of adults, there is no reason why it should be the nucleus.

33 A curious omission in the report's comments on research is any specific reference to university departments or Schools of Education. Here we already have a large number of people professionally trained and committed to research in education.

34 ibid.: 126.

35 Many of the projects in the recent list of grants for the innovations program (in Victoria, SP/29) do not seem to be innovative or concerned with testing the educational effectiveness of certain materials, procedures, etc. In many cases, funds are required for the implementation of existing practices, and usually the aim is to engage in an activity, not to evaluate it (for example, making films, providing a secretarial course at Year 12, establishing an information centre on migrant courses, running a holiday activity centre).

37 ibid.: 36. The Universal Declaration of Human Rights (1948) states that 'parents have a prior right to choose the kind of education that shall be given to their children'. (Article 26).

37 Australia. (1973). op. cit.: 12.

38 ibid.: 15.

39 An early version of the scheme was proposed by Milton Friedman in 'The Role of the Government in Education', *Economics and the Public Interest*, R. A. Solo (Ed.). New Jersey: Rutgers University Press, 1955, Chapter 9.

40 Australia. (1973). op. cit.: 5.

# 2. Changing Society: Some Underlying Assumptions of The Karmel Report*

## P. W. Musgrave[1]

*If administrators and politicians are going to play God with other peoples' lives
. . . they ought at least to get clear what the divine intention is to be.[2]*

## PLANNING SOCIAL CHANGE THROUGH EDUCATION

Mediaeval monarchs may have had god-like powers to change their whole kingdoms, but they rarely seem to have pursued consistent long-term policies of social improvement. Indeed, such policies may only be born of an economic surplus and, hence, may have grown more possible with the birth of capitalism. Certainly, for one reason or another, theorizing about social change became more common in Europe after the late eighteenth century. A crucial figure was Jeremy Bentham, whose method of social planning was somewhat pithily summed up in the words 'investigate, legislate, administer'. This prescription was behind the nineteenth century plethora of royal commissions in Britain and Australia — and in those days royal commissions were not a means of shelving problems, but usually led to action.

The natural successors of Bentham, though with an evolutionary socialist rather than laissez-faire aim, were the Webbs, whose offspring, the Fabians[3], still model their political method upon the Benthamite prescription. These two traditions of reform aimed not to change total societies tomorrow, but to move more slowly by giving attention to one sector of society after another. The conditions of labour in factories, of prisons, and of education all underwent change in Britain, and to some extent in Australia, in this way before 1900. The important point to notice is that at each stage this process was under the full gaze of the public through parliament. The investigation and the consequent legislation were debated, and the relevant minister's administration was subsequently openly evaluated.

During this century two administrative innovations have affected the means of achieving sectoral social change, particularly in education. The first occurred symbolically at the turn of the century, when in Britain by the 1899 Education Act a system of Consultative Committees was set up — to be renamed Central Advisory Councils by the Act of 1944. This system generated such famous reports as the Hadow, Spens, Crowther, Newsom and Plowden Reports. A statutory body of experts, working in a part-time capacity with the support of a small secretariat, reports to the responsible minister on sectoral issues. Such a body can be critical of the status quo and

*Reprinted from the *Australian Journal of Education*, **19** (1):1-14 by permission of the Australian Council for Educational Research.

recommend changes, although the minister need not act on the suggestions. The point to note is that the body is advisory, not executive. Since the 1950s, however, the urgency of the social pathologies of capitalist society, particularly in the USA, have prompted the second innovation, namely the creation of expert bodies with considerable independence who themselves undertake all three processes of the Benthamite prescription for sectoral social change. Examples in the USA are the Poverty Program and, in the educational field, Head Start.

The overall results of Head Start and similar large-scale programs have, however, been disappointing in comparison with smaller experimental projects. Partly this is due to the problems implicit in large-scale operations and partly to the difficulty of recruiting an even quality of keen staff throughout such massive programs. But in addition, there are important differences from the Benthamite prescriptions. Firstly, such programs rarely rest on specific new research, but usually on past academic work that may not be quite relevant and that is often of poor quality and even has very debatable implications — one may here cite the Jensen controversy. Secondly, many of these programs are not closely planned, so that development depends upon local issues or even personal whims. Thirdly, since aims are vague, comparative evaluation is almost impossible; the history of the evaluation of Head Start is a warning to all of this difficulty.[4]

The aims of any sectoral social change are not only important because they are crucial for evaluation. They also indicate the beliefs of the planners about where they see society to be today and where they want it to be tomorrow. Behind the aims which anyone holds for education, or any other sector of society, are a set of conscious or unconscious assumptions of an ideological nature. Underlying these assumptions will be a model of man, that is, a view about such issues as whether man makes his world or is made by it, whether man's capabilities are more influenced by genetic or environmental circumstances, and, perhaps most important of all, about whether man is innately good or bad. This model of man will strongly influence the model of society that is held, that is, the vision of the good society towards which planning is aimed. Both these models will be worked out in such social organizations as educational systems and in schools. In very oversimplified terms, a planner who believes in original sin will probably aim for a more traditional educational system than one who believes that man is innately good.

During the period from 1945 to 1965, broadly the period of attempted post-war reconstruction, planners put their model of society prior to their model of man. This was the age when economists spoke of 'human capital' and educational planners sought to increase the supply of highly trained or skilled labour. During this same period, sociologists, basing themselves on a long English academic tradition, developed the political arithmetic of social class chances. Largely as a result, planners suggested organizing schools so that educational opportunities would be equalized. During the mid-1960s a major ideological shift occurred, the cause and nature of which is still unclear. This was characterized by a movement to give priority to models of man over models of society. In this view, men must no longer be fitted to society; rather society must change to meet the personal needs of individuals. Two good indices, albeit interdependent, of this ideological tendency, which may be called radical individualism, are the rise of the 'hippies' and the recent student movements. These changes have been felt in Australia as elsewhere; yet it is remarkable that, when in 1973 the Labor Party set out to change what was seen to be the massive neglect of education by the Liberals during their 20 years of power, their initiative was in character (though not necessarily in rhetoric) fundamentally that of the 1950s and 1960s, and not of the more recent era of radical individualism. This can be seen if we examine *Schools in Australia*, the Report of the Interim Committee for the Australian Schools Commission, published in May 1973[5], more usually known as the Karmel report. This document forms the basis of the government's educational policy as it affects schools during 1974-5. After a detailed examination of this report as a case study of planning educational change, the discussion returns to the general problem of the means of achieving sectoral social change, more especially in education.

## THE KARMEL REPORT AND EDUCATIONAL CHANGE

### Model of society

The characteristically Australian demand for 'fair go's' has been particularly influential in past educational planning. Fairness has been

> confined to public schooling, and has been interpreted there as an equal and, in the main, uniform provision throughout the State for which each education authority is responsible (3.3).[6]

Certainly up to 1914, if not 1945, 'fair go's' applied on the whole only to what was then known as elementary education and not to secondary schooling. Educational concepts are, however, redefined by successive generations and this definition which was common throughout the world, was based on the aim of giving an equal share of the available resources to all. After 1945, in Britain, equality was interpreted in a meritocratic manner so that planners aimed to give equal opportunities to those of equal measured capabilities. This definition was less powerful in Australia than in Britain, but in Victoria the existence of schools like Melbourne and University High indicated an embryonic meritocratic system. More recently, equality in education has come to be defined in terms that would once have been seen as inegalitarian. 'More equal outcomes from schooling require unequal treatment of children' (3.19). The index of equality here is no longer input, but output; to use the concept associated with the Plowden Report, 'positive discrimination' has become the policy for the planners.[7]

Another facet of equality relates to the plurality of recognized social groupings within Australian society. Ethnic groups, both white and black, and different religious denominations are seen to have equal rights to exist. Rather oddly, one social category, for which many in the last five years have claimed equality, namely women, receives less mention in this connection in the report and is not included at all in the definition of disadvantage in the Schools Commission Act that directly resulted from the report.[8] This view of society as pluralist along specific dimensions extends to the continued toleration of non-government schools, which are largely religious in origin. 'Any variation from this position would, in the Committee's view, require a policy decision on the part of the Australian Government' (7.14).

In the vision of society assumed by the report, schools appear as 'less alienated from their communities than is now generally the case in disadvantaged areas' (9.9). Community involvement and devolution of decisions to schools are considered to be crucial aims for planning. Contemporary Australian society is seen as over-segmented. There is a connection here with the assumption of equality in a plural society. Many 'communities', whatever they may be[9], are to be given equality and power over their schools. Clearly there is a difficult tension here, since the cure for excessive segmentation is the encouragement of an identification with existing segments. The question of overall cultural, rather than sub-cultural, unity may have been begged.[10]

The model of society which the report assumes to be worthwhile for Australia in the 1980s would seem to be one marked by equality within a social system very similar to that existing at present, by the toleration of a wide variety of social groupings, including different religious groups, and by a firm-rootedness in local communities.

## Model of the individual

'A wide range of differences exists among individual children' (10.1) . . . 'the final outcome [of] developed ability . . . is the result of continuous and complex interaction between . . . genetic and environmental contributions' (3.18). Because of this view, attention must be given to achieving equal outcomes by planning for such categories as slow-learners and bright children. Above all, the assumption is that, since many of the differences in children on entering school can be attributed to a structural factor which is taken for granted, namely the unequal distribution of incomes in society,

> there are good reasons for attempting to compensate to some extent through schooling for unequal out-of-school situations in order to ensure that the child's overall condition of upbringing is as free of restriction due to the circumstances of his family as public action through the schools can make it (2.7).

However, the psychological model of man assumed governs the range of strategies of attack available. A genetic view of ability constrains the limits of compensation in a way that neither an environmentalist view nor an appeal to the hidden curriculum of the school does. The report's support for 'complex interaction' has it all ways, but its use of the difficult word 'compensate', despite a relatively lengthy discussion (9.10-9.12), demands some examination before an analysis is made of the report's administrative model for change.

Compensatory education has been questioned on a number of grounds. Recently Jencks has comprehensively reviewed much of the relevant literature and confidently asserted that since the school can do little to offset the inequality born in the unequal structure of capitalist society, attention should be switched from attempting to reform the school to the more radical alternative of changing the structure of incomes. On this view our only aim in schools should be to make them a joyful experience for their pupils.[11] As the report puts it, 'schooling . . . for all children ought to be enjoyable and fruitful in itself' (9.8). However, even if Jencks' use of statistics is beyond question, and that is not an easily answered matter, he still allows some, to me quite large, effects to the schools.

Recent sociological discussion of this concept has focused on the hidden values implicit in the whole idea of compensatory education. Deficits are to be made up, but against which criteria are they to be measured? Usually the aim is to match standards associated with successful pupils who are seen to be middle- rather than working-class and members of the 'Australian', rather than of the migrant or the black, cultures.

Language has come to be seen as central to any discussion of compensatory education. The work of Bernstein in London in the 1960s has led many people to see compensation largely in terms of a shift for disadvantaged children from a restricted to an elaborated linguistic code. Such a view has been increasingly questioned, however, following Labov's analysis, in a paper entitled 'The Logic of Nonstandard English', in which he demonstrates that black English in the USA can be seen as a language in its own right.[12] Yet the ability to operate only in such a language in contemporary American society is a social disadvantage even though it is possible to write, as two American anthropologists have done, 'A disadvantage created by a difference is not the same thing as a deficit!'[13] Such disadvantages are a part of contemporary social reality so that in the framework of the Karmel report countervailing action must be taken.

In a more absolute sense, Bernstein has written, 'The introduction of the child to the universalistic meanings of public reforms of thought is not "compensatory education"; *it is education.*'[14] Thus, if a code other than an elaborated one does not allow entry to full meaning, then the child should be taught elaborated code. In such instances, even if a claim is made that one is merely making an alternative available, a value judgment is operating that puts one mode of thought above another, and, since the correlation between speaking restricted code and being a member of the working class, though not perfect, is high, the mental slip to assuming the middle-class culture superior to the culture of the working class is easy, though unfortunate.[15] In addition, there is evidence to support the view that lower-class children learn more effectively under conditions of extrinsic motivation while middle-class children respond to intrinsic motivation.[16] Thus, the position is reached that, whenever a model of man is assumed that gives great weight to social circumstances in the genesis of individual differences, 'compensatory education' is a valid concept and may have to be undertaken differently for different social groups in any one society.

## The administrative model for change

Although commissions, usually to manage some economic function, have been appointed in Australia before, the report is firmly in the tradition of the post-war era, in that a Schools Commission is to be established, backed by a secretariat (13.11) and consisting of full- and part-time experts, whose members

> should be able to conduct its proceedings on the merits of the business before it, with its members not bound to any particular point of view on specific questions (13.6).[17]

Such a body

> cannot change society directly, but ... its influence must come through recommendations for financial assistance to school and school systems, and thus through the resources made available to schools (5.2).

Indeed, the minister should have power to act on 'the recommendation of the Commission, if the Commission thinks re-allocation is desirable in the light of applications made by non-government schools' (7.20). The experts can be seen to have wide powers over the manner in which resources for change are channelled to the schools in both the government and non-government systems.

At this point comparison can be made with experience in the USA. One of the key problems in implementing programs there has been a tendency to rely overmuch on arguments from rationality and to ignore the political dimension, whether in Washington or at the level of the local ward.[18] Yet in Australia, the central Schools Commission is seen as channelling resources to States through regional boards (13.8) in such a way that 'the direction of developments should be determined by those involved in and having close knowledge of particular schools and particular communities' (9.37). The direction of change is, then, largely at the mercy of local politics. The report rightly comments that 'the traditional process of change in Australian education ... [has] been characterized by the imposition of new policies from above on schools across-the-board' (12.2), so that projects have been

> ineffectual, ... [in part] because the people most affected have been made to feel that they are merely reacting to a particular policy or procedure instead of being actively engaged in formulating it (12.4).

Yet the more that faith is pinned on the local community, the more necessary will it be for the gods to leave their Canberran heavens and descend into the earthly political arena, though the politics played, at least in theory, if rarely in practice, need not be along the dimensions of party.

## Directions of change

The models of society and of man implicit in the report lead logically to recommendations relating especially to equality, plural groups and local involvement. Yet the report, whilst speaking of 'the planning of the strategic development of education on a national scale, as distinct from its centralized administration', can nevertheless claim that

> the Commission should concern itself more with providing incentives for the schools to move in one direction or another, than with delineating a particular model of precise development (13.2).

This picture of a Commission serving as the administrative mechanism for change without any policy which provides direction is belied, however, by the actual programs recommended.

The attempt to make 'the overall circumstances of children's education as nearly equal as possible' (14.3) is largely to be supported by four major programs costing $407 million out of the $467 million recommended for expenditure during 1974-5 (14.10). These programs relate to general recurrent grants to schools, general buildings grants, libraries, and grants to disadvantaged schools. One crucial assumption here is that, although diversity, often recommended using the rhetoric of alternative schooling (e.g. 'ways which enable a hundred flowers to bloom rather than to wither' (2.10)) is to be encouraged, schools are central to the purpose of education. (One can almost say that the report has successfully co-opted the rhetoric of community participation and alternative education to the contemporary structure of education in much the same way as industry has taken over jeans and pop music.)

> Because the Committee believes that schools have distinctive functions for which no other institution in society is specifically responsible, it is considered important that these functions be not only retained but exercised with increasing success (2.21).

Oddly, perhaps, no use is made of an argument provided by Jencks that

> if all elementary schools were closed down, so that growing up became an endless summer ... The cognitive gap between rich and poor and between black and white would ... be far greater than it is now.[19]

Indeed, it is to these groups in our plural society to which the report directs much of the argument and many of its recommendations. As already noted, needs are related to certain disadvantaged groups. The Schools Commission Act, 1973, defines disadvantage in terms of students who are

> members of a community which for social, economic, ethnic, geographic, cultural, lingual or any similar reason [have] a lower than average ability to take advantage of educational facilities.[20]

Yet, no extended consideration is given to the content of education for each social group. Indeed, the whole report is strangely silent about the curriculum, which is surely within its terms of reference as one of the 'appropriate measures to assist in meeting ... needs' (1.1). But the curriculum is either discussed briefly in terms of the attitudes developed as a result of 'the quality of relationships between and among pupils and teachers' (5.4) or as a matter for teachers' choice, often between 'alternatives that curriculum development on a national scale would [provide]' (12.13). The notion that Midwinter evolved in the Liverpool E.P.A. is ignored. His object was to teach disadvantaged pupils to live critically in their environment. Such children must exist in poor conditions for the time being, but need not accept their situation.[21] Such a curriculum is dedicated to changing the social structure from the grassroots upwards. It is fundamentally Fabian in aim, and in the spirit of radical individualism optimistically assumes that man can and will do something to change his environment rather than pessimistically allow it to mould him.

The Karmel report argues very strongly for involvement by the community in the school. This position is supported for three different reasons, namely as 'a means both of extending [the school's] educational influence and of reinforcing pupil motivation' and of bringing teachers and parents closer together (2.19). The Committee acknowledges the 'antipathy' towards and apathy about direct community participation in the governance of schooling' (2.19), and that 'mutual suspicion . . . between administration and teachers' might inhibit 'the devolution of authority' (5. 6). Yet it pressed for some new and participatory version of the democratic myth without ever making clear whether it meant 'citizen participation' or 'interest-oriented participation'.[22] Initial results from a current investigation in Melbourne provide evidence casting doubt on the public's willingness to participate in any general way.[23] By and large, decisions about education are seen as belonging to teachers who are defined as the experts. Furthermore, if those in a locality are to be involved in running the schools, they must be given real decisions to make. In this connection, the Victorian Government would appear to be acting wisely in making money available to schools, if they will take the responsibility to use it, for such purposes as the improvement of local opportunities for leisure.

To make schools more open to parents might have a similar effect to the extension of the welfare state in the UK, where the middle class have proved more competent to use the available opportunities than have the working class. Participation may become more common amongst the middle class. Indeed, it might also be true that the middle class use open and innovatory schools more than the working class.

## Method of change

Some problems and potential conflicts may be discerned as underlying the methods by which the suggested changes are to be achieved. Experts are to define the problems, and both suggest cures and provide resources for change. Yet 'the development of grass-roots initiatives is basic to the success of the enterprise' (9.39). This situation implies the probability both of tension between community and experts, and the possibility that what the experts want may not in fact be accomplished. Additionally, some would say that, when the community does not want to follow the prescriptions of the experts, they have the right to refuse to change their present educational circumstances in the direction desired by the experts. Indeed, this is what happened in the E.P.A. at Dundee in Scotland where some teachers opposed the suggestion of the experts for changes on the grounds that children would be better off under the present educational regime than under that proposed.[24]

Implicit in local participation in the making of educational decisions is a measure of devolution of power from the centre to 'those working in or with the schools — teachers, pupils, parents and the local community' (14.3). The point has already been made that many parents and others do not want to participate in such activities. Many others, again, on our evidence collected in an inner city area in Melbourne, feel that at the moment they do not have the competence to take part in what they see as very complicated decisions. Furthermore, those in power in the educational system can, either consciously or by unconsciously preserving their current attitudes which are unfavourable to 'opening' schools, hinder this policy.[25]

Recognizing the crucial importance of teachers' attitudes when the aim is to change some aspects of the educational system, the report advocates the establishment of 'Education Centres' which 'would serve an important function in stimulating initiatives from the profession . . . and in improving the quality of teaching' (11.18). Rightly the emphasis is put upon in-service training initiated by teachers themselves as being more likely to lead to changes in behaviour than that resulting from courses imposed from above. Thus, while the Committee realized that 'the effectiveness of innovation . . . is dependent on the extent to which the people concerned perceive a problem' (12.4), they gave little attention to publicizing possible or successful changes, though they recognized that Regional Boards would 'serve as a vehicle both for promulgating the views of the Commission and for communicating ideas and proposals to the Commission' (13.7). This could particularly be the case for curricular change.

Furthermore, publicity for successful innovation can act as a reward to the school or teachers concerned. Nowhere does the report consider the wider system of sanctions* working for change and against those who persist in existing methods. The only sanction really suggested is the admittedly powerful one of money. There is, however, an extensive armoury of positive and negative sanctions available to those administering schools to use in order to influence teachers. Promotion, for example, may be dependent upon change. Visits to other countries, States or suburbs can follow or precede changes. Resources, such as materials or even extra staff, may flow from offers to innovate. However, probably the creation of a certain type of professional esteem will most efficiently facilitate change, since no true teacher would then tolerate less than adequate methods.[26]

Under such ideal circumstances, more publicity would negatively sanction tardy teachers and reward those who pioneered worthwhile new methods.

*The word 'sanction' is used here purely in its technical sense and carries no moral overtone.

## PLANNING SOCIAL CHANGE THROUGH EDUCATION IN CONTEMPORARY AUSTRALIA

Despite their disclaimer, the writers of the Karmel report have displayed a view of the 'divine intention', though, perhaps, the theology upon which it rests is arguable. Some, who believe in very different gods, criticize the report as supportive of the present social system[27], but the majority in my view would agree with its 'intention'. In view of my assumption about the majority view, what is at issue here is the method of achieving this 'intention'. Jencks may be right to conclude quite unequivocally that 'equalizing educational opportunity would do very little to make adults more equal'[28], but much evidence shows that education can meet other worthwhile aims, such as making people more literate and numerate than now is the case. Allowing that the Labor Government, purely on political grounds, had to spend and to legitimate the expenditure of much on education early in 1973, one must ask how the results of this expenditure will be evaluated in 1976 when the next planning period must begin, or in 1979 when the Karmel program should be complete. The excuse formerly available to those working in education that resources are scarce will no longer be possible. Unless major differences in the schools are visible to all, the conclusion of the public, those who pay and whose children are our students, must be that teachers, those who train teachers, and administrators are unimaginative and/or inefficient.

The approach favoured by the report appears to rely greatly on experts at all levels of administration. The writers of the report might answer that they have pressed for community action and for devolution to the schools, but communities, wherever they still exist, seem slow to react and in fact the innovatory initiatives of the schools are subject to administrative scrutiny before resources can be made available or are vetoed. What control is there to prevent those in power in the Schools Commission or at state level using their position to further a political position only supported by a small group of intellectuals? If we are to be in the hands of professional planners what code of professional ethics is there to prevent what Moynihan has called 'malpractice with respect to the community'?[29]

Under the Benthamite prescription, administration was expert, but was also open to the political process. Under a system such as that exemplified by the Schools Commission, the manner of allocating resources between competing uses and the monitoring of the program both at central and regional levels can only be seen through a glass darkly. In American cities the political machine took over the anti-poverty programs. In Australia there would seem to be a good chance that the planning of social change through our educational system will be taken over by the administrative system. The Australian educational bureaucracies were possibly beginning to wither under the attacks of radical individualism, but they have now found a new purpose. Furthermore, the new task is of the type for which any bureaucracy is ideally adapted, namely the division of material resources between competing

41

applicants. Power returns to the administrator to be exercised on a type of decision in which bureaucracies can exhibit great efficiency.

In many ways it is odd that politics have been forgotten in the report, since a pluralist society is envisaged in which community groups have some power. If attitudes can be changed so that such pluralities do take part in educational decisions, then the political problems of our society must be immensely more numerous and in addition probably more difficult in that, as has recently been seen in the case of Aborigines, the appeal to the spirit of community often involves ethnic antagonism.

It is the over-reliance on material resources and the under-emphasis on general political activity shown in the report that indicates one possible future new 'divine intention', especially after the main sins of omission of prior ages have been atoned for. There is a need, particularly in a society like Australia where local government is not highly developed and has little or no part to play in relation to educational decision-making, to initiate a continuous and high standard debate over education at national, state and local levels. Then there will be a ferment amongst the public and amongst professionals so that the experts will be forced to render account for their policies and their actions.

It would seem that a large number of action research projects throughout Australia and in every type of educational institution might cause just such a ferment. Research never meant much to the doctor in the hospital or to the industrialist in the factory till he saw results that improved his efficiency. Research will never mean much to the practising teacher till he sees it serving his needs in the school. Projects generated by teachers and open to the view, to the praise and criticism of other practitioners and public alike could serve this end. Evaluation of what is attempted would, unlike in the present large-scale programs, be built into the method used. Such evaluation, though rigorous, need not be strictly scientific in nature, but could be pragmatic and even retrospective. Evaluated action is not the same as experimental method.

The problems examined would presumably be those of local interest so that the involvement of local citizens would go hand in hand with devolution to the school. Because there are many localities with differing problems, there would inevitably be many diverse small programs, though in some cases links would be possible between those studying similar problems, for example, those concerned with migrants or with the possibility that the most academically able might be retarded 'in order to reduce the range of difference' (3.22). Such co-operation could be carried out not only by experts or teachers but also by interested and involved local laymen.

This diversity of approach would, furthermore, match the contemporary variety of educational theory. There is as yet no one answer to most educational problems. Each theoretical approach demands a differing way of tackling the problem. The collection of the results from many diverse programs might enable us to come to a somewhat fuller knowledge of educational theory.

Earlier, an important point concerning most compensatory activity was made, namely that values creep in unsuspected. All such action assumes the right to intervene, usually within what is normally the province of the family. We are not slow to criticize the changes wrought in so-called primitive societies by colonial powers or by missionaries. Yet neither are we slow to plan how to compensate for what we see as the poor familial background of the working-class or migrant child or, for that matter, of the illiterate middle-class child. However, since we are a culturally diverse society, the educational needs or demands of each group will be different and this fact supports the plea for diversity made above. It equally indicates that any vestiges of the old definition of equality must go. Schools will grow to be more and more different and this must no longer be seen as meaning that they are more and more unequal. Yet even in saying this we must remember that seeing equality more in terms of diversity could easily come to be an ideological rationalization for supporting much that today is seen as unfair.[30]

Above all, the results of this action research must be public. Indeed, in the first policy statement from the new Schools Commission there should be a publicity program. Money should be available to finance educational pages in all local and state newspapers, and they should be prepared locally, not syndicated. A national educational monthly might be subsidized. In fact, the single step that might, at least cost, bring more worthwhile change to Australian schools than any other, could be if the Schools Commission were to state that no finance was available to any State for any program whatever unless all vacant teaching and administrative positions were publicly advertised, possibly on a nation-wide scale, though this raises industrial issues of formidable complexity, especially in relation to transferability of pensions. Apart from the dynamic effect upon the principle of appointment by seniority, the payment for such advertising would, as with *The Times Educational Supplement*, finance a worthwhile national journal, thereby substantially raising the level of educational debate throughout the country.

In a footnote to a recent academic paper, Chazan has, half joking, offered us the formula: Frustration=Aspiration/Achievement.[31] The present program of the report, marked by an uncertain divine intention and somewhat weak in theology, will probably raise aspiration more than achievement, thereby increasing frustration, both overall and, perhaps worse, possibly between communities within Australia. The aim must be to seek a firmer theology and in my view, a vast program of well-publicized action research might move us in that direction whilst also ensuring that very varied achievement, paralleling very varied educational need, much more nearly matched the differing aspirations of the many plural groupings in Australia. Some frustration would undoubtedly remain, but it would be a more informed feeling and those concerned, having felt the rewards of successful educational experiment, would be more willing and able to proceed further along the Fabian path of educational change. A society operating in this way in one important social sector would be more capable of generalizing the method to other spheres.

## Notes

1 The author is grateful to his colleague, A. D. Spaull, for a number of valuable comments on an earlier draft of this paper.
2 Moynihan, D. P. (1968). *Maximum Feasible Understanding*. New York: Free Press.
3 As D. White has pointed out, Professor Karmel himself admits to being a Fabian (*The Age*, 19 June 1973). See Chapter 3 of this volume.
4 For an account see Smith, M. S. and Bissell, J. S. (1970). 'Report analysis: the impact of Head Start', *Harvard Educational Review*, 40:51–104.
5 op.cit.
6 Throughout the rest of this paper the report *Schools in Australia* is cited by referring to the chapter and paragraph number in the original document.
7 See Evetts, J. (1970). 'Equality of educational opportunity: the recent history of a concept', *British Journal of Sociology*, 21:425–430.
8 Schools Commission Act, No. 213 of 1973, 3 (1).
9 See Musgrave, P. W. (1973). 'The relationship between school and community: a reconsideration', *Community Development Journal*, 8:167–178.
10 In a Marxist analysis a rather similar point would be made in terms of arguments against 'group solipsism'. See Chapter 3 of this volume.
11 Jencks, C., Smith, M., Acland, H., Bane, M. J., Cohen, D., Gintis, H., Heyns, B. and Michelson, S. (1972). *Inequality: A Reassessment of the Effect of Family and Schooling in America*. New York: Basic Books.
12 See Labov, W. (1969). *Monograph Series on Languages and Linguistics*, 22:1–31. Georgetown University Institute of Languages and Linguistics.
13 Baratz, S. S. and J. C. (1970). 'Early childhood intervention in the social science base of institutional racism', *Harvard Educational Review*, 40 (36).
14 Bernstein, B. (1970). 'Education cannot compensate for society'. In Rubinstein, D. and Stoneman, C. (Eds) *Education for Democracy*. Harmondsworth: Penguin Books, p. 115.
15 There may well be differences in the way these codes operate in Australia. See Davis, D. F. Speaking and writing: a study of some social psychological correlates of skill in and preference for the use of oral and written language. Unpublished PhD thesis, Monash University, 1973.
16 See, for example, Havighurst, R. (1970). 'Minority subcultures and the Law of Effect', *American Psychologist*, 25:313–22.
17 Even in Poland an educational commission, though ostensibly only with advisory powers, has recently been established; see Smolicz, J. J. (1974). 'Some impressions of Polish sociology', *Australian and New Zealand Journal of Sociology*, 10:19–20.
18 Marris, P. and Rein, M. (1967). *Dilemmas of Social Reform*. London: Routledge and Kegan Paul.
19 Jencks, C., et al., op. cit.:87–8. This argument might be deduced from much other evidence on 'the threshold effect' of education, see, e.g., Langton, K. P. and Jennings, M. K. (1968). 'Political socialization and the high school civics curriculum in the United States', *American Political Science Review*, 62:852–67.
20 Schools Commission Act, No. 213 of 1973, 3 (1).
21 Midwinter, E. (1972). *Priority Education*, Harmondsworth: Penguin Books.
22 Bacharach, P. and Baratz, M. S. (1970). *Power and Poverty: Theory and Practice*. New York: Oxford U.P., pp. 201–13 (espec. 202–6).
23 For a preliminary report of this work see Fitzgerald, R. T., Musgrave, P. W. and Pettit, D. W. (1974). 'School and neighbourhood: a case study', *Australian Education Review*, 7 (1 and 2), espec. Ch. 3.
24 Town, S. W. (1973). 'Action research and social policy: some recent British experience', *Sociological Review*, 21:582.
25 Recently the Victorian Education Department allocated more money to Advisory Councils ostensibly so that they had a larger say in the running of the secondary schools. However, the letter announcing this increased grant also advised Councils to allocate these greater resources between themselves and the principal in the same proportions as they had done previously. Not surprisingly this is what some principals seem to have recommended, thereby preserving the status quo and their own power.
26 For the care with which appeals to professionalism should be made see Johnson, L. (1974). 'Is it really important that teaching be a profession?', *Australian and New Zealand Journal of Sociology*, 10:38–41.
27 See Chapter 3 in this volume.

28  Jencks, C., op. cit.: 255.
29  Moynihan, D. P., op. cit.: 201.
30  See Chapter 3 in this volume.
31  Chazan, L. (1968). 'Participation of the poor: section 202 (a) (3). Organizations under the
    Economic Opportunity Act of 1964', *Yale Law Journal*, **75**:627.

# 3. Create Your Own Compliance: The Karmel Prospect*

## Doug White

A currently popular educational radicalism and the desires of the Australian government are in a process of convergence. Involvement, participation and self-management, all key features of much radical education, are becoming also characteristic of official policies, particularly as expressed in the report to the Australian Schools Commission (the Karmel report).[1] On closer examination, it can be seen that the relaxation of older stereotyped patterns is on terms, and within a framework, which are not made by those who take part, except in a local and immediate sense. However, the Karmel report is no mere propaganda exercise; the changes suggested and favoured are profound. This report, and some other initiatives of the Labor Government, hint at a state in search of a grass-roots movement, or of a social system attempting to surround itself with a community. Certainly it appears that many of the policies advocated by radicals in education — community schools, open education, closer relationships between school and external social environment — will now be officially sponsored. Fundamental to one tendency in radical thought is a belief in group subjectivity, the belief that groups of people gathered together can create their own realities. It is this which allows governments to build popular involvement for their own reasons, for such group participation of itself does not lead to an understanding of the social and cultural process as a whole. While people participate in, even control, their localities, central control remains the firmer for being more obscured. To date, the Karmel report has been best known for its recommendations on financial aid. Such a limitation of discussion is unfortunate, for the report is a blueprint for social and cultural engineering on a scale not seen in Australia since the days of planned settlements.

## THEMES IN THE KARMEL REPORT

### The school as a community

The Interim Committee of the Schools Commission (chaired by Professor Peter Karmel) produced a report which it says is a unanimous one, a surprising statement given the radical character of some of its statements. For example,

> Schools can build within themselves a community where both education and people are valued, and where the influences of the market place do not dictate the price placed upon individual talents. Participation in such a caring community which sets out to build social relationships through its method of teaching and

*Reprinted with revisions by the author from *Arena* 32/33: 35–48.

learning can, by reducing the alienation of the individual, be a regenerating force in society.[2]

Many radical critics of education have made similar statements, but with some differences. The mention of 'regenerating society' does not usually figure in the statements of radicals. But a more important characteristic of the Karmel report statement is the deintellectualization of community. There are vast differences between the language of the Martin Report of 1964 (the notorious 'human capital' report) and that of Karmel's committee. The Karmel report appears to go to considerable lengths to avoid such terms as human capital; efficiency is carefully stated only when the discussion is of the distribution of resources and of organization, and the language preferred is of human talent, relationships, participation and individuality. Yet it is hardly likely that an approach to schooling which says so little of intellectuality would be acceptable if earlier work had not been done to devalue the notion.

One of the possible sources of community is that of the community of scholars, and for all the elitism which has come to surround that phrase, a partial truth of the social formation of ideas exists within it. Most of what reality remained in the term as a description of universities was destroyed by the onslaught of central control in the distribution of finance by the Australian Universities Commission. Universities have come to accept the permanence of political institutions and their dependence upon them, and the function of the elaboration of ideas and techniques for the execution of policies made elsewhere. Schools are now to be brought into line, with a three-stage model of control developing; state-appointed committees outline the general policies, academics do the work of elaborating these into workable and ideologically acceptable schemes, schools do the job. Unlike some previous forms of control, in this scheme everyone has a responsible task, and control over their work. The response of university departments of education to the Karmel report is an illustration; criticism has been slight, if existent, and drowned by the noise of meetings arranged to gather in a share of the funds for the kinds of research and development wanted. The universities have accepted that they are to be a source of technical expertise in carrying through a policy made by others. Likewise the schools are not to do with developing intellectuality, if by this is meant an independence of position and an understanding not prescribed by limits which are known to others but not to the learner. The universities, by previous government action and their own complicity, have largely become state agencies. The schools are to socialize the young, and more effectively than in the past by co-operating with other agencies already engaged in the process.

> However education in formal institutions, separated from both the home and the world of work, has proved to be an inadequate means of changing patterns of social stratification or of initiating all young people into society. Unless our conception of education broadens to enable school to forge closer links with other socializing agencies, the possibility of providing equal life chances for children from all types of social backgrounds is severely limited.[3]

The use of the notion of equality will be discussed later; the function of the school (and life) as a socializing process, like the use of alienation (in the previous quotation) as a synonym for unsocialized, is typical of the report. While socialization is not towards the present in an absolutely unchanged form, the structures are in basic form those of today, and the changes are to be gradual, and brought about by the initiative of those in positions of authority. Professor Karmel is, as he declares, a Fabian.[4]

## Decentralization and diversity

The Karmel report comes out for decentralization and local responsibility. For example,

> The Committee favours less rather than more centralized control over the operation of schools. Responsibility should be devolved as far as possible upon the people involved in the actual task of schooling, in consultation with the parents of the pupils whom they teach and, at senior levels, with the students themselves.[5]

There are some qualifications to this policy of decentralization. The money will be distributed from central agencies. The argument for this central distribution is based upon equality of provision, and efficiency in the use of resources, which require that 'certain services need to be organized centrally'. The report encourages diversity; no single pattern is necessarily the best.

> Better ways will not necessarily be the same for all children or for all teachers. This is an important reason for bringing responsibility back into the school and for allowing it to be exercised in ways which enable a hundred flowers to bloom rather than to wither.[6]

Consistent with the idea of diversity, the notion of uniformity of standards, academically, is opposed. In rejecting the idea that equality of social groups means that equal percentages of girls, boys, the working class, the middle class, blacks, whites etc. should gain access to a higher education, the Committee reports:

> The doctrinaire pursuit of equal average outcomes for all social groups could become so expensive as to be unacceptable in terms of alternatives forgone. It could also have undesirable aspects of its own: it admits only one criterion of excellence — an academic one — and assumes that everyone should value the same thing. A further danger is that outcomes might be obtained by retarding the most academically able in order to reduce the range of difference.[7]

There is a strong hint here that the members of the Committee are more knowledgeable than they let on. The only danger they point out is that the academically able may be restricted, which suggests that the Committee puts more attention on that criterion than it wants others to do. The hedging is extremely sensible, for who but the academically able and politically acceptable could write such a report, to tell others that they should be happy on other dimensions. But naturally such a leadership will want to perpetuate itself; it could scarcely conceive of any other way in which the whole could be envisaged or managed. After all, it is still necessary to engage in talent selection. Similarly, there is something other than that which appears in the way 'diversity' is used by the Karmelians. Diversity appears to mean the acceptance of present differences. The argument which tells us that diversity is essentially a good thing is a cover or a justification for the acceptance of the differentials associated with the education of various social groups, when these differences have something to do with one group exploiting another. The appeal of the equality of diversity is used to justify and extend domination, just as alienation means non-socialization.

Hundreds of radicals will applaud the statement that

> The school does not exist to grade students for employers or for institutes of higher learning. Nor should it regard higher education as the only avenue to a life of dignity and worth.[8]

The radicals may not be as much in agreement that there need be no change in the present social organization as implied in the statement, except that perhaps the present must be rethought in terms which give all bits of it their own dignity and worth. The changes planned by the Committee are in the meaning of life rather than in any other reality. To do this, a socially constructed reality must be made, but if it is not made by changing anything else, it must be manufactured. The process of manufacture of a new conception of life is different from the dissemination of propoganda, even to the extent of an intensive Goebbels-like effort; it is also different from those previous historical efforts which involve the rewriting of history. To construct a different social reality, the relationships between persons must be changed; what is envisaged in the report is the manufacture of certain relationships, which change the appearance of reality, though words like appearance and reality already become slippery to the grasp. But the change in appearance is within the manufactured cells of a structure which is itself unchanged.

The diversity and decentralization of control favoured by the Committee are premissed upon an acceptance of the present structures. One way of looking at the report, and some other initiatives of the Labor Government, is as the state and the ALP in search of, and artificially fostering, a grass-roots community. Other parts of the world have the reverse, with a moribund or formal community or locality meeting apparatus being revised, either as a result of radical activity or government initiative; even in the case of Sweden, where a good deal of state activity exists in the production of a centrally managed participatory society, it is said that there are some elements of localized, if paternalist, community from the past which could be used.[9] In Australia these are rare; Scherer has pointed to the exceptional case of Broken Hill, where community activity by trade unions is strong but exists within the confines of an acceptance of ownership of the mines, and, since the mineowners live elsewhere, the union influence and control of everyday life leaves the true controllers untouched.[10] In similar fashion, the arguments in the Karmel report for diversity and decentralization are predicated and dependent upon the acceptance of present structures. The transition is from laid-down structures, which come to be seen as oppressive, to a self- and group-made reality, which obscures the continued existence of these structures. Money allocations will be made, it is recommended, to achieve this.

Attitudes, which are (equally) accepting, but not necessarily approving of, individuals and social groups irrespective of their life styles or accomplishments, and teachers who believe in the capacity for change in all children, cannot be bought.[11]

But this proviso follows the statement:

Human and physical resources do not of themselves ensure a high quality education. Many essential ingredients of good schooling, notably attitudinal and organizational ones, cannot be bought with dollars. But the development of curricular more relevant to the requirements of particular children and to the problems and challenges of the real world, of closer school-community relationships and of active parental interest which is a pre-requisite for increasing school effectiveness, can all be facilitated by the financial backing of new approaches to ways and means.[12]

The funds available are generous by Australian standards. Some will be distributed through the present channels, some through new regional bodies. Funds are also available for special projects of an innovatory kind and will come from a Canberra committee.

Applications for financial support would be invited from individuals and groups, not only of teachers but from the community, so as to provide an opportunity for changes to come from beyond present institutional frameworks.[13]

The overall picture is of diversity within control, a kind of cultural pluralism grafted into the existing structures, with innovations planned or approved centrally. In one hit the report, should its recommendations on the scale of finance be accepted, would wipe out, for the time at least, the old economic-based militancy and would incorporate much of the remainder of radical thought. No longer will simple economic demands, or partial cultural reforms be in opposition to the government policy, nor shake the control over lives that hidden authority exerts. The Karmel committee is a vanguard, one might say, of a new consolidation of authority. To oppose it, groups of people who see that the social and cultural process as a whole are necessary. The radical education movement, in the form which it has taken for the past five or so years, is over; reaction in the form of progressiveness is in the ascendance, and counter meanings and actions require a period of working out. The components of radical thought which have provided the opportunity for the new reaction to elaborate a strategy need some examination. But we have not yet finished with Karmel.

### Equality, community and control

One way of seeing the consistency and the change within education over the last century is in the use of 'equality' — the pursuit of equality has long been said to be a justification and purpose of state intervention in education. Sometimes the introduction of compulsory and free education in each of the colonies is still seen as a victory for democratic and liberal thought, as was said at the time of its introduction. 'In Australia, by contrast with England,' writes Alan Barcan, 'the lower classes already had or were achieving a major share of economic and political power.'[14] A democratic hue became apparent in Australian education, as some of those in power thought it desirable to place a liberal education before the people. The state acted to provide equality of effective education, particularly in rural areas. 'The reforming spirit of colonial democracy also applied itself in the 1870s and 1880s to providing greater equality of educational opportunity.'[15] An historian of Queensland education has expressed the view that the 1875 Education Act for free, compulsory, and secular education 'embodied virtually all the progressive principles of education of the day'.[16] The arguments of the time in that State seem to have been similar to those elsewhere, particularly the difficulty of providing education equally over the territory of the State without centralized control, and the inefficiency of the churches in doing so. In Western Australia, free tuition, the provision of government schools, and compulsory attendance produced the same kind of equality by 1899.[17] Education, Mossenson notes, played a role in consolidation in Western Australia, which was a little different from that in the other States, in the assimilation of 'the children of sandgroper and t'othersider elements'[18], reconciling earlier animosities and hence the breaking down of Western Australia's isolation from the other colonies. This other function of education, that of consolidation, contains the clue which suggests that the liberal talk of equality was alloyed with some other purpose; if not, why compulsion?

Liberal and democratic rhetoric accompanied the passage of state education acts throughout Australia, and is echoed in the work of some of the historians of the period. Austin puts more importance upon efficiency.

> In every colony, theoretical and practical considerations combined to convince the legislatures that the State should see to the education of its children, and that the State alone was capable of doing this, for neither the local communities, nor the Churches, nor the existing boards of education appeared to be capable of discharging this national duty.[19]

The people may have believed in equal opportunity for all, and liberal thought 'recruited the state as the active agent to assist the individual in pursuit of his fair chance to make good'.[20] Political leaders had a different objective in mind, that of a unified society, according to Hyams and Bessant. 'Social cohesion in a community in which the newcomer predominated was to them a vital aim.'[21] Sectarian hostility was a barrier in the quest for a unified colonial society. Denis Grundy, who writes with more concern for the interests of the Catholic minority, argues that centralized state school systems bring about institutionalized powers amounting to coercion.[22] Catholic schools survived, but as a poverty stricken and embattled segment. Other initiatives, particularly of the local groups concerned with the establishment of technical schools, were more effectively suppressed or discouraged. State action, accompanied by a labour movement belief in statism and an anti-Catholic ideology, laid a foundation for popular oppression of the one substantial minority which stood outside a monolithic pro-British nationalism, allowing an outpost of potentially anti-imperialist feeling to be exploited by right-wing ideologues. Its consequences today are the DLP, and, for example, the association with reactionary political groups of a potentially humane position of the Right to Life movement.

Equality of education from the 1970s until quite recently was an equality of provision for those prepared to accept the hegemony of the state in this field, and a means of suppression of those outside. Equality, in so far as there was any, was available only at the more elementary levels of education, and the churches continued to dominate secondary education. Equality was a rhetoric covering dominance, inequality and, possibly, efficiency. The use of education as a means of establishing national unity is still with us, although the particular ways of attempting this have changed. Likewise equality has been given new content, testifying that the appeal of the notion of equal entry into adult relationships remains.

A century ago, equality, where it was applicable, applied only to the provision of minimal educational services for working-class and rural groups. Secondary education remained for long the province of church schools, and therefore of those able to afford fees. Importantly, state secondary schools appear to have developed first in the countryside where a class mix and scattered population meant that there were fewer opportunities for the children of those, who in the cities would have been able to make use of private schools. State secondary schools expanded in number gradually, but it was not until after the Second World War that a different definition of equality developed.

Tom Roper's book, *The Myth of Equality*[23], marks the popular celebration of the new definition, although attention to the inequality had been drawn earlier by groups such as the ACER[24] and the Martin Committee.[25] Equality now became a name for a concern that not all had equal access to higher education, and therefore to the desirable jobs. From one side, this meant access to a mirage of social mobility, and from another an end to wastage and inefficient selection of talent. The change in popular thought to a consideration of education as a means of access to well-paid and influential positions reduced the stability of class-based attitudes, at first noticeable in the decline of traditional working-class politics. But such an instability is dangerous over larger dimensions of society; new limits are not being manufactured, and a Labor Government is merely the harbinger of an attempted new consolidation which will be carried through by future governments irrespective of party.

The dichotomies of classes were unaffected by this provision of educational facilities by the state. The constancy of the class structures did not require intervention of a manipulatory kind of the thought structures of the young, beyond the general acceptance of the notions of the independence of the state as an instrument beyond classes, and the acceptance of a unified society as a desirable state of affairs. The definite uniformity was, as has been shown by Humphrey McQueen and other writers, achieved by specific exclusion of non-whites, particularly the Chinese and Aborigines, and also by the suppression of Catholics.[26] The need for talent selection and the extension of a higher level of general education was associated with an ideological myth, that of social mobility and the absence of class domination. Large-scale expectations of mobility are unreal, and from the point of view of social order, dangerous. The Karmel report plays down such aspects as talent selection and upward social mobility in education, without abolishing them. Equality is now seen as equality of diversity, with a removal of the more obvious signs of financial inequality in this diversity. The attempt to level school provisions has been most noticed in newspaper publicity. The section of the report which led to the policy of varying the amount of aid to fee-paying schools says:

> In respect of recurrent resources, a school is classified as in need of assistance for additional resources if the quantity of recurrent resources per pupil used within it is less than some acceptable standard. A corollary of this definition is that one school is regarded as needing more assistance than another if the quantity of resources per pupil used in the former is smaller than that used in the latter.[27]

This policy is a revival of the long existing theme that the state will act to ensure equality of access to public resources, and extends to the secondary school what in the 1870s was made the policy for primary schools. The state in the nineteenth century, however, excluded certain groups from this participation, notably the Catholic Irish. Those who have built their political power and career on this exclusion have opposed this mode of allocation of funds. But for the first time, savage and open reaction to them has come from official Catholic circles, in this case from Father Martin, director of the Catholic Education Office in Melbourne.

> It's absurd to see this whole matter as a cunning ploy on the part of the present Government which will pave the way for the demise of Catholic schools. This is a typical fear ploy which is often used.[28]

The report, however, does nothing, as it could do nothing, about inequality, except in the allocation of tax money. The government policy is now to extend equality in one direction, to have no groups excluded from the area of operation of the state, and to introduce the theme of equality of diversity. In doing this, the report draws on the theory and program advocated by Christopher Jencks and others.[29] The equality comes across not as a right to obtain resources, or access to power, or to socially favoured jobs. Equality is access to enjoyment and participation.

> Schooling is a significant segment of life which for all children ought to be enjoyable and fruitful in itself, not merely a preparation for life to come.[30]

> Some schools might evolve through successful interaction with their communities into new 'open' institutions, less alienated from their communities than is now generally the case in disadvantaged areas.[31]

Such a proposition supposes that the community does not exist as part of a social structure, but as a local group which has no links with other groups, or if it has these links, that they are of no importance. There is an analogy in the notion of workers' control of a factory. Often this means participation, not ownership. But even where it does mean ownership, nothing necessarily changes, for those who now own the factory are still linked with others through the market, and still produce the commodities demanded within a total system which they have had no say in making. It is possible of course to develop a program of action, including workers' control, which raises these issues; but that requires a program in which new meanings of production and exchange, and widely extended relationships between workers in one place and another, are developed. Workers' control lacks the wider meaning associated with class, and may introduce parochialism under the guise of liberation. The concentration on ownership does not automatically raise these questions. In the schools, the emphasis on community is just as likely to avoid or obscure the questions of why the community exists, its relationship to the wider society, its part in the total social process.

The edifice of community which is elaborated in the Karmel report is in a way imposed by the ALP governed state. Its popular roots are in the Australian version of the liberal welfare state, which looks after the people in its care. Yet something reaching a good deal further than the provision of schools, pensions, child endowment and the like is embodied in this report, and in certain other policies of the Government. What is being planned is the participation of the people, the development of a culture by the state. That culture is fragmented and groupy, enveloping and localized. It is class as culture, an attempt to develop a two-level society with managers and managed, possible because of the continued existence of the framework which has long existed; but that framework still exists, and cannot be overthrown without its accompanying culture. If the plan succeeds, the culture and the society become co-terminous, in a manner which has not existed in earlier capitalism. Nor can it be overthrown in the manner proposed by most earlier models of the overthrow of capitalism; for one thing, it is the culture which must be understood and changed, not merely the structure. While the roots of the present development lie in the needs of the modern capitalist social structure, and use the tradition of state reliance and liberal-welfare attitudes towards the state, they are also dependent upon the popular counter-culture movements. It is no accident that the Karmel report contains much of the language of alternative education.

## RADICAL EDUCATIONAL THOUGHT AFTER KARMEL

The transition of socialist, radical, or critical thought necessary in the working out of educational programs is large. The arguments around more money for schools have been wiped out, or can only be seen as minor. The Catholic solidarity has been destroyed. Already the arguments regarding talent selection and human capital formation have begun to look a little old-fashioned. There are not many now who will raise with such crudity the view expressed recently by a former senior officer of the Australian Council for Educational Research that

> One of the functions (of an education system) is to harness the best resources available in a country to solve the problems being presented to us as we enter the 21st century.[32]

That function remains, but we shall hear it less often expressed, just as we will hear less of the gross national product, economic development and the like, and more of community, participation, ecology; the way in which we are managed changes, in a fashion which at the present time has a basic appeal to many.

The Whitlam Government has disoriented many on the left because it has apparently adopted many of the policies which the radical left has developed over the past few years, and yet there exists an uneasiness that the government could well do something else with these policies. In fact the Australian Government has more than adopted the policies, it has adopted, at least in some areas of its practice, a style which suggests a new mode of capitalist operation. That it is able to incorporate many of the ideas of radicals suggests that these were not in reality the working out of the alternate society that they at times have been thought to be. In education, the freer school, the community school, the school program more related to the outside social environment, the participation of parents, and the independence of the teachers from employing authorities have all been shown to be capable of inclusion in an official state document. The characteristics of such programs need some examination.

A typical modern school program tends to stress the relationship between the persons in the school, the interests of the children, and the non-school experience. An older, 'traditional' school stresses the learning of theories and facts derived from long-established disciplines. In the traditional school, the theories are made to appear to have an objective truth, as if they were not the productions of men engaged in particular social formations and particular forms of interaction with nature. In this sense, school children are tied, unknowingly, into a set of meanings which were not made by them and which make them potentially at the service of others. This education has its own contradictions, however, in that the students are sometimes enabled to enter a wider world than that provided by neighbourhood environments or segments of a particular class. An education of this kind is necessary to a capitalism which in its continual revolution of the means of production extends this to the shaking up of the human factors of production, dragging people from their backgrounds into more flexible and skilled usages. The opposition to traditional education has taken at least two directions, one an attempt to make more conscious the nature of the manner in which ideas are formed, and of the relationship between those and other social processes; the other to resist the domination of established theories by emphasizing personal experience. The emphasis on personal experience leaves untouched the meanings which are used to interpret and generate that experience. A group of children in a progressive school may not be dominated by the structure and established theories of the institution and the teacher; they will be dominated by an experience and habits of thought coming unexamined from the past and the agencies of the media.

In a more extreme form progressive education of this kind produces, and is based upon, a group solipsism. Previously solipsism has been thought of as asserting the primacy of individual subjectivity as a criterion of reality. The new solipsism, however, emphasizes the world of the small group: the individual subjectivity is seen as circumscribed by a reality of limited range; because there is no principle accounting for the interconnection of this multitude of micro-worlds they can appear as self-made. The solipsism of the small group then can have it both ways: by drawing upon the experience of self-determined expression characteristic of the primary group it co-ordinates 'individualism' and the old solipsism. By emphasizing the predominance of the small group it sets the real 'objective' frame within which free individuals make their small worlds. Effectively two traditions are reconciled, but the essence of solipsism is retained as a philosophical rationalization of a status quo.

A world is constructed which is as good as any other world, and has no measure of reality outside its own construction. The production of group-made worlds of this kind is an ideology which suits a class society in which the fundamental structure is obscured, and the existence of nation-wide relationships, based on a feeling of solidarity (such as those of the working class), have been broken. Such an ideology, largely drawn from that of the recent version of the counter-culture, is appropriate to a manipulated society which is perceived as a self-managed one.

The arguments against such solipsism — the chief theoretician of solipsism is Berger[33] and it comes into education theoretically through such writers as Glasser[34] — are of several varieties. Lenin's arguments with the solipsism widespread among intellectuals in Russia after the defeat of the 1905 revolution and the decline of the working-class movement were based on the objective reality of natural phenomena.[35] The rise of solipsism there coincided with the decline of a widespread action-based association between people engaged in a reconstruction of the world, and such movements are themselves an argument against solipsism, for they pose the existence of individual or small-group constructions of the world against a more widely based one. Another kind of argument is that there are bio-cultural bases for the association between persons which prevent any form of association being possible, an argument which is the subject of attack from women's liberation and gay liberation. A further form of criticism of the present solipsism is to be found in the examination of the historically and socially derived meanings and institutions which in fact govern our present experience, and which must be overthrown if our lives are to be changed. This is merely to say that the solipsist view is untrue, and those who act by it in the hope that they form their own lives within the niches of the unexamined present are in truth governed by the present. Obviously a fuller treatment of the social and philosophical foundations of that apparent radicalism which assists domination is necessary.

What is to be done in the present circumstances? Any change of a worthwhile, revolutionary nature requires the elaboration of alternate ways of looking at society and human activity, a movement which in the daily actions of its members lives potentially, and more and more consciously, by alternative and opposing meanings, and some kind of conflict, confusion or division of those in power. There is nothing new in that statement; the recurring argument is about the nature of those who work out the alternative meanings and their relationship with those who are potentially the members of the movement. At times the movement in its actions restates the categories by which people live; the danger of a division of labour between those who act and those who formulate is that the 'vanguard' becomes an incipient new class. Yet a movement which is confined, as the radical education movement is increasingly becoming, to working within conceptions acceptable and favourable to state manipulation achieves nothing. The kind of program which is proposed by the Karmel Committee opens up, even asks for, action and involvement. If thought is given to the limits imposed upon this action, and more far-reaching attempts planned, the Whitlam Government's plans may be merely a part of a process towards further change. But what is needed is a more thoroughgoing criticism and elaboration of alternatives than progressive education nowadays has within it.

## Notes

1 Australia. (1973). *Schools in Australia. Report of the Interim Committee for the Australian Schools Commission.* (Chairman, P. Karmel). Canberra: AGPS.
2 ibid., para. 2.22, p. 14.
3 ibid., para. 2.17, p. 13.
4 *The Age,* 19 June 1973.
5 Australia. op. cit., para. 2.4, p. 9.
6 ibid., para. 2.10, p. 11.
7 ibid., para. 3.22, p. 25.
8 ibid., para. 2.35, p. 26.
9 Huntford, R. (1971). *The New Totalitarians.* London: Allen Lane.
10 Scherer, P. 'Wages: The Management of Labour', *Arena* 31:42–43.
11 Australia. op. cit., para. 5.5, p. 62.
12 ibid., para. 5.3, p. 61.
13 ibid., para. 12.7, p. 152.
14 Barcan, A. (1964). 'The Australian Tradition in Education'. In R.W.T. Cowan, *Education for Australians.* Melbourne: Cheshire. p. 10.
15 ibid., p. 14.
16 Wyeth, E.R. (n.d.) *Education in Queensland.* Melbourne: ACER, p. 128.
17 Mossenson, D. (1972). *State Education in Western Australia 1829–1960.* Perth: University of W.A. p. 95.
18 ibid., p. 99.
19 Austin, A.G. (1961). *Australian Education 1788–1900.* Melbourne: Pitman. p. 177.
20 Hyams, B.K. and Bessant, B. (1972). *Schools for the People?* Melbourne: Longman. p. 47.
21 ibid., p. 48.
22 Grundy, D. (1972). *Secular, Compulsory and Free.* Melbourne: Melbourne University Press.
23 Roper, T. (1971). *The Myth of Equality.* Melbourne: Heinemann.
24 Radford, W.C. (1962). *School Leavers in Australia.* Melbourne: ACER, p. 55.
25 Australia. (1964). *Report of the Committee on the Future of Tertiary Education in Australia to the Australian Universities Commission.* (Chairman, L.H. Martin). Melbourne: AGPS.
26 McQueen, H. (1970). *A New Britannia.* Melbourne: Penguin.
27 Australia. (1973). op. cit., para. 6.1, p. 70.
28 *The Age,* 10 August 1973, p. 5.
29 Jencks, C. (1972). *Inequality: A Reassessment of the Effect of Family and Schooling in America.* New York: Basic Books.
30 Australia. op. cit., para. 9.8, p. 112.
31 ibid., para. 9.9, p. 112.
32 Rechter, B. 'Better-off would gain in ballot for university places', *The Age,* 10 July 1973, p. 17.

33  Berger, P. (1967). *The Sacred Canopy.* New York: Doubleday. Berger, P. and Luckmann, T. (1967). *The Social Construction of Reality.* London: Allen Lane.
34  Glasser, W. (1969). *Schools Without Failure.* New York: Harper and Row.
35  Lenin, V.I. (1952). *Materialism and Empirio-Criticism.* Moscow: Foreign Languages Publishing House.

# Sociological Dimension

# 4. The Needs of Education in Australian Schools

## J. P. Keeves

Any renewal program for education in Australia of the kind which the Schools Commission is attempting to provide must be based either implicitly or explicitly on some conception of the deficiencies of the educational system it sets out to improve. While the report of the Interim Committee for the Australian Schools Commission appears at times to be concerned primarily with lack of finance for education and the unavailability of resources, the Committee at many points in the report sought to link the provision of resources with the intellectual development of the students and the professional development of the teachers in the schools.[1]

This article seeks to identify the conception which the Committee held of the deficiencies in Australian schools and to compare their views with earlier statements prepared by the States. In particular, since a substantial proportion of the program of the Australian Schools Commission has been directed towards remedying deficiencies in schools where disadvantage occurs, this article examines the approach which the Committee took towards the problems of such schools. Alternative procedures are discussed for the identification of disadvantaged schools and corroborative evidence is presented using Australian data for the stance taken by the Committee. It is, however, argued that there is a need to identify cases of schools and students within schools where minimum standards of competence for life in a modern democratic and industrial society are not being achieved. This goal of attaining minimum standards of competence, particularly for students from disadvantaged environments, should not be overlooked in the clamour for better physical facilities and better working conditions for teachers.

Prior to the preparation of the report by the Interim Committee, assessments of the needs of education in Australia had been undertaken at the direction of the Australian Education Council which comprised the Ministers of Education in all the States and the Commonwealth of Australia. In 1960 the Council issued a statement of the needs of Australian education, which was later revised to incorporate further statistical material and was re-issued in 1963.[2] The Council was concerned with the marked disparity between what it saw as the needs of education and what the State Governments were able to provide. The Council's evidence showed the following serious deficiencies:

1 schools are short of qualified teachers;
2 many teachers are inadequately trained and qualified for the job they are asked to do;
3 States are finding it difficult to provide the new accommodation needed;

4 there is a large accumulation of makeshift, substandard and obsolete school accommodation;

5 equipment and supplies of all kinds are required in increasing quantities.[3]

Although the funds available to the State Education Departments had, in the years prior to 1960, increased annually, it was argued that the needs were urgent and that, unless adequate finance were available, the consequences for Australia as a whole would be serious.

Following the Unesco Seminar on planning for education in Australia in 1968, the Australian Education Council early in the next year decided that each State should undertake a survey of its educational needs for a period of five years. A summary statement was published in 1970 under the title *Nation-wide Survey of Educational Needs*.[5] The survey revealed a deficiency of more than $1400 million between what was regarded as desirable for expenditure on education in Australia over the following five years, and what was estimated as likely to be available. The survey calculated what it believed were the necessary capital and recurrent costs of education over the five-year period and made detailed assessments under 11 categories of expenditure: (1) administrative structure, (2) teaching staff, (3) ancillary staff, (4) buildings, (5) land, (6) equipment, (7) pre-service education of teachers, (8) in-service education, (9) scholarships, (10) provision of textbooks, and (11) transport. However, it is important to note that the statements prepared by the Australian Education Council appear to have focused exclusively on the needs of the government-sponsored systems of primary and secondary education and to have failed to consider the needs of the non-government schools. Subsequently, no action was taken by the Commonwealth Government of Australia during the years 1970 and 1972 to meet the needs revealed by this survey.

## THE REPORT OF THE INTERIM COMMITTEE

The Interim Committee for the Australian Schools Commission was appointed in late 1972 and was required by its terms of reference to examine the position and immediate financial needs of both government and non-government primary and secondary schools in the States and Territories. This Committee had access to the documents of the *Nation-wide Survey of Educational Needs*, by then three years out of date. In reporting on conditions in Australian schools, the Interim Committee examined the growth in school enrolments and the growth of the teaching service over the past decade, current sizes of schools and the proportions enrolled in schools of different sizes, changes in pupil-teacher ratios in recent years and the current distribution of enrolments by class size, the qualifications of teachers, the provision of ancillary staff, and the opportunities available for the education of physically and mentally handicapped children. In addition, it reported on trends in the financing of schooling in both the public and private sectors of education.

There were, however, other aspects of the provision for education that were found to be difficult to measure in the limited time available for the preparation of a report. Consequently, the Committee decided to spend several weeks visiting schools throughout Australia and to report on their observations. The impressions they gained from their visits were clear and 10 brief descriptions which they presented of schools in different situations provided telling evidence of contrasts both between and within different school systems. The following paragraph summarized the views of the Committee:

> Members of the Committee were impressed by the magnitude of the need for upgrading and replacement in older schools, both government and non-government, by the lack of facilities necessary for broadening the curriculum, by the generally low level of provision of ancillary and specialist staff and by the wide differences existing in the innovative capacities of teachers and principals. While there are high spots in all systems and types of school, and these bear no necessary relationship to the quality of physical provision, the Committee was left in no doubt, both on the basis of information supplied and on the basis of its own observations, that there was a general need for improved resources and a higher level of educational service among Australian schools, and a special need for help to schools catering for handicapped children and pupils from disadvantaged groups in the population.[6]

The Committee did not attempt to lay down specifications for the servicing of schools in terms of the desirable numbers of teachers and amounts of equipment, arguing a case for fostering new and different combinations in the allocation of resources than had existed in the past. However, to show acceptable target standards in more concrete terms they provided one example of the many alternative patterns for using available resources. These are listed below in condensed and re-arranged form because by comparing them with current practices it is possible to identify more clearly some of the needs which the Interim Committee believed to exist in Australian schools.

1 All teachers should have available one working week annually or its equivalent for professional enrichment purposes.
2 Relieving staff should be provided immediately a teacher is absent from duty.
3 Recognized administrative duties by teachers in school should occupy about 10 per cent of staff working hours.
4 One field consultant should be provided for every 60 teachers in service.
5 New teachers should have a 10 per cent reduction in work load during their first year of service.
6 Maximum sizes of class groups should be 32 students at primary and junior secondary levels, and 25 students in senior secondary forms.
7 Primary classroom teachers should be released from direct classroom duties by specialist teachers for two hours per week.
8 Ancillary staff and the amount of equipment should be increased 100 per cent for primary schools and 75 per cent for secondary schools above the 1972 level.[7]

It is important, however, to emphasize that the statement above illustrated rather than defined the nature of the recurrent resources to be provided for schools.

J. P. KEEVES

With respect to general grants for buildings and for capital expenditure, the
Interim Committee itself did not attempt to define standards; it recommended
the establishment of a national building research centre to undertake a role as a
clearinghouse for information across Australia, to carry out research into
building materials and school design, and to support a building standards
group.[8] The Schools Commission has since prepared a draft statement on
building standards and has recently established a Steering Committee with
representatives from the State Education Departments to assess current needs
for physical facilities.[9] Nevertheless, this would seem to fall short of the
recommendations made by the Interim Committee for research into school
buildings and the definition of standards for such buildings.

In the preparation of the report *Schools in Australia*, the Interim Committee
would appear to have concentrated its attention on the need for a minimum
quantity and quality of resources in schools. It made efforts to assess the nature
of the most effective resources required by schools and to recommend ways in
which perceived deficiencies might be remedied. While the possibility of
assessing need for particular kinds of outcomes from schools, or the need for
resources in regard to their effectiveness in attaining desired goals was rejected
because of lack of adequate data, the Committee does appear to have had an
underlying concern for promoting the intellectual development of children in
the schools. However, documents issued by the Schools Commission since its
establishment do not seem to give the same priority to cognitive and
intellectual development, being more concerned with issues of social equity,
tolerable social diversity and individual worth than with educational
questions.[10]

## THE IDENTIFICATION OF DISADVANTAGED SCHOOLS

The Interim Committee recognized that some schools required greater than
average provision of resources if they were to serve the students within them
effectively. It argued that such schools were best identified using a complex
index of socio-economic level, and work was undertaken by its support staff to
develop such a measure using data from the 1971 Population Census of
Australia. The unit of analysis employed was the collectors' district and the
attributes examined were: occupation, housing, schooling, employment,
migration, residential mobility, family structure, ethnicity and religion.
Unfortunately only a very brief account of the work carried out has been
released, which is insufficient to allow a critical assessment of the
meaningfulness and validity of the procedures actually employed.[11] The
measures derived from the socio-economic scales were used to identify the
relative extent of disadvantage in different States and different regions, and to
identify schools serving collectors' districts and neighbourhoods where there
was expected to be a relatively high level of disadvantage. The extent of
disadvantage assessed by these measures of socio-economic level was employed
in the allocation of money to the States to provide programs which would
compensate for disadvantage.

64

As evidence for the validity of the scales, a brief statement was made which indicated that measures on the socio-economic scale for schools in one region correlated positively with ratings on a five-point scale of the 'educational standing' of localities served by the schools.[12] This evidence would appear to show that the views of the raters on the educational standing of a locality, however this may be defined, is related to the measures on the scale, but which is to be preferred for the identification of disadvantaged schools remains in doubt.

As persons in the State Education Departments came to use the rankings of schools on the socio-economic scale assessing disadvantage, they became dissatisfied with the information they were given. It was argued that the scale was relatively crude, even if it was developed using highly sophisticated techniques, that it was partly obsolete because it used census data which had been collected two years earlier, and that it gave evidence which conflicted with personal judgment for schools on the margins between being disadvantaged and of normal standing. Consequently, while the scale developed is considered to be satisfactory for the allocation of moneys to States and school systems, it has been largely rejected for the purpose of identifying individual schools in need.

## ALTERNATIVE INDICATORS OF DISADVANTAGED SCHOOLS

The proposals of the Interim Committee with regard to disadvantaged schools were similar in purpose to those made by the Plowden Committee in Britain for the identification of 'educational priority areas'.[13] However, in providing assistance to schools in particular areas, different techniques for identifying such schools have been employed in Australia and Britain. The Plowden Committee suggested that in the identification of disadvantaged schools, a trial list of eight possible factors involving occupation, family size, receipts of benefits from the state, overcrowding of houses, poor attendance, and proportion of retarded children, immigrant children, and incomplete families should be used.[14] Subsequently, investigations were conducted by the staff of the Inner London Education Authority to determine an index for schools based mainly on these factors, but which also included teacher turnover and pupil turnover as tentative variables. Attempts to construct an index were not particularly successful, largely because of a lack of knowledge about the nature of deprivation arising from multiple factors.[15]

In Australia, the Supplementary Grants Committee of the Victorian Education Department, having perhaps the greatest amount of deprivation and the highest proportion of disadvantaged schools in the country, undertook a research study to examine a School Priority Index within the constraints of the time available and lack of information on variables that might be considered for an index.[16] Four factors were employed in addition to the ranking of a school on the list of disadvantaged schools prepared by the Schools Commission. These factors were:

**Table 1.** Correlation between School Priority Index Factors and Mean Judgement Ratings in a Sample of Victorian Schools.

| N = 30 Schools | 2 | 3 | 4 | 5 | 6 | 7 |
|---|---|---|---|---|---|---|
| 1  Commonwealth Ranking | 0.23 | 0.52 | 0.12 | 0.21 | 0.64 | 0.25 |
| 2  Socio-Economic Level |  | 0.24 | 0.65 | 0.31 | 0.77 | 0.51 |
| 3  Migrants |  |  | 0.09 | 0.02 | 0.57 | 0.34 |
| 4  Indigents |  |  |  | 0.24 | 0.69 | 0.52 |
| 5  Teacher Turnover |  |  |  |  | 0.53 | 0.11 |
| 6  Summated Rating |  |  |  |  |  | 0.55 |
| 7  Judgement Rating |  |  |  |  |  | 1.00 |

1 *socio-economic level*: the average occupational rating of the fathers of the students within a school;

2 *migrants*: the percentage of migrant students (from non-English-speaking homes) in a school;

3 *indigents*: the percentage of students in the school receiving extra financial assistance from the Education Department;

4 *teacher turnover*: the percentage of teachers at the school in 1973 who were still at the school in 1974.

The ranking provided by the Schools Commission was included to ensure that characteristics of the neighbourhood served by the school were incorporated into the index.

To investigate the strength of this index among schools which were being considered for the allocation of grants, on the basis of the extent of the disadvantage existing within them, a sample of 30 such schools was studied. The five factors listed above were examined in relation to 'judgment' ratings of the degree of disadvantage in the schools assigned by inspectors, special services advisers, field consultants and teachers. Table 1 records the correlations between the five factors and the mean judgment ratings of the assessors.[17] The relatively low correlation between the judgment rating and the commonwealth ranking throws some doubt on the strength of this index, and the much higher correlations between this rating and the average socio-economic level of the school and the indigents in the school suggests the greater utility of these measures. In addition, the summated rating, while only correlating 0.55 with the judgment rating, would appear to be a strong contender for an effective index of the extent of disadvantage existing within a particular school when used across the range within which discriminations must be made.

## ALTERNATIVE APPROACHES TO IDENTIFYING NEEDS

The Interim Committee in making its recommendations believed that a direct approach was impracticable for grappling with some of the needs of education in Australia. Consequently, it concentrated its attention on the need for a minimum quantity and quality of resources in the schools. Moreover, as we have seen, it recognized that students from communities suffering socio-economic disadvantage attended schools which had serious inadequacies both in their resources and in the opportunities they offered to their students. The identification of schools in which the educational deficiences are most acute is not simple, particularly when financial assistance is limited and must be allocated to those in greatest need. As a result each of the six States would appear to have gone about its task of combating need in disadvantaged schools in a different way, each being influenced by its own perceptions of its areas of greatest need .

In the next section of this article, an alternative approach to the identification of the needs of schools and their students is considered. This approach takes as its starting point the central goals of education, examines factors which influence the attainment of these goals and attempts to identify situations in which these goals are not being achieved.

The report of the Interim Committee acknowledged that:

> An important function of education in a democracy is to broaden opportunities for participation in the mainstream of society through the development of necessary skills and credentials.[18]

Yet it also recognized the difficulties which arise in attempting to define goals.[19] Nevertheless, to speak of the deficiencies of an educational system implies spelling out a full account of the aims and purposes of education against which such deficiencies might be seen to exist. However, the Schools Commission does not appear to have recognized the need for the preparation presently or in the future of a detailed statement of aims and goals. In the absence of such a statement, it is necessary to identify those outcomes of education that are commonly regarded to be of greatest importance.

An overseas visitor to Australia, R. W. B. Jackson, writing a little over a decade ago on the needs of Australian education reminded Australian educators and parents that:

> The primary function of the school, and one which alone it can perform, is to provide intellectual development, i.e., to give a good general education, using both academic and non-academic means, in the fundamental skills of communication and in development of understanding of our fellow-man and of the world in which we live. This always has had, and always will have, top priority in the scale of values of the state schools.[20]

More recently J. S. Coleman in the United States has also argued cogently that the schools cannot do all the things being demanded of them.

> Schools are prepared to do what they have done all along: teach young people intellectual things, both by giving them information and giving them intellectual tools, such as literacy, mathematics and foreign languages.[21]

If it is accepted, at some risk of unpopularity when many seek alternative forms of schooling and alternative goals of education, that the schools exist to provide for intellectual learning, then it is not inappropriate to examine the deficiencies of schools in terms of the intellectual outcomes of education which they procure. In the absence of a detailed statement of essential educational outcomes and an assessment of the capacities of schools to obtain these goals, it is necessary to isolate inadequacies within the educational system by comparing schools and forms of education, with respect to specific outcomes of attainment and achievement. If there is a shortfall within a school or within a school system in the performance of its students, then deficiencies exist, and ways and means must be sought to attempt to remedy these deficiencies. This article now turns to assess some of the evidence for deficiencies in Australian education by looking comparatively at the outcomes of education obtained by various groups. From an examination of the differences between schools and school systems in their procurement of specific educational outcomes, we get some view of the location of deficiencies within Australian education. Such a perspective of inquiry would appear to be absent from both the *Report of the Interim Committee for the Australian Schools Commission* and the undertakings which the Commission since its establishment has sought to promote.

The definition and measurement of educational outcomes is a complex task. Nevertheless, it is unsound to abandon investigation into the educational outcomes gained by students in a school system because of the difficulties associated with the enterprise, even if the results of such an investigation must sometimes be examined with caution.

## DISPARITIES IN EDUCATIONAL ACHIEVEMENT AND ATTAINMENT

The evidence presented in this article has been derived from the only study which has been carried out so far to examine the educational achievement of students in all States of Australia and in schools of all types. The testing for this inquiry took place in 1970. The Australian aspects of the study have been described by Rosier[22], and an account of the international aspects has been given by Comber and Keeves.[23] Two tests of educational achievement were used, a short word knowledge test and an extensive test of achievement in science. The testing took place at two levels: the 14-year-old level, which was the last stage at which all members of an age cohort were still at school, and the pre-university or terminal secondary school stage. At both levels the target population consisted of all students at school, whether or not they were currently studying science. The samples of schools were drawn for each State separately, with a probability proportional to size, and were stratified according to type of school and metropolitan or country region. From within each school, 25 students were selected for testing. At the analysis stage the data for the six States were weighted for differences between States and for the very small losses from the designed sample.

While it must be acknowledged that there are other outcomes of the educational process that are important, the two that manifestly influence opportunities for future occupation and income are the number of years of education completed (attainment), and level of performance on tasks of learning (achievement). Consequently, these two outcomes of education are employed to identify the deficiencies in Australian education through an examination of the extent to which different groups reach these goals.

## Differences between the States

In Table 2 the results of one-way analyses of variance are presented using the school as the unit of analysis, as is appropriate for the kinds of comparisons being made. The use of schools as the unit involves the aggregation of the scores of the students in each school to obtain the mean score for each school. Moreover, since comparisons are being made between the mean scores for each State, it is unnecessary to weight the data for differences between States in sampling design. In addition, to permit an examination of differences in educational attainment in each State, between the 14-year-old level when all students in the age group are still at school, and the terminal secondary school stage when differential losses have occurred, the holding power or retentivity of each state group has been calculated from official statistics.

At the 14-year-old level there are no significant differences between States in performance on the word knowledge test, but highly significant differences in achievement in science, with the performance in Queensland, South Australia and Western Australia being high, performance in Victoria and Tasmania being low and that in New South Wales lying between. These results suggest that on the one hand there are few differences between the general ability of the students in the different States, since achievement on a word knowledge test is strongly related to ability, and little difference in their educational programs that is associated with the development of a knowledge of the meaning of words. On the other hand, however, there appear to be clear differences between the States in their provision for the learning of science and in the level of achievement of their students. Moreover, while it may be argued that the variation between States is small in comparison with the variation between students within States, the difference in achievement between the highest and lowest State (4.6 score points) is of the same order of magnitude as the standard deviation of the scores for schools (approximately five points). Table 2 also shows for this age group the proportion of the target population in each State and the estimated holding power, which at the 14-year-old level is necessarily 100 per cent, since this level is below the age when compulsory schooling finishes.

At the terminal secondary school stage the differences between States in performance on the word knowledge test are significant, with the scores of schools in Victoria, Queensland and South Australia being high and those of schools in New South Wales, Western Australia and Tasmania being lower. A reason for such differences does not come readily to mind. The differences between the States in achievement in science are more substantial with the scores for schools in South Australia being approximately a school standard deviation in excess of the lowest of the scores for the other States. The nature of these differences between States in science achievement is of interest, since it

69

**Table 2. Disparities in Educational Achievement and Attainment by State**

| 14-Year-Old Level | No of Schools | Estimated Holding Power % | Proportion of Target Population % | Mean Achievement | |
|---|---|---|---|---|---|
| | | | | Science | Word Knowledge |
| New South Wales | 37 | 100 | 35 | 24.5 | 16.1 |
| Victoria | 39 | 100 | 28 | 22.7 | 15.6 |
| Queensland | 38 | 100 | 15 | 27.1 | 16.7 |
| South Australia | 38 | 100 | 10 | 27.0 | 16.5 |
| Western Australia | 37 | 100 | 9 | 26.7 | 16.5 |
| Tasmania | 32 | 100 | 3 | 22.5 | 14.6 |
| F-Ratio | | | | 0.001 | N.S. |
| Significance p | | | | 6.04 | 1.61 |
| **Pre-University Level** | | | | | |
| New South Wales | 39 | 32 | 37 | 23.6 | 20.1 |
| Victoria | 37 | 31 | 29 | 24.3 | 21.6 |
| Queensland | 37 | 29 | 14 | 25.7 | 21.2 |
| South Australia | 32 | 27 | 9 | 28.1 | 21.7 |
| Western Australia | 31 | 27 | 7 | 24.8 | 20.2 |
| Tasmania | 18 | 21 | 4 | 24.4 | 19.7 |
| F-Ratio | | | | 4.64 | 2.53 |
| Significance p | | | | <0.001 | <0.05 |

is possible that it is related to the conditions under which science is taught in the different parts of Australia. Perhaps, however, such factors as the different proportions of boys and girls studying science may contribute, as may differences in holding power between the States.

The proportion of the target population in each State at the pre-university level is recorded in Table 2, together with the holding power of the school system within each State. These estimates of the holding power are obtained by expressing the size of the pre-university grade as a proportion of the size of the corresponding grade cohort in 1966 when the group were in their eighth year of schooling. Both New South Wales and Victoria have a relatively high level of retentivity, with Queensland, South Australia and Western Australia being slightly lower. In Tasmania it is possible for students to enter university from Year 11, and while it is not easy to make allowance for this in the calculation of estimates of retentivity it has been done by assuming that approximately half of the Year 11 group are able to enter tertiary education in the following year. In spite of these rather liberal adjustments to the Tasmanian data, the evidence still shows that there is a lower level of retentivity in Tasmanian schools at the terminal stage than in other States.

**Table 3. Disparities in Educational Achievement and Attainment by Type of School and Region**

| 14-Year-Old Level | Estimated Holding Power % | Estimated Proportion of Target Population % | Mean Achievement | |
|---|---|---|---|---|
| | | | Science | Word Knowledge |
| **Type of School** | | | | |
| Government | 100 | 77 | 23.5 | 15.0 |
| Catholic | 100 | 16 | 27.1 | 18.5 |
| Independent | 100 | 7 | 32.0 | 21.6 |
| **Region** | | | | |
| Metropolitan | 100 | 59 | 25.7 | 16.8 |
| Non-Metropolitan | 100 | 41 | 23.3 | 15.0 |
| **Pre-University Level** | | | | |
| **Type of School** | | | | |
| Government | 25 | 65 | 24.9 | 20.5 |
| Catholic | 36 | 19 | 23.7 | 21.8 |
| Independent | 70 | 16 | 25.3 | 22.3 |
| **Region** | | | | |
| Metropolitan | 35 | 67 | 25.2 | 21.5 |
| Non-Metropolitan | 24 | 33 | 23.8 | 20.3 |

## Differences between school type and region

Table 3 gives evidence for differences between the average level of achievement on the word knowledge and science tests for students in the three types of schools, government, Catholic and independent, and in the metropolitan and non-metropolitan regions at the two levels of schooling. In addition, the relative percentages of each group in the target population have been estimated from the sample data and estimates have also been calculated for the holding power of each group. No attempt has been made to test the significance of the differences between groups by analysis of variance procedures, because the data have been weighted for differences between States in sampling.

The data presented in Table 3 reveal that at both the 14-year-old level and at the pre-university level the majority of students are in the government schools, and there are more of the remainder in the Catholic schools than in the non-Catholic independent schools. In addition, at both levels as might be expected there are greater proportions in the metropolitan than in the non-metropolitan schools. There are, however, different degrees of retentivity in the schools of different types. The estimates show that the independent schools hold a higher proportion of their students through to the terminal secondary school stage than do either the Catholic or the government schools. Moreover, more students remain longer at school in metropolitan than in non-metropolitan areas.

At the 14-year-old level the students in the independent schools score better on both the science and the word knowledge tests than do the Catholic and government school students. In addition, the Catholic students show better performance on these tests than do the government school students. However, at the pre-university level, the differences between the groups are smaller and no clear and consistent pattern of results is observed.

It should also be noted that the students in the non-metropolitan schools show a lower level of performance on the science and word knowledge tests than is shown by their coevals in the metropolitan schools.

## THE EFFECTS OF THE COMMUNITY IN WHICH THE SCHOOL IS LOCATED[24]

In the previous section, variation between schools has been examined in terms of differences between States, between school types and between the regions in which the schools are located. However, it is important to recognize that disparities in the education provided by the schools must be examined after allowance has been made for the nature of the community in which the school is operating. In the discussion which follows, consideration has been restricted to only one outcome of education, the one measured with greatest accuracy in the IEA Science Project, namely achievement in science. Whereas the Schools Commission employed an indicator associated with the neighbourhood served by the school that was based on census data and assessed socio-economic level, the evidence collected in this inquiry showed that an index associated with the cultural level of the homes of the students within the school was more powerful. Moreover, while it is recognized that neighbourhood and community advantage or disadvantage is many faceted, it is desirable that any measures used in complex analyses should be parsimonious and largely unidimensional. Consequently, the index employed in this study involved relatively few key variables and was formed using simple integer weights to combine those variables.

The six variables selected for this measure of the community served by a school were:
1 father's occupation,
2 father's education,
3 mother's education,
4 use of dictionary in the home,
5 number of books in the home, and
6 family size.
It is assumed in interpreting the meaning of this index that the students in a school will be drawn from a community or neighbourhood which is characterized by the average of these measures for its students of whom the members tested were a sample. When the composite measure was entered into

regression analyses to account for the variance of the achievement test scores in science, with priority over other variables for school type, region and State, it explained 40 per cent of the total variance at the 14-year-old level and five per cent of the variance at the terminal secondary school stage. At the middle secondary school level, before students start to leave school, this measure of the cultural level of the community or neighbourhood served by the school is clearly a very powerful factor. However, at the upper secondary school level where differing degrees of retentivity have operated across the different levels assessed by this measure, it declines in significance. At the 14-year-old level approximately 70 per cent of the total variance between schools in their scores on the science test was accounted for by all variables included in the analysis and at the terminal secondary school level the proportion of the total variance explained was 67 per cent. Thus at the 14-year-old level about half of the variance explained (40 per cent of 70 per cent) was ascribed to the measure of the cultural level of the community, but at the upper secondary school level a much lesser proportion was accounted for by this measure.

In the regression analyses carried out to examine the data for achievement in science using schools as the unit of analysis, attempts were made to assess the importance of State, type of school and region after allowance had been made for community effects, the sex of the student in the school and the type of program offered by the school. While there were significant differences between States, after adjustment in the analyses for the measure of the cultural level of the community, there was no effect associated with type of school at the 14-year-old level and only a slight effect at the terminal secondary school stage, with the government schools and the independent schools showing a higher level of performance in science than the Catholic schools. Furthermore, there were no significant effects associated with urban or rural regions across Australia. However, in subsequent analyses, using students as the unit of analysis, significant regional effects were found in Victoria and Western Australia at the 14-year-old level, with students from rural homes showing a lower performance than those in urban areas.

The evidence from these analyses provided general support for the use, below age 15 years when compulsory schooling finishes, of a measure of socio-economic level of the neighbourhood to assess the level of educational disadvantage experienced by the schools in the neighbourhood. However, it was evident that a school-based measure involving the cultural level of the homes of the students in the school was likely to be more effective than an indicator of the socio-economic level of the neighbourhood of the school. Nevertheless, this superior measure accounted at best for about half the variance between schools in their achievement test scores in science.

It is important to note that the methods of analysis employed allowed the home background factors to have the maximum possible opportunity to account for the variance of the science achievement test scores. More detailed analyses of the variation in science achievement between schools indicated that, at the 14-year-old level, only a little over 13 per cent of the variance explained was unique to the school community measure, the remainder of its contribution being shared with other factors. The causal significance of the estimation of the magnitude of this shared contribution has recently been the subject of some controversy.[25] Many of the points raised in this debate remain unanswered. It is clear, however, that such a measure is the best indicator currently available for identifying schools where there is a low level of achievement, but that it is far from a perfect measure.

## LOW PERFORMING SCHOOLS

An alternative approach to that of identifying disadvantaged schools in terms of socio-economic level would be to identify them in terms of the performance of their students. Consequently, it is of some interest to determine the locality and type of the schools in each State with the lowest level of performance. The *Report of the Interim Committee for the Australian Schools Commission* sought to ascertain where schools holding approximately 15 per cent of the most seriously disadvantaged students, gauged in terms of socio-economic level, were located within metropolitan areas; the figure of 10 per cent was used within non-metropolitan districts.[26] In the investigation that follows we have attempted to identify low-performing schools, from among those in the IEA state samples, that have a level of performance below that defined by the achievement standard of the 15th percentile school. Since the samples of schools were drawn with a probability proportional to their size and were weighted in the analyses to make the total sample representative of Australia as a whole, the schools below the 15th percentile might be expected to represent 15 per cent of the Australian students in the target population, but not necessarily the 15 per cent of students with the lowest performance. Since the target population for the 14-year-old sample comprises all students before attrition by early leaving takes effect, it is an appropriate sample to examine for determining the nature of the schools scoring below the 15th percentile on measures of achievement.

In Table 4 we have recorded for each State the numbers of schools and their locality and type within the samples for the 14-year-old population which fell below the 15th percentile for either the word knowledge or science test. This exercise, while crude and likely to reflect the vagaries of sampling, was illuminating. Suffice it to say there were no independent schools with a standard of performance below this mark. The largest groups of low-performing schools were located in the Victorian metropolitan and non-metropolitan areas and in Tasmanian rural areas. The first group agreed with that identified by the sophisticated techniques employed by the Schools Commission, but little hint of the existence of the Tasmanian and Victorian rural groups emerged from the analyses carried out in the preparation of the Interim Committee's report. Furthermore, an examination of the mean scores for the Tasmanian schools revealed a very low level of performance in some schools, suggesting that not insignificant numbers of students in these schools

**Table 4. Numbers of Schools in States with Performance Level below the Fifteenth Percentile**

| State<br>Number of<br>Schools | NSW<br>37 | Victoria<br>39 | Queensland<br>38 | S.A.<br>38 | W.A.<br>37 | Tasmania<br>32 |
|---|---|---|---|---|---|---|
| **Word Knowledge** | | | | | | |
| Government | | | | | | |
|   Metropolitan | 2 | 7 | 0 | 3 | 0 | 0 |
|   Non-metropolitan | 3 | 4 | 2 | 2 | 0 | 6 |
| Catholic | | | | | | |
|   Metropolitan | 0 | 0 | 0 | 0 | 0 | 0 |
|   Non-metropolitan | 0 | 0 | 0 | 0 | 0 | 0 |
| **Total** | 5 | 11 | 2 | 5 | 0 | 6 |
| **Science** | | | | | | |
| Government | | | | | | |
|   Metropolitan | 2 | 6 | 0 | 2 | 0 | 0 |
|   Non-metropolitan | 4 | 4 | 0 | 0 | 1 | 6 |
| Catholic | | | | | | |
|   Metropolitan | 0 | 0 | 0 | 0 | 1 | 0 |
|   Non-metropolitan | 0 | 1 | 0 | 0 | 0 | 0 |
| **Total** | 6 | 11 | 0 | 2 | 2 | 6 |

may be functionally illiterate. It should also be noted that there were smaller proportions of low-performing schools in the remaining States, and there were only two Catholic schools in the group. These schools were in Victoria and Western Australia and showed a low level of achievement in science but not in word knowledge.

It is not immediately apparent from survey data just what these low-performing schools lack, and a careful examination of the schools might have helped to reveal the nature and extent of their deficiencies. However, from the analyses undertaken by Rosier[27], some evidence is available on the factors which distinguish between schools in their level of achievement in science, apart from those directly associated with the time spent in school in the study of science and the opportunity which the students had to learn the subject matter tested.

Only one factor associated with the resources available to the schools was found to be important. This factor involved the availability of laboratory assistants and other ancillary staff. Moreover, it should be noted that in those schools, where the students perceived that there was a more liberal and less restrictive approach to discipline, the students performed better on the science tests. Furthermore, in schools where the teachers spent more time on preparation, both in the laboratory and in marking assignments, where the teachers stated they made a considerable effort to make the students' practical experience the basis of their scientific knowledge, where the teachers favoured placing emphasis on information as well as teaching students to think scientifically, and where the amount of post-secondary training of the teachers, particularly in physics, was high, the students had higher scores. In addition, in schools where the students spent more time on homework, and where decisions on the content and methods of the courses studied were determined by the head of the science department or by external bodies rather than by individual teachers, there was also a higher level of achievement.

There were many variables concerned with conditions for learning in the schools and with the resources available to schools on which information was collected in this inquiry, that did not emerge from the analyses as being important in accounting for variation between schools and students in science achievement. Such variables of interest to educational planners include size of school and size of class. The failure of variables to enter the regression analyses as significant may have arisen from errors of measurement, from inadequacies in the instruments used, or perhaps more importantly, from lack of variation with respect to these variables in Australian schools.

In some cases the presence of non-linear relationships may have prevented variables which were otherwise important from entering the regression equations. Alternatively, the variables may have been so strongly linked with State, school type, community and home background factors that they failed to make an independent contribution. However, Rosier has been able to direct attention to the conditions under which science might be taught and learnt in Australian schools to yield an optimal level of achievement.

> . . . there emerges a clear picture of a cluster or rosette of factors which influence their level of achievement in science . . . taken together these factors contribute to the overall picture that effective learning of science takes place in a consistent school environment where students receive competent systematic instruction in carefully structured science courses.[28]

It seems likely that, in other areas of school learning, the same class of factors detected by Rosier for the learning of science would lead to a higher level of mastery and to greater cognitive development in these other subjects.

## THE FUTURE PROGRAM OF THE SCHOOLS COMMISSION

In this article it has been shown that the Schools Commission has concentrated on the need for providing an adequate quantity and quality of resources to schools. These needs of the schools cannot be denied, but the desirability of achieving a particular kind of outcome from the schools and the need for directing resources to the schools according to their effectiveness in moving towards important goals also cannot be gainsaid. Evidence has been presented on factors influencing achievement outcomes of schools, which are believed by many to be important, and it is clear that these findings are not inconsistent with some of the more specific needs perceived to exist by the Interim Committee of the Australian Schools Commission. The Commission has, however, up to the time of writing, failed to attempt to identify or to promote a detailed examination of the aims and goals of education for our society.

Without some statement of aims and goals it is difficult to isolate explicitly the inadequacies of Australian schools, although some deficiencies of schooling might be derived from acknowledged deficiencies in the social and cultural life of the country.

Laudably, the Schools Commission has allocated funds to assist students in disadvantaged schools. These schools were identified, initially by a measure of socio-economic level based on an acknowledgment of its relationships with achievement, and subsequently by the judgment of experienced observers or by the use of indices of priority. More recently the Schools Commission has declared that one of the basic values which should underlie the development of its programs is:

> attainment of minimum standards of competence for life in a modern democratic, industrial society.[29]

The Commission, if it were to take seriously its declared basic value of the 'attainment of minimum standards of competence' should direct some efforts into identifying those areas of competence which are believed to be important for life in present-day Australia. Such competence must be stated in explicit terms, with identified characteristics of successful accomplishment of the areas of competence, and the definition of situations in which students can show their attainment or lack of attainment of competence in a specific area.

In this article the location and type of schools where there is a low level of performance have been identified. While there are many limitations associated with the procedures employed, they do suggest schools in which we might expect to find students who are failing to attain the standards of competence referred to above. If it is accepted that only a very few students in Australian schools cannot be helped through education to achieve competence in essential areas, then those who are failing must be identified and assisted. The problems associated with children not learning in the past, and with the low levels of performance on the word knowledge and science tests in some schools, do not necessarily arise from the innate limitations of the children or from the socio-economic disadvantage of the neighbourhoods in which the children and their parents live. They may arise in whole or in major part from a failure of schools to seek optimal instructional strategies to ensure that children from disadvantaged backgrounds attain adequate standards of performance in the essential skills of communication and a knowledge of the world in which they live.

## Notes

1 Australia. (1973). *Schools in Australia. Report of the Interim Committee for the Australian Schools Commission.* (Chairman, P. Karmel). Canberra: AGPS.
2 Australian Education Council. (1963). *A Statement of Some Needs of Australian Education.* Sydney: Australian Education Council.
3 ibid.: 1.
4 See Bassett, G. W. (1970). *Planning in Australian Education.* Report of a Seminar on Educational Planning. Hawthorn, Vic.: ACER.
5 Australian Education Council. (1970). *Nation-wide Survey of Educational Needs.* Reprinted by NSW Teachers' Federation.

6 Australia. op. cit.: 47.
7 ibid.: 63.
8 ibid.: 81.
9 Australia. Schools Commission. (1974). *Newsletter No. 4* (August).
10 See the paper delivered by Ms Jean Blackburn on 'The Role of the Schools Commission in Developing a Contemporary Strategy for Australian Education' to the Unesco 'Learning to Be' Seminar conducted by the Australian Unesco Committee on Education at the Australian National University, 26–30 August 1974.
11 Australia. (1973). op.cit.: Appendix E.
12 ibid.: 166–167.
13 United Kingdom. (1967). *Children and their Primary Schools*. Report of the Advisory Council for England and Wales (Plowden Report). London: HMSO.
14 ibid.: 57–59.
15 For a fuller discussion of this work see Halsey, A. H. (Ed.) (1972). *Educational Priority. Volume 1: E.P.A. Problems and Policies*. London: HMSO, pp. 48–53.
16 Clements, J. M. and Rosier, M. J. (1974). *The Construction and Validation of the School Priority Index*. Melbourne: Supplementary Grants Committee, Victorian Education Department.
17 ibid.: 11.
18 Australia. (1973). op.cit.: 91.
19 ibid.: 49.
20 Jackson, R. W. B. (1962). *Emergent Needs in Australian Education*. Hawthorn, Vic.: ACER, p. 21.
21 Coleman, J. S. (1972). 'How do the Young Become Adults?'. In *Review of Educational Research*, 42 (4): 432.
22 Rosier, M. J. (1973). *Science Achievement in Australian Secondary Schools*. Hawthorn, Vic.: ACER.
23 Comber, L. C. and Keeves, J. P. (1973). *Science Education in Nineteen Countries*. Stockholm: Almqvist and Wiksell; and New York: Halsted (Wiley).
24 For a more detailed consideration of the analyses reported in this section see: Comber, L. C. and Keeves, J. P. op. cit. and Rosier, M. J. (1973). *Variation between Australian States in Science Achievement*. IEA (Australia) Report 1973: 5. Hawthorn, Vic.: ACER.
25 See Keeves, J. P. (1974). *The Effects of the Conditions of Learning in the Schools*. IEA (Australia) Report 1974: 2. Hawthorn, Vic.: ACER.
26 Australia. (1973). op. cit.: 99–103.
27 Rosier, M. J. (1974). 'Factors Associated with Learning Science in Australian Secondary Schools', *Comparative Education Review*, 18 (2): 180–187.
28 ibid.: 186–187.
29 Australia. Schools Commission. Report to the Hon. Kim E. Beazley, MP. Minister for Education. *Supplementary Funds for Programs Administered by the Schools Commission*. August, 1974.

# 5. Teachers, the Public and Educational Change

P. W. Musgrave

## EDUCATION BECOMES A SOCIAL PROBLEM

In the decades immediately following Federation, education was defined constitutionally as a responsibility of the States, but since the 1940s there has been a gradual, but accelerating movement towards the view that the central government should bear more of the responsibility for education at every level. This process began, and is now almost complete, in the field of tertiary education; it was seen next at secondary level in the provision of scholarships and of capital grants for laboratories and libraries and is now accepted for all, including primary schools. What is to be noticed is the way in which the process first showed itself in the tertiary area where per capita costs are highest and gradually spread throughout the whole educational field. In other words, education became a problem largely because scarce resources were demanded and could only be allocated through a political process.

Education, therefore, gradually became more deeply involved in and, hence, dependent upon federal, rather than state, politics. The final stage of this change came when the Labor Party were returned to power in December 1972. For some time they had seen the educational policies of the Liberal-Country Party Government as inegalitarian and insufficient. Throughout the democratic world during the 1960s there was a shift in the definition of educational equality from one that was meritocratic in nature and which led to the organization of wider scholarship ladders for the able, usually discovered by psychometric tests, to a totally different concept that was based on the idea that all should have the same chance to develop their own personality characteristics, even if there had to be positive discrimination in favour of those who began with least advantages. In Australia, a land dedicated to (the myth of) 'fair go's', this ideological change meant a move away from the policy of uniform provision for all by State Education Departments to one in which by some means those who were seen as needy, whether they were poor, immigrant or Aboriginal, should be given more educational resources than their white, Anglo-Saxon neighbours.

As the proportion of the gross national product going to education increased during the 1960s, education was bound to be less taken for granted and to become a topic for political discussion, but what might have been merely a growing concern became a major conflict under the impact of Labor criticism. Education was accepted by the electorate as a, if not the, social problem. One test of this interpretation is that, in the election of 1974, the opposition parties in effect made no attempt to go back on what had been done by Labor during their initial 15 months in office. But, though education may be seen as a problem by most voters, their reasons for now holding this view are probably very different from those of most educationalists and many politicians. There is much evidence that the average parent takes an instrumental view that staying longer at school will 'get Johnny or Mary a better job'. Many of those running schools and school systems, however, believe that more and different education will give people more resources to live a fuller life, thereby making society by their often vaguely specified criteria a better place. It is such confusions over expectations that can lead to frustrations among citizens when the outcomes of political decisions about their welfare are translated into administrative programs by professionals ostensibly working on the public behalf, but actually working towards other goals. What answers, then, were proposed in the field of education, seen by many in the early 1970s as an area of crisis, but largely defined as a social problem by Labor itself?

## THE ANSWER FROM KARMEL

Even where problems generate relatively agreed answers, there can be various methods of translating them into the administrative mechanisms needed to achieve social change. In the early nineteenth century in Britain, one mechanism was that often attributed to Jeremy Bentham. This can be summarized in three words, 'investigate, legislate, administer'. Both in Britain and in Australia, such social problems as those associated with the conditions of labour or in prisons or in the schools have come to be examined in depth by commissions which have led to legislation, which, in its turn, has been administered by public servants subject to the scrutiny of the people through parliament. Furthermore, this method has been adopted by Fabian Socialists and has, therefore, been attractive to many in the Labor Party.

Since the Whitlam Government saw education as one of the social problems requiring rapid attention, it appointed an Interim Committee for the Australian Schools Commission on 12 December 1972, under Professor Karmel, and asked it to report by the end of May 1973 (1.1-2).[1] This political fact must be emphasized in view of the criticisms that will be made later in this article. Something had to be done and done quickly. Indeed, by 18 May 1973, the Karmel Committee produced a document of remarkable quality which has had a major impact on Australian education. The solutions which were suggested were inevitably deeply influenced by the assumptions that the Committee held about man and about the sort of society which they saw as good.[2]

The psychological model of man assumed in any educational analysis dictates the range of strategies available. A genetic view of capability narrows the limits of remedial action in a way that an environmentalist view does not. The Committee have it both ways in that the report claims that 'the final outcome' of 'developed ability ... is the result of continuous and complex interaction between ... genetic and environmental contributions' (3.18).

Thus,

> there are good reasons for attempting to compensate to some extent through schooling for unequal out-of-school situations in order to ensure the child's overall condition of upbringing is as free of restrictions due to the circumstances of his family as public action through the schools can make it (2.7).

Such compensatory action has recently come under strong criticism, particularly by Jencks who, after an extensive review of the literature, has asserted that the school can do little to correct inequality rooted in the unequal structure of capitalist society. On this view, a radical solution would be an attack on the present structure of income.[3]

However, the Committee's model of Australian society in the 1980s is one which, though more egalitarian than today, is nonetheless characterized by a social system very similar to that at present. In addition, high priority is given, on the one hand, to a greater toleration of a wide variety of social groupings, including different religious groupings and, on the other, to a possibly contradictory social characteristic, namely to a strong sense of community. Here again, the direction for change is indicated but the rate is specified in Fabian terms. There is clearly a firm belief that the planning of controlled social change is possible.

The means for change recommended by the Committee fall within the limits specified by these assumptions. Much money must be directed by means of a number of programs, mainly compensatory in nature, to aid all children of whatever grouping or religion who are seen to be in need. Out of $467 million recommended for expenditure in 1974–5, $407 million were to be spent on four programs related to recurrent grants to schools, general building grants, libraries and grants to disadvantaged schools (14.10) with the aim that all schools should have reached an acceptable standard by 1979. An additional $43.5 million was to go to special education. Control was to be exercised by a statutory Schools Commission, backed by a secretariat, consisting of full- and part-time experts. This body was established in 1973 and was granted the finance and powers by and large as recommended by the Committee. Thus, an executive commission of experts with wide powers has control of many resources and the manner in which these are channelled to the schools in both the government and non-government systems so that social change may occur through the schools.

Undoubtedly, the Labor Government had to act quickly in an attempt to begin to solve the educational problem. The Karmel report answered this need and did so in a way that looked rational since the recommendations were based on expert advice and on research of a remarkable quality considering the brief time available. The answer, therefore, appeared legitimate. However, the question that must be asked is whether today, when the first stage of the programs is over, or in 1979, when the total plan is completed, Australians will either be satisfied or even notice any difference in their schools. How will the electorate evaluate the Karmel plan? The position taken here is that, even allowing for the immediate need on both political and social grounds for many material improvements in buildings and equipment, it is to the other two programs, those relating to in-service training and to the encouragement of innovations, that more attention and resources might have been given from the start and must be given in future recommendations from the Schools Commission. This may seem an odd answer to the question just posed, but the attempt will first be made to justify it and then, as a result of this analysis, to give some possible future sailing directions for the consideration of the public and the Commission.

## A CRITICISM OF THE ANSWER FROM KARMEL

In the short term, material resources may be seen as the important factor influencing the quality of education, but in any long-term analysis this totally misses the mark. Education fundamentally is not constrained by the quality of buildings and equipment but by the nature of the teachers and by what children learn. Fine teachers can work without overhead projectors, carpets on the floor and expensively devised kits of material. They create situations within which their pupils both learn so-called academic knowledge and develop into adequate persons. To do this they require some material resources, but above all they require a large measure of public acceptance and support for the direction in which they develop the schools. In a plural society this may mean an acceptance of diversity, though we must be careful not to see this as an excuse for the status quo. This type of analysis switches the focus from compensation to the culture of contemporary society and demands some consideration of (1) the manner in which the general public relates to education, (2) some aspects of the training of teachers, and (3) the implications for administration of this changed focus.

### The general public

One of the implicit assumptions in the Karmel report is that there is a considerable interest in education among some large sections of the public. It is upon this interest that the appeal to community and to grass-roots control rests Research at present under way in Victoria shows such an assumption is unreal in the metropolitan area, and possibly also in the country 'community spirit' is not so strong as often assumed. Most ordinary people are only concerned about education inasmuch as it affects their own children. The form that most people's interest takes is the hope that schooling will lead to a job which pays well and carries high status, though, of course, there are not sufficient such jobs for all who want them. When asked if they feel able or want to help administer their local schools, the usual response is of this order,

> I'm a plumber and wouldn't expect a teacher to tell me how to do my job. I'm not going to tell him how to do his. Anyway, after a hard day's work I'm not willing to go up to the school at night to take part in committee meetings.[4]

In other words, unless support is mobilized in some way, the public are neither very concerned with education either in the way the Committee assumes, nor are they interested except instrumentally, and that is not the way in which many in education perceive what they are trying to do.

There is, of course, nothing wrong in a democracy if those with power or those who wish to be influential propound a view which is as yet unaccepted by or even unacceptable to the majority. Such 'leadership' is one of the ways in which change comes about. However, very often those expecting to lead, that is to change the social situation, have to work at putting forward their ideas. They must persuade the public. Yet to do so they must have a notion of their aims. Unfortunately, in education aims are very vague and slippery. They are rarely discussed with clarity even in educational circles, but at the moment there is no general public debate about the aims of Australian schools. Take, for example, one crucial question: are our schools meant to convert migrants into Australians or in some measure to help to preserve their cultures so that Australia becomes a truly pluralist society? Discussion of this or of similar questions has hardly begun.

In recent years, there has been a beginning to the process whereby discussion about such issues could take place because such newspapers as *The Australian* and *The Age* now carry regular educational features. Yet, although the Committee acknowledged 'the antipathy towards and apathy about direct community participation in the governance of schooling' (2.19), it pressed for participation. Nor did it make clear what the nature of this participation was to be. Was it to be 'citizen participation', whereby all citizens had a chance to play a part in their local school or was it to be 'interest-oriented participation', whereby pressure groups were enabled more easily to influence the schools?[5]

Since there is no great or informed interest in education there must be great difficulty in doing what many consider worthwhile, namely removing the schools from their isolation and rooting them in their neighbourhoods. This last word is chosen advisedly in preference to 'community', because what evidence exists forces the view that the spirit of community in its traditional sense no longer really exists in the large metropolitan areas in which the vast majority of Australians live. Many suggestions to break down the isolation of the school can be made. Thus, local government might be strengthened and given responsibilities for schools as in Britain; local governance of education might be tied to responsibility for raising finance as in the USA or, though at a rather different economic level, Papua New Guinea, or recurrent education might be more readily available as in some provinces in Canada, in the hope that the idea of schooling might never be far from the minds of most adult citizens. These measures could all lead to some opening up of our now isolated educational system.

## The teachers

The climate of schools, especially in a country where education is rather cut off from society, is deeply dependent upon the characteristics and quality of teachers. The teaching force does receive some attention in the Karmel report, but is not given a central position. Teacher development (11.1–21) is given six pages and $10.3 million of the $467 million for 1974–5 (14.10). Some money is set aside for establishing 'Education Centres' in which teachers may do what all fully professional groups do, namely initiate their own in-service training (11.16–20), but the funds are only sufficient to establish 17 centres throughout Australia. Thus, four will serve New South Wales and three Victoria.

Yet in a chapter on 'Fostering Change' (12.1–19), the Committee did realize the importance of stimulating an innovatory climate in our schools. Four pages and $6.0 million were allocated for this purpose. The lack of such a spirit

> has been due largely to lack of resources and because the people most affected have been made to feel that they are merely reacting to a particular policy or procedure instead of being actively engaged in formulating it (12.4).

Both points require comment. Firstly, lack of resources in industry often leads to innovation, to a more efficient way of doing the job. Although the application of economic criteria to education raises the hackles of most educationalists and is, indeed, fraught with philosophical and statistical difficulties, yet there is no logical reason, though it is heretical to say so, why the first argument from scarce resources used by the Committee should be true.

However, the second argument, based on the climate of the organization, carries no such logical objection. Yet, despite their foresight in including this program in their recommendations and their wisdom in retaining direct control from Canberra over this part of the total expenditure, the Committee did not tie this essentially on-service training, which is what attempts at innovation initiated in any one school to some extent must be, into their in-service program. There are no administrative links and no special arrangements are made for disseminating the results of the program of innovation. Just possibly the Committee may have felt that to go further here would have met opposition from the State Education Departments on the grounds that this was carrying the centralizing tendency in educational administration too far and, secondly, though felt, not to be openly admitted, that as far as possible any subsidized and possibly uncomfortable 'stirring' should be in their own control, not in the hands of those in Canberra.

Both programs, and they are connected in that both relate to the nature of our teachers, are not given high priority. Just as in the case of the public, where we have seen that the level of general educational discourse is not high, so here no real attempts were made to create a structure which gives opportunities for all teachers to renew themselves and, according to one's views of the present situation, either to raise the level of expert educational discourse or to keep it at its present level as social and educational circumstances change through time.

## Administration

The structure that was suggested by the Committee and enshrined in the subsequent Act[6] seems to have resulted in an expert executive body that hands out a great deal of money, admittedly to the States for their detailed use, but on criteria decided by the Commission. Despite the Committee's appeal to the grass-roots, both in school and 'community', these decisions and those related to the innovation program seem to be clothed in secrecy.

The need for more knowledge about the nature of and the methods by which decisions are taken is not only based on the ideological arguments in favour of open government that the Labor Government claims to hold. An administrative structure must be created that on *a priori* grounds will support the goals and assumptions of the programs concerned. If this is not done, the chances of success are minimized by the degree by which the administration is an obstacle.

Yet this demand for greater openness in itself raises difficulties. The public discussion must inevitably be a political one since the outcome is intended to influence the allocation of governmental resources. One of the conclusions that might be drawn from the experience of the USA in relation to the running of their educational and poverty programs during the 1960s is that once they become part of the political domain, particularly at the local level, central control becomes difficult, if not impossible.[7] The reformers in the USA seemed to forget that the strict rationality used in planning exercises does not closely match the arguments characteristic of politics.

Once the debate has become public, another problem about the present situation is avoided. What control is there at the moment to prevent those in power in the Schools Commission, or those disembursing the resources allocated to them at the state level, from using their positions to further a political stance only supported by a small group? Their educational prescription may be better medicine for us by even our own criteria, but unless we know the full story we are encouraging the existence of a new form of paternalism. If we are to be in the hands of professional planners there is no code of professional ethics to prevent what has been called 'malpractice with respect to the community'.[8] Widely disseminated public knowledge is the only defence against this. It is also the only way in which administrators ought to enter the political level of the debate.

If the voice of those affected is to be heard there must be some policy that leads to the creation of mechanisms to inform the public at every level so that educational discourse is based on as full information as possible and is reasonably rational. On this argument the Karmel Committee omitted serious consideration of ways by which experts could inform laymen and by which the public could in some democratic mode influence the direction in which the Schools Commission might move. Crucial to this process is the creation of a monitoring process whereby the results, whether success, partial success or failure of the programs now operating can be evaluated. In the political emergency of early 1973 the argument that 'the quality aspects of the resources used in the schools, whether teachers or buildings, defy statistical tabulation' (4.52) may be excused so that, for example, $116 million can be spent in 1974–5 on buildings (14.10), but in the long run not just efficiency of economic allocation but also fairness between schools demands closer analysis developed from a more thorough monitoring of Australian education. This more accurate data will in itself, if disseminated widely, make for a more informed democratic dialogue as it affects policy-making in education.

## POSSIBLE COURSES OF FUTURE ACTION

What has to be realized is that the analysis so far has not by and large introduced new assumptions into the argument of the Karmel Committee. In its second chapter, the report outlined seven 'principal values from which its recommendations (were) derived' (2.3): (1) devolution of responsibility, (2) equality, (3) diversity, (4) public and private schooling, (5) community involvement, (6) special purposes of schools, and (7) recurrent education. Though the focus had to be on the second, fourth and, perhaps, sixth of these values in the early years of the program, much more attention must in the future be given to the remaining values and particularly the first and fifth. In addition, as will be seen later, the last is also relevant to the problem of raising the level of educational discourse amongst the general public and teachers.

### The general public

In any system there are goals towards which those in power aim. Clarity in specifying these goals is needed in education as in other systems for several reasons, all of which have been implied in the analysis so far. Firstly, evaluation of success demands a clear idea of what to succeed means. Secondly, the diversity of a plural society demands specification of what pluralities may exist. Lastly, equality demands the spelling out of the dimensions along which all are to be equal. Discussion of such educational goals at the level of public discourse has not really begun in Australia. Since intellectually, if not emotionally, diversity is accepted, there is no need to accept one set of goals for all education in Australia, but clarity will help to spell out what the alternatives are that are politically acceptable and what are not. For example, the schools of the old religion, Christianity, in its various versions are acceptable. Are those of the new religion, Marxism, in its various versions also acceptable? The alternatives must be stated and clarified so that the political decisions can be made about how our schools will help form the Australian culture of the future.

Debate will be encouraged by publicizing the issues, more particularly as they relate to concrete cases. Here, the place of the innovation program is important. Changes to our present system may be seen as unacceptable, but they can only be rejected as deviant or accepted, and hence no longer seen as deviant, if information about them becomes known both to the experts, the teachers, *and* to the lay public who, in a democracy, like it or not, are their masters. The Schools Commission, then, must act as an agent to publicize what innovations are being attempted, which have succeeded or failed and what criteria are being used for these attempts and for monitoring them. Knowledgeable experts and an informed public increase the chance that the program advocated by the reformers, here the Schools Commission, may be refused by those who are its target. It is not just the public who may reject innovation, but the reformers and those at 'the chalkface' may be at odds as was the case in the Educational Priority Area in Dundee, Scotland where some teachers rejected what was proposed because their experience led them to believe that the children whom they taught and knew would be better off under the old educational regime than under what was suggested.[9]

This refusal is the right of those concerned, but is less likely where the reformers are operating from full information and where those who decide amongst teachers and general public also have full information. This, then, must be one central goal for future action by the Schools Commission. There is, therefore, a need for a publicity program carried on at several levels, but certainly aimed at both teachers and the general public. Funds must be available to ensure that newspapers, national, state and local, can regularly comment on educational issues. Regular features might be subsidized on radio and television to carry the debate to a larger audience. (In all seriousness, a media figure such as Mrs Whitlam might find much useful and interesting work in this field.)

The result of such a constant debate would be an evershifting, but perhaps clearer, definition of education as a social problem. This, if for no other reason, would necessitate a force of teachers and administrators who were up-to-date in their knowledge and flexible in attitude. Since the process of redefinition is dialectical, in that all the parties concerned will take a part in the process of redefinition, there is an even stronger need to make administrative arrangements for the apt initial training and retraining of those working within education.

## The teachers

The initial training of teachers is a topic of great relevance to our argument, but must be excluded here because it is not within the province of the Schools Commission. In-service training, however, is both relevant and in our terms of reference. As already noted, the in-service program is small and funds for Education Centres are sparse. Without in any way lessening the importance of such a program, it would nevertheless seem that many of the aims of in-service work can be achieved by an extended innovation program, because this can act to provide on-service training.

An example will show that this can be so. One of the most fertile areas for change in schools in recent years has been in the area of the curriculum, here including both content and method of teaching the new content. Many large-scale curricular development projects have been undertaken throughout the world. In Australia, an example would be the Australian Science Education Project or the new Social Education Materials Project, the first major expenditure undertaken by the national Curriculum Development Centre. However, curricular materials take two to three years to develop by such methods. Dissemination is usually slow and often five years after the commencement of a project costing tens of thousands of dollars, a minority of schools have adopted what has by now become an out-of-date set of materials. But, if teachers themselves can be persuaded to want to develop their own new materials, many benefits follow. Adoption is nearly inevitable; teachers learn much in the developmental process that they themselves have initiated and grow less alienated from a system often seen as prescriptive and paternalistic; a variety of materials becomes available which, if its presence is known, then becomes more widely available, so that the process of wider choice of more alternatives spreads the process of renewal and learning beyond the initial point of innovation.

What is being advocated is an immense program of teacher-based action research in all educational fields, not just in curriculum. Research never meant much to the doctor till he felt its benefits in the hospital or to the industrialist till he saw increasing efficiency and profits in his factory. Research will never mean much to the practising teacher till he or she experiences its usefulness in his own classroom or school. Evaluation would be built into such a program and though it must be rigorous it need not be frighteningly statistical. Clear thought of a pragmatic and even retrospective nature can tell us much more in qualitative terms about what our pupils have done than we often realize.

There are two needs for such a program. Firstly, some support in the form of advice as well as money undoubtedly will be needed. The present innovation program, though operating in a somewhat closed manner, in that criteria for acceptance or refusal are not yet known, does form a starting point. Ideas for innovation that are put up are encouraged where the idea is seen as good but the method inappropriate. Advice is given, usually by persons wholly acceptable to the teachers, so that initiative is not stunted. An evaluation of the workings of the present program would point up its strong and weak points. What must be established very soon is an advisory and supportive service to encourage a program of grass-roots innovation in the tradition of action research, and to spread throughout Australia the successes *and failures* of this program. Teachers must know not only what went right, but also why failures happened. We rarely are brave enough to publicize where we went wrong.

This publicity raises a second issue. Change does not occur without cost, so that, if rewards can be built into the structure of any system, change is more likely to be accepted. In the past, the reward for innovation has been promotion out of the classroom into administration, the inspectorate, a college or university. In other words, the innovator has been successfully removed from the first line of influence. Clearly, the structure of the career in education is relevant at this point. In Malaysia, Singapore and Hong Kong the salary structure and equivalence of positions in the school, the college and administration has been reorganized to try to avoid the side-tracking of innovators, but the Schools Commission would be brave to tackle the teachers' associations of each State in an endeavour to create rewards for innovators in this way. They can, however, build a variety of rewards, perhaps best termed professional, into their organization. Clearly, a more generous funding of the innovation and the in-service program will reward teachers in material terms, but also the advocated publicity program can be used to reward teachers by widely disseminating the achievements of innovatory schools or teachers. The easiest way to express this aim could be to say that a more professional attitude to teaching was to be encouraged, but this is a dangerous view, since we know that certainly in Australia there may be no necessary 'relationship . . . between the teachers' professional role orientation and their observed behaviour in the classroom'.[10] Therefore, the safest suggestion is that attempts are made to build material and psychological rewards to teachers for justifiable change into a program of action research which is aimed to raise the level of expert discourse on education and, hence, to work as a form of on-service training for teachers and administrators.

**The administration**

There is a tension here in that, as presently organized, much of the work of the Schools Commission must be through State Education Departments. Though these organizations are moving towards a less authoritarian and more decentralized state, the rate of change does not match the desires of many who often fail to realize that some control over the expenditure of public money is essential. Indeed, the very creation of the Schools Commission as a body which largely works through state departments has provided the Education Departments with a new source of bureaucratic fodder. However, the cutting edge of the program advocated here is that part of the Schools Commission's work that is controlled from Canberra, namely the innovations program and a new publicity program, should be based on the Schools Commission. It is, perhaps, worth noting that, unlike the Karmel Committee, the Kangan Committee on Technical and Further Education did set aside about $0.95 million specifically for publicity though apparently only for one purpose, namely the very important one of spreading knowledge of opportunities in vocational education.[11]

This may seem paradoxical in that the appeal seems to be for a less bureaucratic system. Yet the aim of the policies advocated is that a higher level of educational discourse, based on greater knowledge at every level, will result in a more open educational administration at the federal, state and local levels, because teachers and the general public will both demand visibility in decision-making at the levels above them in the necessary, but at present closed and somewhat distant, hierarchy of power.

Finally, one of the original principles of the Committee upon which no program was built by the first report must be taken up and converted into administrative machinery. This is the principle of recurrent education.

> The Committee believe(d) that every member of the society has an entitlement to a period of education at public expense, and that those who leave school early have a claim which they should be able to take out at a later date (2.23).

This belief was justified both on the instrumental grounds that it 'would lead to a continuous upgrading and updating of economically productive skills' but also, and for our argument more importantly, because 'it would contribute to a higher-level awareness of social issues' (2.24), one of which must be education itself. The Committee notes that recurrent education can be the result of a wide range of experiences, 'libraries, museums, theatres, music centres, sporting and recreational facilities and the mass media as well as by formal courses in specialized institutions' (2.25).

Clearly, the direction of future developments to be recommended by the Schools Commission must entail a switch in emphasis from financing schools to the funding of community colleges for life-long education, but this raises a knotty question relating to educational administration. Will such colleges be seen as tertiary institutions and hence, outside the terms of reference of this Commission but controlled from Canberra and possibly related to the forthcoming arrangements for Open Education? Or will they be seen as superior secondary institutions and, therefore, within the control of State Education Departments and staffed largely by members of teachers' associations? Or will they, finally, be seen as within the jurisdiction of the proposed Commission on Technical and Further Education, since the recent (April 1974) report on this subject gave some attention to recurrent education?[12]

## CONCLUSION

Education is now seen as a social problem, but what is the nature of the problem perceived? The need is largely defined as the material renewal of schools and the provision of compensatory programs to offset an inegalitarian social structure. The teachers and the curriculum are almost, though not completely, forgotten. Structure, not process, is the focus. Yet crucial to any educational system is the quality of its teachers, since they control process. The Committee itself produces statistics (4.17–23) to show, without actually saying it, that there are weaknesses in the quality of the Australian teaching force. This situation can be remedied by a conscious attempt at renewal, especially if it is based on the teachers' own process of learning as they, for example, develop their own materials and techniques in their own schools. This process should be open to all, so that the level of educational discourse is raised both among teachers and the general public. Difficult decisions about educational administration, such as that relating to who will control recurrent education, will have to be made, but these problems will only be isolated, clarified, and democratically solved, when the general public are brought into the debate so that democratic decision-making becomes an education in itself.

## Notes

1 Australia. (1973). *Schools in Australia. Report of the Interim Committee for the Australian Schools Commission.* (Chairman, P. Karmel). Canberra: AGPS. Throughout the rest of this paper the convention will be followed of citing *Schools in Australia* by referring to the chapter and paragraph number in the original document.

2 For the full analysis see P. W. Musgrave, 'Changing Society: Some Underlying Assumptions of the Karmel Report', Chapter 2 of this volume.

3 Jencks, C., et al. (1972). *Inequality: A Reassessment of the Effect of Family and Schooling in America.* New York: Basic Books.

4 For some initial results of this research see R. T. Fitzgerald, P. W. Musgrave, D. Pettit, (1974). 'School and Neighbourhood'. In *Quarterly Review of Australian Education*, 7 (1/2).

5 For these concepts see B. Bacharach and M. S. Baratz (1970). *Power and Poverty: Theory and Practice.* New York: OUP, pp.201–13.

6 Schools Commission Act, No. 213 of 1973.

7 Marris, P. and Rein, M. (1967). *Dilemmas of Social Reform.* London: Routledge & Kegan Paul.

8 Moynihan, D. P. (1968). *Maximum Feasible Misunderstanding.* New York: Free Press, p. 201.

9 Town, S. W. (1973). 'Action Research and Social Policy: Some Recent British Experience'. In *Sociological Review*, 21 (4): 582.

10 Johnson, L. 'Is it Really Important that Teaching be a Profession?' In *Australian and New Zealand Journal of Sociology*, 10 (1): 41.

11 Australia. (1974). *TAFE in Australia. Report of Australian Committee on Technical and Further Education. Vol. I.* Canberra: AGPS, para. 4.38.

12 ibid.: paras 1.103–1.115.

# 6. Approaches to the Goal of Educational Equality

## J. P. Keeves

In the Act relating to the establishment of the Schools Commission, the Commission was charged with

> providing increased and equal opportunities for education in government and non-government schools;

and in particular, in the exercise of its functions, it was to have regard to

> the needs of disadvantaged schools and of students at disadvantaged schools, and of other students suffering disadvantages in relation to education for social, economic, ethnic, geographic, cultural, lingual or similar reasons.[1]

'Equality of educational opportunity' has in recent years become a focal point for debate concerned with educational policy-making, both at the national and international level. This article examines the concept of equality of educational opportunity in the Australian setting and considers whether the report of the Interim Committee for the Australian Schools Commission[2] and the programs which have subsequently been introduced will contribute towards the attainment of these ends which the Schools Commission was charged by Act of Parliament to procure.

## EQUALITY OF OPPORTUNITY: A CHANGING CONCEPT

When the Australian colonies were being settled it was considered necessary to provide a traditional classical education for the 'upper' classes but only a bare minimum of education for the 'lower' classes. As the settlements grew it was left to the more wealthy members of these communities to provide education for their children and to religious organizations to extend these educational facilities for other children as best they could. Gradually a system of public education evolved and by the commencement of the twentieth century each of the States had made provision for 'free, secular and compulsory' education. Until such time as free and compulsory elementary schooling had been established, extensive opportunities for education could scarcely be said to exist in Australian society. This is not to deny that for some of the colonists education was important, and as early as 1834, when plans for the settlement of South Australia were being made, the Chairman of the South Australian Company and an influential early settler argued, 'I consider it a duty before even a tent be set up in the new province, to provide for education'.[3] Hard times, however, prevented the implementation of such liberal and enlightened policies.

Approaches to the provision of opportunities for education have changed markedly not only in Australia but throughout the western world during the twentieth century. Coleman has examined the development of the concept of equality of educational opportunity in the provisions made for education in the United States[4], and the growth of the systems of public education within the States of Australia is, in many ways, similar. In this country it is possible to distinguish three stages in the development of the concept and the practice of educational equality.[5]

### Stage 1: A conservative view

At a time when there were perhaps clearer lines between different social strata than exist in Australia today, secondary and tertiary education were provided in the main for those who were to enter the professions as doctors, lawyers and clergy. A majority of the institutions for secondary education were administered by religious organizations and charged substantial fees. It was, however, acknowledged that talented children should be encouraged to develop their abilities and the private secondary schools offered scholarships to those students who would bring credit to them. Within the public sector of education some state secondary schools were established in order to assist those with ability to further their education. Such schools were not, in general, free. Entry to them was highly selective, but scholarships were provided for the more able who could not afford fees.

For the remainder of the children in the community an elementary education was provided, normally to the age of 14 years. However, because of the costs of education to the state, and because parents still had to pay for the upkeep of their children, the age at which it was possible to leave school was lowered and many took advantage of this. These state schools provided a training in the basic skills of computation, reading and writing for those who would become the mass of manual workers in urban and rural areas as well as for those who would be engaged in simple clerical work. As the needs of the community grew for skilled workers who were employed either as clerks or as tradesmen, so the community provided suitable schools, generally with selective entry into them.

Universities were established in several of the Australian States long before the beginning of the twentieth century, but few scholarships were available which assisted the more talented to train for the professions and, in general, students could not attend unless their parents could afford to pay for them. It was, however, possible to undertake university courses as a part-time student and many made use of such opportunities. Moreover, philanthropists from among the upper classes assisted in the establishment of Mechanics Institutes and Workers Educational Associations which enabled members of the working class to undertake further education if they wished to.

### Stage 2: The liberal view

While it is not easy to identify the time when a more liberal view towards education in Australia started to emerge, it would appear that little was accomplished in the democratization of education before the close of World War II. From that time there was remarkable growth in the secondary and tertiary educational systems. Moreover, while the upper age for compulsory schooling shifted only slightly, an increasingly high proportion of an age group continued on beyond this school-leaving age. During this period there was still an emphasis on talent and widespread scholarship programs were instituted to assist students to continue with their education. At the same time, the fees payable in the state school system were gradually reduced or eliminated. Accompanying the expansion of the secondary school system there was marked growth at the post-secondary school level, with the strengthening and development of a wider range of tertiary and sub-tertiary institutions and an increase in the number of scholarships assisting students to enter these institutions. In addition, marked distinctions between preparing for the professions and training for commercial and technical occupations were gradually removed from the curricula of the secondary schools, which were directed towards providing a sound general education for all students.

These changes resulted from societal pressures acting to make educational facilities at all levels available irrespective of social background and financial resources.[6] During this period, attempts were made to provide equality of access to education for all, by the encouragement of talent and by preventing premature selection for special courses. As a result, selective entry on academic grounds to schools of different types has largely disappeared, as has a high degree of selectivity for different courses within schools. Nevertheless, these changes have not produced equality of educational opportunities for all whether they are male or female and whether they come from homes of higher or lower social status. While many of the marked distinctions between the types of education for children of different social strata that characterized the conservative period tended to disappear during this liberal stage, inequalities did not cease to exist and evidence presented later will show the nature and extent of such disparities. Yet in comparison with the educational systems of other countries, the evidence available clearly indicates that Australia has at the present time more egalitarian educational polices and programs than exist in most other western countries.[7]

The government school systems in each State of Australia have sought to provide equally for all children by using across all schools the same formulae for financing buildings and equipment, and for the allocation of teachers, by issuing standard text books, and by ensuring that schools were located so as to be readily accessible. Although non-government schools have existed side by side with the government schools, not all of these non-government schools have fared well, indeed some would appear to have fallen below the minimum acceptable standards of the government sector. In spite of these attempts for uniformity in the level of provision for education with the government schools, more opportunities for education have gone to the more talented and to those whose parents have been able to afford them.

### Stage 3: A needs concept of provision for education

With the publication of the report of the Interim Committee of the Australian Schools Commission, *Schools in Australia*, in 1973, a different concept in the procurement of equality of educational opportunity is emerging. As a result it might well be claimed that a new phase in the provision for education has commenced. In its initial period the Schools Commission will be hard pressed to remedy marked deficiences which exist in certain obvious areas of need. However, in so far as the Commission is required by Act of Parliament to have regard to the needs of students suffering disadvantage in relation to education on a variety of grounds, including social, economic and cultural reasons, then it is clear that something more than formal equality of access to education is involved.

This shift in emphasis in providing for education in Australia is derived in part from developments which have occurred in other parts of the world. Husén has identified three strategies which have been employed at three distinct levels in various countries for bringing about greater equality of educational opportunity.[8] At the pre-school level, particularly in the United States, programs of compensatory education have been introduced for children from disadvantaged home backgrounds. At the primary school level in Britain, the Plowden Report argued that disadvantaged children tend to congregate together in schools in certain areas. It recommended that a compensatory program be developed for such schools and for particular students in these schools. However, the report suggests that:

> What these deprived areas need most are perfectly normal, good primary schools alive with experiences from which children of all kinds can benefit ... But, of course, there are special and additional demands on teachers who work in deprived areas with deprived children.[9]

In a similar manner in the United States special attempts have been made to improve the facilities and to provide more appropriate programs for students in schools in the inner areas of large cities.

At the post-secondary school level, provision is being made in countries such as Sweden for re-entry into formal education, to assist those who left school early, for retraining programs to help those who have become redundant from changing patterns of employment and for a wide range of further education programs to aid those who are seeking new leisure time interests. This so-called provision of 'recurrent education' increases the flexibility of an educational system and increases the opportunities available for further education for those who may have suffered from inequalities earlier in their life. In Britain, the Open University provides similar opportunities for a limited group.

The new educational programs proposed by the Interim Committee of the Australian Schools Commission acknowledge that equality of educational opportunity cannot be achieved by merely removing certain material barriers or by using academic ability to select those who should proceed with education. The proposed approach aims to provide assistance for schools and students who are in need and who are at an educational disadvantage for social, cultural, economic, ethnic and other reasons.

The Schools Commission is also required to have concern for:

> the need to encourage diversity and innovation in schools and in the curricula and teaching methods of schools;

and for:

> the desirability of providing special educational opportunities for students who have demonstrated their ability in a particular field of studies, including scientific, literary, artistic or musical studies.[10]

It follows, then, that equality of opportunity for education in Australia as envisaged under the Schools Commission Act does not mean *identity* of opportunity. What is being proposed is *optimal* educational opportunities for all students in terms of their needs.

The concept of need is not easy to define and it is clear that not all recognized needs can be satisfied by any program of limited duration. Consequently, after the identification of needs, priorities must be established for the assistance, given the finances available. However, a program which aims to provide assistance to those in greatest need is clearly capable, at any point in time, of modification and extension following the identification of other needs and a redefinition of priorities. In the previous paper in this series we have examined the evidence available which reveals the nature and extent of the disparities existing in Australia between different types of schools in the educational outcomes of achievement and attainment. We will now consider whether similar disparities exist between these educational outcomes for different occupational status groups.

## DIFFERENCES IN EDUCATIONAL OUTCOMES BETWEEN DIFFERENT SOCIAL GROUPS

The data examined in this paper were obtained from the IEA Science Project, which is the only study that has been carried out to examine the achievements of students in all States of Australia and in schools of all types. For further details of this inquiry the reports by Rosier[11] and Comber and Keeves[12] should be consulted. Two tests of achievement were employed, a short word knowledge test and a two-hour test of achievement in science.

In Table 1, data are recorded for the performance of students from the six major occupational status groups[13], on the science and word knowledge tests. The estimated holding power at the pre-university level, as well as the proportion of the target population represented by these groups, are also presented.

The evidence at the 14-year-old level, before any dropping out from school has taken place, shows a gradual decline in level of performance from the highest occupational status group to the lowest, with the difference in average performance of these two groups being a little less than one student standard deviation on both the science and word knowledge tests. At the pre-university level, losses have occurred for all groups. Of the students whose

**Table 1. Disparities in Educational Achievement and Attainment by Occupational Status Groups**

| 14-Year-Old Level (N = 5307) | Estimated Holding Power % | Estimated Proportion of Target Population % | Mean Achievement | |
|---|---|---|---|---|
| | | | Science $\bar{x}$ | Word Knowledge $\bar{x}$ |
| Professional, technical | 100 | 13 | 31.6 | 19.7 |
| Managerial | 100 | 26 | 26.4 | 17.2 |
| Clerical, Armed Services | 100 | 12 | 24.8 | 17.2 |
| Skilled Workers | 100 | 18 | 23.9 | 15.6 |
| Semi-skilled Workers | 100 | 19 | 21.6 | 14.0 |
| Unskilled Workers | 100 | 13 | 21.1 | 13.9 |
| **Pre-University Level (N = 4202)** | | | | |
| Professional, technical | 62 | 27 | 26.0 | 22.1 |
| Managerial | 40 | 34 | 24.3 | 20.7 |
| Clerical, Armed Services | 36 | 14 | 24.6 | 22.4 |
| Skilled Workers | 19 | 11 | 24.5 | 20.3 |
| Semi-skilled Workers | 13 | 8 | 24.0 | 20.2 |
| Unskilled Workers | 14 | 6 | 23.0 | 18.8 |

fathers are professional and technical workers, it is estimated that 62 per cent remain at school to the pre-university level, while for those students whose fathers are semi-skilled and un-skilled workers, only 13 to 14 per cent remain to complete their secondary education.

While there are still significant differences in performance on the word knowledge test between the different occupational status groups, the marked change in level of achievement from the highest and the lowest occupational groups no longer holds at this level. Moreover, the differences in achievement between the groups in science are no longer significant.

In Table 2, we have recorded the correlations between the occupational status level of a student measured on the six-point scale and the number of years of further education he expects and his score on a 'like school' scale. For further information on these measures, the reader should consult the report by Comber and Keeves.[14] Results are given for each of the six States and for Australia as a whole for the students in the 14-year-old sample.

Those students from higher status homes expect to have significantly more years of education than those students from lower status homes. In addition, there is a consistent tendency for the higher status students to express more favourable attitudes towards school and school learning. The level of significance of this result is in doubt for several of the States, but is clearly significant for Australia as a whole. It is thus not surprising that the students from higher status homes, who are performing better at school, who like school more and expect to continue longer with their education, should stay

**Table 2.  Correlations between Father's Occupation and Expected Education and Liking School for 14-year-old Students in 1970**

| 14-Year-Olds | Australia | NSW | Victoria | Queensland | S.A. | W.A. | Tasmania |
|---|---|---|---|---|---|---|---|
| Expected Education | 0.24 | 0.28 | 0.20 | 0.25 | 0.19 | 0.27 | 0.29 |
| Like School | 0.09 | 0.09 | 0.05 | 0.10 | 0.13 | 0.09 | 0.12 |

longer at school. It is, however, important not to oversimplify the nature of this educational advantage.

To ascribe differences in educational outcomes to indicators of class and socio-economic status such as occupational rank is to distort partially the nature of the relationships involved. Evidence which has been presented elsewhere suggests that the educative climates of Australian homes, as indicated by the attitudes and practices of the homes, are influenced by a collection of factors which is better described as the cultural level of the home than its socio-economic status.[15] Moreover, the status characteristics of the home would seem only indirectly to influence educational outcomes, while attitudes and practices have a more substantial and direct effect.

The educational advantages derived from homes of high socio-economic status would appear to be of three kinds. Firstly, there is likely to be a genetic advantage, since parents from high status homes tend to pass on to their children genetic endowments which will enable them to perform better at school. Secondly, such parents provide for their children a more favourable home and school environment for intellectual growth. Furthermore, such children are thrice favoured since it is apparent that they can modify to their advantage the environments they experience, whether these environments involve the home, the classroom or the peer group. The evidence from Australian studies indicates that the educational quality of the home and the schooling provided is influenced by the level of ability of the child, and an enhanced environmental effect is observed for students of greater ability from higher status homes.[16]

The type of education provided for a student in Australian schools may not be directly determined by the level of ability of the student as has occurred in the past in British schools. However, in many indirect ways, a student from a more favoured home background, with a higher level of ability learns under more favourable circumstances. The evidence suggests that as an individual at home he has better conditions for learning, that at school he comes together with other students from more favoured home backgrounds, and that they together receive preferential educational treatment. Furthermore, recent analyses show that such factors associated with schooling make significant contributions to student achievement in a subject such as science, even after allowance has been made for factors involving home and student background.[17]

## THE APPROACH OF THE KARMEL REPORT

The Interim Committee was required by its terms of reference to

> make recommendations ... as to the immediate financial needs of schools, priorities within those needs, and appropriate measures to assist in meeting those needs.[18]

It is of some importance to note that these terms of reference directed attention to assisting the schools and not the systems of education operating in each State or the individual students within the schools. Moreover, the terms of reference required the committee to think in terms of the needs of schools and not in terms of societal issues and questions of economic inequality, social equity and tolerable social diversity.[19]

The Committee, before making recommendations to the Australian Government for the provision of supplementary funding for education in the schools, had to examine the needs of the schools. It found the concept of 'need' difficult to define and considered four approaches.

> First, need for a minimum quantity and quality of resources in schools; secondly, need for a particular level and kind of outcome from schools; thirdly, need for resources of varying types and amounts having regard to their effectiveness in moving towards desired goals; and fourthly, need as defined by the extent of the cognitive, physical, social or economic disadvantages of individual pupils.[20]

The Committee acknowledged the difficulty of stating the goals of education in objective terms, which, together with the lack of unambiguous evidence on factors influencing specific educational outcomes, prevented the pursuit of the second and third approaches. The Committee consequently restricted its attention to the first and last of the needs listed above, concerned with resources and the degree of disadvantage experienced by students. Nevertheless, they recognized certain limitations associated with these approaches, and argued that to consider inputs to education in the schools and to ignore outcomes was perhaps unwise, but knowledge of the relationships between possible inputs to schools and their outcomes was very limited.

The fourth area of need concerned with the degree of disadvantage of pupils would appear, on the surface, to require identifying individual students in need, but since such students tend to cluster together in specific schools, it is not impossible to proceed if the schools in which these students are gathered can be identified. Thus, if the needs of these schools containing disadvantaged students could be assessed, it would be possible to develop programs to satisfy these needs and to provide educational opportunities for these students comparable to those experienced by students who were not disadvantaged.

After surveying as fully as possible in the limited time available the needs of the schools along the two dimensions stated above, the Committee recommended a range of programs in seven areas:

1. General Recurrent Resources,
2. General Buildings,
3. Primary and Secondary Libraries,
4. Disadvantaged Schools,

5 Special Education,
6 Teacher Development, and
7 Innovation.

In addition, due to other recommendations made by the Interim Committee, the Schools Commission is directly involved in funding the establishment and operation of education centres primarily for teachers. A further national centre which was recommended by the Interim Committee, the Curriculum Development Centre, has also been established, but is not directly linked with the Schools Commission.

The proposals of the Interim Committee were accepted by the Australian Government and in excess of $650 million was allocated in the first instance to the Schools Commission for the 1974/75 years.[21] Subsequently, in the 1974/75 Budget these funds were increased to allow for inflation and rising costs. In its strategy of funding, the Schools Commission has chosen a middle course between allowing the States complete freedom and flexibility, and a desire to ensure that the funds are ear-marked for particular purposes, by setting up a distinct budget for each program, but with as little prescription as possible within each program. The Schools Commission, in the administration of the money allocated to the first five of the seven areas listed above, makes block grants to the Education Department and the Catholic school systems in each State. However, grants to the independent (non-systemic and non-government) schools are made directly to each school, on the advice of advisory committees except in the allocation of funds under the recurrent resources program. The money available in the areas of teacher development and innovation is available to all schools and all systems and aims to provide financial assistance to enterprising people who will use the grants for the benefit of children everywhere.

Before asking whether the programs in these seven areas will contribute to raising the quality of Australian education or to promoting greater equality of educational opportunity, it is necessary to consider briefly how much money is being spent in each area and the manner in which it is being spent.

**General Recurrent Resources**

In 1974/75 the grants to the government and non-government schools in this area exceed $300 million. These moneys are being spent, with some regard to the needs principle, on the hiring of additional teachers, on the appointment of substantial numbers of ancillary staff, and on the purchase of equipment for the schools. These grants will make some reduction in student/teacher ratios, and will facilitate, through the use of the equipment purchased, the provision of appropriate learning experiences in the schools.

**General Buildings Program**

Approximately $200 million is being made available under existing and new programs and in accordance with the needs principle for the upgrading and replacement of school buildings, including libraries and science laboratories, in both government and non-government schools. It was planned that this money would go approximately one-third of the way towards attaining satisfactory standards of school buildings in all schools, but with rapid inflation, particularly in the building industry, less than originally anticipated will be achieved.

## Primary and Secondary Libraries Program

Because of the block nature of the grants to the State Departments, guidelines for the use of the money (approximately $45 million) available in this area have been prepared on the equipping of library and resource centres to promote the development of student initiatives in learning.

## Disadvantaged Schools Program

This program provides $50 million, in addition to that available from the General Recurrent Resources and General Buildings Programs, to schools identified as having special needs according to criteria of disadvantage. The intention of the program is that schools should not automatically be given grants, but be required to analyse their own problems, propose courses of action and apply for a grant to implement the program.

## Special Education Program

In this program attention has been given to the training of staff to work with handicapped children and to the improvement of physical facilities for the schooling of handicapped children. There have been some delays in providing money to schools in some States because many schools for such children have been outside the state educational systems. In excess of $44 million is available for this program.

## Teacher Development Program

Opportunities have been provided under this program to assist teachers and administrators to raise their level of competence. They are provided in part by courses organized by a joint committee comprising representatives of both government and non-government schools and in part by procedures initiated by teachers themselves. Some difficulties have been encountered in obtaining relief teachers for those who have attended these courses, and some disruptions to the work of the schools have occurred. About $10 million is available for this work.

Linked with this program has been the establishment of 14 pilot education centres which provide in-service education for both primary and secondary teachers from government and non-government schools. Each centre is organized by a governing body. In addition, these centres are involved in the production of locally based resource materials and act as social centres. The interest and enthusiasm shown for these centres has led to an extension of the program and a minimum of 28 centres will be established or supported throughout Australia.

## Innovations Program

The response of the schools to the Innovations Program has been relatively strong and from approximately 10 000 schools in Australia, over 1000 applications were initially received. Out of these proposals about 400 have so far received some support, and it may be estimated that approximately one school in 25 is being influenced by this program. Clearly, the program will leave the majority of schools unaffected unless it is extended beyond the $6 million originally available. Furthermore, in some States, relations have been strained between the administrators of the program and the State Education Departments, arising from the nature of some of the projects which have received grants. Nevertheless, the willingness by so many to undertake innovatory activities is heartening, even if doubt must be expressed about some of the innovations supported.

The movements of the Australian Government in the educational field in the 10 months following the establishment of the Schools Commission, have been accompanied by some fears concerning the infringement of the rights of the States in education. Moreoever, the Commission has encountered some problems in appointing staff to undertake its work. These problems, perhaps only to be expected in the initial stages, may have reduced the effectiveness of some of the Commission's programs.

## WILL THE KARMEL PROGRAMS WORK?

The report of the Interim Committee of the Australian Schools Commission was concerned with identifying the needs of schools and establishing programs that would meet those needs. Three of the programs, the Libraries, Teacher Development and Innovations Programs, were directed towards raising the general quality of Australian education. The remaining four programs have been seen by the staff of the Schools Commission as being concerned with promoting equality of opportunity in Australian education. Both the Disadvantaged Schools Program and the Special Education Program aim to assist schools and to raise the standard of services which cater for students in special need. The former has a compensatory function associated with social, economic and ethnic disadvantage and the latter assists those children who are in some way physically or mentally handicapped and who require remedial and special teaching. In addition, it is probable that some of the aid made available through the General Recurrent Resources and the General Building Programs will be distributed to schools with obvious needs, including some of the schools which are disadvantaged, and so help to compensate for aspects of educational inequalities.

The grants made under the General Recurrent Resources Program for government schools are relatively small when compared with state expenditure on education, and with the grants for non-government schools.[22] If with rising costs the State Governments substitute funds from the Australian Government for money they would otherwise have found themselves, then the effects of this aspect of the program will be negligible. The grants provided under the General Buildings Program seem at first sight to be likely to have more of an impact, since they represent a significant addition to state expenditure.[23] However, with rapidly rising costs in the building industry, the effects of this program will be rather less than originally anticipated.

It must be recognized that the work of the Schools Commission in its emphasis on the needs of schools and through schools to provide for the needs of individual students, has the potential for promoting a new approach in the provision of equal opportunities in education. Under the Act, programs can be set up, both at the present time and in the future, which are compensatory in nature and which help students overcome certain recognized disadvantages. Furthermore, some of the money allocated to the Children's Commission for pre-school and child-care programs in the States may serve a similar compensatory purpose.[24]

Such programs are not completely unknown in Australia, although in the past they have commonly been undertaken by the churches and philanthropic organizations. At a time when there is an increased emphasis on pre-school education it is important to acknowledge that the Free Kindergarten unions in each State were established more than 60 years ago with the expressed aims of assisting disadvantaged children during their years of early childhood.[25] However, governmental policy and programs to provide compensatory education for the disadvantaged are a new departure in Australian education, and is linked with a more radical approach to equality of educational opportunity that has emerged in Britain and the United States in recent years.

In examining whether the Schools Commission programs will work, there seem to be at least four distinct questions which might be asked.

1 Will the grants reduce existing inequalities between schools and systems of schools with respect to physical conditions and staff?

2 Will the grants made to schools improve the quality and general standard of education, as assessed, for example, by level of educational achievement?

3 Will the grants to schools reduce the differences in achievement of different types of schools and of different social, economic, geographical and ethnic groups?

4 Will the grants help to meet the educational needs of cognitively and physically handicapped children?

In the initial stages of the work of the Schools Commission, it is likely that gains will be made through the provision of facilities for special education and the fourth question can probably be safely answered in the affirmative. However, while the reduction of inequalities between schools and systems with respect to the resources available to them, may be regarded at first sight as the easiest to achieve, only time will tell whether the money is being spent wisely and well.

Unfortunately, it is not possible to be confident about the effects on educational achievement of any program which sets out to improve the resources of the schools. Coleman et al. reported from the Equality of Educational Opportunity Survey in the United States:

> that schools bring little influence to bear on a child's achievement that is independent of his background and general social context; and that this very lack of an independent effect means that the inequalities imposed on children by their home, neighbourhood and peer environment are carried along to become the inequalities with which they confront adult life at the end of school.[26]

This claim has been widely publicized, but it has also been very thoroughly examined and supported in the recently published study by Jencks et al. where the findings of several major investigations, carried out in the United States and elsewhere, have been subjected to careful scrutiny and re-analysis.[27] In spite of these gloomy predictions concerning the influence of the schools on education, new ideas and new pieces of evidence have recently come to hand from two directions which suggest that a slightly more optimistic view can be taken.

At the Harvard-IEA Conference in 1973, James Coleman was highly critical of the procedures which he had employed in the analysis of the data from the Equality of Educational Opportunity Survey.[28] Moreover, he rejected the procedures employed in the re-analysis of the data by Mayeske et al.[29] and was critical of those used in the IEA studies.[30] Coleman argued the case for the use of alternative measures that had a direct operational meaning in terms of predicting differences in scores. Variance measures employ the squares of differences, while variation measures are based on the unsquared differences in scores and therefore include the notion of direction as well as magnitude. The emphasis in the analyses he proposed was on the capacity of a variable to predict variation in the achievement test scores rather than accounting for the variance of the test scores. If variation measures were used, the influence of school factors is likely to be seen to be larger relative to the home influence than if the effects were assessed by variance measures.[31]

In previous studies such as the Equality of Educational Opportunity Survey, the criterion measures have been associated with verbal and reading achievement. However, in the IEA science inquiry, the criterion variable was performance on a school-based subject. In general, in the IEA science study some effects of schooling, but relatively few of the many originally hypothesized, did make a difference to achievement in science.[32] In spite of the fact that the analytical procedures employed in the IEA studies, because of the confounding between home and school variables, may have overestimated the effects of home background for the school-based subject of science, some school factors were found to be significant and to be robust across many of the countries which participated in the inquiry. Moreover, as the students grew older, more of the variation in science achievement could be accounted for by school factors.

In the IEA science study, important variables which emerged from the analyses carried out after allowing for the effects of home background formed a cluster of concomitant factors associated with teacher-training, the presence of laboratory assistants, the extent to which teachers undertook preparations out of school hours, and the emphasis placed on practical experience, which required the availability of well-equipped laboratories. Thus it would appear that the General Recurrent Resources Program which is attempting to provide equipment for the teacher and auxiliary staff to free the teacher to prepare his work, the General Buildings Program which is helping to provide laboratories for science teaching, and the Teacher Development Program which aims to provide further training for teachers could have a beneficial effect, if the resources were made available to those schools with the greatest needs. Yet it is necessary to warn that measurable effects will not be large and the gains in achievement may be barely recognizable. However, it is important to state that the expenditure is being undertaken in a way that is consistent not only with the good sense of the administrators but also with the very limited evidence which is currently available.

The attempts being made by the Schools Commission to raise the quality of education in Australia, and to promote greater equality of educational opportunity, are based on the recommendations of the Karmel report. They can, at best, lead to only slight advances in student achievement and to only small reductions in the differences in performance of diverse groups of students from different social backgrounds. Nevertheless, in time the Schools Commission will help to reduce the disparities which exist in the resources available for education in schools of different types serving students of diverse backgrounds. In addition, it will provide a more soundly based education for physically and mentally handicapped children.

The secretariat of the Centre for Educational Research and Innovation in Paris has pointed out, in regard to the quest for greater equality of educational opportunity, that:

> We have learned by experience, if we did not realize it originally, that this is not basically an educational question but a social one, whether it is disparity by socio-economic status or the problem of ethnic or religious minorities.[33]

It is clear that education is not a substitute for economic and social reform. Indeed it may be argued that to divert attention and interest to educational issues, when the real issues associated with poverty and inequality in society involve fiscal policies and housing programs, is to be deliberately misleading. Major educational reforms are a natural outgrowth of social reforms and must follow them.

The Schools Commission in its first year of operation has sought goals which are seen to be educationally sound and it has promoted programs in response to clearly defined educational needs. By continuing to seek areas of evident need in the future, a new concept of equality of educational opportunity could emerge in Australia in which optimal conditions are provided for every child to learn, and for every adult to continue learning throughout his life.

## Notes

1 Australia. *Schools Commission Act* 1973. (No. 213) Canberra: AGPS, p.7.
2 Australia. (1973). *Schools in Australia. Report of the Interim Committee for the Australian Schools Commission* (Chairman, P. Karmel). Canberra: AGPS.
3 Quoted in *Compulsory Education in Australia*. A study by the Australian National Co-operating Body for Education. Unesco, Paris. 1951. p. 15.
4 Coleman, J. S. (1968). 'The Concept of Equality of Educational Opportunity'. In *Harvard Educational Review*, 38 (1):7–22.
5 cf. Husén, T. (1972). *Social Background and Educational Career*. Paris: OECD.
6 For a discussion of these changes see Partridge, P. H. (1966). 'Some Problems of Educational Policy in Democratic Societies'. In *Teachers in Australia*, Melbourne: The Australian College of Education. Cheshire. pp. 1–21.
7 For evidence to support this claim see the reports of the IEA Projects, in particular Husén, T. (Ed.) (1967). *International Study of Achievement in Mathematics*. New York: Wiley; and L. C. Comber and J. P. Keeves (1973). *Science Education in Nineteen Countries*. New York: Halsted Press.
8 Husén, T (1972). *Social Background and Educational Career*. Paris: OECD, p. 158.
9 See United Kingdom, Department of Education and Science. (1967). *Children and their Primary Schools*. Report of the Central Advisory Council for Education (England). (The Plowden Report). London: HMSO, p. 51.
10 *The Schools Commission Act* 1973, loc. cit.
11 See Rosier, M. J. (1973). *Science Achievements in Australian Secondary Schools*. Hawthorn, Vic.: ACER.
12 Comber, L. C. and Keeves, J. P., op. cit.
13 The six-point occupational scale developed by Broom, Jones and Zubrzycki was employed. For details of this scale see L. Broom, F. L. Jones, and J. Zubrzycki. 'Social Stratification in Australia'. In J. A. Jackson (Ed.) (1968). *Social Stratification: Sociological Studies 1*. Cambridge: Cambridge University Press, pp. 212–233.
14 Comber, L. C. and Keeves, J. P., op. cit.
15 Keeves, J. P. (1972). *Educational Environment and Student Achievement*. Stockholm: Almqvist and Wiksell, Chapter 7.
16 Keeves, J. P., op. cit.
17 Comber, L. C. and Keeves, J. P., op. cit.
18 Australia. (1973). op. cit.: 3.
19 These further questions concerning societal issues including economic equality, social equity, individual worth and tolerable social diversity have entered into the writings of the Schools Commission since it was established under *The Schools Commission Act* 1973.
20 Australia. (1973). op. cit.: 49.
21 In preparing this section of the paper the author drew extensively on the paper delivered by Ms Jean Blackburn on 'The Role of the Schools Commission in Developing a Contemporary Strategy for Australian Education' to the Unesco 'Learning to Be' Seminar conducted by the Australian Unesco Committee on Education at the Australian National University, 26–30 August 1974. Other mimeographed documents issued by the Schools Commission have also been used.
22 Segall, P. and Fitzgerald, R. T. (1974). *Finance for Education in Australia. Quarterly Review of Australian Education*, 6 (4). Hawthorn, Vic.: ACER, p. 19.
23 ibid.: 26.
24 *Ministerial Statement* tabled in the House of Representatives by the Hon. Lionel F. Bowen, M.P., Minister Assisting the Prime Minister. *Hansard*, 19 September 1974.
25 As with the further education movements of the past, the Free Kindergartens were sometimes taken over by the more educationally minded middle classes for their own needs.
26 Coleman, J. S. et al. (1966). *Equality of Educational Opportunity*. Washington, D.C.: U.S. Government Printing Office, p. 325.
27 Jencks, C. et al. (1972). *Inequality*. New York: Basic Books.
28 Coleman, J. S. 'Effects of School on Learning: The IEA Findings'. Paper presented at the Harvard-IEA Conference on Educational Achievement, Harvard University, November 1973.

29 Mayeske, G. W. et al. (1969). *A Study of Our Nation's Schools*. Washington, D.C.: U.S. Government Printing Office.
30 See, for example, Comber, L. C. and Keeves, J. P., op. cit.
31 For a full discussion of these issues see Keeves, J. P. (1974). *The Effects of the Conditions of Learning in the Schools on Educational Achievement*. IEA (Australia) Report 1974: 2. Hawthorn, Vic.: ACER.
32 Comber, L. C. and Keeves, J. P., op. cit.
33 Organization for Economic Co-operation and Development. Centre for Educational Research and Innovation (1973). *Policies for Innovation and Research and Development*. CERI/CD (73)9. Paris. CERI. p. 13.

**Political Dimension**

# 7. Autonomy and Control in Educational Renewal in Australia

## W. G. Walker

Education is a political animal.[1] As such it lives, breathes and adapts in every moment of its existence. At times the animal crawls forward like an ancient tortoise, as in the 1930s; at other times, as at the present, it leaps forward with the vigour of a young gazelle.

If we are not far sighted we tend to forget that even gazelles grow old; that they reach a peak of fitness and then slow down gradually, perhaps imperceptibly, over the years before death ultimately claims them.

We tend to forget, too, that as the gazelle grows his survival depends upon his ability to adapt to and come to terms with his environment. So it is with education. The Karmel report, like the Robbins Report in England or the Harvard Report in the USA, means nothing outside the political milieu which conceived it. Not all the recommendations of the report were accepted by the Government; the Schools Commission has introduced new concepts and, incidentally, commissioned new reports, which have inevitably affected the implementation of policies arising from the original report. Furthermore, the decisions of State Governments, the attitudes of teachers' and parents' associations and pressures from Catholic authorities, among other things, have influenced the climate of Australian society since the report appeared.

So complex is the ecology of the environment in which the Karmel report and its implementation have emerged that no single, brief chapter could hope to describe it, much less analyse it in detail or produce taxonomies or systems models sufficient to meet the demands of exacting scholarship. All that can be done is to draw attention to one or two major recommendations of the report, to put these into some sort of systematic perspective, and to attempt to give some probably naive answers to some rather obvious questions. In short, this chapter is unavoidably and unashamedly impressionistic.

## DEVOLUTION OF AUTHORITY

One aspect of the report which has attracted a great deal of attention is its emphasis upon the devolution of authority in a 'grass roots approach to the control of schools'.[2]

Unfortunately, this report, like most other educational reports presented in Australia which have referred to 'decentralization' and 'devolution of authority', fails to differentiate clearly between decentralization of *governance* and decentralization of *administration*. As we shall see, the committee appears to

111

favour both forms of decentralization, but it is notable that it confuses them even with single paragraphs of the report.

To clarify the difference between these two forms of decentralization, and to give point to the discussion which follows, it is proposed to use a model developed by the author while working in the Centre for the Advanced Study of Educational Administration at the University of Oregon.[3] It will be useful to consider centralization and decentralization as end-points of two continua, one (Type A) 'political', the other (Type B) 'administrative'.

Type A ("political")

---

Centralization . . . . . . . . . . Decentralization

Type B ("administrative")

---

Centralization . . . . . . . . . Decentralization´

The model below hypothesizes the intersection of the two continua in such a manner as to describe the extent of centralization and/or decentralization in any country, state or other authority. Point X represents the elected legislature; the line XY — the 'political' dimension — represents delegation of responsibility by the legislature to other elected boards or officials; the line XZ — the 'administrative' dimension — represents the delegation of responsibility by the legislature to its appointed officers. Any country, state or authority may be placed at an appropriate point on each continuum and, if desired, these points may be joined to produce a triangle illustrating that system's reliance on one or the other or both of these varieties of centralization-decentralization. On the model an attempt has been made to show two triangles representing the 'traditional' American state (XAM) and Australian state (XBN) patterns of governance.

The first continuum, *Type A Centralization-Decentralization*, refers to decision-making in the area of public debate and of partisan politics and involves citizen representation in policy-making through the election of legislatures, boards and officials. Close to the centralization pole of this continuum, for example, are the Australian State of NSW and the American State of Hawaii where the only representation of the people in education matters occurs in the state legislature; there are as yet no other elected positions or bodies at state, regional or local level except for the rather primitive parents' and citizens' associations. Close to the other extreme of the continuum are the schools of Illinois where the people elect not only the legislature, the county superintendent, the local school board but, until recently, even the State Superintendent. They also play a role in the election of officers of the PTA which can have a considerable informal influence on the operation of individual schools. In no other English-speaking country is Type A decentralization as marked as in certain areas of the United States.

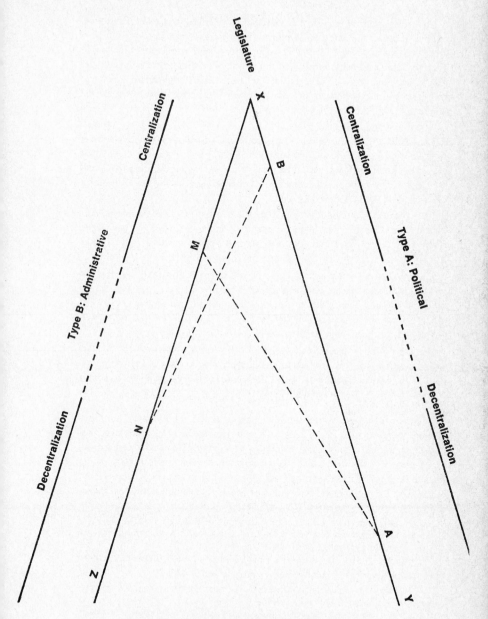

**Walker's Centralization-Decentralization Triangle**

XAM: Traditional U.S. pattern of governance
XBN: Traditional Australian pattern of governance

The other continuum, *Type B Centralization-Decentralization*, refers to the process of decision-making by administrative officers to whom responsibility is delegated by a school system. Thus, in one system the head office might greedily clutch all responsibility to its bosom, while another might delegate much responsibility to officers in the field. This continuum takes no cognizance of elected boards or officials at any level below that of the elected controlling legislature or board.

In the USA, the States have traditionally delegated nearly all responsibility for the operation of schools to local districts, the state supervisors and county superintendents (or their equivalents) playing a minor controlling role. On the other hand, the individual principal has lacked the power and prestige of, for example, the English headmaster, the backbone of the local US system being the superintendent.

The Australian state education systems have delegated considerable powers to inspectors and in most States to regional directors. Principals have been given a considerable degree of freedom and appear to have more power (though they rarely use it) than US principals, for example.

There has been much talk of decentralization in Australia during the last two decades, and this has almost always referred to Type B decentralization, which has usually been achieved through the establishment of area or regional offices. With the exception of the Australian Capital Territory, no serious attempt has yet been made to introduce Type A decentralization.

We are now in a position to analyse more precisely just what the Karmel report has in mind when it refers to 'devolution of authority' and speaks of

> ... the need to broaden the basis of educational policy-making beyond those presently involved and to inform public debate about the operation of schools and school systems.[4]

It is clear from this and several other references that the Karmel Committee favours at least some form of Type A decentralized governance. However, it is also clear that in the complex, entangled ecosystem of Australian education, the members of the Committee were reflecting developments already taking place, rather than breaking new ground. After all, the same point had been put cryptically by the anonymous author of the Unesco publication *Compulsory Education in Australia* a quarter of a century previously:

> The outstanding need of Australian education (is) that every citizen should be made to feel that the state school belongs to him, that it is rendering him a real service, that he has obligations in regard to it.[5]

During the 1960s, the waspish Donald Horne implied the need for both Type A and Type B decentralization when he claimed that

> ... the greatest single reform that seems to be needed in Australian education — and one of the most important reforms that could be made in Australia — is its decentralization to allow teachers to become members of the communities they teach, to allow principals of schools greater initiative, to develop a sense of professional responsibility among teachers, to allow variety and experiment, and to allow more community participation.[6]

Horne has been by no means a voice crying in the wilderness. Kandel[7] in

1937, Butts[8] in 1955, Turner[9] in 1960, Jackson[10] and Barcan[11] in 1961 and the present author in 1964[12], 1970[13], 1972[14] and 1973[15] have all said much the same thing.

Clearly the Karmel proposal *reflected* rather than *initiated* a movement which was already gathering momentum. In Victoria, experimental school boards for primary schools and management committees for high schools were already in existence[16]; in Canberra, stimulated by a series of seminars sponsored by the ACT Council of Parents and Citizens Associations, some principals had introduced their own school councils; the Australian Government had commissioned the Neal-Radford Report which called for dual school boards (one lay, one professional) for schools in the ACT and in the Northern Territory.[17]

Further, there was published contemporaneously with, but quite independently of, the Karmel report, the report entitled *A Design for the Governance and Organisation of Education in the Australian Capital Territory*.[18] The fundamental assumptions underlying the report may be summarized as follows:

Teaching and learning take place largely through personal relationships which are at once brief and fragile, yet of life-long importance. The administrative structures and procedures which provide for these relationships should strengthen and nurture wings, not clip them. Such structures need to take into account not only the child and the teacher, but the parent in the home and the citizen in the community at large.

Shortly before the Committee responsible for the above report had finished its work, yet another important report, *Secondary Education for Canberra*, appeared, in which it was argued

... education must be regarded as a process which takes place outside the special educational institutions as much as within them, and which continues long after a person has left them. A second equally important consequence is that this process is very sensitive to, and is thus deeply affected by, structural changes in society.[19]

But the ACT was by no means alone in its interest in Type A decentralization. Early in 1973, the New South Wales Minister for Education published *The Community and its Schools*[20], sub-titled 'A Consultative Paper on Regionalization and Community Involvement in Schools'. In a foreword, the Minister pointed out that in January 1973 the New South Wales Government had approved in principle the proposal for greater community participation in educational decision-making and he sought the reactions of individuals and organizations to the paper's proposals.

The paper produced an almost immediate furore, especially among members of the New South Wales Teachers Federation, whose official reaction was that

... the proposed system will ensure less participation by the community even at the administrative level, as the power to make decisions will rest with a closed circle ...[21]

Following the receipt of the views of 'several thousand people ... either individually or through organizations', the report was re-written by a review panel[22] and it is a matter of record that even the revised document (which was also concerned with Type B decentralization) had gained little support from the teachers' organization at the time of writing in late October 1974.

Much more could be written about the movement towards community involvement in school governance, and particular attention might be paid by scholars in the future to developments in Victoria and South Australia where the movements towards Type A decentralization were clear and unequivocal by mid-1974.

At the same time, there can be no doubt that the members of the Karmel Committee were also looking for Type B decentralization:

> There have been many changes in Australian society since public schooling through State Education Departments was adopted in the late nineteenth century ... the patterns of control which emerged ... were a response to particular circumstances and to the balance of contending forces operating in Australia at that time. They may not be equally relevant for all time.[23]

Again,

> The size of the units which try to achieve educational goals may not now be inappropriate for efficient and effective operation.[24]

There was, of course, nothing new in this proposal insofar as structures were concerned: decentralization of this type was a quarter of a century old in New South Wales and Queensland, and was already well on the way to development in most other States by 1973. It is doubtful, however, whether the extent of decentralization had reached the stage desired by the Committee.

## NATIONAL PLANNING AND EQUALIZATION

The important point made above is that with regard to both Type A and Type B decentralization the Karmel report was suggesting little that was new *for the States.* A crucial question, however, revolves around its implications for the *Federal Government itself.* It seems clear that, with the exception of the relatively small school systems of the Australian Capital Territory and the Northern Territory, the Australian Government was not seen as operating schools of its own. (It is a point of history that these schools have, in fact, taken the lead in Type A decentralization and have accepted Type B decentralization as well.) Because legally the government schools are the responsibility of the *States,* it is the question of the relationship between the Australian Government and those of the States that becomes most pressing. The Karmel Committee nailed their colours to the mast with the assertion that

> ... a national bureaucracy, being further removed from the schools than the State ones, should not presume to interfere with the detail of their operations.[25]

So far, so good, but what construction can be placed on the following equally unequivocal statement:

> ... the need for overall planning of the scale and distribution of resources becomes more necessary than ever if the devolution of authority is not to result in gross inequalities of provision among regions, whether they be States or smaller areas. The role of the Australian Government in this operation is supplementary to that of the States, but its national responsibility may become increasingly important in ensuring an adequate level of resources and their equitable spread.[26]

This statement is pregnant with meaning. It could be interpreted as 'the mailed fist in the velvet glove'. To some anti-centralists who have watched the growth of federal power in education during the last two decades, this is the only viable interpretation; to those who accept as given that 'he who pays the piper calls the tune', the same interpretation is inescapable.

Such interpretations are not justified when the quotation is taken in context, however. The intention is clear: it is to provide for central, planned funding; to provide for formulae which will ensure an equitable level of funding, and to leave it to 'regions' and individual schools to expend the funds, within certain constraints, as they deem best in the light of local conditions and needs. Of course, only time will tell whether the intentions of the report become organizational realities.

It is important to note that, in world terms, there is little that is revolutionary or even unusual in the Committee's proposal. After all, Strayer and Haig's 'Foundation Program'[27], now common in many US States, dates from the 1920s, while the Rate Deficiency Grant in England and Wales is a well-tried feature of local government. The proposals have aroused concern largely because of the isolation of the Australian educational ecosystem from the world 'out there'.

The Foundation Program for example, richly rewards careful study. It is based on the concept of a 'key district' and the cost of providing a good level of education in terms of children in average daily attendance in that district. Districts within the State receive from state funds

1  a flat grant;
2  an equalizing grant (where necessary) to bring their income per child in average daily attendance up to that of the key district; and
3  a reward grant where earned for effort and innovation.

This scheme, admittedly grossly simplified in the description above, operates at a *state* level in the USA, but there is no reason it could not be operated in an amended form at the US national level as a means of funding States or, if the States were to opt out of education (an unlikely development), individual school districts. Precisely the same could be said of Australian conditions, i.e., the direct 'equalizing' financing of States or regions. It could also apply to the financing of non-government schools, as I demonstrated in some detail in a paper to the First National Conference on the Administration of Catholic Education held in Armidale in 1972.[28]

Clearly, the plan would have had some major advantages over the Government's approach with regard to independent schools in that it would have permitted

1  the continuation of the policy of flat (if reduced) grants to all schools, or systems;
2  equalization grants to those schools and systems which deserved them on the basis of 'need'; and
3  reward grants for effort and innovation to those schools and systems which earned them.

In spite of repeated claims to the contrary, there can be little doubt that the Government's present policies, in the entirely laudable search for equality of opportunity, might also reinforce, once the first flush of enthusiasm is past, the very mediocrity which the Karmel report sought to steer away from.

Of course, it can be cogently argued that both the Foundation Program and the Rate Deficiency Grant are applied in countries where some form of local taxation provides a core of income for school systems, whereas no serious proposal has been made for such taxation in Australia. However, this argument need not apply in the case of federal grants to States, nor, be it noted, in the case of federal grants to the majority of Catholic schools, which need not have been virtually forced into incipient state 'blocs' for purposes of finance.

In any case, the prophets of woe who fear central financing do not have to look very far from Australia to find a nationally-financed educational system which imposes no local taxes, which provides a great many opportunities for local, 'grass-roots' initiative and which has achieved a considerable degree of equality of opportunity. It is an extraordinary but inescapable fact that for many years Australian administrators, scholars and teachers have streamed to England, Scotland, Canada and the USA seeking ideas on such systems while largely ignoring the New Zealand model on our doorstep! That recognition of New Zealand's experience has now been achieved is reflected in the special visits made independently to New Zealand by the members of both the New South Wales and ACT Committees inquiring into the governance and administration of education early in 1973.

It seems that at last the perceptive if somewhat idealized claims made by Lascelles Wilson and others in the 1960s are having some impact in Australia. As Wilson put it,

> The New Zealand system has involved no impairment of ministerial or parliamentary authority. Clearly, the contrary has been the case. The monies expended under the Minister's control by district boards, school boards and committees, have all been public monies voted by Parliament and subject to normal Treasury and Auditor-General's checks. Every Minister of Education presenting his department's estimates to the N.Z. ... has done so secure in the knowledge that supporting his education officers and backing these estimates have been the very large numbers of statutory bodies and their members, well-informed citizens with specific responsibilities to advise him, and through him, Parliament, of the community's educational needs. This is an enhancement, not a diminution, of ministerial prestige, power and authority; an enlargement, not a restriction, of parliamentary responsibility.[29]

## SOME QUESTIONS

At this stage it might prove useful to ask some specific questions which have obviously been puzzling and worrying many in educational circles since the Australian Government adopted the chief recommendations of the Karmel Committee:

1 The Karmel Committee recommends local autonomy in educational

policy-making, yet also implies increasing federal influence over planning and funding. Are these tendencies not contradictory?

Of course they are contradictory — if it naively assumed that governance and administration are not creatures of 'give and take', of 'checks and balances'. The question should not be expressed in terms of contradiction, but of complementarity. England and Wales are excellent examples of countries where local decision-making, national financing and national planning co-exist to the benefit both of the countries concerned and of individual children. As suggested above, an even more relevant example is that of New Zealand, so much closer to our doorstep.

2 Can a centrally conceived and initiated renewal program avoid increasing federal control over educational decision-making?

It is unlikely that with the best will in the world such a program can avoid increasing federal control, even if it wished to do so: it would be naive to believe anything else. Anyone who doubts this statement might read with interest Zelman Cowan's pungent 1968 remarks on the growing power of the Australian Universities Commission.[30] All of this is not to say that certain governments might not try to slough off certain of their powers, as President Richard Nixon sought to do in the USA a few years ago in his relationship with the States. But, given the importance of Section 96 of the Australian Constitution, which has provided the Government with opportunities to intrude into the field of education (and any other field involving financial grants), the growth of central power generally and of control of educational decision-making seems inevitable. The real question, of course, is *how* this power is used, as the following question highlights.

3 Can areas of responsibility be divided, so as to allow increasing federal control in some areas and yet increased local autonomy in others?

The obvious answer to this question is that any attempt to speak of 'pure' centralization or 'pure' decentralization is completely unrealistic.

There have been surprisingly few attempts to study empirically the effects on school systems of centralization and decentralization. However, one outstanding study was that conducted in the late 1930s by Francois Cillie in New York City. Cillie, a South African, saw many similarities between the great (Type B) New York City system and the centralized (Type B) South African provincial systems, which incidentally, were very similar to the Australian state systems.[31] He set out to compare certain health areas within the boundaries of the city system with a carefully matched group of New York state 'villages' adjoining the city which represented the best American tradition of public school administration (i.e. Type A — decentralized, under a superintendent appointed by an elected, fiscally independent board of education responsible to the citizens of the community). The communities were matched with respect to geographical, educational, financial, socio-economic and professional factors.

Cillie set out to test the hypothesis presented by Mort and Cornell in their *Adaptability of School Systems* that

1 certain types of adaptation prosper best in a decentralized (Type A) system of administration;
2 certain other types prosper best in a centralized (Type B) system of administration; and
3 certain further types prosper independently of the kind of centralization or decentralization of administration.

The schools were surveyed by means of Mort and Cornell's *Guide for Self-Appraisal of School Systems*. One hundred and seventy possible types of adaptation ('The sloughing off of out-moded purposes and practices by school systems and the taking on of new ones to meet new needs') were found to be distributed in such a way that, of every 10 studied, about six were found to prosper well in both Type A and Type B communities, about three were found to prosper best in centralized (Type A) communities and more than one were found to prosper best in centralized (Type B) communities.

In a classic statement, Cillie summed up a governmental and administrative reality which should be etched on the hearts of all educational policy-makers:

> Neither centralization by itself nor decentralization, but the centralization of certain aspects of educational administration and the decentralization of others are necessary before the ultimate goal of educational adaptation can be fully achieved in the complete liberation of the potentialities of the individual pupil and the individual teacher.

## STATES' RIGHTS

Questions like those asked above may be readily answered where only two authorities, for example, federal and local governments, are concerned, but the questions are confused mightily in the Australian context by the existence of the States. In brief, the State Governments which emerged from the colonial legislatures retained certain powers and handed over other powers to the Commonwealth. Among the powers retained by the States was the provision of public education. The States continue to guard their powers jealously, but the Uniform Tax legislation of 1942, originally devised as a wartime expedient, handed over all income-taxing powers to the Federal Government and this has virtually emasculated the States financially. The whole situation from a schooling viewpoint has been complicated by the facts that:

1 education has become the single greatest drain on state revenues;
2 education, a labour intensive activity, has increased dramatically in cost in recent years;
3 education has become such a large and complex activity that States have become increasingly anxious to decentralize it administratively;
4 teachers have become so active industrially in their demands for higher salaries and improved working conditions that States have increasingly been anxious to hand over certain powers of employment to local or regional bodies; and
5 education has become politically a 'hot potato', following the powerful actions of parent groups, and especially those in non-government schools.

The Catholic schools, in particular, have vastly complicated the relatively even political tenor of pre-war public education.

In the light of these developments, some specific questions are being asked about the influence of the Karmel report upon school systems, for it is clear that with the exception of a small group of independent non-government schools, the report implies major federal financial relationships with *systems* and only minor financial relationships with individual schools.

The danger inherent in this situation is only too obvious in a country where the state systems have for so long been accused of centralization, mediocrity and conformity. In theory, at least, there is little that the Federal Government can do about this; it *could* be providing funds which merely strengthen at state levels the very characteristics for which they have been so trenchantly criticized in the past and which are contrary to the spirit of the Karmel report. While there have, indeed, been signs of this, the manifestation has by no means been as bad as might have been expected. For one thing, some state governments seem to have shown that they were just not efficient enough to spend the money allocated to them, though considering the legislative lag between the tabling of the report and the passing of the necessary acts, together with the Australian Government's anxiety to show quick results, too much might have been expected of the States. Some appear to have deliberately sought to 'muddy the water' in the hope of making political capital out of the 'States' rights' issue; it is an open secret that one or two have been unco-operative in providing Canberra with statistical data; certainly, some have resented the clear pressures to vary the priorities to which they had committed themselves. But this has not been the general case. For one thing, the innovation grants have encouraged and stimulated thought in schools of all types. For another, by the greatest of good fortune, the availability of large-scale federal funding has coincided with the movement towards decentralization both of governance and administration described above, and this has opened the eyes of senior administrators, teachers and the public to possibilities, whether welcome or unwelcome, which had hitherto been undreamed of. Sometimes this movement has been speeded by the sheer exasperation of administrators attempting to run systems which Jackson had warned were 'grinding to a full stop'[32]; sometimes it has been speeded by genuinely idealistic senior administrators who recognized the need for educational renewal.

Nonetheless, the danger remains. When the excitement of the early-to-mid-1970s passes, will federal funds do more than merely allow the States to do more of the same old thing? Will the gazelle show signs of the pathologies associated with ageing?

## NON-GOVERNMENT SCHOOLS

The Catholic sector is one in which the effect of federal funding is already producing trauma. Until recently the Catholic 'non-system', for all its complexity, internal rivalries, cross-parish, cross-diocese and cross-order networks, provided a useful and different alternative to the state systems. The Catholic non-system had never thought of itself along state lines and this was one of its greatest strengths. The Karmel recommendations virtually forced the establishment of Catholic state boards of education when existing diocesan boundaries could have provided an excellent structure for 'a national system, locally administered'.

Already there are signs of sameness and uniformity creeping into Catholic school administration; already state boards are alleged to be dominated by the capital city boards, some of which seem to be determined to vie with the state for the wooden spoon in the Uniformity Stakes; already the diversity, competition and commitment which were the hallmarks of Catholic education, are in decline.

One must hasten to say that Catholic school buildings are bigger, brighter and better; that teachers are more numerous and better qualified; that finance is more efficiently handled. But the mystique, even the magic, which marked these schools in the past, is dying rapidly.

Of course, the comments above do not apply to the 'non-systemic' Catholic schools, nor to the independent, predominantly Protestant, non-government schools, which have direct links to Canberra. Some of the smaller, marginally economic country schools have been forced to close or combine with neighbouring schools, but the majority of such schools seem to be flourishing, in spite of the occasional *cri de coeur*, under the Schools Commission.

## THE FUTURE

The comparative success of this direct federal government—individual school/group-of-schools relationship has major implications for both the state and independent schools of the future as they develop their boards and councils and seek more and more autonomy.

Elsewhere I have written at length about the humanity, the subtlety of the interaction process we call 'teaching' and I have drawn attention to the innately non-educative, inhumane effects of bureaucracy at its worst.[34] Complexity, impersonality, and organizational rigidity are the fifth column of the educative, as distinct from the instructional, or propaganda process.

I have also presented elsewhere the fundamental thesis that the key administrative goals of educational administration and governance — flexibility and adaptability — are correlates of direct citizen interest and are hence attainable in full measure only through Type A decentralization.[35]

Already the move towards such decentralization is clear and unequivocal at the level of individual schools, government and non-government; already the need for national planning is so widely accepted that the clock cannot be turned back; already there have been sown the seeds of a national system, locally administered. Such a system could be operated through the States, through regions or through individual schools or groups of schools.

Relationships with independent non-Catholic schools could continue on a direct communication basis; relationships with systemic Catholic schools could develop on a truly diocesan, or regional, basis. Relationships with government schools could continue on a state basis, or could be developed on a regional (e.g., Albury-Wodonga) basis.

Yet despite the direction of the move referred to above, it is a matter for regret that the obvious Karmel predilection for Type A decentralization has had to take second place in the case of most programs to a Type B decentralization, all too often on an *ad hoc* basis sadly lacking in evaluative power. This *ad hoc* approach is disappointing in the light of widely-held hopes for high quality national planning. One cannot avoid the conclusion that, although the infusion of federal funds has to some extent changed the administrative directions of the government and non-government schools, this change has too often been based on hasty, day-to-day management decisions rather than on careful, well-researched planning. All of this is sadly reminiscent of the idealistic infusion of federal funds by the United States Government in the 1960s, an infusion which sought to achieve too much, too quickly and did not clearly recognize that it is *people* rather than *money* which are the real change agents in education. This is not to say that the Karmel Committee valued the role of the actuary rather than the visionary, but merely to emphasize that, in the implementation of the report, visionaries seem to be few and far between.

For the great majority of Australian children (assuming that a constitutional amendment transferring the responsibility for education to the Commonwealth is grossly unlikely), the conclusion is inescapable that the success of the Karmel recommendations and of the Australian Government's policies arising from those recommendations will depend in the long run upon the posture taken by the States. What, for example, would eventuate if the Australian Government found itself bolstering state systems which continued to display characteristics criticized by the Karmel Committee? Would it be likely to tie specific *education* conditions to its grants under Section 96? It will inevitably be up to the States either to opt for a future typified by the tortoise of the 30s, or the gazelle of the 70s. The Australian Government, for its part, will need to keep a sharp look-out for ways and means of diagnosing and treating the pathologies of the ageing gazelle not only in the States, the regions and the dioceses, but within Canberra itself. If the Schools Commission is to develop even further as an administrative organization rather than the 'think-tank' type organization of early promise, the most infirm of all gazelles could be in permanent residence right under the nose of the Australian Government itself.

## Notes

1 Walker, W. G. (1970). 'The Governance of Education in Australia: Centralization and Politics', *The Journal of Educational Administration*, 8.
See also Walker, W. G. 'What on Earth is Accountability?'. In P. Chippendale (Ed.) (1977). *Accountability in Australian Education*. St. Lucia: University of Queensland Press.

For an outstanding review of the literature see G. S. Harman (1974). *The Politics of Education: A Bibliographical Guide.* St. Lucia: University of Queensland Press.

2 Australia. (1973). *Schools in Australia. Report of the Interim Committee for the Australian Schools Commission.* (Chairman, P. Karmel). Canberra: AGPS, p.10.

3 Walker, W. G. (1972). *Centralization and Decentralization: An International Viewpoint on an American Dilemma. A Special CASEA Report.* Eugene, Oregon: Center for the Advanced Study of Educational Administration, University of Oregon. But see also: Chapman, Robin (1973). 'Decentralization: Another Perspective', *Comparative Education*, **9** (3), and Walker, W. G. 'Administrative Structure: Centralization or Decentralization', Chap. 10 in G. S. Harman and C. Selby Smith (Eds) (1973). *Designing a New Education Authority.* Canberra: Australian National University.

4 Australia. (1973). op. cit.: 13.

5 Unesco (1951). *Compulsory Education in Australia.* Paris.

6 Horne, Donald. (1974). *The Lucky Country.* Harmondsworth: Penguin. p. 219.

7 Kandel, I. L. (1938). *Types of Administration.* Hawthorn, Vic.: ACER.

8 Butts, R. F. (1955). *Assumptions Underlying Australian Education.* Hawthorn, Vic.: ACER.

9 Turner, I. S. (1960). 'A Plea for Decentralization in Australian Education', *Melbourne Studies in Education 1958–59.* Melbourne: Melbourne University Press.

10 Jackson, R. W. B. (1961). *Emergent Needs in Australian Education.* Toronto: University of Toronto Department of Educational Research.

11 Barcan, A. (1961). 'The Government of Australian Education', *The Challenge to Australian Education.* Melbourne: Australian College of Education.

12 Walker, W. G. 'Educational Administration'. Chapter 9 in R. W. T. Cowen (1964). (Ed.) *Education for Australians.* Melbourne: Cheshire.

13 Walker, W. G. (1970). 'Australian Education: The Next Ten Years'. Chapter 12 in *Theory and Practice in Educational Administration.* St. Lucia: University of Queensland Press. See also Walker, W. G. 'The Governance of Education in Australia', op. cit.

14 Walker, W. G. 'Bureaucracy in Educational Organization: An Overview'. Chapter 2 in W. G. Walker (Ed.) (1972). *School, College and University: The Administration of Education in Australia.* St. Lucia: University of Queensland Press.

15 Walker, W. G. 'Administrative Structure', op.cit.

16 For interim reports on a study of one of these bodies, known officially as an 'advisory council' see David Pettit, 'Community and School', in *ACER Newsletter*, 20 March 1974, and 22 September 1974. The report was published in *Australian Education Review* under the title 'School and Neighbourhood: A Case Study'.

17 Neal, W. D. and W. C. Radford. (1972). *Teachers for Commonwealth Schools.* Hawthorn, Vic.: ACER.

18 Commonwealth of Australia. Assessment Panel on the A.C.T. Education Authority. (1973). *A Design for the Governance and Organisation of Education in the Australian Capital Territory.* Canberra: AGPS.

19 Commonwealth of Australia. Report of the Working Committee on College Proposals for the Australian Capital Territory. (1973). *Secondary Education for Canberra.* Canberra: AGPS, p.8.

20 New South Wales. (1973). *The Community and Its Schools: A Consultative Paper on Regionalization and Community Involvement in Schools.* Sydney: Government Printer.

21 New South Wales Teachers' Federation, 'Submission on The Community and its Schools'. Sydney: 21 September 1973. Mimeo. p.1.

22 New South Wales. (1974). *The Community and its Schools: Report of the Review Panel Appointed by the Minister for Education.* Sydney: Department of Education.

23 Australia. (1973). op. cit.: 10.

24 ibid.: 13.

25 ibid.: 10.

26 ibid.: 10–11.

27 Strayer, George D. and Haig, Robert M. (1924). *The Financing of Education in the State of New York: Report of the Educational Finance Inquiry.* New York: Macmillan.

28 Walker, W. G. 'Centralization or Decentralization? The Key Issue in Catholic Education', Chapter in P. Tannock (Ed.) (1975).*The Organization and Administration of Catholic Education in Australia.* St. Lucia: University of Queensland Press.

29 Wilson, Lascelles. *Canberra Times*, 11 April 1968.

30 Cowan, Zelman. 'The Growth of Federal Participation in Australian Education'. Chapter 1 in W. G. Walker (Ed.) (1972). *School, College and University: The Administration of Education in Australia.* St. Lucia: University of Queensland Press.

31 Cillie, Francois (1940). Centralization or Decentralization? (Contributions to Education No. 789). New York: Teachers College, Columbia University. Note that parenthetical reference to Type A and Type B centralization-decentralization are the author's, not Cillie's.

32 Jackson, R. W. B. op. cit.: 25.

33 This statement, however, is made without the opportunity to observe the effect of a 'system break' — the decision of the Government to reduce the taxation education allowance deductible for each student child from $400 in 1974 to $150 in 1975.

34 For example, see Walker (1970). op. cit., and Walker (1972). op. cit.

35 For example, see 'Administrative Structure', ibid., and Walker (1972). *Centralization and Decentralization: An International Viewpoint on an American Dilemma.*

# 8. Accountability in Education: the Concept and its Implications

## J. V. D'Cruz

### THE 'NEW' ORTHODOXY

On 3 March 1970, the United States Congress was told:

> From these considerations we derive another new concept: *accountability*. School administrators and school teachers alike are responsible for their performances and it is in their interest as well as in the interests of their pupils that they be held accountable.[1]

That of course was a pre-Watergate Richard M. Nixon speaking. But the tarnished reputation of the ex-President does not absolve us from examining the worth of a concept he helped set once more in orbit.

The concept of accountability is really an old one. In some formulations, its defining characteristics are identical despite a lag of many centuries. In Aristotle's day

> Appointments to office by means of the lot ... [were] safe-guarded at Athens in three ways — first by a formal test of fitness before entry on office ... secondly, by a vote in the assembly on the conduct of any officer during his tenure ... thirdly, by a scrutiny at the end of the tenure of office which included not only a financial audit, but also examination before a board of scrutiny.[2]

A current version states:

> Accountability is a regular public report by independent reviewers of demonstrated student accomplishment promised for the expenditure of resources.[3]

Thus, the three elements basic to accountability remain — an accomplishment, independent assessment of results, and public reports.

Nor has the passage of time made any difference to the belief that accountability through inspection and assessment can influence improvements in the teaching performance of a paid teacher. Plutarch's theme was indeed 'results by inspection and assessment':

> Some fathers who, after entrusting their sons to attendants and masters, do not themselves take cognisance at all of their instruction by means of their own eyes or their own ears. Herein they most fail in their duty; for they ought themselves every few days to test their children, and not rest their hopes upon the disposition of a hired person; for even those persons will devote more attention to the children if they know they must from time to time render an account. And in this connection there is point as well as wit in the remark of a groom who said that nothing makes the horse so fat as the king's eye.[4]

A current version states:

> Each teacher and administrator needs to be continually reminded that, by virtue of accepting employment, he has promised each family sending a child to school, each community paying his salary, and each student receiving his service that, in so

far as possible, every student will benefit from his services. Accountability refers specifically to the product of that labour.[5]

Essentially, a performance contract is an agreement by a firm or individual to produce specified results by a certain date, using acceptable methods, for a set fee. The parties may agree in advance that, if the conditions are not met by that date, the firm must continue its efforts, for no additional fee, until they are met; and also that if the requirements are exceeded, either by early completion or by a higher level of achievement, the fee will be increased by specified amounts. Thus, in a contract for additional services, the school has a guarantee that, for the budgeted expenditure, students will acquire certain skills, as measured by an independent auditor; and the supplier of the services has a strong incentive not only to meet but to exceed the contractual requirements.[6]

A funny thing happens to the teacher on the way to accountability; he finds that it sometimes means payment by results. The 'new' orthodoxy is labelled 'accountability', 'stewardship', and so on.

The tenor of the response to demands of accountability depends largely on the climate in which the demands are made. In a context where the loss of public confidence in schools is acute, the demand for accountability carries with it a palpable presumption of guilt. Why else investigate the work of professional teachers in a sense of calling them to account, if there is not the suspicion that there is something amiss with the people concerned or with their work? But where persons or agencies work with confidence, requests for educational or other forms of accountability do not take the form of censure; when work is evaluated, there is an instinctive awareness of the difference between a reasonable conclusion and vindictive judgment.

Having noted that the current demand for accountability is the re-cycling of an old idea and that accountability is best achieved in a climate of co-operation, the rest of this article will concern itself, initially, with the relationships between the concepts of accountability and education and with the differing senses of accountability which can be distinguished; then, with some questions that arise when the concept of accountability is examined, particularly in reference to the Report of the Interim Committee of the Australian Schools Commission; and, finally, with a summary of the main themes and arguments dealt with in this article together with brief recommendations to the Australian Schools Commission.

## ACCOUNTABILITY AND EDUCATION

The link between the concepts of education and accountability is more clearly seen with the aid of some useful distinctions which can be drawn between education, on the one hand, and training and instruction, on the other. With R. S. Peters we might say that education is an activity that must meet the following criteria: the activity must be valuable in itself; the activity must be associated with other activities to provide a wide cognitive perspective; and those who are engaged in the activity must voluntarily come to believe it is worth doing.[7] And that which a teacher does, which we refer to as teaching, is described by Peters as a complex activity which unites together processes, such as instructing and training, by the overall intention of getting pupils not only to acquire knowledge, skills and modes of conduct, but to also acquire them in a manner which involves an evaluation of the rationale underlying them.[8]

Thus, in this process, some outcomes the learner is expected to gain consist not only of habits, skills and performances, but also the capacity to think critically, to reflect constructively, to interpret and to appreciate.

In contrast, training *per se* is closer to performances than to the acquisition of knowledge and beliefs in the context of reflective thinking and critical judgment, because it is concerned with habits, skills and responses. Instruction, with the person learning by following what the instructor says, can also take the form of a carefully reasoned argument; even so, it tends not to stimulate students to think for themselves, though it does not necessarily prevent independent thinking on the part of the pupils. It implies telling on the part of the teacher, without necessarily involving critical understanding on the part of the learner. In both instruction and training, the value of what is transmitted from the teacher to the learner is dependent upon the authority of the teacher and not on the knowledge appropriately justified by the learner to his own satisfaction through reasons, arguments and evidence. While the distinction between educating and instructing-training is real, it would be unfortunate to present it in such a fashion as to allow the distinction to harden into a dichotomy; so I hasten to add and emphasize that certainly a good deal of educating also includes performance-practice, which is derived from the notion of instructing-training.

### The two senses

The notion one has of educational accountability is partly derived from one's understanding of what an educator does, namely whether he is educating or only instructing-training his pupils. On the one hand, if what a teacher does is thought of in terms of our understanding of the concept of education and in terms of our more inclusive concept of teaching, one's notion of accountability would give priority to considerations of whether the teacher's activities were well chosen to involve his pupils in activities valuable in themselves; whether they touched his pupils' imagination, knowledge, beliefs, will and emotions; and whether they involved such educational outcomes as understanding, critical reflection and judgment on the part of the learner. Working from this notion of accountability, any 'accountant' will discover that some of the activities of a good educator will lend themselves to operational description and quantification, while others will defy operational specifications and quantification by any known tests of the activities either of the educator or of his pupils. On the other hand, if what a teacher does is confined only to instruction or training, then one's corresponding notion of accountability need only confine itself to those performances (knowledge, habits, skills) which can be behaviourally identified and easily quantified.

The demand for accountability in educational activities that exclusively comprise training and instruction is more easily satisfied because they involve more easily quantified phenomena; the demand for accountability of activities that comprise education is harder to satisfy because they are a more complex and subtle phenomenon being concerned with bringing about in pupils 'certain states of mind and ways of behaving'[9] that are held to be of value, which in practice, at least, are not entirely measurable as quantifiable behaviour. Thus, part of the notion one has of educational accountability is derived from one's understanding of what an educator does, namely, whether he is educating or only instructing-training his pupils.

Accountability can and does influence, even determine, curriculum design. For instance: Should tests determine only what can be quantified or should tests reflect that which is important? In fact, what is measured becomes important to students, parents and teachers. Thus, if in a school memory is measured but reflective thinking and judgment are not, if rote learning is measured but building a healthy self-concept is not, then, by its very test criteria, the school is indicating what it considers is important and what its priorities are. And the school's curriculum will be designed primarily to cater for those criteria and not others or, at best, give the latter low priority.

It is now clear that the term accountability may be used in two senses. If the objective of the educator is to produce readily quantifiable and easily specifiable, such as behavioural, objectives (e.g., certain examination scores, certificates or achievement scores), then accountability is linked to a type of achievement, which, by definition, can be empirically tested and publicly assessed.[10] On the other hand, if the objectives of the educator are more diverse, with the intention also to involve students in non-operationally defined worthwhile activities, such as appreciating, reflective thinking and judging, and which are therefore more difficult to quantify, then he is thought of as being accountable primarily in respect of having placed students in situations by which those value criteria are met. We do, of course, speak and act in ways which assume that there is achievement possible in non-quantifiable areas of conduct (and education); and we would certainly look askance at someone who claims that he is creating a good learning situation with respect to certain non-quantifiable objectives, if there is no evidence of any sort of student engagement in it or any discernible change resulting from it. In a restricted sense, the demand for accountability is intended to mean proving in a publicly demonstrable fashion the achievement of quantifiable results; in a more inclusive sense, accountability is associated with additional notions such as 'explaining', 'describing', 'making clear', 'justifying' one's intended value criteria and programs of action. The different senses of accountability are logically linked to the differing objectives of the educator, or to the objectives which the person who seeks accountability wishes to impose on the educator. The two senses of accountability, therefore, are a restricted sense which emphasizes the more readily quantifiable, easily specifiable and clearly behavioural aspects of education; and a more inclusive sense which embraces both those elements of education which secure and those which elude precise quantification and behavioural specification.

J. V. D'CRUZ

## KARMEL'S TWO NOTIONS OF ACCOUNTABILITY

It should be stated at the outset that not one, but two notions of accountability are to be found in the Report of the Interim Committee of the Australian Schools Commission, although only one of the two notions is actually acknowledged in the report.[11] One notion is to be found in Chapter 13, the section (13.15–23) formally devoted to 'Administration Accountability' in the final part of the report; here the concept is made explicit and is the dominant notion of accountability which the Committee projects. The other notion is to be found in the first part of the report, especially in Chapter 2, entitled 'Values and Perspectives'; here the concept is left implicit. I intend, firstly, to pinpoint the dominant notion as it is made explicit in the report, and then to extract the second and implicit notion in the report. The extent to which this latter notion approaches my own understanding of the concept will become obvious.

### The notion made explicit

In the second part of this article, I analysed accountability at the general conceptual level; however, discussions on accountability give rise to a series of questions, such as: *Why* be accountable? *Who* is accountable? Accountable to *whom*? Accountable for *what*? *When* is one accountable? When specific answers have been given to these questions, the detailed notion of accountability will have been provided. In this section of the article, then, I shall consider how the report deals with these questions and, in passing, consider whether the Committee's notion of accountability is an adequate one.

*Why be accountable?* In Chapter 13, the Committee argues that the sole reason accountability is necessary is a moral one – money granted for a single purpose must be spent on that purpose alone and on no other. Thus public money must be 'applied properly' (13.15), 'properly spent' (13.19);

> For example, grants which have been recommended to raise the level of services must be shown to have been devoted to improving standards and not say, to providing places for more pupils (13.15).

Does the Committee believe there could be educational or wider social reasons to warrant accountability? There is a vague reference to 'the performance of schools and school systems' (13.16); and there is also the recommendation (13.23 and developed in 13.21–22) that at some stage grants will be available only to schools approved by the Commission — approved, that is to say, 'as capable of providing a satisfactory level *and type* of education' (my italics). But, as we shall see later, these ideas are not sufficiently developed or clear; nor does Chapter 13 go beyond the briefest statement on the necessity for educational accountability, failing to provide any underlying rationale.

*Who is accountable?* The report refers to 'school authorities' (13.16), 'the recipients of grants', who must be accountable for 'financial accounting of all moneys received . . . and statistical returns on the use of human and material resources . . .' (13.17). The group singled out for accountability is school

130

administrators. With this prominence given to them and with the enormous amount of time, energy and human resources expended in accounting, it would not be surprising if the chief executives of schools eventually found themselves increasingly more isolated from the educational aspects of the schools. It follows too that the Committee sees schooling, not education, as the focal content of accountability. Are there not others in education, or even in schools, who should also be held accountable?

*Accountable to whom?* The Committee's answer is that school administrators are accountable to the 'public' through the government-instituted Australian Schools Commission (13.16). But who or what constitutes the public? Obviously, the Committee means the taxpaying and voting public. (Even the Australian and State Governments are seen as intermediaries between the school administrators and the taxpayers.) Are there not other publics to whom the schools are accountable?

*Accountable for what?* According to the Committee, the Schools Commission is there 'not only to ensure public accountability but also to monitor the performance of schools and school systems' (13.16). Public accountability is intended to ensure that public money is not misappropriated, but properly spent on certain 'aspects of pupils, staffing, buildings and equipment' (13.16), i.e., on those things that money can buy. The connection between educational resources and education itself is not inevitable; and administrators and teachers are likely to spend too much time evaluating these material aspects and not the more important and subtle aspects of education.

Next, what precisely is meant by 'performance of schools and school systems'? The relevant section in which 'performance' is invoked gives no criteria by which it is to be evaluated. Does 'performance' refer to some, as yet undisclosed, move by the Commission to set up national, state and regional standards of achievements by which schools and school systems are to be evaluated? If so, where does that place concern for individual differences of pupils and of schools and of school systems? Are not national standards of achievements likely to demand forms of accountability which are of necessity readily quantifiable and ignore those aspects of education that defy operational definition?

Further, with the Government's potentially strong presence on Boards of Trustees of the 'systemic' schools (13.19), and with power to withhold money grants to schools which are not 'capable of providing a satisfactory level *and type* of education' (13.21, my italics), the stage is set for a Commission (acting on the Government's behalf), if it chooses to adopt a tough stance by demanding a restrictive form of accountability, to begin to influence or even determine what that type of education is to be. As we have already seen, forms of accountability can determine the nature of education provided and the type and aspects of subjects which will be given emphasis in schools. When a certain form of accountability is linked with the power to grant or withhold funding, schools and school systems could be facing a potentially threatening situation.

*When is one accountable?* The Committee argues that school authorities are accountable to the public when they receive public funds through the government (13.15–13.17). Does this imply that if school authorities in a country were to conduct schools with no financial help from the public they would be immune from any sort of accountability to the people of that country? For instance, would it be permissible for a school or school system, which claims no share of the nation's tax receipts, to function with the primary aim of training people in the use of violence of any sort as the sole means of resolving disputes?

At this point, two possible objections may be anticipated. It might be said that I have been a bit hard in my treatment of Chapter 13 of the report because that chapter was intended apparently to deal with political rather than educational accountability and, therefore, is understandably and acceptably restricted in scope; and that, moreover, even in Chapter 13 (21–22), there is a hint of a broader concept of accountability in the implication that sooner or later the Commission will be making judgments on other than statistical criteria. My own reactions to these possible objections would be, firstly, that it is not understandable or acceptable for the report to project magisterially the one form of accountability (however necessary that political form may be) as if it were the only one or the most important one in the wide context of education, because it is neither; secondly, that the warning (however welcome, in principle) that some form of *educational* accountability will be demanded sooner or later is not an actual requirement here and now but a statement of intention; and thirdly, that the report only indicates categories of 'specified standards' (e.g., 'the nature of the curriculum' [13.21]) to be met by schools before approval is granted, but gives no detailed indication of what is meant by or subsumed under 'standards' and 'nature'. My general comment here would be that the Schools Commission is not committed in the report to adopt only the restricted notion of accountability, but will come to be identified with it unless the Commission soon provides an unequivocal and clearly articulated richer notion of educational accountability.

## Behaviourism

Embedded in the Committee's dominant and explicitly formulated view of accountability are two concerns that need some examination — the pursuit of the concrete, the exact, and the certain; and the pursuit of what is quantifiably measurable. When applied to education, these pursuits appear in various guises, especially in some form of 'scientific' systems approach. My concern is that these pursuits, which can be quite legitimate and desirable, should not be seen as the only, or necessarily the most important, features of educational evaluation and accountability.

It is important to note some of the implications of behaviourism in education. Behaviourists define learning as behaviour that is changed in conformity with predicted, measurable outcomes and with little or no measurable 'waste'. The idea seems to be that only that which is measurable as behaviour by large-scale empirical tests can really form the basis for the assessment of learning. How long before it becomes the new doctrine that only that which is behaviourally measurable by the current battery of empirical tests should be taught? And where would such a prescription leave much of what goes on in such subject areas as art, music, literature, social studies, religious education? Behavioural objectives foster methods in instruction which are standardized, empirically tested, and aim at measurable results. Learning which is self-centred, uninstructed and unpredictable tends to be eliminated by the behaviourist. Problems arise: what the teacher wants to encourage in students is not always measurable when they are still students and is not always measurable as behaviour. Teachers are also limited by the fact that students are out of their hands in the long run so that they cannot be observed; occasions when the students' behaviour may show that they understand, know or appreciate what teachers wanted of them may be rather limited. Further, while behavioural objectives may sharpen the objectives of instruction, they may also focus on easily defined behaviours which lack scope and significance, thus stressing the inconsequential, the trivial in education. Finally, behaviourism lends itself to modes of teaching which are instruction and training and which fall short of our holistic notion of education.

There is also the danger that insistence on 'performance of schools and schools systems', which might take the direction of measuring students against achievement standards in each subject set for the region, State or nation, may pressure teachers to act in ways unsuited to good educational practices. Students may be manipulated to meet externally imposed standards without regard for their needs and abilities, making a mockery of individual differences. National or state objectives and assessment procedures may influence teachers in their selection of both content and method. Material not relevant to the objectives may be dropped, and methodologies promoting the kind of skills needed in the assessment exercises may be introduced. If tests are to be used nation-wide or State-wide, they are going to be objectively measurable, which means that preparation of students for these tests will more likely take the form of instruction and training rather than education. If the results of national assessment are treated as national norms, some unfair comparisons between groups, States and regions may be made, and some school systems may be presented in a distorted way without due consideration of the complexities in different learning situations.

## The notion left implicit

What we have seen so far has been one view of accountability, located in the final part of the report, which makes explicit the formal conditions that should govern the system of accounting by school authorities. I believe that a close scrutiny of statements in the early part of the report (especially Chapter 2) would provide us with a base from which another more satisfactory notion of accountability may be constructed. As the report does not crystallize completely this alternative notion, a degree of extrapolation is needed. We return to those questions posed earlier.

*Why be accountable?* In Chapter 2, the report suggests that the reasons school authorities must be accountable are both educational and social. The report says that there is an 'obligation on teachers to explain to parents procedures [for example, educational programs] developed through expert knowledge'; this explanation is 'a means', the objectives being 'of extending [the school's] educational influence and of reinforcing pupil motivation' (2.19). The need to be accountable is also placed within a wider social context. The report states that 'it would make good sense to have the school as a nucleus of a community centre' (2.20), urging that it is desirable for there to be 'joint planning, and even conduct, of schools by educational, health, welfare, cultural and sporting agencies', resulting in 'a link ... between school, family, peer group, and the society at large' (2.20). An implication of joint decision-making must surely be joint accountability. Thus, and rightly, the report is saying that rights and duties are correlative, that many groups of people must be held accountable to one another for decisions they have made.

*Who is accountable?* In the first notion of accountability, the report had made school authorities solely responsible for educational programs. If, now, as the report suggests, joint planning and joint conduct of school activities are desirable, then responsibility for those activities must be jointly assumed. Therefore, multiple and joint accountability must be shared by all agents involved in the education of the pupil — the students themselves, teachers, school administrators, parents, state and federal authorities, churches, etc. There is now a basis to call many to account. For instance, are parents of a child not accountable to teachers and school administrators and to parents of other children if, on being admitted to school, their child suffers from acute anxieties, excessive timidity, shyness, temper tantrums or belligerence? — any or all of which may cause learning difficulties. The report accepts the principle that the state is responsible to teachers and parents for adequate material conditions in school; why else would it recommend (2.5) additional funding? While the child is a pupil at school, he or she is also a client of other institutions in society: how then do we mark off the respective positive or deleterious influences each may have on the child? If it cannot be done with any precision, why do we insist on only one of the many institutions (the school) being accountable? It is a fallacy to assume that one can assess, with any kind of precision, where proximate, intermediate, and final responsibility is lodged whenever a child fails to learn the knowledge, skills, values and behaviours which he or she has been promised. Teachers can rightly be held accountable for what *they* teach or do not teach; it is unfair to hold them alone accountable for what the *student* does or does not learn. Others may be responsible for the latter: many out-of-school variables are known to affect learning directly — family stability; economic, educational and nutritional level of the child; and stimulation through his general environment.

*Accountable to whom?* Again, in Chapter 2, the report's answer is more than merely to refer to a taxpaying public; it includes parents (2.19), students and community (2.21). In brief, the report rightly accepts the principle that, in a 'caring community' (2.22), there are many publics to be accountable to. It is a mistake to assume that the public is a unitary entity, sharing a set of identical values and expectations. But there are problems to be resolved. In a pluralist society, with interest groups of varying and opposing expectations, strident calls for accountability have the tendency to politicize the educational process. Which interest-groups ought the teacher to serve? The values he imparts, either of a procedural or substantive nature, may be approved by some and disapproved by others. Should teachers be responsive only to dominant groups in society? Or is every interest-group in the community entitled to feel that it has the right to control the schools for its own ends? Does accountability imply that everybody, regardless of their qualifications and responsibility for the outcomes in education, is allowed to pass judgment on the teacher's competence? Further, is it reasonable to ask teachers to be accountable to their clients when teachers have been for so long rendered impotent by politicians, school councils, administrators, and other external sources? The point needs to be stressed that teachers and school administrators also are a public to whom others (state, parents, pupils, churches, etc.) must be accountable.

*Accountable for what?* In Chapter 2, the Committee spells out the distinctive functions of schools — 'for which no other institution is specifically responsible' (2.21) – which are the acquisition of knowledge and skills, initiation into the cultural heritage, the valuing of rationality and the broadening of opportunities to respond to and participate in artistic endeavours (2.21). These 'traditional', 'special functions' should 'extend ... to acknowledge the importance of confident self-initiated learning and creative response' (2.21). These functions, by and large, satisfy the criteria of education. No one would be rash enough to suggest that all these activities could be quantified or measured behaviourally. Nor can all these activities be carried out in school merely by instruction or training. Nor again is there insistence in Chapter 2 that teachers alone be made accountable for what the student learns; what seems to be asked for is that programs be initiated to provide for activities designed to achieve the special functions of the school. I wish to develop this point a little further.

As we have seen, it would be unfair to hold teachers entirely responsible for a student's learning, because the reasons that could inhibit learning may stem from a source outside the school. What a teacher can and should primarily be held responsible for is the provision of educational programs deemed to be worthwhile. He should be made notably responsible for what he does, not fixedly for what the student learns. When a teacher's accountability is seen in this light, much of the frenzy goes out of the process of evaluating the teacher's contribution: worthwhile educational activities and outcomes become the important thing, not exclusively examination results, systems approaches, achievement tests, behavioural objectives. However, it would be unwise, if not destructive of the whole task of education, to treat behavioural and non-behavioural approaches as opposite poles on a continuum, for they complement one another. The tools we use to evaluate must be appropriate to the tasks that confront us. As Carmel Leavey insists, 'the whole evaluation procedure needs to match the richness and complexity of the whole educational situation'.[12]

If we accept the argument that the major focus should be away from activities designed to bring about specific behavioural changes (while recognizing at the same time that all teachers generally need to do some teaching for objectives), then on what basis can activities be justified for inclusion in the curriculum? The following value criteria extracted from James Raths' work[13], though not exhaustive, might suggest appropriate forms of activity a teacher might undertake:

All other things being equal, one activity is more worthwhile than another

1 if it permits children to make informed choices in carrying out the activity, and to reflect on the consequences of their choices; . . .

2 if it assigns to students active roles in the learning situation rather than passive ones; . . .

3 if it asks students to engage in inquiry into ideas, applications of intellectual processes, or current problems, either personal or social; . . .

4 if it involves children with reality; . . .

5 if completion of the activity may be accomplished successfully by children at several different levels of ability; . . .

6 if it asks students to examine in a new setting an idea, an application of an intellectual process, or a current problem which has been previously studied; . . .

7 if it requires students to examine topics or issues that citizens in our society do not normally examine — and that are typically ignored by the major communications media; . . .

8 if it involves students and faculty members in 'risk-taking' — a risk of success or failure; . . .

9 if it requires students to re-write, rehearse, and polish their initial efforts; . . .

10 if it involves students in the application and mastery of meaningful rules, standards, or disciplines; . . .

11 if it gives students a chance to share the planning, the carrying out of a plan, or the results of an activity with others; and . . .

12 if it is relevant to the expressed purposes of the students.

As Raths explained elsewhere, teachers, parents and students should be asked to share in the development of alternative sets of criteria of worthwhile activities, other than the ones he presents.[14] It might be added that often parents are bamboozled by specialist chatter over the technical aspects of education, whereas, perhaps with some coaxing, they can be quite clear and articulate about what they value in education. I suspect that, to some extent, what is described as 'parental apathy' in the educational context is a form of parental bewilderment, frustration and withdrawal from technical discussions in which they are not trained to participate.

In the inclusive sense of accountability, teachers must find ways 'to explain' (2.19) or to describe, expound, make clear, in terms meaningful to non-teachers, their relevant value criteria of the educational situation and the appropriate teaching programs. Parents and other non-teachers in education are likely to play a more meaningful and effective role in first helping to formulate the value criteria of education and then in generally commenting on and evaluating the appropriateness of the programs designed by teachers to promote those values, than in the more detailed and specialist assessment of the programs. If the movement towards 'more open patterns of control' (5.6) is to succeed, then school doors must be unlocked, in more ways than one, to many legitimately interested publics.

In summary, while the more restricted sense of accountability first seeks to determine the operational objectives and then to design tests which can measure those objectives, the more inclusive sense first seeks to determine the value criteria of worthwhile activities and then to decide appropriate procedures by which measurable and non-measurable components may be accounted.

*When is one accountable?* The report's comment, implicit in Chapter 2, is that people are accountable for activities when they are in a position to determine what those are to be: the Committee believes that

> responsibility will be most effectively discharged where the people entrusted with making decisions are also the people responsible for carrying them out, with an obligation to justify them . . . (2.4).

This is quite different from the sort of bureaucratic answerability demanded of school administrators in the report's explicit statements in Chapter 13. Quite simply, if we only carry out what someone in higher authority has decided, we would not be accountable for that decision. And if for some reason we are forced to carry out that externally imposed decision in certain ways specified to us, then the one in authority who made the decision is *accountable* for it, while we are *answerable* to him for carrying it out in the prescribed manner. When the teacher freely enters the teacher-pupil relationship, he becomes accountable for the aims, content and methods of his programs and shares some responsibility for the outcomes. If parents, pupils (2.4), and 'other socializing agencies' (2.17) are to be jointly involved with teachers in some forms of educational decision-making, then they must also be held accountable and be jointly held responsible for the outcomes.

## SUMMARY AND RECOMMENDATIONS

The themes dealt with in this article were, firstly, that the notion one has of educational accountability is derived partly from one's understanding of what education means; and, secondly, that two senses of accountability may be distinguished — a restricted sense which emphasizes the more readily quantifiable, easily specifiable and clearly behavioural aspects of education; and a more inclusive and richer sense which embraces both those elements of education which secure and those which elude the quantifiable.

The central arguments in this article are, firstly, that the notion of accountability in terms of bureaucratic answerability of educators, which is explicitly projected by the report in Chapter 13, is too narrow to serve a concept of education that is complex and subtle; and secondly, that more, not less, accountability of an enriched kind, expressed in implicit and muted tones in Chapter 2 of the report, is required in education. This enriched notion of accountability is one that demands of *all* the agents of education (e.g., teachers, pupils, parents, the state, churches, etc.) that they provide for optimum conditions for worthwhile learning to occur and that they be accountable to one another for the provision of those conditions.

My recommendations then are, firstly, that the thrust of future concern over accountability should shift from being only a bureaucratic check that fiscal misappropriation has not occurred in educational spending, to include as well a concern for research evaluation that seeks to gauge the effectiveness of the professional educators' aims and programs to provide optimum conditions for worthwhile learning to occur; secondly, that attempts be made to provide some appropriate institutional framework within which *all* the agents of education are encouraged to accept their responsibilities for the formulation of the value criteria of educational goals; and, thirdly, that attempts be made to develop structures through which *all* the agents of education accept and fulfil their respective accountabilities to one another, with respect to the provision of optimum conditions for worthwhile learning to occur.

I cannot see such a shift of thinking about accountability occurring until the many publics with an interest and a desire to participate in educational decision-making first come together in serious dialogue; it cannot be achieved by *fiat*.

## Notes

1 Message on Education Reform to the Congress of the US from Richard M. Nixon, 3 March 1970, Part I, p. 3.
2 Barker, Ernest. (Ed.) (1962). *The Politics of Aristotle.* New York: Oxford University Press, pp. 193–4.
3 Lessinger, Leon M. 'Accountability, etc.', in E. D. Allen and E. Seifman (Eds) (1971). *The Teacher's Handbook.* Illinois: Scott, Foresman and Co., p. 73.
4 Plutarch, 'Education of Children', in *Moralia*, New York: Putnam, 1972, pp. 43–5.
5 Lessinger. op. cit.: 81.
6 Lessinger, Leon M. (1970). *Every Kid a Winner: Accountability in Education.* New York: Simon and Schuster, p. 18.
7 Peters, R. S., 'Education as Initiation', in R. D. Archambault (Ed.) (1967). *Philosophical Analysis and Education.* London: Routledge and Kegan Paul. Also, Peters, R. S. (Ed.) (1973). *The Philosophy of Education.* London: Oxford University Press. Chs. I and XII.
8 *Ethics and Education.* London: Allen and Unwin, 1966, pp. 39–40.
9 Snook, I. 'Philosophy of Education', in J. V. D'Cruz and P. J. Sheehan (Eds) (1975). *Concepts in Education: Philosophical Studies.* Melbourne: Longmans, p. 6.
10 'Assessment' and 'evaluation' are often used interchangeably, but they can be usefully distinguished. Very briefly, assessment has to do with 'taking stock' of something, while evaluation has to do with asking the overall 'worth' of the stock.
11 Australia. (1973). *Schools in Australia. Report of the Interim Committee of the Australian Schools Commission.* Canberra: AGPS. This document is commonly referred to as the 'Karmel report', after the Chairman of the Interim Committee which issued the report, Prof. P. Karmel. Throughout the rest of this chapter the convention will be followed of citing *Schools in Australia* by referring to the chapter and paragraph number in the original document.
12 Leavey, Carmel. 'Evaluation and Education', in J. V. D'Cruz, and P. J. Sheehan. (Eds) (1975). op. cit.: 96.

13 From Raths, James D. (1971). 'Teaching Without Specific Objectives', *Educational Leadership*, 28:714–20.
14 Raths, James D. 'Worthwhile Activities', in J. D. Raths, J. R. Pancella, J. S. Van Ness (Eds) (1971). *Studying Teaching*. New Jersey: Prentice Hall, p. 133.

**Economic Dimension**

# 9. The Macro-economics of Educational Renewal

## C. Selby Smith

### INTRODUCTION

Since the Report of the Interim Committee of the Australian Schools Commission, referred to subsequently as the Karmel report after its chairman, Emeritus Professor P. H. Karmel, is available to the public, no attempt is made here to set out in any detail the various grants recommended.[1] The discussion in this chapter concentrates rather, in the brief space available, on some of the report's major implications from a macro-economic perspective.[2] Suffice it to say, however, that the phrase 'educational renewal' may well both raise and reflect unrealistic expectations about what the Karmel programs can be expected to achieve. Despite the shift they represent towards greater federal involvement in primary and secondary education, and the increased emphasis they lay on a 'needs' criterion when allocating funds between schools or school systems, the Karmel recommendations are essentially 'more of the same' for Australian education rather than a radically new departure.

The tests applied here to the Karmel programs are essentially the traditional trinity of the economist's pantheon: efficiency, equity and stabilization policy effects. The efficiency test is concerned with achieving maximum output from given inputs (or conversely, with achieving a given output using a minimum of inputs). The equity criterion is concerned with whether those in similar circumstances are similarly treated, and whether those in dissimilar circumstances are treated dissimilarly — and appropriately, which in the case of the Karmel programs clearly incorporates a movement towards more substantial assistance for those with greater 'needs'. The difficulties of rendering this latter part of the criterion sufficiently precise for operational use are not to be underrated, neither are the difficulties of reconciling it satisfactorily with the other criteria. Although these problems are not pursued further here, they need to be borne in mind throughout this chapter.[3] The third test is the contribution of the Karmel programs to stabilization policy, which in the circumstances of 1974 (the only year in which the programs have so far operated) means essentially their relationship to inflation.[4] It is frequently possible when discussing a particular program, whether in the public or the private sector, tacitly to ignore its (relatively minor) effects on overall stabilization policy. It is not a satisfactory approach when discussing the Karmel programs, partly because of their magnitude, partly because they directly contributed to exacerbating wage increases and the particularly serious pressure on resources in the building industry, partly because of the seriousness of the current inflationary pressures and their links with these educational initiatives (among others) and partly because the Federal Government in its Budget of September 1974 argued that, rather than take the unpopular measures which were urgently required to slow the rate of growth of prices, it preferred to press on with its program of social reforms of which the Karmel programs were a major component. This is not, of course, to argue that inflation was caused by the Karmel programs — that would be nonsense — but merely that since they had some effect in exacerbating inflation, any macro-economic assessment of their impact which did not take it into account would be incomplete.

The chapter is divided into seven parts of which this introduction is the first. The second section discusses some aspects of the real cost of implementing the Karmel recommendations, the third section the relationship between inflation and the extra grants for education, the fourth section some effects on federal-state relations in Australia, the fifth section some aspects of the Karmel programs in relation to the tax system and the sixth section some effects on the use of labour, especially highly skilled labour, in the Australian economy. In the final section of the chapter, the Karmel programs are discussed more generally in relation to the threefold criteria of efficiency, equity and contribution to stabilization policy.

Two other preliminary points should be made. Firstly, on many matters relevant to the topics discussed here, the full story was not known when the chapter was being prepared.[5] Although based on the best information available then, either in published documents or from private discussion, the conclusions reached here should be regarded as tentative pending a longer period of operation for the Karmel programs and fuller information about their implementation and effects. Secondly, the chapter largely concentrates on difficulties and problems associated with the Karmel recommendations. This is a conscious decision, reflecting the conviction that it is in these areas that discussion can be most fruitful. However, it might lead the unwary reader to believe that the author was, on balance, substantially critical of the overall program. This is not so: the vision and energy of Professor Karmel and his Committee have laid the basis for substantial improvements in Australian schools. What is crucial now is that the best use be made of this great opportunity.

## THE REAL COST OF THE KARMEL COMMITTEE'S RECOMMENDATIONS

The Interim Committee recommended grants of some $660 million for the two calendar years beginning in January 1974. However, only some seven-tenths of this represented additional assistance, because a variety of previously existing schemes of commonwealth aid to education were incorporated in the total program. Some $461 million was recommended for government schools, some $179 million for non-government schools and some $20 million for programs which were not specifically allocated between the sectors.[6] Most of the funds were provided for general assistance with recurrent or capital expenses ($309 million and $196 million respectively), although the very substantial sum of $155 million was allocated to a variety of particular programs.[7] In August 1974, supplementary funds were requested by the Schools Commission for both capital and recurrent expenditures.[8] The money cost of the program being administered by the Schools Commission is thus very substantial. On the other hand, the programs might have important resource-creating effects, while the increased expenditure will be partially offset by large rises in receipts (for example, through taxation on the additional income and expenditure).

Furthermore, the political constraints are such that the money must be spent, at least by the end of 1975, but preferably at approximately the rate at which the Federal Government makes it available to State Governments, Catholic education authorities and individual schools. The State Governments, for example, have frequently argued during the postwar period that the funds they receive from the Commonwealth together with the revenues they can raise themselves are inadequate to properly fund the important responsibilities with which they are vested under the Constitution, and among which education is particularly important, both politically and economically. The difficulties of spending the additional funds efficiently are exacerbated by the specific purposes for which much of the money must be spent, the shortage of competent and experienced administrators, by the very rapid rate of growth of expenditure and the complexities of integrated planning in large educational systems — especially if the use of outside consultants, architects, builders, etc. is in practice discouraged. A more fundamental obstacle to optimal resource allocation in education is inadequate knowledge of the relationships between inputs and outputs. Furthermore, education is a means whereby more fundamental social goals are pursued rather than an end in itself, yet the Commonwealth Government has little constitutional power over education in the States, and its financial influence only provides an uncertain means of achieving its educational purposes (and hence its more basic social goals). In the circumstances, considerable waste is almost inevitable.

The real cost of a particular economic activity is the other opportunities which are foregone in order to undertake it, whether other programs elsewhere in education, elsewhere in the public sector or in the private sector. The massive funds being made available for education are involving sacrifices elsewhere, yet many of those in Australian education do not perceive the need to justify their use of additional public money or to demonstrate how it is enabling them to pursue social goals more adequately. There is a real danger that the multiplying examples of conspicuous waste and the absence of many instances of obviously improved results could damage the public commitment to more generous funding for education (as has already happened in some overseas countries). Obtaining value for money would be much more likely if the growth rate of expenditure was lowered. This would require the rate of increase to be maintained over a longer period if given real targets are to be

achieved, but it could — as the next section emphasizes — render the
achievement of those real targets more likely.

## THE RELATIONSHIPS BETWEEN INFLATION AND THE ADDITIONAL GRANTS FOR EDUCATION

The Federal Government is responsible for macro-economic management, and
the implementation of the Karmel programs from early 1974 coincided with
the worst bout of sustained inflation that Australia has suffered in over 20
years.[9] The fundamental causes of inflation are a matter of contention among
economists and this is not the place to explore this fascinating question in
detail. Suffice it to say that major social changes involving rapid growth in
government expenditure over a short period are almost certain to contribute
to inflationary pressures in a fully employed economy given the circumstances
of the early 1970s, that the additional taxation required to finance such
programs tends to exacerbate pressures in factor and product markets which
contribute to inflation (as well as giving the Government a vested interest in
the revenue consequences of continuing inflation), that these additions to
inflationary pressure are likely to be  significantly more serious if the
Government is committed at the same time to other major initiatives in the
public sector (whether in health services, social welfare or urban
improvement), but that it is a wild overstatement to claim that, of themselves,
the additional grants for education are more than a contributing factor to
inflation in Australia.

The rapid growth of costs and prices is reducing substantially the expansion
in real educational services which can be achieved from the financial outlays
allocated by Parliament. Inflation renders more serious any tendency for
spending from the additional grants to be delayed, but very rapid growth of
expenditure on education raises its own problems (as the previous section of
this chapter emphasized). It should also be borne in mind that, large though
the funds appropriated as a result of the Karmel recommendations are, they
still represent only a minority of the expenditure on Australian schools —
even for those schools which are organized and financed by governments. Yet
inflation tends to reduce the real value of all the resources represented by
particular money outlays, whether they are expenditures by State Education
Departments, Catholic education authorities, or individual schools and
parents, not just the additional funds provided by the Australian Government.

Educators may feel there is an obvious solution to these problems, i.e., that
as the Schools Commission recommended to the Australian Government in
August 1974, the Government should agree to 'accept the principle of
supplementary Schools Commission programs to maintain the purchasing
power of grants legislated by the Parliament from time to time'.[10] As
mentioned in the previous paragraph, this is only a partial answer, since
Schools Commission grants only represent a minority of the funds available to
Australian schools. Supplementation of only this assistance to State

Governments is quite inadequate to enable them to maintain the real value of the resources they provide for primary and secondary education if inflation continues at the rate now anticipated. Indeed, the effects of inflation tend to be particularly serious for labour intensive industries, since the rate of growth of wages and salaries is even faster than the present rate of growth of prices in Australia — and education is a labour intensive industry *par excellence*. Yet there is a still more fundamental problem from the viewpoint of macro-economic management. While the supplementation of grants to maintain their real value is obviously desirable from the point of view of those in each program seeking supplementation, supplementation of all such programs will merely intensify the inflationary situation. In theory, this could be largely avoided by supplementing only the education grants, but in practice it seems hard to argue a strong case why supplementation should occur for education, but not for other activities such as law and order, roads, health services or social welfare. There is also a problem of incentives, since the knowledge that any increases in cost can be virtually automatically recouped through grant supplementation is likely to accelerate cost increases.

Salaries and associated expenses (especially teachers' salaries) and building works account for the bulk of recurrent and capital expenditure respectively in both primary and secondary education. In both these areas, the implementation of the Karmel programs has tended to strengthen inflationary pressures. The negotiations over salaries and conditions for teachers in government schools (the largest group of teachers), which have substantial flow-on implications for teachers employed in non-government schools, are generally conducted at state level and the Schools Commission is not a party to the negotiations.[11] Yet the additional federal funds for education are providing educational authorities with greater room for financial concessions. Although complete data on movements in the salaries of teachers and other comparable categories of highly skilled labour are not yet available, it seems probable that one result of the Karmel funds has been to accelerate the rate of growth of teachers' salaries.[12] Not only is this an important contributory factor to inflation in itself, but it is likely to have flow-on implications elsewhere given the traditional methods of wage and salary determination used in Australia, the size of the teaching workforce and its particular importance for relativities in state public services (and perhaps for women, too). In its editorial on the Federal Budget, the Melbourne *Age* said that most Victorians 'would welcome more positive indications that the enormous outlay is enhancing the quality of education and not mainly the prosperity of the teaching profession'.[13] These were strong words, especially coming from a newspaper which has in general been well-informed on educational affairs and a strong supporter of the Federal Government's educational initiatives.

So far as the capital program is concerned, it has added to the strains on the construction industry, which in early 1974 was already overextended. The result was to strengthen demand relative to supply, to raise the rate of growth of prices and to lower both the quality of educational building and the terms on which it could be carried out. However, with the sharply reduced rate of growth in the money supply, the tightening of credit, the fall in business expectations and the rise in interest rates, the pressure on the building industry has been easing markedly during 1974. The full decline in activity has probably not yet emerged, but scope is beginning to appear for substantial shifts of resources from the private to the public sector. This could be to the advantage of educational capital programs, which are a major component of the Karmel recommendations.

Difficulties, however, are still likely to occur in using State Departments of Public Works for a rapid expansion of educational construction, or in obtaining non-government builders experienced in educational construction in adequate numbers, while the Federal Government still seems liable to overestimate the speed with which resources can be shifted between different uses. Better value for money would almost certainly be obtained if the shift of financial resources into educational construction occurred more slowly — and, in order to achieve similar real targets, it would then need to continue for a longer period. These changes would have the further advantage of contributing to less fluctuating demands on the building industry and hence of easing the task of macro-economic management for a significant part of the economy.

## FEDERAL-STATE RELATIONS AND THE KARMEL PROGRAMS

The present structure of the Australian Federation causes major problems for the satisfactory implementation of programs such as those recommended in the Karmel report. There is a serious imbalance between the revenue sources and the expenditure functions of the different levels of government. Education is the largest single expenditure responsibility of the State Governments, and consequently any major shifts in federal-state relationships in education have substantial implications for the structure of the Australian Commonwealth. It is the opinion of the writer that some functions such as overall funding, strategic planning, and redress of regional inequalities are those with which the Schools Commission should be primarily concerned, while the details of educational administration require less centralized control. The Schools Commission should not become too heavily involved in the administrative regulation of educational details.

During 1974, the Schools Commission has displayed an ambivalent attitude to those with whom it will have to co-operate if the possibilities for educational renewal are to be realized in Australia. An obvious example concerns its relationships with non-government schools; since there is considerable fear that the Commission could become another Department of Education for non-government schools, there is a widespread realization that at least some of its members are opposed in principle to the existence of private schools, and a member of the Commission, Mrs Joan Kirner, is one of the plaintiffs in a court case designed to test whether the Australian Government has constitutional power to provide funds for non-government (especially religious) schools.

Another basic question revolves around the respect to be paid to the sovereignty of the components of a federal state. Of the Australian States, all but two have non-Labor governments who tend to view any Federal Labor Government with suspicion and whose suspicions are currently further fuelled by the realization that at least some members of the Federal Cabinet and Caucus are opposed, in principle, to the continued existence of State Governments holding their present powers. Yet if the best long-term results are to be achieved in the schools, genuine co-operation between State Governments and the Schools Commission is essential. A pre-condition of this from the viewpoint of the States, it should hardly be necessary to emphasize, is that their constitutional rights and their ability to determine their own priorities are clearly acknowledged. Financial assistance and other co-operative ventures are different in spirit (and are likely to be different in result) from attempts to take over state functions or to dictate lines of policy against local preferences when constitutional power lies locally.

The determination of priorities raises major difficulties in most States, especially for those expenditure areas where responsibility and initiative are not wholly confined to one level of government. The Karmel recommendations restricted state priorities, in the sense that the resources were to be additional to those already provided and were to be specifically for education, but the bulk of the funds were for general recurrent or general capital purposes, free of detailed restrictions. They combined this with a number of less substantial but more specific programs in areas where they perceived a special priority and a particular national concern. However, the question of maintenance of effort by States (and other schools and school systems) is far from clarified; indeed, there is a danger that precipitate action by any of the parties could fundamentally endanger that fragile co-operation which is so essential for the success of the whole endeavour. There are also major inconsistencies in underlying assumptions and serious practical problems inherent in the prevailing arrangements whereby a general agency with interest in regional equalization (the Grants Commission) matches overall needs, efforts and resources between claimant and standard States but explicitly leaves each State free to determine its own expenditure (and revenue) priorities, while at the same time another commonwealth agency concerned with a specific though important area of state responsibility is attempting to equalize resource use in its own area of special interest. The two approaches are not compatible and they are leading to contradictory flows of resources. For example, the Grants Commission has been providing additional (untied) grants to the claimant States relative to the standard States of New South Wales and Victoria, while at the same time the Schools Commission, another aim of the Commonwealth Government, is bewailing the condition of inner city schools in Sydney and Melbourne and recommending (tied) grants to help remedy what they see as a deplorable state of affairs. Even within the commonwealth bureaucracy itself, machinery for determining educational priorities is inadequate, requiring development of a stronger co-ordinating role for the Department or a consolidation of the Commissions. The complex results of these unsatisfactory arrangements for the national determination of priorities in public expenditure in general, and education in particular, are compounded by differing priorities between States and the varying relationships between State and Commonwealth. The result is that neither efficiency nor equity is necessarily pursued either rationally or consistently.

## THE KARMEL PROGRAMS AND THE TAXATION SYSTEM

In general, the Karmel report made little attempt to integrate more closely the system of educational finance with the general taxation structure, although it might be argued that its substantial expenditure recommendations imply a higher tax burden than would otherwise have existed, or the sacrifice of some other public goods or services, or some combination of the two. The implications of the higher tax burden are difficult enough to estimate, but the real costs (and benefits) of foregoing alternative public goods or services are even harder to evaluate. In principle, however, it seems likely that substantial improvements could be made to equity in education by a closer meshing of the taxation system with the methods of providing and financing education.

The Karmel Committee examined the provision of education through the funding of schools and school systems. Yet the needs of children should be the touchstone of educational policy rather than the needs of educational institutions or systems. Individuals differ widely within school systems and even within individual schools. To speak of rich schools rather than schools attended by children whose parents are wealthy is a fundamental error with far-reaching implications. In fact, government schools, Catholic schools and other independent schools do not generally cater exclusively for the rich or the poor, but for pupils whose parents vary widely in income, wealth and taste for education.

There are dangers in using a needs criterion to differentiate institutions rather than individual pupils or their parents — and some of the unfortunate effects could be exacerbated by inflation. For example, the great majority of Australian school children attend government schools, but in general (despite some exceptions such as the disadvantaged schools program) the additional funds will not necessarily bias provision more heavily in accordance with a needs criterion. It is far from clear that for the majority of schools or school children inequalities are being reduced: they could even be increasing. Similar conclusions apply to the non-government schools. The lower grants per pupil to schools which the Interim Committee classified more highly in terms of resource use do not differentiate between pupils who are from poor or wealthy homes. The long-run result will be to make such schools more exclusive in social and economic terms, which was surely not the intention of the Interim Committee or the Labor Government. Furthermore, the adoption of resource use as the criterion for graduated government assistance, though understandable, is likely to have an unfortunate long-term effect on incentives, rewarding those who provided least themselves and penalizing those who provided more. The recommendations of the Interim Committee are also leading to dissimilar treatment of individuals whose parents are in an equivalent socio-economic situation but who favour a different type of education, say Catholic rather than secular. The actual policy also appears to be inconsistent with the Interim Committee's stated preference for greater diversity in Australian education.

In short, the failure to integrate the taxation system more effectively with the provision and finance of education, coupled with the decision to examine the needs of schools and school systems rather than of individual pupils and parents is leading to inequities within the government sector, inequities within the non-government sector and inequities between them. Individuals in similar circumstances are not being treated similarly, individuals in dissimilar circumstances are being treated similarly and both of these situations are inequitable.

Four other points are made briefly. Firstly, although education can provide a means for individual advancement, the redress of educational equalities in itself is unlikely to result in any radical restructuring of the pattern of income, wealth, prestige and power in Australia. To the extent that the Federal Government sees the Karmel program as a potent means to transform society, it will almost certainly be disappointed. Education is too weak a tool to accomplish this task alone. Secondly, to the extent that the additional educational benefits are disproportionately concentrated on the disadvantaged members of society, they may tend to reduce slightly the dispersion in earned incomes (by relatively raising the lower end of the distribution) and this could have implications for the incidence of the tax structure. Thirdly, to the extent that the actual incidence of the Australian tax system is largely proportional to income, as some submissions to the Asprey Committee suggest, and if the benefits from the educational services provided through the additional funds are distributed among pupils approximately in proportion to their previous distribution, then the overall distribution of costs relative to benefits will not be substantially affected by the implementation of the Karmel recommendations. The available information is inadequate to support definite conclusions, but if this approximation is close to the truth, the 'needs' criterion may be more rhetoric than substance. Finally, the Budget decision to cut the deduction for education expenses allowable for income tax purposes from $400 to $150 will improve equity among some taxpayers (since the deduction was more valuable to those with a higher taxable income), but may reduce it when comparing other groups (for example, those with children in government rather than in non-government schools).

## EFFECTS ON MANPOWER SUPPLY AND DEMAND

Primary and secondary education in Australia is a labour-intensive industry. The additional financial resources for schooling are tending to be largely used for payments to labour, albeit to highly skilled labour. The Karmel programs are having, or are likely to have, some important influences on the labour market, on the relative demands for and supplies of particular categories of highly educated labour. In this section, five aspects are emphasized.[14]

Firstly, there was the impetus given to labour market certification through education. The expansion of the number of teachers implies expansion in an area of the labour market where competence in achieving particular goals is difficult to demonstrate and certification through formal educational achievements (or experience) has become the recognized route to more senior and more highly paid positions. Coupled with this is the relatively rigid hierachical pattern of organization which appears to be built into the structure of most Education Departments in Australia. Not only may the expansion of an area where these attitudes are so strong be held to be undesirable in itself, but it could be argued to be inappropriate for the world of tomorrow in which co-operation, flexibility and openness are likely to become more highly valued traits — and doubly inappropriate for educational activities which are essentially concerned with the preparation for tomorrow of the children of today.

Secondly, the implementation of the Karmel programs is likely to produce changes in the labour market because of their influence on relative salaries and conditions. One example which has already been emphasized concerns the increased willingness to allow a more rapid improvement in teachers' salaries and conditions than would otherwise have occurred. It is also not impossible that the Karmel funds might enable changes to be made in the career structure of teachers' earnings.[15] This could have significant effects: for example, in reducing wastage from the teaching profession, in expanding the intake of mature entrants to teaching, or in rendering educational administration less of a closed shop.

Thirdly, the Karmel programs could result in a shift in the relative labour market positions of men and women. Teaching has become increasingly dominated by women in the post-war period, although less so at secondary than at primary level and much less so for more senior administrative positions than in the classroom. Thus, improving the financial position for school staff will tend to benefit women disproportionately — although the exact results depend substantially on a variety of other decisions largely made by men in key administrative positions. Furthermore, if many of these teachers would have had little choice than to work in primary or secondary education (and were happy to do so rather than not to work) then the increase in their salaries and conditions is substantially analogous to monopoly rent and inefficient in the sense that a similar bundle of goods and services could have been achieved at lower cost.[16]

Fourthly, there is likely to be an increase in the national influence on wage fixation. The major negotiations on teachers' salaries and conditions now occur for State-employed teachers at state level. However, the increasing federal interest in the outcomes of schooling, the importance of teachers in the education process and their dominating influence on recurrent costs are likely to lead to growing Australian Government concern with the escalating cost of teachers. The inter-State leap-frogging of wage claims and the effect of increased federal grants on the bargaining backbone of State Governments seem likely to cause the Schools Commission to become more intimately involved in the process of wage determination for staff in schools. One possibility would be the calculation of national teacher salary scales to which recommended grants could be related, any excess to be borne by the particular school or school system involved. The pressures to move in this direction would tend to be intensified if the Commission decided, in the light of inflation and other factors, to relate future financial assistance for non-government schools to the costs of education in government schools.

Finally, the implementation of the Karmel programs has coincided with the Federal Government's assumption of the full financial responsibility for tertiary education throughout Australia. This has resulted in a major shift in the relative interests of State and Commonwealth, of which the situation with respect to teachers' colleges is of particular interest here. Prior to July 1973, the single-purpose government teachers' colleges were almost wholly financed by State Governments, for the last six months of 1973 they were jointly funded by the Federal and State Governments according to the formulae then ruling for CAEs and universities, while from January 1974, they have been wholly financed by the Commonwealth.

The previous interest of the States was to secure an adequate balance between the provision of teachers (the bulk of additional staff came straight from tertiary institutions) and the demand for them in the schools. In 1974, however, their interest in the cost of supplying teachers is sharply reduced: their predominant concern now is with the total supply of teachers and in obtaining 'a fair share' for their own State. The result of these changing pressures in higher education in general, and in the preparation of teachers in particular, is not yet clear. What is obvious is the changed situation, the greater role for the commonwealth authorities, the enhanced need for co-operation (whether within the federal bureaucracy or between the Commonwealth and the States), and the effects which could occur in the relative supplies and demands of different categories of highly skilled labour. Although very little discussed, the Karmel programs could have significant implications for the Australian labour market.

## CONCLUSIONS

There are four main conclusions. Firstly, the apparent cost may be an over-statement, since the program could have resource creating effects. For example, if education results in higher output or if the reduction of educational inequalities causes significant additional productive capacities to be liberated, the net cost may be significantly lower than it appears initially. Looking at the programs from another perspective, it is clear that inflation is reducing the intended increase in real resources for education, while much of the additional outlay on education is returned to the exchequer (e.g., higher salaries for teachers resulting in significantly higher tax revenues, and similarly for the Budget's reduction in the allowable deduction for education expenses). Nevertheless, on plausible assumptions it appears that the Karmel programs involve very substantial additional federal expenditure on schooling and a significant (though smaller) increase in the real resources devoted to education.

Secondly, in terms of efficiency, the implementation of the Karmel recommendations leaves much to be desired. There is a lack of clear goals and a frequent lack of common purpose or co-operation in pursuing them. Furthermore, there is a basic lack of knowledge about the relationships between inputs and outputs in education. In practical terms, the rate of growth in expenditure is proving too rapid for the established systems to handle effectively. There is a particular shortage of experienced administrators with co-operative attitudes. There is a real danger that the multiplying examples of educational waste will endanger that public support on which additional finance for education must be based in the long term.

Thirdly, in terms of stabilization policy, the Karmel programs have tended to exacerbate inflationary pressures while inflation has, in turn, undermined the possibility of achieving the intended objectives. In particular, the Karmel programs have tended to raise the rate of growth of teachers' salaries and to increase the pressure on resources in the building industry. Nevertheless, these educational initiatives have been no more than a factor contributing to inflation in Australia: they are very far from being its major — let alone its sole — cause. The excessive rate of growth of expenditure has complicated stabilization policy, just as it has contributed to inefficiency. Note that the dual objectives of maintaining the real value of education grants and reducing inflation may not be wholly consistent.

Fourthly, the strongest justification of the Karmel programs probably lies in their equity aspects. Equity can be viewed from many perspectives. The allocations between schools and school systems largely reflect broad social value judgments. The Karmel programs attempt to raise resource use in government schools closer to that in the more fortunate non-government schools. They also attempt to apply a needs criterion in the non-government sector, but much less so for government schools where despite some attempts to reduce inequalities (for example, through the disadvantaged schools program) the bulk of the funds are for general recurrent and general capital grants.[17] The Interim Committee chose to base its funding procedures on schools and school systems, rather than on individual pupils or parents, and this has caused substantial inequities between individuals and inadequate links between the tax structure and the additional grants for education. The allocation of grants between States was only approximate, was based on attempts to equalize between States and is inconsistent with Grants Commission procedures both in theory and in practice. If the benefits from the additional resources are roughly proportional to the previous distribution[18] and if the costs of providing these resources are approximately proportional to income (as evidence to the Asprey Committee suggests) then — in aggregate terms — the programs are probably causing little reduction in educational inequalities. Equity can also be considered from the viewpoint of educational producers and consumers respectively. So far, at least, the main benefits from the implementation of the Karmel recommendations appear to have accrued to politicians, teachers and educational administrators rather than to the children in schools whom the system is presumably primarily intended to serve.

Overall, the programs appear to have slightly compounded the difficulties of economic management, to be open to more serious objections on efficiency grounds and to have both advantages and disadvantages in terms of equity. Even if there are net equity advantages, it is far from obvious that they are sufficient to justify expenditure of $350–$400 million per annum in terms of the alternatives foregone.

## Notes

1 See Australia. (1973). *Schools in Australia. Report of the Interim Committee for the Australian Schools Commission.* (Chairman, P. Karmel). Canberra: AGPS.

2 For a recent systematic exposition of the financial aspects of the Karmel programs see P. Segall and R. T. Fitzgerald, 'Finance for Education in Australia: An Analysis', *Quarterly Review of Australian Education*, **6** (4).

3 For some further discussion see Chapter 1 by Professor Crittenden, Chapter 10 by Brother Mortensen, in this volume.

4 An interesting feature of the programs is their very low import content.

5 During late October 1974.

6 See Australia. (1973). op. cit.: 142.

7 $50m. for disadvantaged schools, $45m. for libraries, $44m. for special education, $10m. for teacher development and $6m. for special projects.

8 $64.47m. for recurrent expenditure and unquantified assistance for capital grants based on the principle of supplementation to maintain the purchasing power of grants previously legislated by Parliament. See Australia Schools Commission. (1974). *Supplementary Funds for Programmes Administered by the Schools Commison: Report to the Minister.* Canberra. Mimeo.

9 The only period in which prices rose at a similar rate since 1945 was during the Korean War in the early 1950s and even then it might be argued that the inflationary problems were less intractable than now.

10 Australia. Schools Commission. (1974). op. cit.: 5, recommendation (a).

11 The ACT and Northern Territory are relatively minor exceptions to this generalization.

12 A cynical observer of the political scene might argue that this acceleration of teacher salaries was not coincidental, given the significant support Labor has received from the teachers' unions.

13 *The Age*, 26 September 1974, Editorial, p. 9.

14 Three more general points should be borne in mind: that, when the Labor Government took office in December 1972, there was a small though declining volume of unused resources in the Australian economy, but when the Karmel programs began to be implemented in early 1974 the macro-economic problems were of restraining inflation rather than of stimulating demand: that the Labor Government was committed to major programs in other areas as well as in education, for example in health, social welfare and urban affairs, and that, in practice, it tended to be committed to their speedy implementation; and that there was a particular

shortage of sufficiently competent experienced administrators to manage the substantial changes envisaged for education without inefficiency or inequity.

15 For a discussion of the structure of earnings in teaching see C. Selby Smith. (1973). 'An Economic Approach to Teacher Loss and Retention', *Australian Journal of Education*, **17** (2): 142–152.

16 Or a larger bundle could have been purchased at the same cost.

17 Note that some funds (e.g. for special projects) are likely to increase inequalities rather than reduce them.

18 As may well be the case in government schools (especially if the relatively minor disadvantaged schools program is neglected). Unfortunately the use made of general Karmel grants is not clear for all States.

# 10. Finance for Independent Schooling

K. G. Mortensen*

## Background

In the 1950s and early 1960s, revenue-sources in a non-government school included fêtes, raffles, beer-bottle and paper drives, finance from fees and from State Junior Government scholarships, won after fierce preparation. There was no other government funding. Then came December 1 1963, a gala day. Capital grants for science building and facilities were introduced, making final parity with high quality secondary schools, at least in science laboratories, at last possible. Again, in 1967, the Victorian Government made per pupil grants; the Federal Government followed in 1969. These grants increased over the years, enabling non-government schools to hold fees reasonably steady and, even, to improve working conditions.

On 12 December 1972, the Australian Labor Government, to secure 'equality of opportunity' in education for all children, set up an Interim Committee of a proposed Australian Schools Commission. This committee, meeting under Professor P. Karmel as chairman, was to identify need and recommend allocation of federal money in certain defined categories of assistance.

The Report of this Committee was greeted with enthusiasm by the Universities, state school organizations (teachers and parents), and the media. The non-Catholic independent school community and many Catholic elements viewed the findings with a combination of praise, distrust and protest — praise for measures that cared for the disadvantaged and handicapped, protest and distrust that the Committee had rejected the principle of basic per pupil grants and that it had adopted a basis for assessing needs which did not consider 'the plight of parents'.[1] The criteria for available recurrent resources also happened to divide Victorian secondary schools in such a way that practically all in Categories A to D were non-Catholic; all in Categories F to H were Catholic.

The reaction of the Catholic community was confused. The response of the hierarchy was concerned, but restrained. The Catholic Education Offices considered that equitable funding was being approached. The executives of religious congregations took the grants without comment or with expressions of gratitude, but some teaching religious disapproved of various assumptions determining the Karmel recommendations. Religious who were members of the Headmasters Conference or the National Council of Independent Schools

*The author is grateful to Mrs Margaret C. Gartland for her generous assistance; also, to his colleague Mr K.W. Gould for helpful discussion.

stood firm with these organizations. Their non-Catholic colleagues showed patience, tact and discretion in dealing with domestic Catholic issues which were, however, related to the good of the whole non-government school community.

It has been claimed that one great effect of the Karmel report was to destroy the unity of organizations involving Catholic parents, e.g., the Australian Parents Council and affiliated Federations of Parents and Friends. There was division in Sydney, but of more import was concern at the possible effects of parent dissent from the assessment of clerics and from ecclesiastical response. Forthright comment could have been interpreted as division within the Catholic community and as a usurpation of the role of the official leadership.

The net effect of current policies has been that the continuing efforts of schools which have resources equal to or better than that of state schools have led to reduction, even threat of forfeiture, of aid. It now appears that the continuing efforts of schools operating on low fees will never attain the 'required' standards without substantial government support and threat to their independence.[2]

**Parameters of this article**

It is not the purpose of this article to discuss 'absolute' equity or to answer the popular question of the 1974 Monash lecture series: What is the price of choice?[3]

The discussion is limited to the problem of 'relative' equity using ratios and indices which show relative benefits accruing to the government and non-government sectors and which serve as a guide to change. Thus Section 1 considers the ratio of the total expenditure through state budgets and federal grants on the non-government sector to that on the government sector; specific ratios are provided for the primary and secondary sectors and for the different 'categories' of school in each sector. Section 2 examines the extent of a Total Resources Gap (in money and in proportional terms) in government funding of government and independent schools. The proportional index relates the money gap to average weekly earnings per male unit (after tax). In Section 3, ratios and gap indices are developed to compare benefits in recurrent grants flowing to independent schools under the States Grants (Schools) Acts 1972, 1973 and 1974. The secondary and primary sectors are dealt with separately; in the latter instance, the analysis concentrates on Catholic systemic schools. The distribution of grants for building, including science laboratories and libraries, is considered in Section 4. Grants for disadvantaged schools, which in Victoria are being applied to renovations, are included.[4] Section 5 comments on the distribution of grants to such schools. Section 6 considers the joint impact of recurrent grant funding *and* recent changes in allowable taxation deductions for educational expenses. The article concludes with a general commentary.

The conclusions have political implications. If there is a significant increase in relative benefits (recurrent and building) to the non-government school, and also a diminishing gap between government expenditure on government and independent schools (in money and proportional terms), this would show that the non-government sector was receiving more favourable treatment under Labor than under Liberal-Country Party government.

On the other hand, if there were no appreciable increase but, rather, perhaps a decrease in relative benefits, an increasing resources gap, other policies such as taxation changes directed generally against parents in the non-government school sector, this would suggest that the public had been misled by those who refer to 'massive aid' for Catholic schools.

The Karmel report was first introduced to Catholics in such a way that many thought they 'had never had it so good'. They now have to examine their position critically and in depth.

## TOTAL GOVERNMENT FUNDING

There are two indicators relevant to determining whether assistance to independent schools is equitable relative to the funding of government schools, viz., assets and money flow to enable continued operation. This article uses, in subsequent sections, a *Building Ratio* and *Index* to assess new accumulated assets and a *Recurrent Ratio* and *Index* of expenditure to assess flows in support of current operation. While no attempt is made to assess existing possessions, a *General Ratio* (including all sources of expenditure) is used in the present section as a guide to changes in relative equity.

The General Ratio is the ratio of total government expenditure on primary and secondary education (Federal and State Budgets) per pupil in an independent school to the corresponding expenditure per pupil in a government school. This ratio can be calculated in two ways — by using published aggregate data for government expenditure divided by the respective school populations; or by considering components of per pupil expenditure in the primary and secondary sectors and in the different categories of schools.

If we except Category A schools, the data in Tables 1 and 2 show rises — of the same order in primary and secondary sectors — since 1972-73. A rise suggests an improvement in 'relative' equity, but must be interpreted in conjunction with indices of 'continuing effort'. (See Table 7.) Study of Tables 1–4 enables the following further conclusions to be drawn:

1 The Karmel Supplement ($467 million as at May 1973) represents only 12 per cent of the total estimated government expenditure ($3919 million) on primary and secondary schools of all types during calendar years 1974 and 1975.
2 Total federal grants for 1974 and 1975 together were expected to fall just short of $700 million according to the 1973–74 budget reckoning. This figure, which includes 'existing grants' under legislation passed by the former Liberal-Country Party coalition, is 18 per cent of the total.

**TABLE 1** Government Expenditure on Primary and Secondary Education — Victoria

| | 1971-72 | | 1972-73 | | 1973-74 | | 1974-75 Budget estimates | | 1974-75 Estimates of actual payments | |
|---|---|---|---|---|---|---|---|---|---|---|
| | Govt. | Indep. | Govt. | Indep. | Govt. | Indep. | Govt. | Indep. | Govt. | Indep. |
| 1. Expenditure from State sources only, $m | 302 | 10 | 358 | 12 | 420 | 16 | 501 | 20 | 543 | 20 |
| % age of total | 96.8 | 3.2 | 96.8 | 3.2 | 96.3 | 3.7 | 96.2 | 3.8 | 96.5 | 3.5 |
| 2. Federal Grants, $m | 6 | 12 | 8 | 15 | 23 | 23 | 76 | 39 | 76 | 39 |
| % age of total | 33.3 | 66.6 | 34.8 | 65.2 | 50.0 | 50.0 | 66.1 | 33.9 | 66.1 | 33.9 |
| 3. Total from State and Federal sources, $m | 308 | 22 | 366 | 27 | 443 | 39 | 577 | 59 | 619 | 59 |
| % age of total | 93.3 | 6.7 | 93.1 | 6.9 | 91.9 | 8.1 | 90.7 | 9.3 | 91.3 | 8.7 |
| 4. General Ratio (calculated from "3" and school populations) | 0.22 | | 0.23 | | 0.28 | | 0.32 | | 0.30 | |

1. Data are derived from "Schools in Australia", the Hon. L. Bowen (C.P.D., November 15, 1973, pp. 3401-2), the Federal Budget of 1974-75 and Victorian State budgets, statements of Education Department Expenditure, and annual reports of the Minister.

2. Allowances from State sources for teachers in training for government schools are included. However, expenditure on teachers' colleges (including those approved in the non-government sector) is now funded by the Federal Government and has been omitted. This provides a better base for comparing expenditure on schooling over the years. Transportation costs, payroll tax and expenditure on "special groups" (aboriginal, migrant, isolated and soldiers' children) are also excluded in all analyses of Victorian figures.

3. The actual Victorian **recurrent** expenditure has been greater than the estimate by 13 per cent (1972-73) and 5 per cent (1973-74). The October 1974 rise in teachers' salaries suggests an increase (1974-75) of 13 per cent in budget estimates of recurrent expenditure. A further salaries increase before June 30, 1975 is probable but, as it will come late in the financial year and may be counterbalanced by spending below estimates on building, no further adjustment is made to total expenditure. (See Table 1).

4. The estimate for the increase in **total** expenditure in **Victoria** (1973-74 to 1974-75), not allowing for post-budget increases in teachers' salaries, is 31 per cent. (See Table 1). This is consistent with trends revealed in The Schools Commission Report to the Minister (August 1974) where the 1975 recurrent allocations were increased by 21 per cent 'to maintain the originally planned programme momentum'. This statement should be read in conjunction with the Hon. L. Bowen's assumption (ibid., p. 3405) of a rise in operating costs of 10 per cent per year; also the Hon. K. Beazley's statement (C.P.D., November 19, 1974, p. 3665) that Karmel had allowed 'a compounding inflation factor of 6 per cent'.

---

The 1974–75 budget adjustment for inflation increased the figure to 20 per cent.

3 The States Grants (Schools) Act 1974 provided some additional $78.9 million for the period to 31 December 1975, as 'supplementary grants to allow for cost increases'. If these are regarded as increases to the Karmel Supplement (rather than to programs in existence prior to 1 January 1974), the amended specific 'Karmel' contribution represents about 14 per cent of the total expenditure.

4 In 1972–73, the non-government sector in Australia received 7.9 per cent of the total federal-state expenditure on primary and secondary education. This figure has over two years (1973–74 and 1974–75) increased to about nine per cent for Australia (and Victoria).

5 The Report of the Interim Committee recommended 11 per cent of the $467 million money cake of May 1973 for pupils in non-government schools. In 1972, 21.5 per cent of Australian pupils (primary and secondary) were in non-government schools.

6 The Committee therefore aimed to redress the balance in distribution of direct federal aid under the Liberal-Country Party coalition of 1972. As shown in Table 5, it did this by a larger proportionate increase in the government than the non-government sector. This met the 'needs' of government schools and the demands of the state school lobby.

However, the Committee still retained a balance in total federal government expenditure in favour of the non-government sector. Break-up of the States Grants (Schools) Act 1974 indicates that the final figure may now be 31 (non-government) to 69 (government). Hence, the non-government sector's proportionate share of federal direct allocations is greater than its share of the school population.

The implication is ostensibly that this is a more than equitable treatment meeting the 'needs' of Catholic schools particularly and satisfying the demands of the Catholic school lobby. However, when the Australian Labor Government of today refers to expenditure for primary and secondary education, it persistently emphasizes federal program grants. It considers that it should not be held responsible for the financial allocations of State

**TABLE 2** Government Expenditure on Education per pupil Government and Independent Schools — Victoria

| | 1971-72 | 1972-73 | 1973-74 | | | | 1974-75 (Est.) | | | |
| --- | --- | --- | --- | --- | --- | --- | --- | --- | --- | --- |
| | | | Category | | | | Category | | | |
| | | | A | E | H | Syst. | A | E | H | Syst. |
| **1. Primary Education** | | | | | | | | | | |
| (a) Independent Schools, $ per year | 83 | 102 | 126 | 136 | 144 | 170 | 152 | 189 | 223 | 277 |
| (b) Government Schools, $ per year | 401 | 469 | 548 | 548 | 548 | 548 | 699 | 699 | 699 | 699 |
| (c) Ratio (a) to (b) | 0.21 | 0.22 | 0.22 | 0.24 | 0.26 | 0.30 | 0.22 | 0.27 | 0.32 | 0.40 |
| **2. Secondary Education** | | | | | | | | | | |
| (a) Independent Schools, $ per year | 144 | 186 | 228 | 265 | 287 | — | 262 | 362 | 437 | — |
| (b) Government Schools, $ per year | 698 | 829 | 1022 | 1022 | 1022 | — | 1346 | 1346 | 1346 | — |
| (c) Ratio (a) to (b) | 0.21 | 0.23 | 0.22 | 0.26 | 0.28 | — | 0.19 | 0.27 | 0.32 | — |

1. The ratios for 1974-75 should be reduced by at least 7 per cent to allow for rises in teachers' salaries granted in October, 1974.

2. Government funding of education for a child in an independent school has two components: recurrent and capital for building. The first component is unambiguous; the methodology of approach to estimation of average building grants, $ per pupil, in each sector and category is discussed in the section on building.

FINANCE FOR INDEPENDENT SCHOOLING

**TABLE 3** Government Expenditure on Primary and Secondary Education Government and Independent Schools — Australian States

| | 1971-72 Govt. | 1971-72 Indep. | 1972-73 Govt. | 1972-73 Indep. | 1973-74 Govt. | 1973-74 Indep. | 1974-75 (Est.) Govt. | 1974-75 (Est.) Indep. | 1975 (Last half only) (Est. Total) Govt. | 1975 (Last half only) (Est. Total) Indep. |
|---|---|---|---|---|---|---|---|---|---|---|
| 1. All State Government Expenditure, $m | 920 | 32 | 1058 | 45 | 1270 | 53 | 1524 | 65 | 914 | 38 |
| % age of total | 96.6 | 3.4 | 96.2 | 3.8 | 96 | 4 | 96 | 4 | 96 | 4 |
| 2. Federal Grants, $m | 21 | 36 | 26 | 48 | 90 | 70 | 258 | 121 | 187 | 70 |
| % age of total | 36.8 | 63.2 | 35.1 | 64.9 | 56.3 | 43.7 | 68.1 | 31.9 | 72.8 | 27.2 |
| 3. All Government Expenditure, $m | 941 | 68 | 1084 | 93 | 1360 | 123 | 1782 | 186 | 1101 | 108 |
| % age of total | 93.3 | 6.7 | 92.1 | 7.9 | 91.7 | 8.3 | 90.5 | 9.5 | 91.1 | 8.9 |

3919 (the estimated sum for total expenditure in calendar years 1974 and 1975).

Calculations of State budgets for 1974-75 are based on the increase in the Victorian budget estimate, i.e. 20 per cent. The figures are conservative, for they do not allow for rises in teachers' salaries during the financial year.

163

**TABLE 4** Recommendations of Karmel Committee and States Grants (Schools) Acts 1973 and 1974 for Australian States

| | Total | Govt. | Indep. |
|---|---|---|---|
| Estimated Expenditure from State and Federal Govts., 1974 and 1975 combined, $m | 3919 | 3563 | 356 |
| % age of total | — | 90.9 | 9.1 |
| Summary of grants in Interim Committee's recommendation for the States, $m (Table 14.3) | 660 | 460 | 179 |
| % age of total | — | 72.0 | 28.0 |
| Summary of net costs of Committee's recommendations ("Karmel Supplement"), $m (Table 14.1) | 467 | 396.5 | 50.2 |
| % age of total | — | 88.8 | 11.2 |
| Thus, "Existing Programmes", according to Karmel, $m | 193 | 64 | 129 |
| % age of total | — | 33.2 | 66.8 |
| Final estimates after Federal Budget of 1974-75, $m | 774 | 511 | 229 |
| % age of total | — | 69.1 | 30.9 |

1. 'Existing Grants' in Table 4 does not include $32.5 m covered by other legislation cited in **Schools in Australia,** Par. 14. 14 (pp. 144-5); also, see Tables 14.1 (p. 141) and 14.3 (p. 142).
2. Regarding Special Programmes for teacher development and innovations, the Interim Committee designated these as 'Joint Programmes'. It did not allocate the funds between government and non-government schools. Hence, total expenditure of Karmel recommendations does not equal the sum of allocations. (Also note 1974-75 Budget Paper No. 7, Table 19, p. 55).

**TABLE 5** Federal Grants for Primary and Secondary Education, $m
All Australian States

|  | 1973-74 | 1974-75 |
|---|---|---|
| Non-government sector | | |
| Grants due from continuing, unvaried policies of Government of the Right Hon. W. McMahon, 1972 | 70 | 84 |
| Grants under the policies of Government of the Right Hon. E. G. Whitlam, 1972-75 | 70 | 121 |
| Government sector | | |
| Grants due from McMahon policies | 45 | 44 |
| Grants under Whitlam Government | 89 | 257 |

Governments. If allocations for education in the budget of the Liberal Government for Victoria are a guide, the non-government sector will still get less than four per cent of the state budget funds. By determining grants and loans to the States, the Federal Government certainly largely determines the latter's capacity to fund. Whatever the cause, the issue is or should be, the total moneys flowing to primary and secondary schools from all sources.

## THE TOTAL RESOURCES GAP AND CONTINUING EFFORT

It has been fashionable to indulge in attacks on so called 'wealthy' secondary schools, with nominal maximum fees over $1000 per annum. The cost (financial year 1973/74) of educating a pupil in a Victorian government secondary school was $1022 per annum (excluding teacher training, transportation and payroll tax). This was made up of $807 recurrent cost, $163 capital cost and $52 for allowances to student teachers in training.[5]

Space does not permit some relevant analysis, for example, a correlation of Karmel Index and fees, but one thing is certain — the margin between expenditure per pupil on a child in a government school and maximum parent's expenditure on a child in an independent non-Catholic school is closing.

A Resources 'Gap' can be calculated from the difference between total expenditure of public moneys on a child in a government and non-government school. This quantity can be expressed in dollars, $, or as an index, taking 1971–72 as a base year, 100.

To use this index as a requirement for 'continuing effort' assumes that costs per pupil are to be set at the same figure for students in both government and non-government schools. This ignores various economies and diseconomies associated with recurrent operations in each sector; also, differing rates of expansion and capital costs. Where the work load and salaries of teachers in

165

**TABLE 6**—Teacher Costs per pupil, $, in a Victorian Government School

|  | 1971-72 | 1972-73 | 1973-74 | 1974-75 (Budget Estimate) |
|---|---|---|---|---|
| **Primary** |  |  |  |  |
| $ | 250 | 290 | 345 | 421 |
| Teacher Costs Index | 100 | 116 | 138 | 168 |
| Total Resources Gap, Index (Money Terms) | 100 | 115 | 131 | 158 |
| **Secondary** |  |  |  |  |
| $ | 410 | 485 | 605 | 722 |
| Teacher Costs Index | 100 | 118 | 147 | 176 |
| Total Resources Gap, Index | 100 | 116 | 137 | 168 |

The 1973-74 and 1974-75 Gap Figures are for a Category E school.

non-government schools have not kept pace with conditions and 'going rates' respectively, the index should be related to the amount both parents *and* teachers have to provide.

A significant item in the rise of the requirement for 'continuing effort' is the increase in teachers' salaries and the decrease in the pupil to teacher ratio in state schools. The Index for teachers' services appears as a major factor in the first term of the Gap. As expected, it moves with this Gap, which is not closed effectively by the increases in grants. (See Table 6.)

If the requirement for continuing effort in money terms grows at the same rate as the average weekly earnings (after tax), then the proportional effort required of parents with children in non-government schools remains the same, i.e. they would need to expend the same proportion of their disposable income as before to bring expenditure per pupil to the same figure for independent and government schools. These statements assume, firstly, that the incomes of parents are similar to the overall pattern of similar families in the population and secondly, that the gap in money terms is met entirely by parents.

The requirement for continuing effort (in proportional terms) is obtained by dividing the Index in money terms by the Index of average weekly earnings per male unit (after tax). The indices are shown in Table 7. It is evident that, if improvement of standards correlates with money expenditure, the Catholic parent with a child at a systemic primary school would have had to find an additional $55 between 1972–73 and 1974–75 to close the gap; for a child in a non-systemic Category H primary school, receiving proportionately less of building grants and no possibility of entitlement to a disadvantage allotment, the figure is $109. The sum for any secondary school pupil is not less than $250. In addition, the Index (in proportional terms) indicates an increased

**TABLE 7** Requirement for Continuing Efforts in the Independent Schools of Victoria

| | 1971-72 | 1972-73 | 1973-74 Category | | | | 1974-75 (Est.) Category | | | |
|---|---|---|---|---|---|---|---|---|---|---|
| | | | A | E | H | Syst. | A | E | H | Syst. |
| **Primary** | | | | | | | | | | |
| 1. Total Resources Gap, $ | 318 | 367 | 422 | 412 | 404 | 378 | 547 | 510 | 476 | 422 |
| Index in money terms | 100 | 115 | 133 | 130 | 127 | 119 | 172 | 160 | 150 | 133 |
| Index in proportional terms | 100 | 104 | 107 | 105 | 102 | 96 | 114 | 106 | 100 | 88 |
| **Secondary** | | | | | | | | | | |
| 2. Total Resources Gap, $ | 554 | 643 | 794 | 757 | 735 | — | 1084 | 984 | 909 | — |
| Index in money terms | 100 | 116 | 143 | 137 | 133 | — | 196 | 178 | 164 | — |
| Index in proportional terms | 100 | 105 | 115 | 110 | 107 | — | 130 | 118 | 109 | — |
| 3. Index of Average Weekly Earnings | 100 | 109 | 127 | | | | 157 (Est.) | | | |
| Index of Average Weekly Earnings after tax | 100 | 111 | 124 | | | | 151 (Est.) | | | |

1. Categorisation did not apply before January 1, 1974.
2. In estimating tax, the family unit is assumed as wife and three children, one at primary, one pre-school; other concessional deductions are set at $200. Fluctuations in the relative movements of Average Weekly Earnings before and after tax are associated with variation in deductions for dependents and in tax scales.
3. The estimate of Average Weekly Earnings (1974-75) is based on preliminary figures of the Institute of Applied Economic and Social Research, Australian Economic Review 3-1974.

K. G. MORTENSEN

requirement for all categories of schools in the secondary sector. The Prime Minister's terms of reference to the Interim Committee requested that there should be no 'substitution for continuing efforts'; he did not ask for 'increasing effort'.

While an increase in the Index (in proportional terms) suggests a need for expenditure of a greater proportion of income at equal standards, the Index does not specify that such an effort is being made. Assessment of the actual effort to close the Resources Gap requires information on the changing proportions of contributions by parents (through fees and voluntary activities) and teachers (through lower rates of pay and heavier working loads). The latter factor is also related to the quality of service provided.

## RECURRENT EXPENDITURE AND GRANTS

This section separates the component of recurrent expenditure from total expenditure and considers 'relative' equity in terms of the ratio of public moneys in grants per non-government school pupil to the recurrent expenditure per government school pupil. The secondary and primary sectors are considered separately.

### Secondary sector

The recurrent expenditure per pupil in the average Australian government school has been assessed by the Australian Government at $640 for the financial year 1973–74, 23 per cent greater than 1972–73. Under the States Grants (Schools) Act 1972, each child in a non-government secondary school would have received 20 per cent of this figure, i.e., $128 in 1974. Under the current dispensation, after the 1974 Federal Budget, the sum of $120 was received by a pupil in a Category E school (Karmel Index 90–102 per cent of the resources in an average Australian government school).

Following indicators cited under 'Total Funding', an increase of 31 per cent can be expected in recurrent expenditure in the average Australian secondary school from 1973–74 to 1974–75. Under the States Grants (Schools) Act 1972, all secondary school pupils would have received $168, one-fifth of $837. In fact, Category E schools are to receive $169 in 1975.

The 'needs' assessment of schools, even with the A.L.P.–C.P. compromise of December 1973, happened to save the Federal Government $3.4 million in 1974 in recurrent grants to secondary schools. The budget adjustment (1974–75) increased the 1974 recurrent grant to non-government schools by $3.0 million so that the whole exercise still saved the Australian Government $0.35 million over what would have resulted from application of the 1972 Act. Benefits to schools in Categories F to H over and above the $128 due in 1974 under this Act were about $2.9 million, which the Catholic sector gained at the expense of the non-Catholic sector. Schools in Categories A to E lost $3.2 million.

The percentage of federal moneys flowing directly in 1975 for recurrent

168

expenditure in non-systemic secondary schools with an index above 102 is 0.6 per cent of the total expenditure (federal/state) on primary/secondary education. Federal recurrent grants per pupil to 50 schools in Category A, educating three per cent of Australian secondary pupils, constitute 0.15 per cent of the total expenditure. An estimate for a continuing 1972 Act is 0.28 per cent. Whichever figure is taken, it is ridiculous to blame the deficiencies in secondary education on movement of federal financial resources to Category A schools.

By departing from the principle of a basic percentage recurrent grant[6], the Interim Committee and the Labor Government have encouraged the States to introduce legislation that offers no security or stability to non-government schools.[7]

The Hon. L. H. S. Thompson, Minister for Education, Victoria, stated that, in 1974, 'equal amounts will be paid by both the State and Commonwealth Governments'.[8] In the ACT, the Commonwealth met its obligations by paying per pupil grants of $76 (primary) and $128 (secondary) based on 20 per cent of the average Australian recurrent expenditure for 1973–74. Victoria provided grants of $62 (primary) and $104 (secondary) based on the national average for 1972–73. The state grants of $80 (primary) and $135 (secondary) for 1975 are set according to 'a specifically Victorian standard' to quote the 1974–75 budget speech of the Hon. R. J. Hamer, Premier of Victoria. The per pupil grants in 1974 (16 per cent) and 1975 (estimated as 16 per cent) are less than that due under the McMahon formula.

A Ratio for Recurrent Grants can be derived as a guide to equity. The term may be defined as the ratio of total grants per pupil from Federal and State Governments to the recurrent expense of educating a child in an average Australian government school of the same type.

The current figures for Victoria are shown in Table 8. All categories of school show an increasing Recurrent Resources Gap in money terms. Movements (1973–75) in the Ratio and Index (in proportional terms) for Category H schools show an improvement. Movements in the Index for Category E schools and above suggest an increased demand for 'continuing effort'. The Ratio for a Category E school has improved slightly, but, because of failure of the State to fund according to the McMahon formula, such schools did not obtain a total 40 per cent of the average government school recurrent cost in 1974; nor will they secure this proportion in 1975.

**Primary sector**

In the primary sector, most of the children are in Catholic parish schools and these are now organized on a systemic basis. The statement of the Hon. L. Bowen suggests that Catholic systemic schools were block-funded at the per pupil level of a non-systemic, Category H primary school.[9] The actual figure seems to allow for a proportion being taken up in the administration of Catholic Education Offices.

**TABLE 8** Recurrent Expenditure and Grants per Secondary Pupil — Victoria

| | 1973 | 1974 Category | | | 1975 Category | | |
|---|---|---|---|---|---|---|---|
| | | A | E | H | A | E | H |
| **(a) Grants to Independent schools, $ per year** | | | | | | | |
| Federal | 104 | 92 | 119.5 | 152 | 94 | 169 | 260 |
| State | 72 | 104 | 104 | 104 | 135 | 135 | 135 |
| Total | 176 | 196 | 223.5 | 256 | 229 | 304 | 395 |
| **(b) Government schools, $ per year** | | | | | | | |
| Total | 519 | 640 | 640 | 640 | 837 (Est.) | 837 (Est.) | 837 (Est.) |
| **(c) Ratio of (a) to (b)** | | | | | | | |
| Totals | 0.34 | 0.31 | 0.35 | 0.40 | 0.27 | 0.36 | 0.47 |
| **(d) Recurrent Resources** | | | | | | | |
| Gap, $ per year | 343 | 444 | 416.5 | 384 | 608 | 533 | 442 |
| Gap Index (in money terms) | 100 | 129 | 121 | 112 | 177 | 155 | 129 |
| Index (AWE) | 100 | | 119 (Est.) | | | 146 (Est.) | |
| Index (AWE after tax) | 100 | | 114 (Est.) | | | 138 (Est.) | |
| Gap Index (in proportional terms) | 100 | 113 | 106 | 98 | 129 | 113 | 94 |

1. Estimates for average weekly earnings (1974 and 1975) are from the Institute of Applied Economic and Social Research, Melbourne University.
2. It should also be noted that the ratios are inflated and the indices distorted by two factors which act unfavourably against the non-government sector, viz.
(a) it is considered that the calculation of recurrent expenditure per government school child is reduced by failure to include head office administration, debt charges, depreciation or components of teacher training.
(b) the grants apply to a calendar year, e.g. 1975, whereas the recurrent expenditure is calculated for a financial year set back six months, e.g. 1974/75.
(c) the figure for recurrent expenditure is calculated according to provisions in the regulations associated with the States Grants (Schools) Act. Its value is decided at a meeting of State Ministers of Education.. There is an agreement among the States that only the Australian average figures are made available. The expenditure in a large state such as Victoria is higher than the average, e.g. $696 for 1973-74 (The Hon. L. H. S. Thompson, Questions on Notice, October 30, 1974, p. 1793). When based on this figure, the Ratio for a Category H school is 0.37, not 0.40.

**TABLE 9** Calculation of Recurrent Ratio and Indices for Systemic Primary Schools — Victoria
(Excluding grants for Disadvantaged Schools)

|  | 1973 | 1974 | 1975 |
|---|---|---|---|
| (a) Average per pupil grants, $ per year |  |  |  |
| Federal | 62 | 102 | 163 (Est.) |
| State | 51 | 62 | 80 |
| Total | 113 | 164 | 243 |
| (b) Average recurrent expenditure per Australian government primary pupil, $ per year. | 309 | 379 | 498 (Est.) |
| (c) Ratio of (a) to (b) totals | 0.37 | 0.43 | 0.49 |
| Recurrent Resources |  |  |  |
| Gap, $ per year | 196 | 215 | 255 |
| Gap Index (in money terms) | 100 | 110 | 130 |
| Index (AWE) | 100 | 119 (Est.) | 146 (Est.) |
| Index (AWE after tax) | 100 | 114 (Est.) | 138 (Est.) |
| Gap Index (in proportional terms) | 100 | 96 | 94 |

In granting $62 (1974) under Act No. 8495 (1973), the Hon. R. J. Hamer's Victorian Liberal Government supplied $14 less than that due under this Government's previous Act No. 8378 (1972). The wording of the latter Act would have led to a grant of about $100 per pupil in 1975.

Table 9 gives per pupil recurrent grant data on Catholic systemic schools.

In assessing the grants to systemic primary schools in Victoria, one may note the following:

1 *All* moneys flowing under the 1972 Act were distributed to schools on a per pupil basis.

2 If the Victorian figures are typical of other States, about 93 per cent of the $8.91 million under the 1973 Act flowed directly to the systemic primary schools. In 1974, 90 669 pupils in these schools received $8.26 million and it is estimated that the average distributed after the budget supplement will be $102 per pupil.

3 Approximately 2462 pupils were in Victorian parish systemic secondary schools receiving $265 835.

4 Of the 343 parish primary schools in Victoria, before budget adjustment, 60 received less than that due under the States Grants (Schools) Act 1972, 58 received an equivalent amount; 225 schools received more.

During this year, a non-systemic school in Category H received less than many systemic schools. If such a school was sponsored by a different religious faith, this anomaly could well be raised as a matter offending against Section 116 of the Constitution. On the other hand, many Catholic schools which would have been assessed as Category H in the non-systemic classification

171

received less than the $97.5 per pupil due to such a school in 1974; the same situation persists in 1975.

In the first year of application of the Karmel report, Victorian Catholic systemic primary schools did not obtain massive recurrent aid. In fact, they received only an average of $26 per pupil more than they could have secured under the States Grants (Schools) Act 1972 of the McMahon Government. Estimating total Victorian expenditure on primary and secondary education in calendar years 1974 and 1975 as $1260 million, the recurrent grants for disadvantaged Catholic schools were about 0.1 per cent of this total. On an average, $9 will flow per pupil in a Catholic systemic school or $50 to each child declared disadvantaged.

In conclusion, one may note an improvement in the Average Recurrent Ratio and the Resources Gap Index (in proportional terms) for systemic schools during 1974 and 1975. The movement is similar to that apparent in Category H secondary schools. However, in both years, there is an increase in the gap in money terms.

## BUILDING GRANTS

Federal aid for building (excluding science laboratories and libraries) in schools in 1974 and 1975 combined was planned to be: government $164 million, non-government $34.5 million.[10] The latter's share (17.3 per cent) approaches an equitable distribution. In addition, Mr. Bowen stated that 'up to 50 per cent of the total . . . may be applied to new pupil places'.[11]

The total Victorian state budget estimate (1974–75) for school buildings and sites is not less than $107 million. State sources are to supply $65 million of this sum. The only state allocation for the non-government sector is $0.5 million subsidy on interest for building secondary schools.

Table 10 presents figures for building. During 1973–74, as a result of initiatives of the McMahon Government through the 1972 Act and the Karmel allocations, moneys for primary school building became available for the first time. There was a consequent reduction in the Building Resources Gap (primary). Despite this relative improvement, there were delays in consideration of building grants during financial year 1973–74 and, at the time when approvals came through, there were upwards movements in the Victorian Building Cost Index.[12] For example, the Index rose by 9.26 per cent in April 1974, a further 2.78 per cent in May and 8.63 per cent in June. In attempting to help as many applicants as possible, the Schools Commission made inadequate grants and schools had difficulty in obtaining building finance at reasonable rates of interest.

Indicators suggest that heavy federal funding and large, unmatched allocations from state sources towards building government schools will widen the secondary 'gap' considerably in 1974–75.

The current situation in Victoria is that the State Department of Education failed to spend more than $9 million of moneys available in estimates for

**TABLE 10** Ratios of Equity and the extent of Continuing Effort (Building) in the non-government sector (Victoria) State and Federal Capital Funding, $ per pupil (Av.)

| | 1971-72 | 1972-73 | 1973-74 | 1974-75 |
|---|---|---|---|---|
| **Primary** | | | | |
| Ratio | | | | |
| $ non-govt. school children | $\dfrac{0}{40} = 0.00$ | $\dfrac{0}{48} = 0.00$ | $\dfrac{16}{45} = 0.36$ | $\dfrac{38}{88} = 0.43$ |
| $ govt. school children | | | | |
| Building Resources Gap, $ | 40 - 0 = 40 | 48 - 0 = 48 | 45 - 16 = 29 | 88 - 38 = 50 |
| Index (in money terms) | 100 | 120 | 72 | 125 |
| Index (in proportional terms) | 100 | 108 | 58 | 83 |
| | | | | |
| **Secondary** | | | | |
| Ratio | $\dfrac{30}{116} = 0.26$ | $\dfrac{30}{130} = 0.23$ | $\dfrac{42}{163} = 0.26$ | $\dfrac{62}{292} = 0.21$ |
| Building Resources Gap, $ | 116 - 30 = 86 | 130 - 30 = 100 | 163 - 42 = 121 | 292 - 62 = 230 |
| Index (in money terms) | 100 | 116 | 141 | 267 |
| Index (in proportional terms) | 100 | 105 | 114 | 177 |
| Index of Average Weekly Earnings | 100 | 109 | 127 | 157 (Est.) |
| Index of Average Weekly Earnings after tax | 100 | 111 | 124 | 151 (Est.) |

173

## Notes to Table 10

1. The analysis is based on government budgets and statements of expenditure; 'Schools Commission Programs 1974' (September, 1974) giving a progress report on expenditure; 'Schools 1973' (Australian Bureau of Statistics, ref. 13.5) and releases from the Catholic Education Commission of Victoria.

2. During the three financial years prior to 1974-75, the per pupil expenditure on government building has varied from 27 to 22 per cent primary, 73 to 78 per cent secondary. There is no official statement as to allocation for 1974-75; my calculations assume a per pupil distribution of 23 to 77.

3. Totals include capital grants for general building and libraries; for secondary science laboratories; also, disadvantaged schools (Federal, systemic schools only).
The subsidy for payment of interest (State, secondary only) on capital loans is a recurrent cost and is omitted. It amounts to an average of $4 per pupil and has been included in calculation of the Total Resources Gap (Tables 2 and 7).

4. In Victoria, funding for 'general buildings' in the non-government sector was distributed equally between primary and secondary schools. Where funding is not specific to a sector, this principle has been adopted. There are more primary (109,537 in 1973) than secondary pupils (83,900), so the allocation per pupil is less in the primary sector.

5. In considering grants for 'general building' within the primary sector during the first nine months of 1974, the average per pupil allocation was in the ratio 22 (non-systemic) to 78 (Catholic systemic).
The average per pupil allocation for secondary children in categories was in the ratio 14 (A, B and C) to 40 (D, E and F) and 46 (G and H). These figures have been applied to Categories A, E and H respectively.
The above data have been used in Tables 2 and 7 in assessing distribution of budget estimates into types and categories of school.

6. Grants for disadvantaged schools in the first nine months of 1974 (therefore, overlapping over two financial years) amounted to $758,920. This is about $9 per systemic primary child or approximately $115 per pupil for the 6500 children in the 21 schools receiving building benefits as "disadvantaged". Calculations in Tables 2 and 7 allowed $0.8 per systemic child in 1973-74 and $7.9 in 1974-75, from a budgeted total of $846,000.

1973–74. While the Building Index rose at an average monthly rate of two per cent in the three months ending October 1974, funds are not available for the non-government sector to meet basic extension needs (classrooms and toilets) in the majority of schools with legitimate claims. At the present level of grants and with the high building standards demanded by the Schools Commission, a generation of children could pass through some schools without the benefit of a modern library. In contrast with the 1960s and early 1970s, there are no or few major projects underway, and there is an insufficiency of work for builders normally active in the Catholic school sector.

## DISADVANTAGED SCHOOLS

The Karmel Committee allocated $50 million (11 per cent of its total 'supplement' of $467 million) to disadvantaged schools. This sum is about 1.3 per cent of the total moneys spent on Australian primary and secondary education during calendar years 1974 and 1975 combined.

The distribution of moneys for both building and recurrent expenditure (as discussed in the text) is 88 per cent to government schools and 12 per cent to Catholic systemic schools. *Schools in Australia* states that 'it can be seen that the Catholic systemic schools were operating in 1972 at an average standard of some four-fifths of that of government primary schools.'[13] This fact does not appear to be recognized in the distribution ratio of 88 : 12.

Secondly, one might also wonder at the complete absence of non-government secondary schools seeing that, to quote Karmel, 'the typical Catholic secondary school uses about 70 per cent of the resources used per pupil in an average state school.'[14] If a low letter in the Category system is to replace a right (recognized by the Australian Government) based on 'disadvantage', this might have been spelt out more clearly.

## TAXATION DEDUCTIONS FOR EDUCATION EXPENSES

*The Herald*, 16 October 1974, states: 'Mr Whitlam told caucus that the decision on school deductions was the unanimous decision of Cabinet arrived at after studying a report by Dr Coombs'.

If this statement refers to 'Review of the Continuing Expenditure Policies of the Previous Government', June 1973, pp. 258–259, it is a poor justification for action.

The Coombs case rests on certain correct principles and evidence, viz., that the tax deductions are a type of 'disguised expenditure in the form of a subsidy' operating in a manner that gives more saving in money terms to those on higher incomes.

There is nothing novel about this interpretation. In the absence of an equitable return of taxation to parents paying independent school fees — therefore not subsidized by governments through funding in the measure offered to parents with children at state schools — the Income Tax Assessment Act (Section 82J) formerly offered indirect assistance through an allowance of expenditures up to $400 per student. Only part of this sum, say $250, offered a relative concession to a parent with a child at an independent school. A parent with a child at a government secondary school could claim $150 without question — for uniforms, incidental fees, fares, books, music and sport, excursions organized by the school etc.

The $400 deduction allowed parents some reduction in taxable income in respect to part or whole of the fees paid. Although individuals on higher income, at higher rates of taxation, benefited most, the bulk of the support went to those of moderate or modest income.[15] The estimated savings (1974–75) of $30m will not flow from parents of children in state schools; it will flow from all parents in non-government schools, perhaps primarily Catholic parents for the simple reason that their children are in non-government schools in great numbers.

The former Treasurer, the Hon. F. Crean, has stated: 'This Government has gone further than any other government in the abolition of fees generally . . . There are less fees payable now in the system than were ever payable before'.[16] This statement was made after clear evidence that fees in Catholic parish schools are rising steeply. This affects the parents of children (17.55 per cent of those in Australian primary schools in 1973) who attend Catholic primary schools; only 2.26 per cent of children attend non-Catholic non-government primary schools.[17]

Fees are rising in independent secondary schools where the main impact will come on the parents of Catholic (16.62 per cent) and non-Catholic (7.67 per cent) children.

In failing to recognize such facts, the Review's treatment of education expenses is quite inadequate. Dr Coombs recognized that the deduction 'would ideally be better replaced by a system of rebates on taxation'. He then goes on to regret that 'this is a matter going beyond the compass' of his Task Force. While Mr Crean recognizes that 'an ossified pattern cannot suddenly be changed in a very short space of time'[18], he did not employ this principle. Dr Coombs' argument that 'the taxpayers most affected would for the most part be those in the higher income brackets' was re-echoed by Mr Crean. It is unsound. In fact, the lower income earner with children at a non-government school will be penalized more as a percentage of his income than a higher income earner who can better bear the loss from an annual income of $20 000. If a family contains a number of children attending non-government schools, the chance of movement into a new taxable income level is increased.

The underlying philosophy is made clear in Treasury Taxation Paper No. 7 (November, 1974) which states (p. 18):

> From an equity viewpoint it would be difficult to argue that education expenses reduce the capacity of an individual to pay tax in a country where education is provided free of charge by a system of State Schools; heavy expenses are an *option*, not a necessity. [My italics.]

It is evident that the Treasury does not consider that 'the prior right of parents to choose whether their children are educated at a government school or at a

**TABLE 11** Money Flows per pupil to School/Parent Partnership Alternative Government Policies
Category H Secondary School/Parent on Average Weekly Wage

|  | Continued and Unvarying Policies Pre December 1972 | | | Current Policies | |
|---|---|---|---|---|---|
|  | 1974 | 1975 (1st half) | | 1974 | 1975 (1st half) |
|  | $ | $ | | $ | $ |
| Federal Govt. | 128 | 84 | (Est.) | 152 | 130 |
| State Govt. | 128 | 84 | (Est.) | 104 | 67 |
| Estimated Savings from maximum taxation deduction | 128 | 64 | | 88 | 24 |
|  | 384 | 232 | | 344 | 221 |

1. For the Victorian Government, see State Hansard, The Hon. L. H. S. Thompson, November 16, 1972, p. 2113; November 13, 1973, p. 1946; The Hon. R. J. Hamer, October 24, 1973, p. 1450 and the 1973-74 Budget Speech.
2. Junior Government Scholarships amounted to an average of $15 per child in the period 1 Jan., 1974-30 June, 1975. The sum is common to both tables and is omitted.

non-government school' (Schools Commission Act, 1973, p. 7), has economic implications!

In the debate of 16 October 1974, the Hon. A. H. Lamb stated: 'We cannot isolate this debate on the right to a $30 million taxation deduction for education expenses from the full thrust of the Australian Schools Commission'.[19] I agree. Table 11 gives a listing, for a Category H school-parent partnership, of benefits due under continuing federal and Victorian Acts (1972) and unamended taxation deductions compared with benefits under the 1973 Act as amended by the 1974–75 budget and by Cabinet decision on the figure of $150 for deduction of educational expenses. The figures apply to a man earning the average wage, $125.90, in Victoria in the June quarter of 1974.

During the period, 1 January 1974 to 30 June 1975, the school-parent Country Party policies of 1972 and the commitments then made (later modified) by the State Liberal Government of the Hon. R. J. Hamer.

The data may also be considered in the light of Table 8. Table 11 shows that, for the instance cited, the payment in tax was decreased by $40 for the education of each child at an independent secondary school for the first half, but not the last half of 1974. If this sum is regarded as a debit against the recurrent per pupil grants of $256 (1974) for a Category H school, the real 'Ratio' is 0.34, to be compared with 0.40 (apparent). If current taxation policies continue until 31 December 1975, the 1975 'Ratio' will drop from 0.47 to no more than that sought by the McMahon formula.

## GENERAL COMMENTARY

Any appraisal of the work of the Interim Committee must consider its terms of reference which made explicit mention of the 'financial needs of schools'.[20] The Committee interpreted its role narrowly as concern 'with the resources used in the schools and not with the financial situation of the parents of pupils'. Justice to the taxpayer with children at non-government schools was not the issue. He had made his contribution to funding of education but, according to the terms of reference, there was to be no substitution for his 'continuing effort'.[21]

It follows that *Schools in Australia* should be regarded as an emergency document dealing with disadvantage, not a primer of principles on justice to parents or pupils. When the Committee phased out grants for schools in Category A and Cabinet decided to terminate these grants from 1 January 1974, their action could be justified as within the terms of reference. If assessment of 'needs' by Karmel had been coupled with Cabinet decision to give a base recurrent grant according to the McMahon formula, the Government would have presented a coherent plan.[22]

The Interim Committee sought, by 1979, to secure schools of high standard, offering 'equality of opportunity' to all students. For 1974 and 1975, the Committee recommended 'funds aimed to go to about one-sixth the way in each year towards reaching the 1979 targets'.[23] At the opening of 1975, all schools in the non-government sector are involved in a holding operation, with threat of parent withdrawal because of the reduction in taxation deductions for educational expenses.

It is submitted that the economic contribution of the Karmel report to solving the problems of education in the non-government sector has been exaggerated.

1  In allocating recurrent grants for 1974, the report has brought increases to only some non-government schools and at the expense of other schools, with erosion of the principle of parents' rights in educating their children. The latter schools are almost entirely non-Catholic and any worsening of their position must narrow the social class from which their pupils come. Such policies cannot promote the 'equality' that the Government seeks.

2  When judged by the Total Resources Gap in money terms, $ per pupil, government support for independent secondary schools is declining; this applies to Category H schools also. The Index of required continuing effort, in proportional terms, has also increased for all categories of secondary school. (See Table 7.)

3  When judged by the Recurrent Expenditure Ratio, a Category H secondary school derived no overall benefit from the combination of Karmel *and* state (Victoria) policies in 1974; the position improves in 1975. However, in both 1974 and 1975 a Category E school with resources below that of an average Australian government school is worse off than under continuing (and unvaried) Liberal-Country Party federal

practices and the 1972 commitments of Mr Hamer's State Government (See Table 8.)

4 The recommendations of the Interim Committee, accepted by the Labor Government, have created new avenues of benefit for Catholic primary schools. Many running at a deficit, but certainly not all, have obtained significant help. (See discussion on Table 9.) However, if 'needs' judged by Karmel formula evaluating school resources is to be the criterion, the Catholic parish schools have not obtained 'massive' aid, even after favourable distribution of general building grants to ordinary systemic schools and by supplementary allocations to disadvantaged schools.[24]

5 The school-parent partnership in even Category H secondary schools (1974) with a Karmel Index of less than 67 and a parent on the average wage is worse off during (1974) and the first half of 1975 than under the recurrent funding of Federal (and State) Acts, 1972, and an unamended taxation deduction. (See Table 11.)[25]

6 The Karmel report failed to recognize the support required if state sources were to fund the non-government sector equitably, particularly in respect to building costs for both secondary and primary schools. (See Table 10.)

In the final analysis, adherence to sound principles protecting the independence of schools in the non-government sector will be just as important as equitable financial support from governments. Until both are achieved, it will be necessary for parents, and the schools founded to serve their children, to accept financial disability, give mutual support and maintain morale.

### Notes

1 Australia. (1973). *Schools in Australia. Report of the Interim Committee of the Australian Schools Commission.* (Chairman, P. Karmel). Canberra: AGPS, para. 6.38 (p. 67). See also, 1.4 (p. 4) and 5.14 (p. 50).

2 See McKinnon, K. R. (Chairman of the Schools Commission). 'Some Problems of Finance in Education'. Meeting of Australian Parents Council, 24 August 1974; and address to ANZAAS Congress (*The Canberra Times*, 23 January 1975). Also Ross Warneke (*The Age*, 12 December 1974) citing R. Costello, member of the Schools Commission.

3 Public Lectures Program (March-May 1974), 'Labor, Karmel and the Schools'. 'Absolute' equity may be defined as that equity which is full justice after considering all the factors involved. This has never been analysed adequately. Hence, I aim only to consider 'relative' equity which can be inferred from movements in economic indicators.

4 This paper does not discuss 'Special Education' — provision for the handicapped. The Interim Committee (Section 10.27, pp. 115-116), by not providing for direct funding of special schools in the non-government sector, envisaged some absorption of 'voluntary' schools by the government administration. While the Australian Government has provided a grant towards recurrent costs of non-government schools in 1974 and 1975, the Karmel recommendations have inhibited the development of those special schools which have decided to remain independent.

5 The figure for recurrent cost (1973-4) is based on the Report of the Minister of Education for that year. The Minister's figure is $864.69, but when calculated according to the principles observed in this paper (see Table 1, note 2), the figure is $807. This sum includes debt charges and an estimate for head office administration. Another estimate, $696, cited by The Hon. L. H. S. Thompson (Questions on Notice, 30 October 1974, p. 1793), is according to an accounting practice also followed by the Australian Government. The Federal Minister for Education has not yet released estimates for 1974-75 and this paper uses estimates (primary

and secondary) based on a 31 per cent increase from 1973-74. (Cf. footnote 4 to Table 1.) A critique of this judgment, involving comparison with official figures, would only be possible if the States publish all data used in calculation, including a full statement of actual expenditures in the previous financial year. (Also, note footnote 2 to Table 8.)

6 The Rt. Hon. W. McMahon, *Commonwealth Parliamentary Debates*, House of Representatives, 11 May 1972. The figure according to the McMahon formula was 0.40. The Federal Government pledged to contribute at the level of 0.20 and appealed to the States to match this.

7 I suggest comparison of Victoria: Education Grants No. 8378 (19 December 1972) and its inbuilt formula with No. 8495 (4 December 1973), where this is eliminated.

8 Victorian *Hansard*, 16 November 1972, p. 2113.

9 The Hon. L. Bowen, *C.P.D.*, op. cit., 15 November 1973, p. 3405.

10 The 1974-75 federal budget increases grants towards all building in government and non-government sectors combined by $10.5m for the period 1 January 1974 to 30 June 1975. The distribution of total moneys for science laboratories and libraries (some $70m) is essentially in accordance with the school populations.

11 The Hon. L. Bowen, ibid., p. 3402.

12 The Building Cost Index is used for purpose of cost adjustment on contract sums in accordance with the Cost Adjustment Agreement, September 1970. A labour-materials ratio of 45:55 applies. See, *The Australian Builder*, November 1974, p. 456.

13 Australia. (1973). op.cit.: 67.

14 ibid.: 70-71.

15 For example, during 1969-70, in the school of my domicile, a Lorenz analysis of the economic status of parents (averaging about four children) showed a close similarity with the Australian spectrum of families of the same structure. For data on the relation of income to deductions claimed for educational expenses, see Mortensen, K. G., *The Age*, 25 September 1974, and Gould, K. W., *The Age*, 10 December 1974.

16 The Hon. F. Crean, *C.P.D.*, op. cit., 16 October 1974, pp. 2403, 2405.

17 Australia. (1973). loc. cit.

18 The Hon. F. Crean, ibid.: 2404.

19 The Hon. A. H. Lamb, ibid.: 2407.

20 Australia. (1973). op. cit.: para 1.4 (p. 4).

21 ibid.: 3.

22 This was apparently the general intention of the Minister for Education, the Hon. K. E. Beazley: 'My view was that every school in the country, including the Geelong Grammar School, should receive a basic grant from the Commonwealth and that the Commonwealth should have an identity with the education of every child.' (*C.P.D.*, 30 May 1973, pp. 2844-2845).

23 Australia. (1973). op. cit., para. 6. 12, (p. 62).

24 Cf. McKinnon, K. R., 'The financial situation of Catholic schools was, I think, appreciated but not sufficiently highlighted by the Karmel Committee. Catholic authorities, even with this massive additional federal government support, have now been forced to review fee structures', Monash Public Lectures Program. ('The Next Steps from Karmel') op. cit.; also address to ANZAAS, op. cit., where he stated: 'Although the funds provided to non-government schools for 1974 and 1975 were thought to be generous, the submissions of interested parties for the needs of the next three years seek a vastly greater proportion of equivalent government-school costs'.

25 Another benefit which has been withdrawn is the opportunity to compete for Commonwealth Secondary Scholarships. The Liberal/Country Party coalition doubled the number of scholarships for 1973 and boys in Form 4 of my school won 70 awards, 42 per cent of the total enrolment of these classes.

The Labor Government has abolished the scholarship system. It introduced a Secondary Allowances Scheme in early 1974. Families with an adjusted income (gross for family, minor deductions) of more than $5675 (as at October 1974) are not eligible for any aid and this will cut out parents of moderate means who previously benefited from the hard work of children of average ability who, with the school's assistance, were able to win scholarships. It may also be noted that the new 'allowances' scheme involves disbursement of less than $3 million where $11 million was distributed in scholarships.

## II. The Schools Commission:
## Programs and Issues

**Overall Evaluation**

# 11. Renewal in Australian Education — a Changing Prospect

J.K. Matthews and J.P. Keeves

## THE KARMEL INITIATIVES

The Interim Committee for the Australian Schools Commission, under the chairmanship of Professor P.H. Karmel, was appointed 11 days after the election, in December 1972, of the first Australian Labor Party Government for 21 years. It produced its report, *Schools in Australia*, in the very short period of five months.[1] The Committee's terms of reference reflected to some extent the ideology of the Labor Party, in particular its commitment to the promotion of equality of opportunity.

These terms of reference required an examination of the needs of schools, priorities within them, and the recommendation of appropriate measures to meet these needs. The Committee was required to work towards establishing acceptable standards for all schools, taking into account the particular needs of disadvantaged groups. This gave Committee members broad scope for developing their own framework of values and establishing their own goals for education in Australia. In doing so, they have largely influenced the context of debate on Australian schools for the foreseeable future.

The terms of reference also reflected, in their stress on the needs of schools and on priorities within these needs, the compromise reached within the Labor Party on the question of state aid to non-government schools. By accepting 'needs' as the basis for the allocation of funds the Party could quite comfortably accommodate both government and non-government schools within the framework of its egalitarian ideology. However, the terms of reference were remarkably free from ideological dogma or prescription. The Committee of experts was left to decide what needs and priorities should be considered important and what measures would best meet them.

As can be seen above, the Committee was required to think in terms of the needs of schools, and not of social issues such as equality and diversity. Its programs reflected its stated goal of bringing all schools up to an equal and much higher level of physical provision and operation by the target date of 1979. However, they also reflected the values the Committee considered to be important in the development and advancement of Australian education. Chief among these values were equality, diversity, and devolution of responsibility to those most closely concerned with the process of schooling.

Equality was interpreted as providing opportunities for all individuals, irrespective of socio-economic or physical handicaps, to acquire the basic level of skill considered necessary for living and participating fully in the communal life of a complex society. Beyond that, it was seen as providing a wide diversity of equally valued paths to personal satisfaction and fulfilment.

This interpretation of equality required that more resources should be devoted to those who were less likely to reach an acceptable level of skill. It also led to the 'needs' approach in the allocation of general recurrent grants. The allocation of more funds to those States whose schools lagged behind the national average and those categories of non-government schools which were below target levels was, in part, an attempt to equalize the conditions of learning, so that children previously suffering from adverse school environments might be enabled to learn in the more advantageous surroundings enjoyed by everyone else. No crude correspondence was assumed between school conditions and educational outcomes. However, it was considered that all children should enjoy a high level of provision, both to maximize the possible effects of resources on learning and to demonstrate that all children should be equally valued, no matter where or how they lived.

More directly related to the Committee's interpretation of equality were the Special Education and Disadvantaged Schools Programs. In the former, children with obvious physical and mental handicaps were to be provided with extra resources in an attempt to raise their level of cognitive and social competence towards the level considered desirable. In the latter, schools serving areas in which there was a predominance of people with social disadvantages (for example, low-status occupational groups, migrants, Aborigines and single parents) were to be eligible for extra funds to mount programs aimed at increasing the levels of competence, and widening the horizons, of their pupils.

Diversity of educational provision and approaches was a logical corollary of the interpretation of equality that placed equal value on a variety of lifestyles and interests. This pluralist view of society was reflected in the acceptance and support of various kinds of non-government schools. It was perhaps more evident in the Special Projects (Innovations) Program, in which the development of new and different curricula, teaching methods and systems of organization were to be encouraged by grants to individuals and groups for experimentation in these areas.

Devolution of responsibility to those most closely involved in the day-to-day running of schools and school systems was encouraged by the requirement that school personnel themselves should put up programs to be approved and funded, for example in the Disadvantaged Schools and Special Projects Programs. It was also reflected in the fact that general capital and recurrent grants were made to state and systemic educational authorities without firm prescription, to be allocated as they saw fit.

Thus, although the primary aim was to meet the assessed material needs of schools and raise their levels of operation, the Committee, in the programs it recommended to achieve this goal, sought to influence the direction of Australian education in the light of the three major value orientations of equality, diversity, and devolution of responsibility.

## The programs

The programs recommended by the Karmel Committee and continued by the Schools Commission reflected a fine balancing of the values and priorities expressed in the Karmel report. In particular, they were intended to reconcile the somewhat conflicting aims that those closest to the schools should decide priorities, and that the areas considered by the Committee to be of high priority should not be neglected. The general purpose capital and recurrent grants were expected to achieve the first aim, while it was hoped that the special purpose grants would achieve the second.

It was not only the specific programs of the Schools Commission that were put into operation over the next few years. The more general recommendations advanced in *Schools in Australia* for improving the quality of the educational enterprise also influenced developments. One of these was that the Commonwealth Government should expand its support for educational research activities.[2] This was one of the factors influencing the strengthening and reorganizing of the Australian Advisory Committee on Research and Development in Education, now called the Education Research and Development Committee. This body was given greatly increased resources and a permanent chairman.

The establishment of a national Curriculum Development Centre, suggested at an earlier date by the Australian Education Council, was influenced by the Karmel report's support for curriculum development on a national scale to supplement and aid state, local and teacher initiatives and provide alternatives.[3] The Centre was established in 1974 and became a statutory authority in July 1975.

Another result of the Interim Committee report and programs, was the restructuring of the loosely connected Catholic schools into a stronger and more co-ordinated system. The Karmel report recommended that State-wide bodies be formed to disburse and account for funds granted to Catholic systemic schools. The Catholic authorities themselves realized that strengthened co-ordinating machinery was a necessary response in order to obtain financial assistance from the State and Commonwealth Governments. Consequently, State Catholic Education Commissions have been established as educational policy-making and administrative bodies, serviced by State Catholic Education Offices. A National Catholic Education Commission met for the first time in 1974. This rationalization and restructuring of Catholic educational administration has greatly increased the effectiveness of the Catholic school sector in political terms, and in 1976 it became one of the strongest advocates for the retention of the Schools Commission at a time when the existence of that body appeared threatened.

## Problems encountered

By May 1975, all the original funds recommended by the Interim Committee had been committed and more than 65 per cent had been expended. In its

*Report for the Triennium 1976–1978*, the Schools Commission examined the implementation of the policies and programs proposed by the Interim Committee.[4] It has become evident that several major problems were encountered in carrying out these recommendations. Some of the problems would be inherent in any program of planned educational change. As Porter has pointed out, policy-makers must give attention to the reality that both personal needs and organizational requirements equally affect the process of change.[5] This means that political and structural protection of innovation must be built into any program attempting change in education. This was not done as effectively as it could have been in some of the Schools Commission's programs. Good relations between government and non-government education authorities and personnel in the States, and the agents of the Schools Commission were not necessarily ensured by the procedures developed, and the fact that Australian education operated in an ongoing political system meant that some difficulties were bound to arise. Some of the more specific problems are discussed below.

*Rises in teachers' salaries.* The salary levels of teachers increased by 82 per cent in the period 1971–74 at a rate roughly equivalent to that of average male wage increases.[6] There were major salary awards at approximately 18-month intervals in all States during this period. Since salary costs constituted 80 per cent of recurrent expenditure in education[7], this restricted the number of options for which recurrent resources could be used. The number of possible extra staff was itself restricted by the increased salary costs and by the fact that teachers with high professional qualifications and longer experience constituted an increasing proportion of the total teaching force.

Since 1974, teachers' salaries have stabilized, with no major awards or variations other than those associated with national wage indexation. However, salary costs continue to account for the major proportion of recurrent resources used in all programs, even with cost supplementation, as the growth rate in the total funds available has been restricted.

*Inflated building costs.* Most capital expenditure on schools in the decade to 1973–74 went to accommodate an expanding and mobile population. A huge backlog of needs for the improvement and upgrading of facilities, that could not be met in a triennium, had been built up over the earlier years. Emergency increases in funds voted for 1974–75 were not enough to offset the growing proportion of state funds needed for new places rather than improvement, and less than an estimated one-third of all funds available in 1974–75 were devoted to upgrading.

In the five years 1969–70 to 1974–75, building costs had escalated in all States. By 1975, for each $1.00 spent on educational buildings in 1969, $1.75 was required to purchase the same facilities.[8] Although a supplementation provision was attached to capital grants from the Federal Government, in so far as the state government and Catholic systems were not able to contribute their full share of the rising costs, facilities completed necessarily diminished proportionately. Because of this, the hoped for improvement in the physical conditions of learning for Australian children has not been as marked as it might have been if full supplementation could have been found.

Inflation, in general, has inhibited progress towards achieving the original aims. The primary reason has been, of course, that it has eaten into the real value of additional funds, thereby reducing the effort that could be put into the improvement of facilities. Consequently, the expected level of improvement in sub-standard school buildings could not possibly eventuate in anything like the planned time. A second and less tangible effect of inflation has been that it has distracted attention away from the needs of education as a political issue and concentrated it on more readily recognized economic issues.[9]

These two facets of the effects of inflation have contributed to a backlash against high levels of educational funding. The qualitative goals and outcomes of the Schools Commission programs are not easily measured, and as inflation has inhibited improvement in levels of physical provision which can be measured, some sections of the community have expressed disquiet at the lack of tangible results for the money expended, and have favoured concentration by the Government on the eradication of inflation rather than on programs from which they can see little measurable benefit. Concern with the problems of inflation resulted in the postponement of triennial funding in the 1975–76 budget, and has subsequently put beyond possibility the achievement of the initial capital expenditure programs of the Schools Commission by the target date. The potential for educational development during the next half decade has obviously been seriously diminished.

*Federal-state relations.* In recent years there has been a major shift in control over education, with administrative responsibility remaining with the States but financial responsibility being increasingly assumed by the Commonwealth through increased grants to the States, both under the general purpose vote and under Section 96 of the Constitution. This tendency was accelerated by the programs of the Whitlam Government in the years 1972–1975, which in effect amounted to the development of a nation-wide educational plan. Through the establishment of specific purpose programs of financial assistance, the Federal Government has become a primary decision-maker in the field of education. However, while the Karmel programs may have resulted in the States losing some independence in the making of broad policy for their respective systems, they have also expanded the resources, opportunities and possible effectiveness of some state activities in a relatively non-prescriptive manner.

The major problem which arises from a situation where policy-making and administrative responsibilities are dispersed between federal, state and non-government authorities and institutions is that the complexity of the provisioning arrangements may lead to a distortion between educational aims and their realization. The Schools Commission programs have had two major aims, first, to augment funds available to the States for schooling in order to raise the level of resources available, and second, to support specific developments considered nationally important. However, the influence of these programs on schools has been limited by three factors:

1 Federal funds amount to approximately one-fifth of total expenditure on schools by governments, the balance being provided from the general revenue of the States.

2 The Commission has no executive mandate outside the limits of financial accounting for expenditure, and has to rely on other educational authorities to implement programs.

3 Because the Commission is a statutory authority established to advise the Federal Minister, the implementation of its programs must depend on political decisions at the federal, as well as state, level of government.[10]

It was evident that the States did not need necessarily to expend Schools Commission funds in the spirit of the Commission's recommendations. For example, in some States, there has been some questioning as to whether General Buildings and Recurrent Grants were spent where the needs were greatest. In specific purpose programs which have required co-operation between state and federal authorities, the amount of red tape to be dealt with has been a source of complaint, for example, during the early stages of the Teacher Development Program. This has also been the case in the implementation of the General Buildings Program, where state departments have strongly established lines of authority and responsibility and have not welcomed any notion of the isolation of federal funds or the suggestion that they should be used according to criteria other than those already determined. State Governments politically opposed to the Federal Government have been tempted to magnify problems and use resources differently from the ways intended. Accounting procedures, in general, have been rather poor, and it has been difficult to tell how the States are using the allocated resources. This has been especially true of the General Recurrent Program.

Of course, the original objectives of a program were not only at risk of being distorted at the state and system levels, they also had to pass intact through the Federal Government's decision-making processes. An early example of how aims were changed at this level was the decision forced on the Labor Government by a hostile Senate in 1973 to maintain a certain level of per capita recurrent support for Category 1 and 2 independent schools, in spite of the Government's intention to stop such aid to these schools immediately and the Karmel report's recommendation to phase it out gradually.

In general, the division of responsibility between Commonwealth and State Governments became no longer clear. Nevertheless, with the establishment of the Commission there has been a shift of political accountability for education to the Federal Government while the States have remained responsible for most of the day-to-day operation of their school systems and for the allocation of most of the federal money they received.

*The change of government in 1975.* The previously mentioned problems in translating the Karmel ideals into educational practice were minor in comparison with the changes which resulted from a change of government in late 1975. The Schools Commission created out of the original Interim Committee had produced its *Report for the Triennium 1976–1978* in June 1975. Because of the adverse economic conditions of the time, the then Labor Government decided to treat 1976 as a year outside the normal triennial progression, which was to be resumed at a later stage. The new Coalition Government decided to stop triennial funding altogether, replacing it by a system of 'rolling' triennia. This meant that, as each year of a triennium was completed, plans for the following two years were to be reviewed and revised and initial proposals made for the next triennium. The Commission, in its *Report: Rolling Triennium 1977–79* suggested that this might lead to unsettling short-term arrangements.[11] Unless minimum levels of growth were guaranteed over the whole of the period this policy would be patently detrimental to long-term planning and would negate the gains in stability which the introduction of triennial funding arrangements had brought to the schools area.

The new coalition Government was committed to decreasing the use of specific purpose grants and increasing the general revenue to the States. This 'new federalism' meant that the Commonwealth Government sought to withdraw as much as possible from financial responsibility for schooling, which was to be seen more as a responsibility of the States. It did not imply, however, that the Government wished to withdraw from the financing of non-government schools, to which the Liberal Party had a traditional commitment. The platform on which it was elected foreshadowed the provision of per capita grants for recurrent purposes to all independent schools as a proportion of the cost of education at a government school. The redemptive egalitarianism of the previous few years was not part of the Liberal philosophy. The first step towards this goal has been taken by the instruction, in the most recent set of guidelines to the Commission, to increase per capita grants to the top two categories of independent schools as a first step towards raising these grants to 20 per cent of the running cost of educating a child in a state school.[12] Additional capital funds of $3 million were also to be granted for building non-government schools in growth areas.

These instructions would seem to have two major consequences. One is the apparent erosion of the 'needs' principle established by the Karmel Committee and continued by the Schools Commission. The other is that in a situation of no real growth, it foreshadows a reallocation of funds from state to independent schools. This would appear to be in keeping with the general intentions of the present Government as mentioned above. However, it would not be in keeping with the Schools Commission aims of 'topping up' funds available to both state and independent schools on the basis of need in order that overall a much higher level of provision might be attained.

Under a direct application of the 'needs' approach some reallocation of funds from government to non-government schools would be necessary in any case. This has arisen because, on the one hand, the States, rather than merely

191

maintaining their existing expenditures on education, have increased them, thus bringing state schools closer to target levels. On the other hand, Catholic parochial schools have fallen further behind, partly because of a fall in private inputs, and partly because of the employment of an increased proportion of non-religious staff. In a no-growth situation, this makes some transfer of funds necessary and reopens the question of the basis of aid to non-government schools in general. However, the decision of the Federal Government to raise the level of per capita grants to the top two categories of independent schools, already well above target levels of provision, would seem unrelated to the principle of needs, and made no contribution to easing the position of the Catholic parochial schools.

In the guidelines for the 1977–79 rolling triennium, the Government ordered that expenditure should be restricted to two per cent growth for each year of the triennium.[13] In the most recent guidelines applying to the remaining two years, it has prescribed a situation of no growth at all.[14] Apart from the uncertainty generated by such changes the role of the Commission has become restricted to determining a reasonable allocation of a limited amount of funds for one or two years in advance. In its 1977–79 report, the Commission expressed a concern that maintaining existing standards while also introducing other initiatives was too ambitious within the funds allocated.[15]

The major effect on the operation of the Commission and the implementation of its ideals stems from the introduction of the system of guidelines itself. By presenting guidelines to the Commission before it makes its evaluations and deliberations and presents its reports, the Government influences and restricts what the Commission can do. The opportunities for open planning and for consideration of wide-ranging submissions are severely limited. Rather than operating as an independent assessor of needs and recommending to the Government what ought to be done to meet those needs, the Commission must of necessity merely act as a distributor of prescribed funds in a semi-prescribed manner within limits outside its control. This restricts its competence and severely comprises its independence. Policy recommendations are not advanced by the Commission but decisions are made by the Government before the Commission has been able to assess any evidence on which they could be based. An example has been the decision by the Government to limit funds available to the Development and Special Projects Programs.[16] This decision was handed down to the Commission in a set of guidelines without explanation rather than being a considered decision taken by the Commission itself within the framework of its consistent set of values and its priorities for achieving its goals.

By providing the Commission with guidelines in this manner the Government avoids the political odium of publicly rejecting the recommendations of an independent, expert body. Instead, it tells the body what it can recommend and receives the sort of report it wants. As the policies of the Government do not necessarily concur with the priorities of the

Commission based on perceived needs, this is the most insurmountable obstacle yet encountered in the implementation of the Karmel ideals. The most recent report of the Commission, outlining its proposals for the triennium 1979–81, plans for a five per cent growth in expenditure in real terms in 1979 compared to 1978, a further four per cent growth in 1980 and 3.3 per cent growth in 1981. These recommendations have been made in advance of the issuing of firm guidelines for 1979, and it will consequently be of interest to observe governmental reactions.

## Evaluation

One of the Schools Commission's objectives has been to provide for the evaluation of the effects of its programs in order to obtain evidence of how best to proceed towards its defined goals.[17] Formal evaluations by independent researchers are being carried out for the specific purpose programs, in particular, the Disadvantaged Schools, Libraries, Services and Development, and Special Projects Programs. While none of these evaluation studies have been published there is enough evaluative material available to give a sound impression of how the programs have been operating. It would also be useful to evaluate the effects of some of the Schools Commission programs in terms of such things as amounts of money and class sizes.

However, a possibly more valuable approach to evaluating the effects of the Schools Commission programs would be to address oneself to the values and conditions of schooling the original Karmel report sought to promote and to ask oneself to what extent the programs had contributed towards these aims. As we have seen, the Karmel Committee's programs were formulated within a framework of values, chief amongst which were equality, diversity and devolution of responsibility. The Committee also expressed adherence to the principles of private and public schooling, community involvement, the special purposes of schools and recurrent education.

## EQUALITY

In its attempts to promote equality, the Commission's programs aimed at improvement and equalization of the quality and general standards of all schools. It is now doubtful whether these aims can be achieved in full. While improvements have been made in the standards of buildings and facilities and the recurrent resource levels of schools, inflation and other problems have made progress towards acceptable levels for schools extremely slow. Also disparities in educational provision can still be observed between and within States and systems. For example, it was estimated that, in spite of Schools Commission funds and the previous Science Facilities Program, approximately 15 per cent of government schools were still without adequate science laboratories in late 1975, when programs in this area were terminated.

Capital funds associated with the Disadvantaged Schools Program have been less effective than hoped, largely because of difficulties in integrating these funds with other resources, including the General Building Grants, and with the programs adopted by the school under the Recurrent Grants section of the program.

While it has become apparent that funds from the Schools Commission have not been able to eliminate inequalities in physical conditions and staffing, it could also be asked whether the programs have contributed towards a reduction in differences in educational outcomes between schools of different types and between different social, economic, geographical and ethnic groups.

It would not perhaps be surprising that the Schools Commission's programs could not be seen to have greatly altered levels of achievement or differences in achievement between social groups. The Interim Committee and the Commission were asked to make recommendations based on the needs of schools and of disadvantaged groups and it formulated its programs accordingly. For example, the Disadvantaged Schools Program was aimed at improving the standards of provision and resource use in schools in disadvantaged areas. Levels of disadvantage were initially assessed using socio-economic characteristics of the school's catchment area rather than levels of achievement of pupils within the school itself. Thus the thrust of the program was not to raise achievement levels in low-achieving schools, but to provide compensatory resources to schools whose pupils came from backgrounds not conducive to academic achievement in order to equalize the physical conditions that might lead to success. In general, the recommended improvements in facilities and resource use of the Schools Commission's programs could be said to aim at a necessary, though not by any means a sufficient, condition for improvement in the quality and equality of educational outcomes.

## DIVERSITY

The stated value of diversity would be less dependent for its realization on large amounts of money and more on changes in attitudes than are those of quality and equality of provision, and the Schools Commission's programs must be seen to have contributed to some extent to the promotion of changing attitudes. The Special Projects (Innovations), Disadvantaged Schools, and Teacher Development Programs, in particular, have led to an awareness and discussion among teachers and administrators of different approaches and their effectiveness. While the Special Projects Program has accounted for only a relatively small amount of money and could only affect a limited number of teachers and students in a relatively few schools, in many situations, for the first time, it became possible for people with new ideas to try these out. The chief effect of this has been the creation of a climate in which change and experimentation were seen to be desirable and possible, and this effect has spread to schools and systems not themselves affected by particular programs funded by the Commission.

Response to the Special Projects (Innovations) Program has been enthusiastic. By mid-1977 approximately 2000 projects had been funded since the inception of the program and it had only been possible to fund less than a third of all applications received. As this program has been controlled by the Schools Commission itself with less requirement for co-operation from authorities in the States, there has been less possibility of conflict and distortion of aims than there has been in many other programs. However, this autonomy has possibly been irritating to state authorities, as it has sometimes fostered developments which have run counter to established practice and, more importantly, because it has potentially shifted some of the influence over future trends in educational practice outside the scope of the state authorities' policy-making machinery.[18] The extent to which this has occurred has not yet been documented.

## DEVOLUTION OF RESPONSIBILITY

Devolution of responsibility to regional and school levels could only be encouraged and implemented effectively at the state level. Over the last few years, all States have been actively involved in regionalizing their administration. Schools Commission's programs, such as the Teacher Development Program which has a regional basis, have supported and contributed to this trend. Decision-making at the school level has also been encouraged by the Disadvantaged Schools and the Special Projects Programs in which proposals must be put up from the school community itself.

Perhaps the most important program for the encouragement of devolution of responsibility to the school level has been the Disadvantaged Schools Program, which in some States has affected schools catering for up to a quarter of the school population. It is clear that the opportunities provided by this program have greatly affected the ideas and practices of the teachers involved and that this effect has spread with the transfer of teachers to other schools not affected by the program. Like the Special Projects and Teacher Development Programs, the Disadvantaged Schools Program would appear to have encouraged a re-evaluation of approaches and goals among teachers and has improved morale considerably. It has also encouraged a willingness to make decisions and take responsibility at a local level. The degree to which these school-based initiatives have been encouraged has varied between States and once again the degree of autonomy actually granted to schools has varied according to the policies and preferences of the State Education Departments and Catholic education authorities.

With the change of government in 1975 and the revived stress on state initiatives, State Education Departments have been given a strengthened role in the administration of all programs. The State Minister for Education, has, in one State at least, assumed more direct control over the criteria for declaring schools disadvantaged and over which schools are actually listed, as well as over the specific projects funded. This has led to quite marked changes of direction. The Schools Commission recommendation that a small percentage of general recurrent funds be allocated directly to all schools for deployment as the schools see fit does not appear to have been put into practice in most States. Thus, while it would seem that a more favourable climate for devolution of responsibility to individual schools has been created by the Schools Commission programs, progress towards it, because of state and federal political factors, has been somewhat retarded.

The first and most obvious effect of the Karmel recommendations was to depoliticize the educational debate, shifting its focus from the long-standing controversy over state aid to the more basic questions of equality and need. As has been suggested elsewhere, the Schools Commission has started to become the major embodiment of a new consensus.[19] It has managed to work towards an equitable scheme of provision for all schools according to need rather than deteriorating into a battleground for various sectional interests. It created a framework within which different groups could discuss the progress of education rather than merely resorting to raising conflicting opinions. It has now been generally accepted that need was a sound basis for funding, that it was possible to assess need, and that the judgments of a group of experts open to public scrutiny provided an effective way to undertake educational planning.

The second great achievement of the Karmel programs has been that they energized and improved the quality of the debate on education in Australia. The Commission has increased the availability of information concerning educational matters, thereby furthering well-informed discussion on educational issues. Evidence relevant to decision-making has been made more readily available and more people have been offered the possibility of becoming involved in the decision-making process through participation in particular projects and by the devolution of responsibility.

Related to this have been the increased possibilities for professional activity that the Karmel programs have offered teachers and others involved in the schooling process. As well, parents have been given enhanced opportunities for increased knowledge and in some cases involvement in activities. These developments have added to the confidence and enthusiasm of teachers, with consequent effects on morale, particularly in schools where morale was previously low. This rejuvenating effect on the teaching profession should have far-reaching ramifications that could only work to the benefit of pupils in all schools.

A third major effect has been in contributing to a change in the Australian view of the social function of education. Until recent years a narrowly academic, meritocratic model of schooling was widely held to be the norm. The chief aim of the school system was seen as providing opportunities for those who would become leaders in society and in various walks of life to develop their talents to full capacity. According to the basic assumptions underlying this view, inequalities in provision, treatment or outcomes did not matter as long as those who had the talent were not prevented from achieving what they were capable of by extrinsic factors.

The revised and more egalitarian view of the social function of education gave everybody an equal claim on resources, treatment and possibilities for various kinds of success. Education was seen as involving the development of every individual, not just those marked out for social or occupational leadership. Those with intrinsic or extrinsic barriers to the development of competence, in this view, deserved more rather than less of the community's help and support. This changed perception of the educational endeavour both influenced the Karmel report's recommendations and was influenced by the Karmel report. The report became the embodiment and the definitive statement of this new view of the social function of education, and in fact was the first national statement of what schooling should be that had been produced in this country. Educators were provided with a philosophical and theoretical framework within which to discuss the aims and outcomes of schooling in Australia, and this provided them with a sense of purpose previously lacking in this field.

## SOME PERCEIVED SHORTCOMINGS

The Schools Commission in its first major report emphasized the importance of ensuring that all children should achieve a basic plateau of competence to enable them to exercise the options open to a citizen in society.[20] While disparities between different social groups in educational achievement were acknowledged, there was scant recognition that problems of some consequence would be found to exist in Australian schools. At the same time as the Commission was preparing its first report, the House of Representatives Select Committee on Specific Learning Difficulties was conducting an inquiry into important aspects of the work of the schools. This Committee, sensing that a problem existed, commissioned the ACER to undertake an investigation into student performance in the areas of literacy and numeracy. Using the findings of this research study[21], and from the evidence submitted to it, the Select Committee prepared a significant report — *Learning Difficulties in Children and Adults.*[22]

The evidence from the study of literacy and numeracy has indicated that, while in general the work of the schools should not be disparaged, a significant proportion of Australian students were not achieving an acceptable level of basic competence in the skills of reading, writing and number work before they reached the minimum school-leaving age. The report of the Select Committee drew attention to deficiencies in educational practice and in the preparation of teachers which meant that children with learning handicaps did not receive the help that they needed.

A further inquiry into education conducted by the Poverty Commission and the research studies sponsored by this inquiry have drawn attention to difficulties faced by many young people during their later years of schooling and on their emergence into the workforce.[23] This inquiry also demonstrated that school retention rates were lower for Aboriginal students, for Southern

197

European migrants, for the children of lower socio-economic groups and for children in rural areas than for other Australians. The ACER study of literacy and numeracy found that similar differences applied in the achievement of basic skills.

The reports of the Schools Commission have recognized these groups as disadvantaged in our society but they would not appear to have acknowledged the nature and extent of the problems encountered by these groups. Moreover, relatively little of the funds and the effort of the Commission has been directed towards the improvement of the quality of teaching and the increasing of the effectiveness of student learning of these and other disadvantaged and handicapped groups in the area of the basic skills.

In this context, the questions to be asked are not whether these above-mentioned groups have been able to achieve educational outcomes commensurate with those of other social groups, but whether they have been enabled to reach the level of competence necessary to operate effectively in society and whether their educational progress beyond that level has been in accordance with their needs and preferred role in society. Further questions to be asked concern whether the members of disadvantaged groups are able to find employment and achieve economic independence or whether they are destined to years of aimlessness and life without a recognized role in society.

The evidence from these inquiries raises further questions about educational provision extending beyond the years of schooling into the area of post-school and recurrent education. While the principle of recurrent education was endorsed by the Interim Committee as being one of the values that influenced its decisions, none of the Schools Commission's recommendations have dealt with this area or with the problems of school-leavers. Indeed it may be asked whether they recognized the existence of such problems of critical importance to Australian society. It would appear evident that if one body or Commission were permitted to establish priorities and rationalize educational developments across the whole of Australia, then the dangers of critical problems being ignored would be too great. A diversity of approaches would seem essential for the welfare of the nation.

## THE FUTURE

In spite of these shortcomings, the Karmel and Schools Commission reports and programs have had a far greater and more valuable effect on schooling in Australia than any analysis of physical provision and particular programs would indicate. The general rejuvenation and improvement in quality of the educational debate; the vastly improved morale, enthusiasm and involvement of those concerned in the schooling process; the increased willingness to grapple with basic philosophical questions about the functions of schooling; and the more positive climate for educational activity must all be attributed to some extent to the effects of these reports.

Nevertheless, as has been seen, the functioning of the Schools Commission as an independent assessor of needs and adviser to the Commonwealth Government has been severely curtailed and is likely to be more so in the future. This is largely because of the imposition of guidelines which limit the competence of the Commission to fulfil either of these functions. Instead, it must carry out the instructions of the Government within a predetermined framework. In this role it cannot hope to have the impact on educational thought and practice it originally had, and must diminish in importance in the Australian educational context.

The introduction of the 'rolling triennium' may exacerbate this trend as it virtually limits the Commission to making decisions and calculations for one year ahead. This is a time-consuming process and may prevent the Commission from studying and reporting on long-term trends and educational issues. It cannot fulfil an important role in the generation of educational thought if it has to leave important questions unanswered.

There are also likely to be further changes in the composition of the Commission to include direct representation of various educational interest groups. This could have the effect of diminishing its status as an independent, expert body and reduce it to a bargaining ground for competing groups in the allocation of scarce resources.

A closer examination of some of the recent guidelines of the Commonwealth Government reveals further patterns for the future. The foreshadowed concentration on funding non-government schools and erosion of the needs principle by linking per capita grants to costs in government schools has already been mentioned. The guidelines also indicate a stronger role for state government authorities. The Commission is required to consult with them in developing its own recommendations and state authorities are to have strengthened responsibility for the administration of all programs. Growth in federal funding is to be non-existent in 1978 and the indicative planning guidelines will restrict it to one per cent for the following two years.[24] It is suggested that savings of about $4 million be made on the programs for Services and Development and Special Projects, thus restricting these programs significantly.[25]

These guidelines indicate directions for the future which run counter to the goals of the Schools Commission so far. They foreshadow a gradual diminution of the still limited federal financial involvement in state schools. They indicate the presence of a conservative backlash against spending on the promotion of change and diversity in education. While the Special Projects and Teacher Development Programs only involve a tiny proportion of total funds they have been of some importance in broadening horizons and indicating possibilities for future action to cope with changing social perceptions concerning education. Together with erosion of the needs principle, the destruction of a favourable climate for diversity and experimentation may herald a return to traditional views of what schooling is for.

In general, the major effect of the guidelines imposed on the Schools

Commission has been to destroy the carefully built-up consensus on education and make educational debate once more a political game. Because allocation of funds and continuation of programs is once again based on the policy decisions of political parties rather than the deliberations of independent commissioners, debate is beginning once again to split along party and interest group lines and the main issue is once again division of the cake rather than more basic questions of need and equity. Consequently the State-aid and State-rights issues may once again dominate the centre stage in educational discussion in Australia.

## Notes

1 Australia. (1973). *Schools in Australia. Report of the Interim Committee for the Australian Schools Commission.* (Chairman, P. Karmel). Canberra: AGPS.
2 ibid.: 126.
3 ibid.: 129. Mr A. W. Jones, the Director-General of Education in South Australia and a member of the Interim Committee for the Australian Schools Commission, may well have influenced both the Commission and the Australian Education Council in their support for a national curriculum development centre. After a visit to Britain in late 1972 he stated:
'I was impressed with the work done in curriculum by the Schools Council in England, so much so that I believe we should copy it on a national basis using the Australian Science Education Project as a basic structure.'
See Jones, A.W. (1973). *Report on Overseas Visit, 2 October, 1972 to 7 January, 1973.* Adelaide: Department of Education.
4 Australia. Schools Commission. (1975). *Report for the Triennium 1976–1978.* (Chairman, K. McKinnon). Canberra: AGPS.
5 Porter, P. (1977). 'Models of Fostering Change in Educational Systems: A Comparative Perspective', *Australian Journal of Education,* **20** (3): 241–259.
6 Australia. Schools Commission. op. cit.: 265.
7 ibid.: 15.
8 ibid.: 204.
9 See Tomlinson, D. (1977). *The Liberal Party. Politics and Education Policy. Australian Education Review No. 8.* p. 66. Hawthorn: ACER.
10 Australia. Schools Commission. op. cit.: 3.
11 Australia. Schools Commission. (1976). *Report: Rolling Triennium 1977–79.* (Chairman, K. McKinnon). Canberra: AGPS, p.3.
12 Australia. Schools Commission. (1977). *Rolling Triennium 1978–80: Report for 1978.* (Chairman, K. McKinnon). Canberra: AGPS, pp.27–28. Appendix A.
13 Australia. Schools Commission. (1976). loc. cit.
14 Australia. Schools Commission. (1977). loc. cit.
15 Australia. Schools Commission. (1976). loc. cit.
16 Australia. Schools Commission. (1977). loc. cit.
17 Australia. Schools Commission. (1975). op. cit.: 25.
18 See Anderson, D.S. (1976). 'Labor's Achievements in Australian Education 1972–1975'. In *New Directions in Australian Education.* Melbourne: Australian College of Education. p.43.
19 ibid.: 36.
20 See Australia. Schools Commission. (1975). op. cit.: 7.
21 See Keeves, J.P. and Bourke, S.F. (1976). *Australian Studies in School Performance. Volume I. Literacy and Numeracy in Australian Schools: A First Report.* Canberra: AGPS.
Bourke, S.F. and Lewis, R. (1976). *Australian Studies in School Performance. Volume II. Literacy and Numeracy in Australian Schools: Item Report.* Canberra: AGPS.
Bourke, S.F. and Keeves, J.P. (1977). *Australian Studies in School Performance. Volume III. The Mastery of Literacy and Numeracy: Final Report.* Canberra: AGPS.
22 Australia. (1976). *Learning Difficulties in Children and Adults. Report of the House of Representatives Select Committee on Specific Learning Difficulties.* (Chairman, A. G. Cadman). Canberra: AGPS.

23 Australia. Commission of Inquiry into Poverty. (1976). *Poverty and Education in Australia. Fifth Main Report.* (Commissioner, R. T. Fitzgerald). Canberra: AGPS.
and
Wright, A.F. and Headlam, F. (1976). *Youth Needs and Public Policies.* Melbourne: Department of Youth, Sport and Recreation, Victoria.
24 *Guidelines for Education Commissions 1978–1980. Rolling Triennium.* Statement by the Minister for Education, Senator the Honorable J.L. Carrick. Duplicated. June 1977. Clause 4.
25 ibid., Clause 6.

# 12.  The McKinnon Prescription*

## A Critique of the Schools Commission's Future Society and School Curriculum

Merv Turner

Within weeks of its electoral victory late in 1972, the Whitlam Labor Government set up the Interim Committee for the Schools Commission. The Commission proper was established as a statutory authority in December 1973. Three major general reports have been published to date. The Karmel report, *Schools in Australia*[1], was issued in May 1973, and had been prepared as a matter of urgency in order to set the policy guidelines for a massive increase in federal financial support of education in Australia at primary and secondary school level. The recommendations, supported almost entirely by the Government, became the basis for funding in the 1974 and 1975 calendar years.

The first triennial report of the Commission (for the triennium 1976–78) was tabled in June 1975.[2] It was immediately caught up in the aggravated economic problems of the Whitlam Government. The report was 'received but not accepted'. Proposed expenditure for 1976 was reduced to a level sufficient to sustain prior levels of recurrent expenditure but which would limit new initiatives and capital expenditure. The Government called for revised recommendations by March 1976, for a 1977–78 triennium which would be within financial guidelines to be framed by the Government.

The political defeat of Labor led to a delay in the framing of the financial guidelines and these were eventually handed to the Commission by the Fraser Government in May 1976. These guidelines set a two per cent limit to the annual growth of expenditure (in real terms, calculated on a 1976 base), with a commitment to 1977 but with only a forward planning concession for 1978 and 1979; that is, a 'rolling' triennium was instituted. The report for the rolling triennium 1977–79 was issued in July 1976.[3]

Until 1975, the Schools Commission's programs needed no defence and drew very few critics. The popular acclaim accorded the Karmel report reflected the significance of education as a (the ?) major electoral issue which brought the Labor Government to power in 1972 and to the period of 'heady' days following the election, when expenditures created the impression that the problems (real or imagined) under which education had laboured for so long

---

*This title was used previously for an article published in *Arena*, **40**:101–111. That article forms the basis of this chapter, which also takes into account a later report of the Schools Commission. 'McKinnon' refers to Kenneth McKinnon, first chairman of the Commission.

were to be wiped away. Of course, this popular acclaim has to be properly interpreted. Despite the electoral significance of education in 1972, the subsequent acclaim was limited largely to the 'professionals' — the administrators, educational academics, teachers, and leaders of certain groups of ancillary parents — who appeared united principally by a common faith in the power of money but who were divided in their focus on what constituted Australia's educational ills. To a significant degree, dogmatic and sycophantic expertism prevailed and the educational bureaucracies and privatized intermediaries flourished.

However, some doubts — both financial and educational — must have penetrated the Commission prior to its first triennial report since, although it recommended the expenditure of an unprecedented $2000 million, this represented a contraction on the growth rates projected by the Karmel report, and since it also clearly acknowledged, even if it failed to resolve, some of the more serious criticisms that had been raised by the few against the Karmel report.

By the time of the Fraser Government guidelines, the public acclaim was muted and defence of the Commission had shrunk to more limited proportions. Defenders included some Directors-General of Education, the leadership of some parental and teacher organizations, and the Commission itself through its Chairman, Kenneth McKinnon. By the time of the federal elections of December 1977, the Commission was 'invisible' and education was no longer an electoral issue. To be realistic, it was not because the critics had been influential but rather because the economic depression had converted education from a necessary to a desirable commodity. 'Do you think Labor might give some more to education?' became the occasional and half-hearted pre-electoral question along the scholarly corridors.

It might be thought that this episode was but a spasm and that education has now returned to its prior style and trends. The Commission, however, continues to spend very large sums of money (in excess of $500 million in 1977) even if subject to constraint. Perhaps more importantly than this, but partly because of it, the Commission remains an organization of considerable influence in encapsulating and promoting a still professionally popular view of the desirable directions of educational change. For this reason alone, its pronouncements, programs, and policies deserve continuing critical attention.

## REACTIONS TO THE KARMEL REPORT

Musgrave[4], Crittenden[5], and White[6] provided significant criticisms of the Karmel report. These critiques are all included in this volume.

Musgrave characterized the report as being 'marked by an uncertain divine intention and somewhat weak in theology' — a reference to its 'there-is-something-in-it-for-everyone' financial largesse and its apparent lack of any clearly formulated process to make a real difference in education. Crittenden pointed out 'the piecemeal character of its educational theory', the fact that it

203

tried 'to find a place for most of the conflicting interpretations of the role of the school at the present time', and argued that it was uncritical, misleading, confused or supportive of contradictory positions.

Both Musgrave and Crittenden, however, appeared to be co-operative. Musgrave made a number of suggestions from his sociological perspective calculated to make 'those concerned ... more willing and able to proceed further along the Fabian path of educational change'. Crittenden, from his philosophical perspective, urged that appropriate analysis of 'important aspects of its statements of theory (which is) vague or ambiguous or inconsistent' could lead to 'a more satisfactory synthesis', but he acknowledged that it would be impossible 'to unite the conflicting claims ... in a perfectly harmonious system'. They both forgot that a major implicit, and increasingly explicit, intellectual project in the socio-cultural domain is in fact to attempt to unite conflicting claims in a perfectly harmonious system.[7]

Musgrave and Crittenden constructed their criticisms within a sectoral evolutionary model of social change. Musgrave spends some little space establishing a particular part of the history of the extension of intellectual participation and control in government and administration. He recognizes the Schools Commission as a very advanced modern type — 'expert bodies with considerable independence who themselves undertake all three processes ("investigate, legislate, administer") of the Benthamite prescription for sectoral social change'. The three functions have tended to come together only in the period since the 1950s in response to 'the urgencies of the pathologies of capitalist society'.

Their critiques are essentially those (the one sociological, the other philosophical) of the internal consistency of the Karmel report. Neither critic provides an account, or even a hint, as to why the 'social pathologies of capitalist society' have come into existence or become more visible, nor why they are regarded as urgent, nor who regards them as urgent and for what reasons, nor why a Schools Commission was seen as providing the possibility of a means of amelioration.

White's critique had a different basis. He did not take for granted much that remained unexamined by Musgrave and Crittenden. Thus, for example, he provided an account of the Karmel report in the context of the expression in it of historical developments linking society, culture and education within capitalist development in general, and in Australia in particular.

## THE SCHOOLS COMMISSION REPORTS: THE FUTURE SOCIETY

The first triennial report of the Schools Commission is important to those who are concerned to extend their criticism of the Karmel report for several reasons. For example, the first triennial report did acknowledge criticism and attempt to reconcile it to the themes of the Karmel report. A typical instance is provided by the concept of community. Both White and Crittenden pointed out that the Karmel report had assumed the nature and existence of communities that do not, in fact, exist in reality. The first triennial report apparently responds to this by acknowledging that 'no ready made close community of any size or variety exists in industrial societies'.[8] Yet in many later parts of the report the word continues to be used as if such communities do exist (as well as being used in other ways).[9]

The first triennial report is more important, however, for its attempt to develop a more coherent picture of two things — the future society and the future school curriculum — than did the Karmel report. It is also apparent that the curriculum is not only ameliorative of present problems but is also at least a partial means towards the end of the future society.

By paraphrasing (and often almost directly quoting) parts of the report, one can characterize the future society as follows:

The future society will be a sophisticated industrial society in which access to the ideas and forms of higher and further study will remain closely allied with power, income, and status. The job or occupation will become more vital to every individual and more dependent on education since, among other things, unskilled occupations will continue to decline, along with an increase in the number of jobs requiring higher degrees of literacy and mathematical skill. Paid work will play a more important part in the life experience of women and, in complementary fashion, men will increasingly share domestic and childrearing responsibilities.

This increasing sophistication will produce tendencies to further fragmentation of society and increased frequency of occurrence of social problems. However, these will be overcome since education will also produce a respect for persons, an obligation to take the wishes and interests of others into account, and a more widely dispersed capacity to reason one's way through personal and social issues, which, together with participation with others in the give and take of collective decision-making, will enable ordinary citizens to consider alternatives and evidence and to accept the provisional rather than the absolute nature of social arrangements and solutions.

Important among these provisional matters or contingencies facing people in industrial societies will be the nature of the job. There will be increased provision of vocational training throughout working life aimed either at upgrading skills of the workers in a particular industry as part of a scheme to modernize that industry, or to increase inter-industry mobility.

In all of this, the society will be an equal society since students at senior secondary levels and beyond would be representative of girls and boys, of city and country, of various ethnic backgrounds, religious affiliations and the like in the identical proportions to those represented in the population at large. Thus there will be no categorical attribute of a person that will be differentially associated with the denial of access to power, income, and status.

This equal representation in its institutions will arise because society will value all its children, and institutions, most importantly the schools, will positively raise the aspirations of children from any of those categories now generally less powerful, or with lower incomes, or with reduced status within the existing social structure, and by encouragement sustain and recognize the authenticity of the cultures of these social groups.

Such sustained cultures, however, will not be necessarily part of the mainstream culture. It will be the total society which will arrange the redemption of those whose own culture puts them on the margins of the mainstream culture, at the same time recognizing and sustaining that disadvantaging but authentic culture.

Similarly, society's institutions must be viewed in analogous ways to its individual members. They must not become museums (cultural or social non-functional or dys-functional artefacts of earlier times), but must be given that constant re-appraisal and refurbishment that will make them highly adaptive to changing circumstances.

More could be added. But enough!

It is clear that this future society is our present society projected into the future and made more internally secure. Schools are used for the direct social end of providing that security, through training a voluntary but uncritical malleability in all its members at the same time as extending the graded and constantly re-processed work skills required for the expansion of production.

Amplification of some aspects of the model will make this abundantly clear. Consider, for example, equality as it enters the model. Participation in schooling at all levels must be completely representative of all possible sub-groups of the population. Achievement of this, it is asserted, is equivalent to saying all social sub-groups will have equal access to power, incomes, and status. Thus the Commission is on the side of the elimination of inequality. But the Commission says nothing about how power, incomes, and status would be more equally distributed within as well as between social sub-groups. Or, what would be better, of how power, incomes, or status might be eliminated as expressions of significant but fetishized forms of social relationships between people.

Thus the version of equality espoused by the Commission is but a thinly disguised version of meritocracy hopefully to be freed from accusations of racism or male chauvinism or the like by the techniques of compensatory education. Women Aboriginal Prime Ministers, managing directors, and professors are obviously desirable products of the program.

Consider the obligatory respect for persons, their wishes and interests, the give and take of collective decision-making and their alliance with the provisional rather than more absolute nature of social arrangements and solutions. This is clearly a consensual model of acquiescence in social change made palatable by release of restraint on personality. Apparently there will be no persons deserving our disrespect in the future society. All wishes and interests will be good (but, presumably, some will be 'gooder' than others). The separation of respect, wishes, and interests from any concrete situation is at best naive, and at worst suggests deliberate manipulation of people to eliminate any critical response they may otherwise have to other people's wishes or interests and which could represent a reality of exploitation or domination.

Consider the cultural aspect. There will be a mainstream culture — the culture of the total society — in which all will share. In addition, all, or at least many, members of society will share in one of a number of other cultures. The Commission appears to have confused national or ethnic styles — as exemplified, say, in food preferences or dress — with cultural difference. Almost all Western societies now have significant national/ethnic minorities (significantly a consequence of the labour mobility which the Commission accepts as an essential feature of the future society). But, with some limited exceptions, cultural differences expressed between the mainstream and the minorities are minor and residual.

These grounds of culture are everywhere increasingly the same — namely those of Western materialist-ideological culture. Whatever distinguishing significance the artefacts, symbolic forms, and other cultural elements may have had they tend to be either destroyed or to enter the realm of the mainstream market as a new commodity, a new leisure form of pure novelty and momentary significance, and the like. The view that there is but a single culture in Western societies (and probably in all industrial societies) — and which is everywhere the same — is increasingly more valid than the view that such societies are mainly and increasingly multi-cultural. The multi-cultural view, if maintained, seems only to promise a fetishized existence of personal transience amidst immense variety.

Mainstream culture has an enormous capacity to destroy the grounds and fetishize the forms of other genuine cultures (within a history of the territorial extension and internal development of the mainstream). The continuity of another culture thus depends upon the denial of the mainstream. But other genuine cultures are dependent for their continuity on the mainstream because of its destructive capacities. This is a profound contradiction and accounts for the inability of the Commission to handle the problem of Aboriginal education and also explains why, in its own terms, handling the migrant national/ethnic groups is not a problem.

Consider those Aboriginals still in possession of significant elements of a culture different from mainstream culture. The Aboriginal Consultative Group of the Schools Commission was also conscious of the tensions if not the contradiction when it wrote to the Commission:

> We see education as the most important strategy for achieving realistic self-determination for the Aboriginal people of Australia. We do not see education as a method of producing an anglicized Aborigine but rather as an instrument for creating informed human beings with intellectual and technological skills, in harmony with our own cultural values and identity. We wish to be the Aboriginal citizens in a changing Australia.
>
> It would be a tragedy to destroy one of the last remaining people who do not worship material values. Our vision of education is not compatible with overemphasis placed on manpower oriented goals that most Australian people know.

We see the need for a change in education for both the aborigine and non-aborigine, their teachers, and their children; to create an Australia where the values and cultures of both people thrive.

The process of achieving this will require many major changes in direction for your education. It is also ours, but it does not serve us as well as it does you; nor do we completely understand it, but at least we are aware of where it most fails us.[10]

If the Commission's pointing to a pluralist multi-cultural vision extends to Aborigines, the prospects for a genuine Aboriginal cultural recreation are bleak. Rather, there would be a continuing erosion of the Aboriginal cultural remnants until at most some cultural vestigial artefacts would survive; and the Aboriginal people would have joined us in being dominated by mainstream culture. Perhaps corroborees accompanied by didgeridoos will have their modish popularity like highland dancing to bagpipes, square-dancing to a fiddle, or Zorba-dancing to an accordian; and, of course, we can all take part if that is our desire.

The pluralist multi-cultural vision mystifies the contradiction. It appears to be authenticating other cultures when in fact it is destroying them.

## THE SCHOOLS COMMISSION REPORTS: THE FUTURE CURRICULUM

Further aspects of the Commission's view of the future society could be developed, but consideration now turns to the future school curriculum as seen by the Schools Commission in its first triennial report. Views on the curriculum are much more explicit than in the Karmel report although they stand in a direct line of descent from it.

Demands of job skills and the increasing difficulties of survival in a more sophisticated society, according to the Commission, oblige the schools to upgrade literacy and mathematical skills significantly in all children (save for those with severe physical or mental disabilities). The first triennial report, in its only direct reference to a piece of educational research, quotes with approval the American Survival Literacy Study for its conclusion that

a reading age of thirteen years was required to permit reasonable comprehension of the simplest newspaper article, and other studies indicate that the simplest form in which complex material (for example hire-purchase agreements and medical claim forms) can be presented requires a reading age of about fifteen years.[11]

Education must ensure learning outcomes sufficient for independent (?) functioning and occupational choice among all children. Literacy is, however, alternatively described as effective English usage in standard language form. Thus literacy is the acquisition of pure skill devoid of context or cultural reference.

Logic, mathematics, science, art or any of the other ways through which the human race has reflected upon or sought to order understanding ... may be learned and applied in any value framework and should be so learned.[12]

Presumably these too have entered the realm of disembodied or decultured technique.

The old-fashioned meaning of curriculum as a prescriptive selection of knowledge of some substantial and even enduring significance has apparently disappeared into prehistory. The skills of effective English usage and of value-free logico-rational technique are supreme and universal. Cultural knowledge — for example, of those necessitous aspects of human existence and continuity which any culture must handle — is debased to a matter of taste and the word 'taste' is used in a denigrative sense by the Commission. However,

> it is more than a matter of taste whether they become literate or acquire in other fields competencies in life and in the exercise of options in a sophisticated society.[13]

The Commission may be right in matching areas of competence as value-free technical skills with sophistication as the art of quibbling. Unfortunately, the Commission takes sophistication for granted. Those who know Bloom's taxonomy of abstract universalized cognitive skills might regard the Schools Commission promotion of 'skill' as its zenith of significance in Australia.[14]

Further, teachers are invited to turn 'cultural (and other) differences to educational advantage' in this promotion of skill, thus killing two birds with one stone by avoiding conflict with home culture. What is intended here is that where skills dominate and where knowledge, as their vehicle, is only a matter of taste, the teacher may as well use that 'cultural' knowledge with which the school child is familiar. Thus skill outcomes would be assured and at the same time a feeling of confidence would be engendered that the child's disadvantaging 'culture' is valued.

Beyond this the curriculum must be supported by appropriate compensatory actions to the degree that all children should at least reach a defined 'basic plateau of competence' around 15 or 16 years of age.

There are two other important elements for the curriculum. The first is a component geared explicitly to job choice. The Commission evidently subscribes to the established sciological concept of 'cooling out' — apparently too many schools have persuaded too many children in aiming too high (that is, seeking access to higher power, incomes, or status). There is a touching faith in work experience programs, exchanges between city and country schools and the like in effecting this 'cooling out' and which is equated, euphemistically, with more realistic job choice. The converse result is much more likely.

The second additional element concerns those 'learnings' that arise from more immediate social networks. The nuclear family is not good enough since it consists in this day and age of too few adult and sibling models. Schools may be the only place, the Commission asserts, where many students can gain this association with a wide range of adult models (beyond those provided by teachers). Hence the school must deliberately plan for such association. That is, planned association with adults would be part of the curriculum. Not surprisingly, although the Commission refers to a wide range of such adults, its principal practical suggestions involve the representatives of welfare, medical, and dental services. The Commission's examples are limited to models of professional, intellectual skills.

Hence, the Commission provides a picture of the curriculum that looks like:

1 language instruction for effective standard English usage,
2 logic, mathematics, science for rational value-free problem-solving skills,
3 additional locally based 'cultural' studies,
   (and where in the above three areas since substantial content is only a matter of taste, if the content is drawn from the child's immediate experience it will serve the additional purpose of validating the child's 'culture'),
4 vocational orientation and experience of a realistic 'cooling out' kind, all finally larded by,
5 contact with other adults,
   (but not of discordant kinds — they should be models of the pinnacles of the skills represented in the first three areas or, possibly, of the child's 'culture').

What can be added to or subtracted from this account by reference to the 1976 (rolling) triennial report?

Much of this second report, as befits the economies of the time of its preparation and submission, is an exercise in bureaucratic/financial management, but there is an entire chapter on perspectives

> which recapitulates the basic positions discussed in previous reports and expands this presentation while re-affirming the Commission's commitment to the directions of change identified as important (and) these changes are grouped around two general themes, equality of opportunity and openness and participation.[15]

Those concerned with critiques of internal consistency will find no overall improvement in this chapter. As but one example, consider the following three extracts:

> Schools do not have the power to make society more equal, guarantee everyone jobs, or make all jobs equally pleasant and self-directed. If these ends are desired they must be pursued through direct social action.[16]

> All young people should leave school with the confidence that they are able to make sense of the world as they experience it, to act upon it, and participate in directing it. The generalized intellectual competencies which give power to that confidence are the special business of schools.[17]

> Options in life are wider than they were. There is no single model of right living. This requires that schools assist young people to acquire a capacity for making choices through an understanding of society, through exercising choice in learning, through access to information relevant to life choices confronting them and through relationships which make it more likely that they will take the interests of others into account in the choices they make.[18]

Ignoring the naivity of the implied social objectives such as making all jobs equally pleasant and self-directed, and ignoring, for example, whether generalized intellectual skills, if they exist, do give power to the confidence to act, the statements are confused and contradictory.

On the one hand, the schools have no power to make society more equal and yet, on the other hand, schools should prepare young people to act on the world and change it (and clearly the Commission would not wish them to act to make it more unequal). But, in any event, why do we need to worry about this at all if the world is moving towards such complete relativization as is implied in the third statement.

## CONCLUSION

Despite internal inconsistency such as indicated above, the Commission does reaffirm a continuing commitment to directions of change identified as important and sustained over the three reports. And beyond the debate about the consistencies, strategies, and tactics, the reports do have a cohesion and this cohesion is centred on a pattern of social relationships.

Consider the repeated, central, and sustained use of word-themes such as equality (of access, of opportunity, and the like), of openness, of participation, of community, of criticality as expressed in a value-free technical-rational form, of enlarged tolerance for others' wishes, and more.

Taken together, these social relational elements paint a portrait of the set of social relational elements of a form of intellectual culture which emerged more clearly about the turn of the century and which has since extended to become the pervasively dominant form. The most significant single generalization that can be made of the views of the Schools Commission, as represented in its three major reports, is that it wishes to project on to schools, and directly or indirectly on to the whole society, this intellectual cultural form as the generalized social relational form. Crudely, the Commissioners are saying that if everybody lived within the relationships they experience, or that they imagine or wish they could experience, the world would be a better place.

The elements of this social relational form taken at face-value do have an appeal. But it is important to realize that the developing trend in this century is for them to be distorted or inverted or turned into personal attributes of people rather than be expressive of a genuine relationship between them. Put simply, the social relational elements do not now represent that more fundamental basis (or at least part of it), or a means to a better understanding of the world and hence of the possibility of reconstructing it. Rather, they represent the end-point of another process. An equal, open, participatory, community-oriented, rational-critical, infinitely tolerant person becomes a kind of ideal type. As an ideal type, these elements, as attributes of the person, take on an absolute quality and are clearly conflictual. No wonder then that in this century personality has moved towards a momentary or transient character — as observed and even celebrated, for example, in much modern literature. The operational corollary of the momentary personality is 'doing your own thing' within the extending variety of a commodity form.

Those that take on explicitly the production of that ideal type are taking on the management of culture. The curriculum of the Schools Commission could hardly be better framed in its intent for that purpose. Hence, the Schools Commissioners and all those others who subscribe generally to those directions that they have repeatedly affirmed have assumed the role of cultural managers.

For this reason they should be opposed.

Resistance will only become a real choice if the implications of the meritocratic system are examined and exposed and if the meaning and consequences of 'doing your own thing' in an instrumental and commodity-fetishist mainstream culture are comprehended. There could hardly be a better place to begin this effort than with the reports of the Schools Commission. The social and cultural assumptions of the Schools Commission, and the existing and emergent realities to which they are linked, will have to be transcended if cultural management is to be defeated. Questions of cultural alternatives assume validity to the extent that the culture so central to our self-formation is subjected to critical reflection.

Such an effort already goes a long way to suggest a curriculum different to that of the Schools Commission. This task and the teaching which would go with it would have to be undertaken without the support of the Schools Commission.

## Notes

1 Australia. (1973). *Schools in Australia. Report of the Interim Committee for the Australian Schools Commission.* (P. Karmel, Chairman). Canberra: AGPS.

2 Australia. Schools Commission. (1975). *Report for the Triennium, 1976–1978.* (K. McKinnon, Chairman). Canberra: AGPS. (Referred to in the *Arena* article, and sometimes elsewhere, as the McKinnon report.)

3 Australia. Schools Commission. (1976). *Report: Rolling Triennium, 1977–1979.* (K. McKinnon, Chairman). Canberra: AGPS.

4 Musgrave, P.W. (1975). 'Changing Society: Some Underlying Assumptions of the Karmel Report', *Australian Journal of Education,* **19**(1):1–14. Also Chapter 2 of this volume.

5 Crittenden, B.S. 'Arguments and Assumptions of the Karmel Report: A Critique'. In J.V. D'Cruz and P.J. Sheehan (Eds). (1975). *The Renewal of Australian Schools: Educational Planning in Australia after the Karmel Report.* (First Edition). Richmond: Primary Education. Also Chapter 1 of this volume.

6 White, D. (1973). 'Create Your Own Compliance: the Karmel Prospect', *Arena,* **32/33**: 35–48. Also Chapter 3 of this volume.

7 Readers are invited to consider the contents of the many 'futurologies' now being written. In particular Emery, F. (1974) *Futures We're In,* Centre for Continuing Education, Australian National University, might be taken as an example of the working out in a 'futurology' of the general systems perspective. There is an oppositional literature. *Arena* might be taken as a source of a particular oppositional thesis as well as introducing the interested reader to others such as that of Jurgen Habermas.

8 Australia. Schools Commission. (1975). op. cit., para. 2.14.

9 See, for example, ibid., Chapter 11, 'The School and the Community'.

10 ibid., para. 9.18.

11 ibid., para. 2.3.

12 ibid., para. 2.10.

13 loc. cit.

14 Bloom, B. (Ed.) (1956). *A Taxonomy of Educational Objectives; Cognitive Domain.* London: Longmans Green.

15 Australia. Schools Commission. (1976). op. cit., para. 2.1.

16 ibid., para. 2.4.

17 ibid., para. 2.9.

18 ibid., para. 2.10.

**Aspects and Emerging Problems**

# 13. Innovation Programs

## G.W. Bassett

A critique of innovation schemes in education such as those proposed in the reports of the Karmel Committee and the Schools Commission can be profitably approached within the broad context of school-society relationships, since in its most significant connotation, innovation in education is a planned attempt to alter these relationships.

The direction of the proposed change may be from the outside in (by trying to bring the schools more closely into line with social needs or pressures), or from the inside out (by trying to change social practice through school programs). The first could be called a social-needs model of educational innovation, the latter a social-reform model. A simple example of the first is a change in school curriculum to meet the social need of metrication. Examples of the latter do not spring so readily to mind, as it is difficult to conceive of an educational innovation designed to bring about social change which is itself quite independent of social objectives. One can, however, conceive of an innovation of an essentially educational kind which seeks to produce social change by strengthening some existing social attitude or practice, or by making it more widely prevalent. A significant traditional example of this is the schools' attempt to cultivate the values and skills of inquiry. These values and skills are by no means universally accepted, understood, or practised in the community at large and, in pursuing them with students, schools could be considered to be attempting an innovative social change. This distinction in the way the school-society relationship is interpreted, and the emphasis placed on one interpretation or the other, makes a significant difference to any innovations program attempted, and also to its implementation.

The most common innovation pattern in education fits the social-needs model best. Most Australians take for granted that the school exists for socially useful purposes, and that its aims should be authorized by social needs and values. Social needs are commonly expressed in vocational terms (particularly at present when there is substantial unemployment), and sometimes in terms of civic responsibility, leisure, and the like. When school and society get out of step, the dysfunction is interpreted as a failure on the part of the school to meet its obligations because of inadequate resources, poor leadership, unsuitable teaching methods, or other disabling factors. The innovations needed to improve the effectiveness of the schools from this point of view are primarily methodological, not philosophical, since the objectives are determined externally. Many critics of the present system believe that the most desirable innovations needed to bring the schools into line with social needs would be a return to didactic teaching, drill in the basic scholastic skills, and firm discipline.

215

The social-reform model of innovation is more concerned with improving the quality of social life than with merely meeting its material needs. It aligns itself with social causes such as equality and freedom, and seeks to strengthen them by new approaches in the schools. Thus, while it too is concerned with methodology (administration, teaching methods, curricula, resources etc.), it is also oriented towards new objectives. It is this model that best seems to fit the innovation schemes of the Karmel report and the Schools Commission.

The central theme of the Karmel report is the role of the school in strengthening the social goal of equality of opportunity. It was to make this goal more of a reality in Australian society that the Committee proposed to improve the quality of education by such measures as financial assistance to schools according to their need, special assistance to disadvantaged schools and handicapped children, improving the quality of the teaching force, and fostering an innovative climate in schools.

It is in connection with this last objective that the innovation program was proposed. For this program a $6 million fund was recommended to encourage innovations at the national, system, and school level. Only examples of innovations are suggested in the report, the emphasis being on the stimulating effect of the additional resources in raising the quality of schooling. School level projects were aimed mainly at individual teachers. In this report the scheme is linked with teacher development, with the substantive value of the innovation being played down. The experience of innovation was regarded as a form of professional therapy, leading to an improved quality of education in the schools, and through this to the greater equality. There is no doubt that a scheme of direct assistance to teachers is likely to have a stimulating effect. Typically, individual teachers have had little sense of independence and influence. This scheme gives them both.

The Schools Commission *Report for the Triennium 1976–78* endorsed the main features of the innovations program outlined above, but went beyond it in two significant ways.[1] Firstly, it placed greater stress on the evaluation of projects, thus shifting the emphasis from the value of the innovation to the teacher as a personal experience to the value of the innovation as a product. This change of emphasis obviously poses increased difficulties for those charged with the task of judging the proposal. Secondly, it guided (if not directed) the innovator's choice of project, thereby concentrating innovative effort in specific areas. Thus, whereas the features of the social-reform model were evident in the Karmel report in the major programs (assistance to schools according to need, disadvantaged schools, etc.) and less so in the Innovations Program, they emerge quite clearly in the Commission's thinking in the Innovations Program also. Would-be innovators are encouraged to undertake projects dealing with such matters as community participation in education, the education of girls and women, rural students, migrants, handicapped students, and culturally deprived students. The positive nature of the reformist character is evident from the wording of the topic regarding the education of girls and women: to 'reduce the educational disadvantages of girls and women'[2], rather than the more open form: 'exploring problems in connection with the education of girls and women'. It is clear that the Commission had already made its mind up about the trends in social changes affecting women — 'The Commission . . . accepts the need for schools to reflect more directly in their curricula and organisational arrangements the changing role of women in Society'[3] — and wished to bring the schools in as an ally. In fact, the role of women in Australian society, and related questions concerning the home and work force, are quite controversial, and scarcely offer the schools clear guidance for changes in their program.

The spelling out of 13 priority areas for innovative projects raises quite a fundamental question regarding the innovations program. Why these 13? In the section of the report dealing with the role of the Commission, there is a bland statement that could be indirectly regarded as the Commission's answer. 'Emerging trends in Australian education at the present time largely coincide with those the Commission also sees as desirable'.[4] This is disarming, but it still leaves one in doubt about the basis for a policy for innovation. Actually the 13 themes listed offer a wide range of options for aspiring innovators, and there is the further option of making proposals outside these guidelines, but the problem of justifying the direction which that innovation should take remains.

The evaluation of educational policy is a complex process involving both public and professional opinion, but its articulation ultimately is a matter for governments, particularly if public funds are involved. It must be one of the most dramatic ironies of educational administration in Australia that educational policy is vested in the State Governments, yet the most prominent scheme for changing education is administered by the Federal Government. It is realized of course that state authorities are also concerned with innovation through various in-service programs, but the innovations scheme of the Schools Commission has attracted most attention in the profession, probably because of its policy of direct funding. Comment on this curious anomaly is not meant as a criticism of the Schools Commission, but rather of the tortuous pattern of educational administration that has emerged in our federal system.

## INDUCEMENT FUNDING OF INNOVATION

I have argued elsewhere that the use of inducement funding could be self-defeating by encouraging the error that innovation can occur only when financial assistance is given.[5] A realistic consequence of this is that innovation will falter or stop when the money runs down, as it may well do. In this respect the PACE program of the United States in the 1960s, which probably was the model for the scheme in the Karmel report, should have provided a warning.

In fact, quite significant changes could be effected within all the Commission's priority areas without the use of any additional funds, and particularly in the following:

    (a)  improve the learning of basic skills, and in particular deal with the problem of illiteracy.

(c) explore ways of opening up or modifying the traditional structures and patterns of activity within the school.

(d) find ways in which students can participate in making decisions about their own education and the conduct of their schools, and encourage participation in the development of projects.

(g) give reality to the value of cultural pluralism in schools, and affirm the cultural identity of students from other cultures and their value as members of an integrated society.

(j) relate the school to the community it serves, and increase parent and community participation in the school and in the process of innovation.

(l) reduce the educational disadvantages of girls and women.

(m) provide special educational opportunities to students who have demonstrated their ability or interest in a particular field of study, including scientific, literary, artistic or musical studies.[6]

Innovation in these matters (and others not included in the list) requires more than anything else, dedication, imagination, hard work, and a striving towards self-improvement. Undoubtedly, many new ventures require additional resources, and it would be foolish to adopt the spartan attitude that improvisation is always possible. Funds should be available when they are needed, but as an integral part of maintaining a progressive education program rather than as a prize to be won in a kind of educational competition.

## THE INNOVATIONS PROGRAM IN ACTION

No comprehensive evaluation of the scheme has yet been made. It probably never can be made because of the difficulty of isolating influences in a complex situation, and in finding measurements for some of the more subtle outcomes. We can look around us, and talk to teachers enjoying the unusual experience of having money to spend. In my experience this has been very satisfying, mainly because of the professional gleam in the teachers' eyes as they explain what they are doing. We can look around us, and talk to teachers whose proposals have not been accepted. Dr McKinnon, the Chairman of the Schools Commission, has hinted that there is evidence that disappointed teachers have proceeded with their project as proposed, or in a limited way.[7] I hope this is correct. We can also consult the Commission's publication, *National Directory of Innovations Projects Funded by the Schools Commission* (Revised Edition, April 1977).

This publication covers the years 1974–75 in detail, and 1976 in less detail. The 1974–75 projects are classified by level (national, system and school). The school level, which accounts for the greatest number of projects, is classified into the following: audio-visual, teaching methods and class organization, curriculum, remediation, disadvantaged groups, teacher support, extra school activities, community involvement, learning networks. Most of these areas are subdivided, thus presenting a usefully detailed category for each project. Each entry gives the name and address of the person to whom the grant was made, the amount granted, and a brief description of the project. There are also two alphabetical indexes, one for the persons receiving the grants (grantees, ugh!), and a brief description of the project. The document is thus a very useful one, both as a record, and a means of stimulating the spread of ideas. I assume that it is readily available to teachers.

By far the most popular category is Curriculum, reflecting what might be considered the teachers' most vital professional interests. The scheme obviously was manna from heaven for those who wanted to get a kiln and potters' wheel, to secure equipment to introduce letterpress printing into the Art curriculum, to start organic gardening, to set up an office complex for commercial teaching, to develop a theatre building, to erect a log cabin on an environmental studies area, to set up a nursery of native flora, to prepare a basic kit for Economics, to acquire the facilities to teach Japanese in the primary school, to set up a Mathematics work-shop for individualizing teaching, to develop computer studies, to enlarge the school orchestra for students in Grade 8, to establish an animal house, to introduce the course 'Man — A Course of Study' for two Grade 7 classes, to develop individualized materials in the humanities, to introduce foundry as an industrial arts subject, etc.

The categories Teaching Methods and Class Organisation, Extra Curricular Activities, and Audio-Visual also account for a substantial number of projects, whereas there are relatively few projects in Remediation, Special Classes and Schools, and Disadvantaged Groups, although with respect to the latter, it is realized that there is a separate disadvantaged schools program.

One gets the general impression from a perusal of these lists that teachers want to experiment in the familiar professional areas of curriculum, method and organization more than in the more socially oriented areas of disadvantaged schools and students, and community relationships. The projects supported in 1974 and 1975 reflect the Karmel Committee's emphasis on the value of the process of innovation to the teacher, rather than the value of the innovation itself. It would be an interesting exercise to reclassify these projects into the 13 areas nominated by the Schools Commission. Without actually doing this exercise I suspect that they do not fit well into the new pattern. The same point could be explored by comparing the projects approved for 1976 with those for 1974–75. As has been pointed out, these are not classified except by level (national, system and school), and by State. The special projects approved for schools, systems and organizations (and the occasional individuals) appear to follow the guidelines closely, with great emphasis being given to girls' education, aboriginal education, educational disadvantage, country education, and community education. From an inspection of the school level projects, there appears to be a shift in the range of projects towards the 13 specified areas, but it is not clear cut. Left to themselves, that is, by pursuing a policy of change for the sake of change (and interpreting this as change for the sake of the teachers' professional development), it seems likely that teachers will engage in new versions of existing pedagogical ideas (especially those made possible through securing equipment), rather than see their role as spearheading social reform.

How innovative are the projects? The Karmel report defined innovation as the creation of change by the introduction of something new. Based on this criterion the task of administering an innovations program must be very difficult, since clearly at the time judgment has to be passed on the proposal, the latter could not possibly have brought about change (unless perhaps it were based on some pilot experiment). The phrase 'something new' also presents difficulty. New to whom? New in what way, as means or end? Surveying the list of approved projects it seems clear that novelty has been interpreted relatively, and that the opportunity for a person to do something that he has read about, or seen elsewhere, has been judged to be innovative for that person. If this is the Commission's interprepation of innovation — and it certainly is a defensible one — it could be said that the scheme is really achieving the dissemination of new ideas by a strategy of financial encouragement, as well as no doubt helping some genuinely new ideas to be born. Pusey (a member of the Schools Council Innovation Committee, but writing independently) claims for the individual project scheme a diversity at the 'grass-roots' level of education that 'appears to be the best solvent of structures which impose restricting uniformities on the educational process'.[8] If the hidden process in the innovations program is dissemination, its curious long-term result may be convergence in greater uniformity, as new ideas become the new orthodoxy. The stereotyping of practices at present occurring in open-plan schools is an example. Whether this uniformity, if it is achieved, is on the basis of the Commission's priorities, or on other criteria, remains to be seen.

## STRATEGIES OF INNOVATION

The Commission's strategy is to work through organizations, systems, federal bodies and individual teachers, but the main thrust of the scheme is through individual teachers. Seventy-one per cent of available funds committed by early 1975 was devoted to school level projects. The point is made in the report that attempts to change teachers and schools by a power strategy, when the initiative for change lies outside the school, have been remarkably unsuccessful. There can be no quarrel with this. The Commission program is based on the assumption

> that worthwhile change is most likely to occur when action is based on the active participation of those involved, especially teachers, and therefore on their perception of the school situation.

It claims 'that problems should be defined and solutions developed, by those who will have to convert ideas into effective action'.[9] One need not quarrel with this either; but it can be interpreted in different ways. One way is to stress the role of the individual teacher in defining problems and developing solutions; another is to stress his membership of a school staff, and to take all the collateral institutional relationships fully into account in planning the innovation. I would wish to stress the second interpretation. The Commission appears to stress the first, in spite of the reassurance about 'creating a supportive environment for the projects'.[10] Pusey describes the scheme as a 'grass-roots' program in which teachers, students, and people from local school communities themselves define the problems and propose their own solutions. He claims that

> it rests on one basic principle: individual, and not governments or government agencies, should define an innovation according to their needs and aspirations. It is a self-help program, returning initiative to teachers, parents and the community.

Again one is left with the uneasy feeling that teachers are being encouraged to act individually, and on projects that are separate from the mainstream of their school's program, adding embellishments, rather than contributing to the main task facing the school of making its whole operation more effective.

A school is a complex institution in which individual effort and initiative, interdependence, formal and informal structure, facilities and community relationships are all involved. To be effective it needs to be planned as a whole, with each function compatible with others. What one teacher does affects others, what the principal does affects everybody, and the kind of organizational setting and community relationships that are established facilitate or constrain what each member can achieve.

If the quality of education is to be improved, it will be done most effectively through the improvement of the school as an organization, including such unspectacular matters as these:

1 clarifying the school's goals;
2 careful and frank appraisal of the degree to which the curriculum, organization, evaluation, discipline, and relationships with the community are compatible with the goals;
3 experimenting with individual methods of teaching that cater for the distinctive characteristics of the students;
4 using time and space in the school more flexibly;
5 experimenting with procedures for decision-making and communication to raise the morale of teachers and students;
6 making the best use of the particular quality and qualifications of staff.

To state this is not to undervalue individual initiative, but rather to attempt to make best use of it in a particular setting. Much of what teachers are taught, both in training and in in-service courses, remains inert or frustrated in the particular schools in which they work.

If the whole school were to become more the focus of innovative effort the present emphasis in in-service and innovations programs on attempts to influence individual teachers should shift to organizational development.

This is, in part, a power strategy, in that it involves the use of individuals or teams from outside the school, and thus would most likely be included among the strategies that the Commission regards as unsuccessful. But it is in no sense a coercive strategy, since it comes into play only at the schools' request, and operates on a co-operative basis between the school and the development team. It is a blend of school initiative and outside help, and as such seems likely, given the Australian tradition of centralized control, to have more chance of success in the long run than one which relies wholly on individual teacher initiative. A scheme to help individual teachers, no doubt, is likely to have quick results as a stimulant, or in complementing what might be done with whole school programs, but by its very nature it cannot deal with situations involving the functioning of institutions.

Organizational development is by no means a simple prescription for reform. There are overseas models from business and education, but idiomatic versions of it have to be worked out for Australian conditions by experiment and research. Some obvious elements of this task are these:

1 To design projects that can run for two or three years so that there is sufficient time for diagnosis and remedy to work, given the complex problems involved in them.
2 To experiment with different kinds of school — small, large, city, country, primary, secondary, disadvantaged, affluent, etc.
3 To experiment with different types of development teams, working from outside the school. A possible new role for inspectors of schools in such a strategy would be an important consideration, perhaps crucial to this position in the future. The role of advisory teachers, academics, and other consultants would need clarification.
4 To experiment with different modes of intervention.
5 To clarify the kind of infra-structure needed in schools for them to co-operate effectively with external members of a development team, and to carry on independently afterwards.
6 To experiment with different arrangements whereby staffs could be enabled to give sustained attention to the schools' problems, deliberating on such matters as objectives, problems, disciplines, resources, assistance from consultants, etc. Steps such as freeing a whole staff for a week for planning, which has already been done in some schools, are suggestive.
7 To develop materials to assist schools with self-analysis and assessment, covering such features as school climate, decision-making, communication, staff and student morale, community relationships, curriculum objectives, evaluation methods, etc.

If the Commission is not disposed to encourage such projects, they should be taken up by state education authorities as an important part of their in-service programs. Commission projects, or at least some of them, might then be related to the overall development plans in which schools are engaged.

## CONCLUDING COMMENT

Innovative fervour seems to come and go with an erratic rhythm. In the USA, the ferment began in the late 1950s, sparked off by a wave of national insecurity in the cold war. It first manifested itself in the fields of science and technology, but soon became linked with the new thrust of the Kennedy regime towards social reform. It reached its zenith in the mid-1960s, but by about 1970 a conservative reaction had set in, 'accountability' replacing 'innovation' as the fashionable word.

In Britain, the educational revival came later, undoubtedly being influenced by America, particularly in the new curriculum development movement. Notable events were the publication of the Plowden Report (1967), documenting and encouraging the new primary school movement, the various Nuffield curriculum projects, and the creation of the Schools Council (1964), charged with reform in curricula and examinations. The force of that movement has slackened, if not spent itself, following the customary backlash. Austerity and accountability have effectively contained it politically, and there has been public disquiet about the effectiveness of the new methods.

In Australia the move came even later, partly in response to influences from both America and England, and partly from the social reform policies of the Whitlam Federal Government. The landmarks in this period, as it affected the schools, were the Karmel report[12] and the creation of the Schools Commission in 1973. But we are already in the reactionary phase, before many promising movements have had time to succeed. Political conservatism, inflation, and unemployment have created an unfavourable social and political climate for innovation, and there is strong public criticism of the school system for alleged low scholastic standards and poor discipline. For us the period of euphoria has been pitifully short.

It appears that this cyclic (or spiralling) configuration of educational reform is inherent, beginning with complacency and passing through an innovative phase, then reaction, and finally to complacency again.

Perhaps, if educationists can keep their nerve in the face of present widespread criticism, it might be possible to sustain a quieter kind of innovative movement, without any of the pretentious labelling of what we do, and free of any bandwagon effects, by trying to turn our schools into educational communities, and making a reality of old ideas like catering for individual differences, making school work relevant and enjoyable for students, encouraging independence, self-discipline, and a pride in achievement. For this schools need to have a large measure of autonomy, but they also need resources and help. How this help can be best given is no doubt controversial. Probably a variety of strategies is needed to best meet the different needs that there are. The one advocated in this commentary, providing professional support, as distinct from material support, and aimed at raising the level of effectiveness of the school's regular program, is at least one. What is innovative about this is that it subjects to critical examination routine tasks and procedures that are taken for granted, with the likelihood of significant change to follow.

### Notes

1 Australia. Schools Commission. (1975). *Report for the Triennium 1976–1978.* (Chairman, K. McKinnon). Canberra: AGPS.
2 ibid., para.17.7 (1), p.197.
3 ibid., para.7.17, p.86.
4 ibid., para.2.19, p.11.

5 Bassett, G.W. (1975). 'Innovation in Australian Education', *Administrators Bulletin*, **6**(8). St Lucia: University of Queensland.
6 Australia. Schools Commission. (1975). op. cit., para.17.7, p.197.
7 Australia. Schools Commission. (1977). *National Directory of Innovations Projects Funded by the Schools Commission*. Canberra: AGPS.
8 Pusey, M.J. (1976). 'Innovating: a Profile of the Schools Commission's Innovations Program', *Education News*, **15**(10):4-13. See p.8.
9 Australia. Schools Commission. (1975). op. cit., para.17.2, p.195.
10 ibid., para.17.8, p.197.
11 Pusey, M.J., op. cit.:4.
12 Australia. (1973). *Schools in Australia. Report of the Interim Committee for the Australian Schools Commission*. (Chairman, P. Karmel). Canberra: AGPS.

# 14. Equality and Education*

Brian Crittenden

## EDUCATION AND THE PRINCIPLE OF EQUAL OPPORTUNITY

The nineteenth century's optimism about the power of formal education to effect social reform has been dampened but by no means extinguished during the course of the present century. The optimism has probably been most persistent in relation to the role of the school in promoting equality. This point of view is very clearly illustrated in the first two reports of the Australian Schools Commission (1975, 1976) and in the.. forerunner, *Schools in Australia*, prepared by an Interim Committee and published in 1973.[1] In each of these documents, the advancement of equality in schooling and, through schooling, in the general life of the society, is the fundamental concern. Despite the economic difficulties and a change in government, they have significantly influenced the shape of public policy in education. It is useful, therefore, to examine at least some of the issues that arise from the way they interpret equality as an ideal and relate it to the practice of education.

It should be noted in passing that the first report of the Schools Commission sets out its theory on equality in less than four pages (paragraphs 2.2 to 2.10). The second report is somewhat less cryptic: it devotes about eight pages (paragraphs 2.2 to 2.19) to a more selective and detailed discussion of the position taken in the first report. But even if we presuppose the nine or so pages on equality in *Schools in Australia,* it still amounts to a rather compressed treatment of so complex a question — especially as the reports of the Schools Commission touch on a number of other important topics in the course of dealing with equality. The running together of rather different notions of equality in all three documents may be due, in part, to brevity, but I think it may also reflect some theoretical confusion. There have been some important modifications and changes of emphasis on the question of equality and education in each succeeding statement (particularly the most recent). However, I shall assume that the doctrine set out in *Schools in Australia* has not been changed substantially. Certainly, it is clear from the two reports of the Schools Commission that this is its own view.

In applying equality as a human value to education and to social life more generally, it is crucial to keep in mind some important differences between advocating on the one hand, the principle of equal opportunity, and on the other, an ideal of an egalitarian society. The Schools Commission, following

*An abbreviated version of this chapter appeared in the *Australian Journal of Education*, 21 (2): 113–126.

225

the position taken in *Schools in Australia,* has treated these two ways of interpreting equality as though they were facets of the same thing, or at least entirely compatible. This assumption is far from correct.

It is true that even in a thoroughly egalitarian society (e.g. one in which the total of significant human goods enjoyed by each member is the same), there is a place for at least some version of the principle of equal opportunity. The principle comes into play whenever commonly desired goods are in short supply, or are of the kind that presuppose for their possession the attainment of certain qualifications. The principle does not simply reiterate rules of fairness (for example, that the conditions to be satisfied are indeed relevant or that those who acquire the desired goods do in fact satisfy such conditions); it also requires that when the reasonable grounds that apply here and now for discriminating among individuals have their origins in arbitrary social arrangements, these arrangements should, as far as possible, be eliminated or offset by the members of the society as a whole.

But what must be noticed is that, even when the principle of equal opportunity is interpreted at its full strength, it is thoroughly at home in a social order in which there are vast differences in the goods that members enjoy (particularly in income and property, social status, and political power). In fact, it is in the so-called free enterprise economic system, informed by liberal, individualistic social theory, that the principle has the fullest scope for application. In the psychology of liberal capitalism, primacy is given to individual competition and to profit as the incentive for encouraging the skills and effort on which the system is thought to depend. Granted, then, that there is a broad scale of financial rewards and that each level is to be occupied by the most deserving individuals judged on the basis of ability and effort in free and open competition, it is obvious that there should be a pervasive concern with equality of opportunity. For the principle prescribes that, insofar as it is physically possible and morally permissible, the conditions under which individuals compete for the rewards of the system shall be equal, and thus the rewards shall be distributed in proportion to personal merit.

The actual extent of social manipulation that the principle enjoins depends, of course, on what is thought to be physically possible and morally permissible. In liberal-capitalist societies, the scope was greatly enlarged, as the nineteenth century assumption that the laws of supply and demand had the character of natural laws came to be abandoned. The degree of enthusiasm for the principle of equal opportunity has also tended to wax or wane depending on the state of the perennial debate over the relative importance of genetic and environmental factors. (Although the environmentalists were triumphant during the 1960s, the pendulum seems to have swung somewhat against them in recent years.)

The main point to be stressed in the present discussion is that when the principle of equal opportunity is being applied to its fullest extent in the context of a liberal-capitalist society, it does nothing in itself to promote a more egalitarian social order. The disparities of wealth, power and prestige remain exactly as they were. The outcome that the principle does promote, when rigorously applied, is a society stratified according to merit rather than on the basis of patronage or hereditary privilege.

From their beginning, one of the main purposes of the public systems of education has been the development of a work-force that would meet the needs of an industrial economy. Even when the range of schooling undertaken by most people came to include several years at the secondary level, the occupational purpose tended to overshadow the objectives of a liberal education (that is, of a broad and integrated intellectual, moral and aesthetic development). The instrumental way of thinking about education was so entrenched that even purely liberal studies had to be given a market value. We reached the point where, regardless of any real connection between formal education and a particular job, the level of scholastic attainment, or at least the number of years spent at school, generally determined the level of occupational income and prestige to which one would have access. Whether our extended system of formal schooling has much bearing on job efficiency or not, it has certainly come to play a crucial role in selecting where people are to be placed in the economic hierarchy.

Given this selective role, it is obvious why advocates of equal opportunity within the liberal-capitalist system would concentrate their attention on the school. If, through various forms of social engineering and pedagogic intervention, differences in scholastic outcome can be made to depend mainly on individual ability and effort, then to use such differences for occupational selection ensures that economic and other advantages are apportioned according to merit.

In its discussion of equality, the first report of the Schools Commission asserts: 'Schooling is not a race; its major objective is not to identify winners and losers . . .'.[2] But this is more the expression of an ideal than an accurate description of the role that schooling has played in our social and economic system. It is precisely because the race for the positions of advantage in the system begins with formal schooling that the advocates of equal opportunity have concentrated so much energy on pre-school remedial programs.

In its most generous interpretation, the principle of equal opportunity as applied within the liberal-capitalist system extends to what the Plowden Report called 'positive discrimination'. In this view, the principle is not satisfied even by providing *comparable* conditions of education for everyone (itself an extremely formidable task); it also requires that those who experience serious learning difficulties should receive relatively more financial and pedagogical assistance than others. There are obvious problems in reconciling this interpretation with the central theories of liberal capitalism. Certainly, it cannot be taken as advocating a kind of handicapping system so that, through adroitly applied differential treatment, all students, regardless of ability and interest, would be educated to the same extent. What is being assumed, apparently, is that not everyone needs the same pedagogic and other help to realize his potential for education. The point and justification of positive discrimination is not, therefore, to promote an equal educational outcome by the end of formal schooling, but to provide the maximum help that is needed, and can be given, to enable each individual by that time to reach the highest level of educational attainment of which he is capable.

It is beyond my purpose to engage in a detailed critical assessment of the principle of equal opportunity as it is applied to education in our kind of social order.[3] However, at least a few summary comments should be made. In favour of the principle, it can be said that it has provoked action that has led to a significant reduction of the gross differences in the conditions under which people were educated. Moreover, in a society characterized by a substantial range of incomes, it seems preferable that entry to the more lucrative and interesting jobs should depend on personal scholastic merit than on some form of privilege involving such factors as family, sex, class, ethnic group, religion. This is not to imply, of course, that there are no better alternatives.

On the negative side, it should first be noted that the rhetoric of equal educational opportunity (or equal economic opportunity through education) is somewhat misleading. Even if the external conditions affecting education were the same for everyone, as long as the educational outcome depends on abilities that vary greatly among the participants, it cannot be literally claimed that everyone has an equal chance of reaching, through education, the highest levels in the social and economic order. To suggest otherwise is like saying that a person in poor health has an equal chance of winning a race against a champion athlete, just because they both compete under exactly the same conditions.

In the second place, even when the principle of equal opportunity is applied in a thoroughly efficient way, it does nothing of itself to change the character of society. If there are inequitable differences of income or a stratum of poverty at the bottom of the social pyramid, these remain untouched. What the operation of the principle is designed to affect are the occupants of the various levels of income and power. While particular ethnic groups may no longer be disproportionately represented among the poor, still poverty remains. Those who attempt to achieve social justice through equal educational opportunity not only overestimate the role of the school as an agent of social reform, but tend to divert attention from the need for a direct, and more effective, attack on poverty and related problems.

Finally, the principle as applied to education accepts and reinforces the questionable role that schooling plays in determining one's place in the social and economic hierarchy. More generally, the principle emphasizes almost exclusively the instrumental value of education, its pay-off in socio-economic advantage. In this atmosphere, it is easy to forget that the process of education should be a worthwhile experience in itself and should play a fundamental part in shaping the overall quality of human life. It is not surprising, then, that when the school in difficult economic circumstances fails to be an effective means of job opportunity, there should be widespread scepticism about the value of education.

## EGALITARIAN MODIFICATIONS OF THE EQUAL OPPORTUNITY PRINCIPLE

Until fairly recently, even egalitarian-minded reformers were inclined to support equality of educational opportunity as an effective and desirable means for advancing their ideal of social equality. During the past decade or so, many egalitarians have witnessed the limited practical success of efforts at achieving equality of educational opportunity, and have become convinced of the powerlessness of the principle to change the liberal-capitalist system radically. In fact, some have mistakenly assumed that the principle belongs exclusively and essentially to this system, and as such they reject it entirely. Short of an outright rejection of the principle, various reinterpretations have been proposed that are intended to make the principle better serve the ideals of social equality. Two of these reinterpretations in particular deserve some comment. There is an attempt to accommodate at least some aspects of both of them in the reports of the Schools Commission (and in *Schools in Australia*).

The first revision claims that the ideal of equal educational opportunity is achieved only when the outcome for each individual is as nearly as possible the same or equivalent. Equality in the initial conditions of schooling and during the process will not do, because it results in an unequal educational outcome and thus inequality of social and economic opportunity. Instead of arguing for the equal right of all to the good we call education, this view supports a radically different claim, namely, the right of all to the same (or equivalent) educational attainment. Failure to give due weight to this difference is one of the main weaknesses in the treatment of equality in the documents to which I have been referring.

Whether the objective of equal educational outcome is defensible or not, it should be emphasized that, like the traditional principle of equal educational opportunity, it assumes the connection between schooling and socio-economic opportunity. Its strategy is to neutralize this influence by ensuring that everyone is equally schooled. The practical effect of such a strategy, however, can only be to exacerbate the situation in which an increasing number of people engage in more and more years of formal education while at the same time the scholastic qualifications required for entry to an ever-widening range of jobs are continually rising.

A more fundamental point, however, is that the attempt to implement the policy of equal educational outcome (assuming it is taken seriously) encounters severe moral and practical difficulties. The massive social engineering that the application of the policy entails could not avoid violating the ideals of freedom and justice to an extent that would be out of all proportion to the good that may be achieved. And it is at least arguable that to educate everyone to the same level, no more nor less, is not for the good of a society. Of course, as long as the genetically determined differences of ability that are relevant to educational outcome cannot be controlled, the policy itself cannot in the strict sense be implemented.[4] Even in regard to interest and motivation, which may

229

depend largely on environmental conditions, it is practically impossible to control effectively their influence on educational outcomes.

Proponents of the objective of equal educational outcome have not been blind to the practical obstacles. A not uncommon way of attempting to avoid these obstacles is through the use of verbal magic. All activities undertaken in the name of education and at whatever level of achievement are declared to be of equal value. The move is sometimes supported by the claim that each individual determines for himself what is to count as knowledge, so that attempts to assess learning against objective standards of achievement are not only morally objectionable but epistemologically mistaken. Even if this pretence successfully ensured that, in relation to schooling, everyone competed equally for jobs, it is patently a betrayal of educational values. No one would try to justify such a subterfuge if it were a question of making equal provision for health care or for adequate food and shelter.

The second main reinterpretation of the principle of equal opportunity calls for a social order in which the various sub-groups of the society are proportionately represented at whatever levels the goods of the society (including education) are distributed. One of the main reasons for the recent stress on equal treatment for groups rather than individuals has been the recognition of the political effectiveness of such an emphasis. It also has a strong appeal because it provides individuals who fail with an escape from personal responsibility; they can always blame their failure on prejudice against their group.

In discussing this view, as it relates specifically to education, the report of the Interim Schools Committee quotes from A.H. Halsey:

> ... the goal should not be the liberal one of equality of access but equality of outcome for the median member of each identifiable non-educationally defined group, i.e., the *average* woman or negro or proletarian or rural dweller should have the same level of educational attainment as the average male, white, white-collar suburbanite.[5]

The attitude of the report to the objective of equal *average* educational attainment is not entirely clear. It toys with the idea, but is also somewhat critical. The main tendency of the report is, I believe, finally opposed to anything like a strict doctrine of equal educational outcome, whether the units being considered are individuals or groups. In its first report, the Schools Commission seems to differ from its predecessor in this matter. It introduces the first of its basic themes in this way:

> The first is equality — an emphasis on more equal outcomes from schooling, laying particular stress on social group disparities and attempts to mitigate them, and on social changes and their effects on desired outcomes.[6]

It should be noticed in passing that this group approach to equal outcomes from schooling is not quite consistently or clearly elaborated in the report's subsequent discussion of equality. On some aspects of the matter, the Commission's second report is less ambiguous. In general, it focuses attention on improving the educational achievement of individuals rather than of groups. In fact, it speaks of the 'demonstrated incapacity (of education) substantially to alter the relative position of social groups'.[7] Despite this, the report is still concerned about the education of social groups as such. Thus, it calls for a greater effort to give 'under-achieving social groups' a better chance of success at school.[8] While the second report explicitly repudiates the objective of equal individual outcomes in education[9], it makes no comment on the question as it affects groups.

A number of weaknesses in the attempt to achieve equal average outcome among social groups have been pointed out in a recent article by A.R. Jensen.[10] The attempt is, as Jensen puts it,

> unfortunate for education, not only because the individual is the essential unit of all the factors involved in educability, but because none of the ethnic or social groups in question is sufficiently homogeneous in the characteristics involved in educability to warrant its being treated as the unit for any educational prescription.[11]

Jensen also stresses how mistaken it is to assume that differences in educational outcome can be resolved by concentrating on social and economic factors, for there are roughly the same individual differences of scholastic performance and income among siblings as among different social classes and races.

In relation to the practice of 'reverse discrimination' in which social group quotas govern the process of selection, Jensen raises several criticisms:

1 There is the problem of deciding what groups are to be included, and where to place the quota.

2 For applicants who are near the selection cut-off point, the use of group quotas frequently leads to the rejection of better qualified individuals from one group in favour of less qualified individuals from another.

3 The very highly qualified members of groups protected by a quota tend to be seen as beneficiaries of the quota system rather than in terms of their personal merit.[12]

## SUMMARY: ASSESSING THE PLACE OF EQUALITY IN EDUCATION

In the present century, schooling has been valued mainly as an instrument in the service of political, economic and social ends. These ends have been significantly shaped by a widespread commitment to equality as a social ideal — interpreted by some as actual equality in the total goods of life and by others as equality of opportunity. It is hardly surprising, therefore, that schooling should have been so influenced by the social ideal of equality. From what has already been said, it will be clear that I believe the concern for issues of social equality in and through schooling has played an altogether disproportionate part in educational theory and practice. It has reinforced the purely instrumental approach to education and the often artificial connection between schooling and economic status, and has distracted attention from questions about the specifically educational quality of what schools achieve as distinct from their usefulness as social levellers or escalators (depending on how one interprets equality).

Historically, the ideal of equality has been applied to education mainly in relation to the principle of equal opportunity. There is, I believe, a clear, if modest, place for this principle in the conduct of education. It can justifiably be argued that, where two people are equal in characteristics that are relevant to the attainment of what is judged to be a generally desirable level of education, they should have equivalent opportunities for achieving such an education. Whether the effort to offset various kinds of obstacles to education can, or should, be justified in terms of equal opportunity is, I think, more doubtful. I shall return to this point later.

On the question of equality of treatment as a general policy in the practice of education, there is no serious argument at the present time. Everyone acknowledges that, in relation to learning, human beings are in fact unequal in their capacities, interests and motivation. To treat everyone in the same way would only exacerbate the differences. Proponents of equal educational outcome have for a long time been strong supporters of unequal treatment in the process.

But the case against equality of outcome — whether it refers to individuals or average group performance — seems to me almost as obvious. If the program were to be taken seriously, it would first be necessary for every child to be made a ward of the state at birth and to be raised under virtually identical conditions.[13] But even when all the controllable environmental factors have been accounted for, human beings remain unequal in their capacities for educational attainment. As I have already noted, an equal outcome could not be achieved without seriously compromising principles of justice and freedom. In any scheme of this kind, there are also the evident questions about who the social engineers are to be, how they gain access to their position, what controls they are subject to. Apart from the totalitarian character of the political system, there would be a serious loss to the culture as a whole. If the objective were effectively achieved, the standard of intellectual, aesthetic and moral excellence would at best be what a majority of people in the society could, in fact, through various kinds of educational effort, be brought to achieve.

The inappropriateness of aiming at equality of outcome is particularly clear when one reflects on the nature of education as a human good. In contrast to food and clothing, property, wages, annual leave and even aspects of health care, education is not like a simple product that can be neatly packaged and distributed. As an achievement, it is a highly complex and intangible set of goods — beliefs, attitudes, ways of thinking, acting, feeling, imagining. It is never possessed once and for all, and it admits of an enormous range of possible levels of attainment with virtually no upper limit. In particular, it is not the kind of good that one person can bestow on another, treated as a passive recipient. However helpful pedagogic intervention may be, education depends directly and finally on each individual's efforts at understanding and on the extent to which these are successful. It is a moral ideal of teaching to use whatever knowledge and skills one has in order to enable each individual learner to achieve the fullest understanding of which he or she is capable at the time.

In summary, then, whatever interpretation is placed on equality as a social ideal, it seems to have only marginal bearing on the practice and objectives of education.

## ASPECTS OF EQUALITY IN THE HUMAN RIGHT TO EDUCATION

There is a rather different question about equality and education from the kind we have been considering — one which is often obscured, or at least confused, by a preoccupation with the school as an instrument of social equality. It is the question of whether there should be a common curriculum; that is, whether everyone should have access to a liberal or general education that is the *same* in its objectives and the main features of its content. This question leads into a large and complex topic that I shall not attempt to take up in any detail in the present context. However, I must comment on it to the extent that it is related to another way in which the moral ideal of equality has a bearing on education.

### An argument for a common curriculum

If we assume that everyone has a human right to education, we are granting that everyone has, in some sense, an equal claim to acquire the good we call education.[14] We are also asserting in effect that what we call education is necessary for the welfare of each human being as such. Thus, more specifically, the right is a moral claim on the group of human beings that make up a society (and perhaps ultimately on the whole human community) to do what it can to ensure that each of its members becomes educated. Given the characteristics of education that were noted above, this moral claim is still a very obscure one. Apart from the babel of conflicting opinions on precisely what the good called 'education' consists in, there is the obvious problem of different natural capacities for learning. Do we mean that each person makes a moral claim to obtain the fullest education of which he is capable? Or, if we focus literally on equality, are we to say that the moral claim extends only to the level of education that the least capable members of society can attain? I believe a middle ground between these extremes can be justified. It is here that the question of a common curriculum enters the picture. I shall not attempt to fill out the details of the argument, but shall merely sketch its main outlines.

1  In the transmission of the whole culture of a society from one generation to another, education (in the sense associated with schooling) has a relatively specific role to play. Its proper function is limited not simply to those aspects of the whole culture that are worth preserving, but among them, to those whose acquisition depends on, or at least is facilitated by, a deliberate and sustained program of teaching and learning. There are many worthwhile aspects of a culture that can be acquired just as well, or

233

better, through direct experience in various social practices — e.g. as the member of a family or other close-knit group, at work, at play, through religious and other celebrations.

2 The content that satisfies the foregoing conditions has often been called the 'high' culture. It is that part of the total way of life of a people that is systematically and self-consciously developed in the light of rigorous standards of excellence. At its core are those activities that attempt to embody and express the highest intellectual, moral and aesthetic ideals. This form of culture is (to use Raymond Williams' phrase) documented in a body of intellectual and imaginative work.[15] It is the central business of education as schooling to introduce each generation to this body of work as a living tradition.

Not all societies have realized a high culture in the sense in which I am using the term. Among those that have done so, the ideals and achievements have varied in quality — both between and within cultural traditions. But broadly speaking, the tendency in high culture is towards universality, towards the standards of truth, rationality, objectivity, moral and aesthetic excellence and so on that apply to *all* human beings. In Arnold's well known phrase, the concern is with 'the best that has been thought and said in the world'.

3 The high culture is to be distinguished from other manifestations of culture that may form part of the whole way of life of a society. In particular, it is unlike 'mass' culture, in which the emphasis is on entertainment, escape, the thoroughly predictable response that has been drained of any serious mental effort. But it is also unlike 'folk' culture which is largely unselfconscious and integrated into the entire fabric of the life of those who participate. Obviously, the high culture affects, and is affected by, such other forms.

The high culture must also be distinguished from the characterizing values of the so-called social classes — assuming that such groups can be distinguished independently on criteria of birth or income. It is true that the high culture has often been the preserve of a privileged class, has often been valued more by one class than another, and has often borne the unmistakable influence of this or that particular class. But of itself the high culture is the inheritance of all the members of a society because it is concerned with the standards of general human excellence in the intellectual, moral, and aesthetic domains. It is precisely in this sense that it is a common culture and provides the substance of a common curriculum. The sense of 'common' is qualitative not quantitative, that is, not what the culture of the majority actually is or what remainder of beliefs and values the members of a society happen to share when all their differences have been subtracted.

4 To become acquainted with the content of the high culture as I am interpreting it is evidently worthwhile. But whether it should be the object of a human right is perhaps less clear. Can it be said that each

individual's welfare as a human being depends on it? An argument for an affirmative answer can be set out in general terms as follows. The development of a distinctly human character depends on learning the main symbolic systems of a culture. These systems provide different ways of describing, explaining, interpreting and appreciating the human and physical world. To the extent that an individual is ignorant of any of these systems, he is thus limited as a human being. Hence all members of a society need to be adequately initiated into each of the main symbolic systems. This condition cannot be satisfied unless it includes at least a general introduction to the content of the high culture, for the latter is the conscious development of these main symbolic systems according to the most adequate available standards of truth, objectivity, moral and aesthetic excellence.

Whatever else it might include, the human right to education may, therefore, be interpreted as a moral claim that all individuals make on their society to be provided with the opportunity for gaining an adequate general introduction to the content of the high culture, the common curriculum in the sense already indicated. What constitutes an 'adequate general introduction' would of course need to be determined in detail. It would set out the level of general or liberal education that it is fitting for any person to achieve. Such a program would certainly go beyond the basic skills of literacy and numeracy and an elementary knowledge of the social order to which one belongs. However, the engagement in mathematics, science, literature and the other elements of the high culture would just as clearly not be undertaken as a basis for scholarly work but in order to develop a broad framework for understanding, interpreting and appreciating human life.

The providing of opportunity would have to take account of the diversity of abilities and interests affected by environment and heredity. Ideally, each individual should be enabled to go as far towards achieving the desirable level of liberal education as his or her personal abilities and efforts will allow. In practice, of course, the assistance that can be given will depend on the full range of claims, based on human rights and other moral grounds, that are being made on the resources of a particular society.

## The Schools Commission on a common curriculum

Although the reports of the Interim Committee and of the Schools Commission are not concerned in detail with the question of education as a human right, they do take up two crucial elements of the foregoing argument: the questions of a common culture and curriculum and of a desirable standard of educational achievement.

The former is touched on in the Commission's first report.[16] What we find is hardly a systematic discussion. Still, there are at least some hints of an

235

argument hidden among the thickets of several dense and diffuse paragraphs. The main features may be set out in the following points:

1 There are certain broad intellectual skills that everyone should acquire. However, the development of such skills does not depend on being initiated into 'traditional subject fields, or high culture' (2.7). The skills are content-free.

2 At the same time, although such modes of understanding as logic, mathematics, science and art have been historically associated with the middle class, they in fact possess general human value and should be made available to all. They are value-free in the sense that 'they may be learned and applied in any value framework' (2.10).

3 At present, the cultural values typically reflected in Australian schools belong to only certain of its social groups. This is an undesirable situation. The full spectrum of social and cultural diversity in Australia should be reflected and encouraged by the schools. Indeed, every child should find the values of his family (his 'reality') reflected in the school (2.8).

4 But the school should also provide everyone with adequate opportunity to enter what the report calls 'the mainstream culture'.

In summary, the report seems to favour an extensive form of educational pluralism for the purpose of reflecting and encouraging every variation of values in the society, yet it also wants the schools to provide a kind of common curriculum. There is no clear indication of how these objectives are to be achieved simultaneously. But a clue is given in two assumptions made by the report: that the range of desirable intellectual skills can be acquired independently of any particular body of knowledge and belief; and that even when logic, mathematics, science, art and so on are the objects of schooling, their study is compatible with any framework of values.

One can hardly engage in a systematic critique of the report's position when there are so many aspects of it that call out for clarification. For example, what are the cultural values that the schools generally reflect? Are they some sort of defining values of the so-called middle class or, perhaps, values of the high culture that the middle class has in fact supported? What is the claimed historical link between the middle class and such systematic modes of thought as logic, mathematics and science? What is the 'mainstream culture'? How is it related to what schools generally profess, to the values of the middle class, to high culture, and to what the report refers to as 'popular and commercial culture'? For any rigorous discussion, the notions of class and culture would have to be used with more precision than is evident in the report of the Schools Commission.

Granted the obscurities and terseness of the report, I think there are nevertheless at least three points relating to the question of a common curriculum on which the report should be criticized.

1 The acquisition of important intellectual skills cannot be divorced from bodies of knowledge and belief or, more generally, the traditions of systematic inquiry in a culture. How we perceive a situation, the

questions we ask, the hypotheses we form are shaped by the concepts, beliefs and theories we possess. Problem-solving or any other intellectual activity is not simply a matter of employing certain technical skills of inquiry that exist independently of any particular cultural context and can be learned as such. It is significant that the report seems to treat literacy as simply a 'word game', having no integral connection with social and cultural practices. Apparently, it wishes to treat all intellectual skills in an analogous fashion.

2 Although the report claims that the range of intellectual skills that the school is designed to foster can be acquired by other means than through 'the traditional subject fields, or high culture', it argues for the general human value of 'logic, mathematics, science, art or any of the other ways through which the human race has reflected upon or sought to order understanding' (2.10). The saving qualification is that these modes of understanding 'may be learned and applied in any value framework'. But here the report introduces its second dubious dichotomy: between the public forms of knowledge or understanding and value frameworks. While the practices of logic, mathematics, science, art and so on may be engaged in by people who hold conflicting value perspectives on the nature of man and society, these perspectives will at least affect what is done in the name of the various forms of understanding; when such perspectives enter into the substance of a form of understanding (as, for example, in history, social science and literary criticism) they may make a radical difference.

There is also a limit to the tolerance which logic, mathematics, science, etc. can have towards diverse value frameworks. The intellectual and moral values involved in the serious practice of the public modes of thought are simply not compatible with *every* value framework. To take one conspicuous example: the tradition of critical rationality which has informed the public modes of thought in the recent history of Western culture may be valuable for human beings generally, but it is certainly not valued highly in every culture, or even by every group within Western culture. In regard to the report's policy of educational pluralism, whatever the schools may be able to do to accommodate the diversity of values in the Australian society at large, they cannot consistently reflect or respect the fairly prevalent range of values that are fundamentally anti-educational.

For at least some children the 'reality' (to use the report's word) of their family background is shaped by such factors as racial or religious prejudice, superstition, crude materialism, dissension between parents, cruelty and violence. It is naive, therefore, to suggest that there should always be harmony between the values of the school and those of each child's family. Schools inevitably encourage some values rather than others from among all the values that are in fact held in a society at any time — and indeed they ought to be carefully selective. But even when the values supported by the schools are chosen according to the most justifiable criteria of educational value, it is almost certain to be the case that some children will, in the words of the report, 'feel more confident and supported in the school than do others'. The reason is simply that some families will be committed to encouraging what meets the criteria of educational value, while others will be indifferent or hostile. Whether such families form identifiable social groups in the society is a contingent matter.

3 Where the report favours a common curriculum, it seems to rely mainly on a utilitarian argument. That is, the emphasis is not placed on the intrinsic value of the activities that constitute the common curriculum or the contribution they make to the living of a worthwhile and satisfying human life, but on the pay-off they have in our society in terms of political and social power, and economic advantage. Thus the report wants everyone to become literate in standard English, not because it will enable them to gain access to the great artistic achievements of English literature or even to read serious contemporary journalism, but because it is the language in which the business of everyday life in our society is conducted. According to the report, forms of non-standard English are just as valid as means of social exchange, but their scope is limited to sub-groups within the society. (Oddly enough, the report also notes that standard English is more sophisticated and generalizable, but the point is not developed.)

The report may seem to modify its utilitarian position when it argues that a grasp of standard English is necessary for gaining entry to the 'forms of higher and further study'. As we saw earlier, the report speaks of the forms of knowledge as having general human value, as being 'the ways through which the human race has reflected upon or sought to order understanding'. One might expect that here the report would have stressed the place that such understanding has in the quality of any human life, and that therefore it should be accessible to everyone. But the report is still preoccupied with the cash nexus. In its view, a crucial limitation of non-standard forms of English is that they do not 'give access to the ideas or forms of higher and further study with which power, incomes and status are closely allied in industrial societies' (2.10).

## Desirable level of educational attainment

In regard to the question of a desirable standard of education that everyone should have the opportunity to achieve, I believe the position of the Schools Commission is more satisfactory. In each of the three documents to which I have referred, the priorities for government action in education are directly related to the task of ensuring that all members of the society reach a certain level of achievement over a range of common educational objectives. This general approach is clearly consistent with the interpretation of education as a human right suggested above. There are, however, two main qualifying comments I would make on the Commission's argument.

Firstly, the stress seems to be placed on a *minimally* adequate educational attainment. (The first report of the Commission speaks, for example, of 'threshold levels' and a 'basic plateau of competence'.) If the level of expectation has been placed too low it is, perhaps, because of the undue weight given to instrumental criteria (such as occupational needs and social efficiency). Admittedly, the two reports of the Commission seem to go further than the report of the Interim Committee. However, they are ambiguous on whether the kind and level of education they believe everyone should attain require an initiation into the high culture. One basic difficulty in assessing the adequacy of what is envisaged is that none of the documents provides even a general description of the program — not even of the kind that Raymond Williams, in *The Long Revolution*, proposes for a common curriculum.[17]

Secondly, contrary to the Commission's belief, the policy of using public resources selectively in an effort to ensure that everyone will at least reach a certain standard of education does not depend on or necessarily promote principles of equality. If the policy succeeded, the quality of formal education for a large proportion of the society would be raised to a satisfactory level. It is possible that for a majority of people in the society the gap between their level of education and that of the best educated would be narrowed. But unless very able and interested students were in some way prevented from exceeding the proposed desirable standard, there would still be very significant differences in educational achievement. It is conceivable that in a situation where everyone had the opportunity to attain at least a good standard of education, the upper limits of achievement might be advanced.

It is misleading, therefore, to speak as *Schools in Australia* does, about promoting 'a more equal basic achievement between children', or to claim, as the Commission's first report does, that the development of independent learning abilities in everyone will advance greater equality of educational outcome.[18]

The policy may be linked more closely with equality of opportunity than with the ideal of an egalitarian society. This is the connection that is highlighted in the Commission's second report. But it seems to me that the policy can be better defended on the grounds that were proposed above in examining education as a human right. This approach avoids the difficulties raised in the first section of this article against using the school as an instrument of equal economic opportunity. But it is also more consistent with the policy that the Commission is really advocating. The objective is not to provide everyone with an *equal* opportunity to reach the desirable level of education, but to give each individual the assistance he or she needs in order to reach that level. The objective might more accurately be described as the promotion of appropriate or sufficient opportunity.

## CONCLUSION

To return finally to the general question of equality in the human right to education, it seems that equality is involved in two respects. Firstly, stress is placed on a curriculum of general education that is the *same* for everyone in its objectives and the main features of its content, and secondly, every individual is held to be equally entitled to the fullest possible assistance he or she needs in order to attain the desirable educational level. Beyond these features, however, education as a human right is by no means dominated by the notion of equality. In the process of education, the right requires substantially unequal treatment of individuals according to their particular abilities, interests, and social circumstances. It does not imply that everyone will, in fact, reach the quality of liberal education considered appropriate for any human being. Nor does it prescribe that no-one should go beyond this level of educational attainment. What it does require is that everyone should certainly have a sufficient opportunity of at least gaining an adequate introduction to liberal education. Education viewed as a human right has nothing to do with equality of outcome; the whole emphasis is on the responsibility of a society to ensure that, as far as possible, no-one fails to gain the range and quality of education that befits the dignity of a human being.

### Notes

1 Australia. (1973). *Schools in Australia. Report of the Interim Committee for the Australian Schools Commission.* (Chairman, P. Karmel). Canberra: AGPS.
  Australia. Schools Commission. (1975). *Report for the Triennium, 1976–1978.* (Chairman, K. McKinnon). Canberra: AGPS.
  Australia. Schools Commission. (1976). *Report: Rolling Triennium, 1977–79.* (Chairman, K. McKinnon). Canberra: AGPS.
2 Australia. Schools Commission. (1975). op. cit., para. 2.4.
3 For a very critical account of the principle of equal opportunity, see John H. Schaar, 'Equality of Opportunity and Beyond'. In J. Roland Pennock and John W. Chapman (Eds) (1967). *Equality,* New York: Atherton Press. I have discussed Schaar's position and other aspects of the principle of equal opportunity in *Education and Social Ideals,* 1973, Chapter VI. Toronto: Longman Canada.
4 Apart from what can be done to control genetic factors, there are of course the complex moral questions of what ought to be done in this area.
5 Australia. (1973). op. cit.: 22.
6 Australia. Schools Commission. (1975). op. cit., para. 2.1.
7 Australia. Schools Commission. (1976). op. cit., para. 2.4.
8 ibid., para. 2.19.
9 ibid., para. 2.13.
10 Jensen, A. R. (1975). 'The Price of Inequality', *Oxford Review of Education,* 1 (1): 59–71.
11 op. cit.: 61.
12 The recent DeFunis case in the US illustrates the legal and moral problems of applying racial quotas in the selection of applicants for educational programs. Not only does this policy attempt to offset the effects of racial discrimination by using race as a principle of selection, but as one Negro scholar (K. Clark of New York University) has noted, 'For blacks to be held to lower standards, or held to different standards, or in some cases to no standards, is a most contemptible form of racism.' Quoted in Maurice Cranston, 'Compensating for Disadvantage', *The Times Higher Education Supplement,* 9 July 1976, p. 14.
13 The point is emphasized by James S. Coleman in commenting on the implications of John Rawls' theory of equality. 'Rawls, Nozick, and Educational Equality', *The Public Interest,* 43: 122.

14 I have discussed the nature of the human right to education in *Education and Social Ideals*, Chapter II.
15 Williams, R. (1961). *The Long Revolution*. Harmondsworth: Penguin Books, p.57.
16 Australia. Schools Commission. (1975). op. cit., paras 2.7–2.10.
17 Williams, R. (1961). op. cit.: 174–175.
18 Australia. Schools Commission. (1975). op. cit., para. 2.7.

# 15. Transition from School to Work — An Emerging Problem

## J. P. Keeves and J. K. Matthews

While the Interim Committee for the Australian Schools Commisson and the Schools Commission itself, when established, were grappling with the many problems confronting Australian ed·· \tion, particularly those advanced in the 1970 statement of educational nee·' , there were new issues emerging which they do not seem to have recognized. Nevertheless, among the Western industrialized nations there was a growing awareness, in response to accumulating evidence, that the comprehensive secondary schools, particularly at the upper levels, were failing to meet important objectives. As a consequence there was increasing debate both in the United States[2] and in Europe[3] on the future of institutionalized schooling for youth.

Within Australia, the education section of the Poverty Inquiry, with Dr R. T. Fitzgerald as Commissioner, turned its attention to certain aspects of the problem and commissioned research studies to obtain the necessary evidence.[4] The Report of the Poverty Inquiry has, in part, been instrumental in focusing attention on this emerging problem in Australian education.[5] However, it has been a review by the OECD panel of examiners that has highlighted critical issues which have been exacerbated by growing unemployment among youth in Australia. Their report[6], together with the background document *Transition from School to Work or Further Study in Australia*[7], which was prepared by the staff of the Commonwealth Department of Education, would appear to have been the stimulus for the establishment of the Committee of Inquiry into Education and Training under the chairmanship of Professor Williams.[8] The report of this Committee, due to be completed by mid-1978, is awaited with considerable interest.

It is already apparent from the debate currently taking place that new educational policies will be required during the coming decade to meet emerging conditions that have arisen from the impact of societal changes within this country on the educational programs of the schools and tertiary institutions. Moreover, it is increasingly apparent that future financial support for education will be limited by economic circumstances and that new programs will only be implemented at the expense of existing ones. These are questions that the Schools Commission will, in the future, have to examine. As a consequence, the Commission will need to reassess its priorities and redirect its allocation of resources.

In this article some of the issues associated with the education of youth and their transition from school to work are examined. In addition, suggestions are made for solutions to these problems and the consequences of these solutions for education in the schools are discussed.

## FROM CHILDHOOD TO ADULT LIFE

Every society faces the problem of providing for the development of its children through adolescence to adult life. There are three main areas in which growth takes place. Firstly, there is the development of the cognitive and intellectual capacities of the individual. Whereas in the years of early childhood this aspect of growth is largely fostered by the home, as the individual moves through childhood and adolescence, provision for growth in this area is increasingly undertaken by educational institutions. Associated with the development of the intellectual skills of the individual is the transmission of knowledge from one generation to the next, so that such knowledge is conserved, and future development of knowledge is made possible. This has in the past been seen as the prime role of educational institutions.

The second area in which growth occurs is the preparation for and selection of an occupation or career through which the individual may achieve economic independence. Musgrave has recently drawn attention to the possibility of following an 'un-career' in which an individual can work if he wants, in the way that he wants and for as long as he wants.[9] Furthermore, Musgrave argues that such an approach, which is being selected by many, is socially defensible under present economic conditions when suitable employment is limited. The further alternative of a 'non-career' in which work is seen as meaningless and perhaps irrelevant, may also be gaining greater acceptance in our society. However, the consequences of following such a course for an individual who becomes unable to achieve economic independence would seem to be tragic. The preparation for and selection of an occupation has in the past been shared between the educational and employing institutions, but is currently being relegated to educational institutions because of the costs incurred by the employers. The consequences of what is argued to be greater efficiency have been the building up of more extensive senior secondary, tertiary and sub-tertiary educational institutions in which youth is segregated from the adult world.

In the third area we would place those aspects of development that are associated with creative living and are outside the fields of learning and work. Included within this area are the achieving of mature relations with persons of all ages and of both sexes, the acquisition of a set of values together with an ethical system that serves to guide behaviour, and the preparation for marriage and family life.[10] A further frequently over-looked but important component of this area is the preparation for and selection of creative leisure-time pursuits. Such activities cannot be divorced from interpersonal relationships or from the acquisition of a system of values. Nevertheless, with greater provision for more flexible working hours, longer vacation periods, and extended long-service leave at regular intervals, the development of creative ways to use leisure time becomes of increasing importance. Unless each individual in his transformation from childhood to adult maturity acquires the capabilities for self-fulfilment in all three areas, we would argue that he is being denied to a greater or lesser extent development as an individual, and constructive participation in society. While provision for individual growth is a far greater task than can be left to educational institutions, our schools are increasingly being required to supply the necessary opportunities for personal development in all three areas.

## THE CHANGING PURPOSES OF SCHOOLING

Over the past decade there has been considerable debate about the quality and needs of schooling in Australia and these issues have been examined in the reports prepared by the Schools Commission.[11] This questioning has been brought about by several factors, including the increased pressure for provision of educational facilities occasioned by migration and the post-war rise in the birth-rate, and by changed perceptions of what education is for. Notions of equality and comprehensiveness in education have replaced meritocratic goals of selection of talent and, as a consequence, attempts have been made to foster the intellectual development of an entire age group rather than selecting and fostering the few chosen on intellectual criteria.[12]

In addition, a greater awareness of, and faith in, the personal and social benefits of education had led to a marked increase in participation in education among youth over the last 15 years. In 1964, 38 per cent of the 16-year-old age group and 17 per cent of the 17-year-old age group were enrolled full-time in school. By 1972, the corresponding figures were 55 per cent and 30 per cent.[13] The rate of growth in upper secondary enrolments slowed down after the early 1970s, but there are signs that it is again increasing.[14] At the present time, it is estimated that some 35 per cent of secondary school students continue to Year 12, the terminal year of schooling. Approximately 22 per cent proceed to universities or colleges of advanced education, and an estimated further 30 per cent enter technical and further educational institutions.[15] The expectations of young people have been for more and more schooling, as has been the experience in other industrialized nations, notably the United States, Japan, and Sweden.

Until recently the benefits of extended periods of education have been unquestioned and it has been assumed that lengthy education was intrinsically good for the individual. Moreover, given the increasing complexity of technological development in the workplace, it has also been considered beneficial for productivity and the economy in general. The different educational institutions provide the young with three main types of skills or qualifications.[16] Firstly, they develop such basic skills as literacy and numeracy; secondly, they produce specific skills to meet the particular requirements of the labour market, ranging from the learned professions to the manual trades; and thirdly, formal educational qualifications, such as the Higher School Certificate and tertiary degrees and diplomas, are used by employers in the recruitment of staff. It has become evident, however, that the educational qualification demanded for a particular job is often unrelated to the skills needed to carry out the tasks required by the job. The qualification relates more to the level of the increasingly highly credentialled pool of labour from which selection has to be made and acts therefore as a selection threshold rather than as an indicator of actual skill. In addition, studies such as the ACER Survey of Literacy and Numeracy have shown that the acquisition of basic skills is by no means as universal by the minimum school-leaving age as had been previously assumed.[17] However, training in specific marketable skills has frequently been seen by schools and other educational institutions as not being part of their function.

The value of extended periods of formal education for the personal development and socialization of young people into adult social roles has also come into question.[18] For increasing periods after physical maturity, youth are cut off from adult society and from responsibility and are set within an age-segregated subculture where objectives and activities are contrived and bear little relation to either the developmental needs of youth or the wider goals of society. The decreasing size and greater homogeneity with respect to age of families exacerbates this tendency towards age segregation. As a consequence, young people are presented with few adult models or activities for interacting with adults.

It is clear that formal education can no longer be viewed as intrinsically beneficial under all circumstances. Institutionalized schooling must be seen within the framework of the wider society and the place of individuals within that society. As a consequence it is necessary to re-examine the nature and extent of education that will allow individuals to find a satisfying and productive role within this context.

## UNEMPLOYMENT AMONG YOUTH

A problem apparently associated with a lack of congruence between school and society, or education and work has been exposed by the current economic recession. The evidence from the labour force survey for August 1977 revealed that there were 118 200 persons aged 15 to 19 years unemployed, and the unemployment rate for this group was 16.3 per cent, being slightly less for males (14.6), and slightly greater for females (18.3 per cent). By way of comparison, the same survey revealed that there were 204 300 persons aged 20 years and over who were unemployed, with an unemployment rate of 3.7 per cent. With the rate of youth unemployment at this level, with an estimated 140 000 to 150 000 teenagers unemployed and with an estimated unemployment rate of 20 per cent and above by August 1978, there is clear evidence of a serious social problem.[19] However, this problem is not unique to

Australia. It should be noted that an International Conference at the Aspen Institute in Berlin in 1976 stated that

> Youth unemployment was identified as the most acute problem facing school and society, not only because of its magnitude in some countries, but also because there does not appear to be a short-term solution to the problem.[20]

While the problem of youth unemployment is readily exposed it is much more difficult to understand. Sheehan has recently clarified several issues in the debate on the origins and nature of the problem.[21]

1  The share of youth aged 15 to 19 in total unemployment and the ratio of unemployment rates for youth to rates for adults has remained relatively constant over the past decade. However, there has been some upward drift in this ratio for females during the decade, indicating that recent structural changes in employment patterns may contribute to an explanation.

2  In addition to the difficulty faced by the recent school-leaver in seeking a job, there was some evidence of four factors that would explain why difficulties were encountered in finding employment. These factors were (a) the existence of severe skill imbalances in the junior labour force, (b) the existence of geographical imbalance between rural and metropolitan areas in the supply and demand for labour, (c) the inability of the economy for several years past to absorb the early school-leaver, and (d) the difficulty experienced by some ethnic groups in finding employment.

3  There was also evidence that increases in the relative wage rates for youth and the displacement of youth by married women entering the workforce contributed to youth unemployment in a minor way. It was also possible that the large increases in unemployment benefits for youth which have been granted in recent years would affect their work-seeking behaviour, but this could not be seen as a cause of the current high levels of unemployment among youth.

Other factors which have been advanced as causes of the difficulties encountered by youth in gaining employment are as follows:

1  There is a tendency for employers to prefer experienced workers whose productivity is considerably higher.

2  Youth are believed to have undesirable attitudes to work, with greater turnover and increased selectivity in jobs. However, apart from a relatively high turnover rate there is little evidence for such assertions.

3  There is an increase in the use by employers of educational credentials as selection instruments which concentrates unemployment among youth who lack both qualifications and experience.

The evidence presented by Sheehan would seem to imply that the primary cause of the present youth unemployment problem is the impact of the economic recession on the labour market, which is traditionally adverse to youth and which has traditionally shown much higher rates of unemployment among youth than among adults.[22] It is, however, easy to assume that with an upturn in the economy the problems of youth unemployment will recede.

Nevertheless, there is increasing evidence to indicate that the problems associated with the unemployment of the unskilled in Australian society are not cyclic in nature but are related to long-term structural changes in the workforce. As a consequence we may anticipate that it will become necessary, although perhaps undesirable, for successively greater proportions of youth to be withdrawn from the labour market. Experience in other advanced technological societies, such as the United States, Japan and Sweden support this view. Consequently we may expect continued increases in school retention rates in Australia which are caused by young people who would have left to take jobs if they had been available, but who persist at school and at tertiary institutions in the absence of any other option. Many of these students will gain few additional and marketable skills from the prolongation of their education. They will merely add to the trend in credentialism which further disadvantages the youth leaving at lower levels.

While there is an economic recession, the prospects are not promising for those with higher credentials, but they are even worse for early school-leavers without any qualifications at all. In general, those with post-school qualifications find some form of employment, even if it does not come up to their expectations or skill levels. However, for many without qualifications, a state of affairs accentuated by the demise of both the Intermediate and Leaving Certificate Awards, or their equivalents, the alternatives are a period of several years with little or no employment, or several years of additional education of dubious worth.

## LACK OF FIT BETWEEN SCHOOL AND WORK

It is clear that many young people leaving school in Australia today have reduced access to employment and thus to full participation in the life of our society. The transition between the world of school and the world of work is neither smooth nor automatic, and the damage to the self-concept and morale of young people may well be considerable. The institutions of economic activity and of education in our society no longer appear to complement each other, and thus both merit searching examination. Any investigation of the problem of lack of fit between the world of work and the world of education must address itself to the following three questions:

1 To what extent do schools equip students with the attitudes and competence necessary to gain and maintain employment and useful social functioning in society as it is now constituted and is likely to be in the near future?
2 To what extent do the labour market and particular occupations provide opportunities and experiences commensurate with the talents, qualifications and experience of the young people entering the workforce and to what extent do employers foster the continued growth and development of their young employees?
3 What are the most appropriate means for inducting youth into the adult

society and to what extent should the socialization process be the responsibility of institutions such as the school?

In any discussion, the focus must be primarily upon those who leave school at or before the end of secondary schooling rather than those who continue to study at the post-secondary level. This is for four main reasons. Firstly, they constitute a majority of entrants to the workforce from educational institutions. About two-thirds of the age group leave school at Year 11 or lower, and about half of school-leavers do not proceed with any form of post-secondary education. Secondly, it is this group whose needs and experiences have been largely ignored in the past. The attention of educational planners has been focused on expanding opportunities for further tertiary study, irrespective of the social and personal costs of such a course of action, while ignoring the needs of a majority of Australian youth for whom it is neither appropriate nor desirable. The emergence of the problem of unemployed youth would seem to indicate that it is time the balance swung in the other direction. Thirdly, it is this group on which the burden of the lack of correspondence between the education and the labour systems falls most heavily. These are the young people most prone to unemployment, underemployment and dissatisfaction. To such youths, whose adult life begins in this fashion, permanent harm could well be done. This could provide a focus and breeding ground for wider dissatisfaction and could generate long-term problems for Australian society. Finally, this group contains the younger generation of groups already most disadvantaged in our society, such as Aboriginals, non-English speaking migrants and those growing up in poverty. It is thus a logical point for attempting to break into the cycle of disadvantage and for improving the quality of life of groups for which it has previously been low.

Bearing in mind this primary focus on those who enter the workforce without post-school qualifications, we will address ourselves to each of the three questions stated above.

## AREAS OF BASIC COMPETENCE

Firstly, in the basic skills area, as we have already indicated, approximately 25 per cent of school-leavers, especially those leaving at or around the minimum legal age, do not have the literacy or numeracy skills necessary for employment in many occupations.[23] The *Youth Needs and Public Policies* report showed that there was considerable agreement among early school-leavers about the need for basic skills and preparation for work and a career.[24] However, these young people tended to see educational institutions as unresponsive to their needs and generally they had negative school experiences. They left at the end of the period of compulsory schooling, which was the most crowded and impersonal stage. Pressures for academic achievement, the apparent irrelevance of much of the curriculum, and the aggravation of petty rules and restrictions led them to reject school and made them less likely to return to formal education in the future. The early-leavers listed dissatisfaction with school as the major reason for leaving, rather than such factors as financial difficulties. As well, these students were often in lower academic streams or terminal courses. In effect, a 'push-out' by the school occurred. Seventy per cent of the young people in the 'Youth Needs' sample who left school at Year 10 or below had no idea of what they wanted to do when they left school, thus demonstrating a marked inadequacy of vocational guidance at this level.

The student leaving school without a terminal secondary certificate would also be greatly disadvantaged in not having the formal qualification which has become the basic minimum requirement for entry to many jobs, particularly in the white collar-clerical area, and to almost any form of post-school training. Twenty years ago, the possession of a Junior or Intermediate certificate gained by success in an external examination at Year 10 of secondary schooling was a guarantee of consideration for a wide range of jobs. Today, certification at this level has been either abandoned or has declined in importance with the growth of credentialism and the terminal secondary certificate has taken its place. This stress on higher credentials has reduced the options of school-leavers at levels below the final secondary year irrespective of their skills and competence. Improving their cognitive performance and range of skills would be of no benefit in gaining employment unless it could be recognized in some way at the point of hiring labour in the market place. More flexible selection criteria for entry to both jobs and post-school study, based on the actual skills and qualities required, would appear to be needed if young people are not to be forced into persistence at school against their inclination or to be severely disadvantaged for failing to continue at school.

The production of specific skills to meet the requirements of the market place would not appear, at the present time, to be seen as the function of the school at any level. However, Victorian technical schools and most comprehensive schools in other States do provide some training in practical skills which would be of use in later apprenticeship programs or practically-oriented occupations. Many schools also offer optional courses in typing and commercial subjects as well as other specific skills which should be of use in gaining employment. These courses should be valuable, particularly for potential early-leavers and could well be extended. However, if schools provided training at a basic level which was too narrowly restricted to the skills required for particular occupations they could close off their students' options rather than opening them. Schooling at the lower secondary level would probably be of most use to these students if it concentrated on the inculcation of basic skills, not only of literacy and numeracy, but also the social and personal skills and the knowledge necessary to function effectively in society. It should also provide basic training in practical and technical skills which could be of use in future employment and perhaps some practical work experience in putting these skills into effect.

The OECD Panel of Examiners were impressed with a widespread desire throughout Australia

> to enlarge, improve and enrich the information, guidance and placement services for young people who must make important educational and occupational decisions at the end of their compulsory education and in the years that follow.[25]

Moreover, while they noted the wide variety of procedures being tried in different parts of Australia, they argued that there was a major problem of increasing the total amount of services provided and of developing a coherent program of effective services to meet the needs of particular groups of young people.[26] It is, however, for the early school-leavers that programs of career education, guidance and placement services are urgently required, since such early-leavers are likely to be most vulnerable to the vicissitudes of the labour market.

## THE EMPLOYMENT SYSTEM

The second question relevant to the school-work interface focuses on the employment system and the extent to which it matches the needs and talents of entrants to the workforce – and indeed workers in general. Industrialization in the western world has been accompanied by segmentation of work into small and repetitive tasks. This is not only true in manufacturing but also occurs in many clerical and service occupations. This process is now being questioned as it creates boring and alienating work experiences for employees and does not necessarily promote higher productivity. For the early school-leaver trapped in a series of physically unpleasant and exhausting repetitive tasks in a factory, it thwarts opportunities to learn and develop on or off the job and provides no obvious avenues for advancement. For the better credentialled entrant to the workforce the situation is almost as bad. After persisting with education in order to gain a qualification, the school or tertiary graduate finds that he has only gained a position that involves working on minor and repetitive clerical tasks, which do not satisfy the increased expectations that further education has given him. Neither situation is healthy and it is of value to consider whether the educational system should adjust to meet the needs of the labour market.

Manpower needs can be viewed from the stance of the availability of different types of labour as well as from that of the technical requirements for particular jobs. It may be more appropriate to re-fashion the job and concomitant training programs provided by industry and commerce to the kinds of workers available, rather than demand that the education system fashion the potential workers to the kinds of jobs which have been created. This would require a basic reassessment of the purposes and operation of most public and private enterprises and a partial shift in their benefits from shareholder and manager to those engaged in production. Elements of an occupation conducive to job satisfaction have been variously described as independence, control and initiative, good relationships with fellow workers, appreciation of work done, variety, and opportunities for learning and personal growth. The redesign of jobs incorporating some or all of these features could include horizontal and vertical job enlargement and whole process team-work. These are being tried out on a small scale in some industries and government departments with apparent success. However, there is no indication at this stage of any large-scale adoption of such practices in Australia.

It has been consistently noted over the last few years that, of the 15-22 age group, the best satisfied, both educationally and occupationally, are apprentices and others in fields such as nursing, which combine work with further education. The 'Youth Needs' study found that apprentices had identified vocational goals and followed clearly defined steps towards attaining them. They felt they were achieving something and could see results for their efforts. In contrast to young people in dead-end jobs and those remaining at school, apprentices felt that they were learning a great deal and could see the practical application of their study.[27] It would seem that an extension of the apprenticeship model or the development of variations on it would be most conducive to job satisfaction among the young. This type of combination of work and education might well be the most satisfactory way of meeting the needs and expectations of many teenagers leaving school and inducting them into the world of work and adult society.

The OECD Panel of Examiners has pointed out, however, that in Australia small and medium firms are having increasing difficulty in providing satisfactory practical training for apprentices and absorbing increasing costs, in spite of government subsidies.[28] There are growing demands for technical colleges to provide a greater proportion of the practical training associated with apprenticeships. The system has also been criticized on the grounds that it is too costly, that the indenture relationship is outmoded, the training is too long, and that industries no longer need all-round craftsmen. None of these problems is insurmountable and it would seem desirable that the apprenticeship system should not be discarded, but should be restructured, better organized and more closely related to training needs and to complementary programs provided by educational and training establishments. It would seem essential that the features which have made apprenticeships an attractive option for school-leavers should be developed in any extension of the system.

## SOCIALIZING YOUTH INTO ADULT SOCIETY

The third question to be examined concerns the most appropriate means for socializing the young in our society. It is this question which has received most attention in overseas studies of the problem, notably the United States and the other OECD countries. One major report which is relevant to the Australian situation is that of the Panel on Youth of the President's Science Advisory Committee in the United States.[29] This report, named after its Chairman J. S. Coleman, points out that segregation from others of different ages has increasingly come to characterize the social and economic position of youth in

251

American society. This segregation is accompanied by a youth culture which has become a surrogate for maturity. There has been a shift in the options available to young people. Opportunities have increased in areas of consumption, leisure and formal education, but have declined in other areas. Opportunities to carry out responsible work and to engage in efforts important to the welfare of others have been deferred until the end of an increasingly long period of schooling. The proportion of young people at work has declined sharply and changes in occupational requirements have excluded youth from some of the most challenging jobs. Deferment of economic rewards has as a corollary a decline in options concerning the path to adult working life. Social and sometimes legal pressures make it difficult to resume education after several years out in the job market. The world of education is clearly and markedly divorced from that of work.

Some of the reasons for this segregation of youth have been that families no longer sanction the early commitment of the young to productive activity; trade unions and professional organizations fear large-scale incursions by youth into their labour markets; humanitarian sentiment opposes the exploitation of youth; and professionalization and bureaucratization have narrowed the range of youth's contact with adults. Ideas and institutions which once served genuine and explicit needs have been uncritically extended to the point where they deprive youth of experience important to their growth and development.

This analysis has been corroborated by Australian findings. The poverty and 'Youth Needs' studies demonstrated that the young see schooling as separate from the real world and unresponsive to their needs. Fitzgerald reported that the expressed concerns of adolescent students were to achieve a sense of purpose, a feeling of competence and to find a career.[30] Extended periods of schooling did not necessarily help many young people to achieve these goals. Wright and Headlam found youth wanted more emphasis in their lives on personal and social development and more responsible involvement in the real life of the community.[31] Extended periods of schooling led to a concentration on the intellectual aspect and to a neglect of other facets of developing maturity.

The recommendations of the Coleman report to remedy this situation are of considerable interest. They concentrate, however, on designing environments appropriate for the all-round development of youth and largely ignore the wider social and economic structures of the society within which youth must live and grow. Briefly, the recommendations are that the school should cut down its own functions to the purely academic and act as an agent for facilitating other experiences for youth; that alternation between school and work should be encouraged; that work organizations should undertake educational functions; that youth communities and adult-sponsored youth organizations should be encouraged and taken more seriously; that legal and administrative constraints on the work activities of youth should be reviewed; that education vouchers should be issued at the end of compulsory schooling to be used at the discretion of the individual at any period in his life; and that opportunities for public and community service should be expanded.

These recommendations make great sense in relation to the developmental needs of adolescents and the human needs of all age groups. However, they operate in a societal and economic vacuum. They do not attack the basic problems of why the economy no longer needs youth labour and what can be done to change the nature of all jobs and economic relationships, including those of the young, so that a fuller and more equitable part may be played by all, with everybody's talents being used and developed to the full. The Coleman report assumes an economic and societal status quo and seeks to make it more palatable and in keeping with the developmental needs of youth. However, we would argue that for the solution of the problems that have recently emerged in Australia, certain societal changes must precede educational change and not proceed from it.

Within an Australian context, the problems of the transition of young people from education to work must be examined with regard to the economy and the institutions of society as a whole. Moreover, the interests of all other age groups and members of the workforce must be taken into account if the measures are to be successful in a lasting sense.

## SOME PROPOSED SOLUTIONS

### Youth unemployment

Up to the time of writing most of the newly initiated policies in Australia have tackled the problems of youth unemployment. While the programs being undertaken serve an immediate need, they are, at best, short-term solutions. One important step has been to establish a Special Youth Employment Task Force in each State with representatives from the Commonwealth Department of Employment and Industrial Relations, State Governments, employers and trade unions. In addition, a Youth Employment Bureau has been created within the Department of Employment and Industrial Relations with offices in each State. The Task Force will undertake a major campaign to encourage employers to engage additional young people, and the Bureau will provide backup to the campaign.

In addition, a diverse and comprehensive range of programs has been developed for unemployed youth. The programs include the provisions of (1) subsidies to employers to take on young unemployed and to assist them to establish themselves in the workforce, (2) community groups to support young unemployed people by helping them to improve their job-seeking skills and to maintain their readiness for work, (3) courses in literacy and numeracy, personal development, communication skills, and job skills to assist young unemployed people with low educational qualifications, and (4) rebates for employers releasing apprentices to attend technical colleges for training.[32]

Those programs that involve training seek to raise the basic competence and skills of youth, making employable some who are at present unemployable. However, such short-term training programs do not create additional jobs and at best are only temporary solutions to the problems that exist. Action to solve the youth unemployment problem can only be effectively taken within the context of the economy as a whole. Without substantial changes, there is bound to be fairly serious youth unemployment whenever a high level of economic activity is not maintained.

## Staying Longer at School

Action to meet the educational, developmental and employment needs of young people can be taken from a number of directions. One is the school. As has already been suggested, action concentrated on the school alone cannot be expected to achieve much for the majority of adolescents. Attempts to keep them longer in school will only exacerbate the unfortunate trends already in existence. Also any attempt to further enlarge the functions of the school are of doubtful value. Already, whenever there is perception of a social ill, the school is expected to take some part in solving it — thus we have drug education, driver education, sex education, and a whole host of other particular programs aimed at lessening perceived problems of socialization into adult life. The effectiveness of these attempts in altering attitudes and actions has not been conclusively demonstrated by the evaluative studies that have been made. As well, the school has been called to take on a host of social therapeutic functions. It is expected to cure social inequality, juvenile delinquency and a range of other social and emotional ills. The problem with further enlarging the functions of the school is that its aims become diffuse and it ends up achieving none of its functions well. It is also true that adolescents see the activities of the school as being contrived and divorced from the real world. Programs to develop work experience, maturity, and social responsibility, which are based in the school, therefore run the risk of not achieving their aims, simply because they are connected with the school and are therefore perceived as being removed from reality.

## Youth Employment Programs

A further proposed course of action is the creation of special kinds of jobs for young people, particularly in relation to community service. However measures such as this have disadvantages from the point of view of the young people for whom they are designed: they are temporary time-fillers which merely postpone the problem of finding more permanent employment in an ongoing situation. They could also suffer from a problem of unreality, similar to that endemic in programs attached to schools. If such work programs contain only young people, are for a limited period, and provide work which does not appear to be integrated with the normal economic life of the community, they solve neither the long-term employment problems of youth nor the socialization problems of isolation from adults and adult responsibilities.

Such special work programs for young people could also create problems in the general workforce in these areas. Presumably there are agencies and government departments already operating in the fields of community service which these programs would encompass. What would be their reactions to this intrusion into their fields? What would the unions think of an influx of temporary labour at possibly quite different rates of pay outside union control? Would the clients of such services feel they were being downgraded or used to solve other people's problems?

Perhaps a better solution than creating special short-term job programs would be to expand government assistance to agencies working in these fields enabling them to employ more staff and extend their functions. This would require an understanding that the majority of new employees would be young entrants to the workforce and that a training component would be built into their work.

Other measures could include subsidizing the employment of certain categories of young people, as is already being done with apprentices, and revising terms and conditions of employment to make young people more competitive in the job market.

**New Educational Programs**

Refreshment, updating and retraining is usually provided by post-school institutions as well as by in-service courses in such institutions. This sort of continuing education should be encouraged and expanded, but more importantly, much training of this kind might take place at the workface. This would, however, probably involve subsidizing such programs from government funds.

A substantial number of industrial and commercial organizations currently conduct training programs for their staff. Relatively little is known about such programs, their purposes and scope, their effectiveness and value, and the extent to which they interest and attract workers at different levels in an organization. We believe that a marked expansion of such programs could well take place, and cite as evidence the range of such programs in operation in Sweden and in Scotland, countries with similar problems to those currently existing in Australia. Courses conducted close to the workface have, we believe, a greater chance of serving the needs of individuals as well as the organization and thus will be seen to be more relevant both by those taking the courses as well as by those conducting them.

The growth of programs being conducted by the trade unions in the training of their members would also seem to be an important development that should not be starved of funds and could well be expanded and diversified. Moreover, it is possible that much desirable flexibility would be lost if such programs were incorporated into the TAFE sector. We suggest that an important development to which the unions should give every consideration is the further education of their members to advance their personal development in every possible way.

It is clear that if the educational needs and employment prospects of the majority of young Australians are to be met and enhanced, the existing educational institutions on which to focus are not the schools, the universities or the colleges of advanced education, but the TAFE institutions and community colleges. TAFE enrolments, of which a majority are part-time, are more than double those in other post-secondary insitutions and 63 per cent of total TAFE enrolments in 1974 were in vocationally-oriented courses. In all TAFE streams, 44 per cent of enrolments were of students under 21 years of age.[33] This indicates the importance of TAFE as a study option for school-leavers, both for vocational training and for basic education. This is a trend which should be encouraged, especially for students who leave school at the end of the compulsory period. Study in a TAFE institution, especially part-time and combined with work, does not have the disadvantages of isolation, unreality, perceived irrelevance and petty restrictions which are inherent in the school situation for these students. They can concentrate on acquiring the skills and competence which they see as relevant in their jobs and their personal lives and which form a basis for employment and further training.

A large number of part-time enrolments of people under 19 in the trades stream of TAFE institutions are apprentices, who would appear to be among the most well satisfied of all adolescents. The current problems in the apprenticeship system and its possible expansion should be thoroughly investigated, particularly with a view to maintaining the enormous advantages of apprentices being based and gaining their practical experience in the workplace.

There is, however, a tendency for other occupations, such as nursing, which have traditionally combined training with work, to base their training almost completely in educational institutions and to demand educational pre-requisites such as the HSC for entry to training courses. This is unfortunate and closes off options for many young people. If it does occur, and we suggest it should be strongly resisted, it is essential that bridging courses should be provided for nursing aides to equip them to undertake nursing training, and it could even be of value to provide courses to equip nurses for entry to training courses for medicine or social work or related fields. The rise of arbitrary educational credentials for entry to various levels of occupational activity has closed off options for people to work their way up in a field and has produced what almost amounts to a caste system of occupational choice. Whereas once it was possible to work one's way up from messenger boy to managing director, it is now highly likely that the managing director will be recruited from entrants to the firm at a high level determined by the possession of particular credentials. Meanwhile the messenger boy can progress only to a defined ceiling beyond which he cannot go without acquiring these credentials. A system of on-the-job training or closely integrated part-time study in TAFE institutions would be preferable to the imposition of credential-based ceilings and would enable every worker to develop his talents to the full and progress as far as he was able. Movements in this direction might help to overcome some of the educational and work problems of young people.

Recurrent education and opportunities for upgrading skills should be available to all age groups, not just the young. If those engaged in educational activity were more evenly spread throughout all age groups, it would ease the transition from education to work because this education would not be so heavily concentrated on the young. With more older workers temporarily out of the workforce for educational purposes it would be necessary to spread existing work between more people on a more equitable basis, and more young workers would need to be brought in.

## PREPARATION FOR CREATIVE LIVING

In the preceding sections, consideration has been given to proposals for the solution to the current problems of youth that involve further education and employment. In both areas, the dangers of segregating youth from people of other ages have been discussed. As both Smith and Orlosky[34] and the Panel on Youth of the President's Science Advisory Committee in the United States[35] have pointed out, the benefits of integrating youth with adults would seem to greatly outweigh the benefits of segregation by age in the socialization of youth. However, neither formal education nor employment and the gaining of economic independence cover fully all aspects of personal development in the transition from childhood to adult life. There is an area of preparation for creative living concerned with the development of interpersonal relationships with people of all ages, with the acquisition of a system of values and with the selection of creative leisure-time pursuits that is being largely ignored in the present-day provision for the socialization of youth. While this area is not divorced from those of learning or work it is not adequately covered by the proposals we have made. We argue that programs that will provide for individual development in the area that we have elected to call 'creative living' are required. Nevertheless, it is important that such programs should not divorce the youth who participate in them from the rest of society but should lead them into closer involvement with other people across the whole of the age range.

In Australia, we have had little experience with Youth Service Organizations such as the Peace Corps of the United States or Volunteer Service Overseas in Britain and we have little direct knowledge to draw upon in this area. However, we note that these schemes have provided opportunities for few young people to employ their energies in making a contribution to society. Furthermore, we question the value of the emphasis on service overseas when there are equally valuable but different contributions to be made nearer to home. Nevertheless, we argue that these service organizations could provide a model if correctly directed for promoting the development of youth in this third area of preparation for creative living.

In Australia, there are many institutions that have programs of service that atrophy for lack of energy and manpower to sustain them. We have in mind institutions that serve an expressive and integrative role which include such organizations as churches, museums, galleries, theatres; institutions that provide services to individuals, which include care of the aged, the very young, the infirm and the handicapped; institutions that are concerned with community services, such as those responsible for parks and gardens and the conservation of the environment, or with the provision of recreational facilities; and finally institutions that foster general welfare, such as the defence services, and emergency services. It is advocated that extensive service programs should be promoted that will provide opportunities for youth to undertake work with such institutions.

We would not envisage that a complex administrative organization should be established that would carry out work in these areas, but rather that programs should be developed by existing service organizations that will receive financial support provided young people aged 15 to 24 years are engaged in such work. It would seem important that participation in such programs should not be seen as a temporary expedient filling the free time of youth while unemployed, but rather as planned service of six to 12 months duration or longer, alternating with a period of study and training or with a period in the regular workforce.

## CONCLUSION

If the assumption is correct that the current high level of unemployment is not just the consequence of a short-term cycle of events, but the outcome of structural changes in the labour force, then the problems of unemployed youth will remain for an indefinite period. Some of the envisaged 100 000 to 200 000 youth who cannot find employment will return for further schooling or for training programs in TAFE institutions, some will find gainful work as employers are encouraged to engage a higher proportion of youth. Nevertheless, there will remain a very substantial number for whom alternative programs that foster personal growth and development will have to be established.

There are already in existence organizations that are directed towards the service of youth such as the Outward Bound Movement, the Scout and Guide Movements, the YMCA and YWCA, and Rural Youth. These organizations grew and flourished under different circumstances. If new programs are to be set up to cater for the changing needs of youth, then these organizations should also be encouraged to redevelop their programs away from those of leisure time pursuits towards sustained programs of service, adventure and preparation for creative living. However, the problem is too great for such organizations to handle.

A possible solution would appear to be a Youth Service Movement supported from public moneys, through which youth undertake sustained service activity for periods of six to 12 months or more. Such activity should be alternated with education and/or work, and should not involve the segregation of youth from other age groups, but should serve to bring youth into closer contact with people of all ages.

However, we recognize that other possible approaches to solving this major problem could well be evolved, and some potentially valuable programs could have a greater educational component. Nevertheless, we believe that it is necessary to warn against the ever-present danger of viewing such programs in terms of courses conducted by institutions established by the educational bureaucracy for a specific purpose. Such institutions are over-concerned with their staff establishments and their building programs so that they have insufficient flexibility to meet changing needs and changing circumstances. Too little is known about the wide range of educational programs run by industry and commerce for the training of staff on the job. We would argue that these also provide a hopeful area for future development.

It is of some concern to us that the magnitude of the problems that appear to be forming in Australia and have already emerged overseas, are not being appreciated in this country. Educators, employers and politicians have not as yet accepted that the problem is one of considerable proportions and significance for the future of this country. Yet it has become increasingly obvious to us that no long-term solutions to the problems of youth education and employment or to the broader questions of general unemployment and worker dissatisfaction can be found in Australia without the active co-operation of both employers and trade unions. Trade unions in Australia, in particular, are in a position to influence the working conditions and terms of employment for the majority of Australians as well as to promote or hinder the development of young people and their smooth absorption into the workforce. Any government wishing to address itself seriously to these problems must seek the opinions and the help of the trade union movement and attempt to ensure that all measures taken will be supported by the unions. Otherwise there is a strong risk that the best of policies will not meet with success, and the present and future generations of youth will fail to make a satisfactory transition from the restricted world of schooling to the wider world of gainful employment and creative participation in adult life.

### Notes

1 Australian Education Council. (1970). *A Statement of Some Needs of Australian Education.* Sydney: Australian Education Council.
2 See Passow, A. H. (1976). *Secondary Education Reform: Retrospect and Prospect.* New York: Teachers College, Columbia University, and W. Van Til (Ed.) (1976). *Issues in Secondary Education.* Chicago, Ill.: National Society for the Study of Education.
3 See Bulcock, J. W. (Ed.) (1976). *The Future of Institutionalized Schooling.* Report on an International Conference, Aspen Institute, Berlin, September 13-17.
4 Australia. Commission of Inquiry into Poverty. (1976-1978).
— (1976). *Lifelong Education and Poor People: Three Studies.* Canberra: AGPS.
— (1977). *Aspects of School Welfare Provision.* Canberra: AGPS.
— (1977). *School Leavers: Choice and Opportunity.* Canberra: AGPS.

— (1978). *Outcomes of Schooling: Aspects of Success and Failure.* Canberra: AGPS.

— (1978). *School, Community and Work; Urban and Rural Aspects.* Canberra: AGPS.

5  See Australia. Commission of Inquiry into Poverty. (1976). *Poverty and Education in Australia. Fifth Main Report.* (Commissioner, R. T. Fitzgerald). Canberra: AGPS.

6  Organization for Economic Co-operation and Development, Education Committee. *Review of Educational Policy in Australia. Examiners' Report and Questions.* Paris: OECD (draft). October 1976.

7  Australia. Department of Education. (1976). *Transition from School to Work or Further Study. A background paper for an OECD Review of Australian Education Policy.* Canberra: Department of Education.

8  For the Terms of Reference for the Committee of Inquiry into Education and Training under the Chairmanship of Professor B. Williams, see *House of Representatives Weekly Hansard*, 9 September 1976, pp.878–879.

9  Musgrave, P. W. 'Educational Aspects of Youth Unemployment'. In R. F. Henderson (Ed.) (1977). *Proceedings of the Second Symposium of the Academy of the Social Sciences in Australia on Youth Unemployment. November 7 and 8, 1977 — Canberra.* Canberra: Academy of the Social Sciences.

10  These components recorded in this area are derived, in part, from Havighurst's study of developmental tasks. See R. J. Havighurst. (1953). *Human Development and Education.* New York: Longman, Green and Company.

11  Australia. Schools Commission.

— (1975). *Report for the Triennium 1976–78.* Canberra: AGPS.

— (1976). *Report: Rolling Triennium 1977–79.* Canberra: AGPS.

— (1977). *Rolling Triennium 1978–80: Report for 1978.* Canberra: AGPS.

12  See J. P. Keeves. 'Approaches to the Goal of Educational Equality: Will the Karmel Report Work?'. See Chapter 6, in this volume.

13  OECD Education Committee. op. cit.: 21.

14  Australia. Department of Education. (1977). *Major Trends and Developments in Australian Education in 1975 and 1976.* Canberra: Department of Education.

15  Karmel, P. (1977). 'Education and the Workforce', *Education News*, **16**(1):12.

16  ibid.

17  See Keeves, J. P. and Bourke, S. F. (1976). *Australian Studies in School Performance. Volume I. Literacy and Numeracy in Australian Schools: A First Report.* Canberra: AGPS.

Bourke, S. F. and Lewis, R. (1976). *Australian Studies in School Performance. Volume II. Literacy and Numeracy in Australian Schools: Item Report.* Canberra: AGPS.

Bourke, S. F. and Keeves, J. P. (Eds) (1977). *Australian Studies in School Performance. Volume III. The Mastery of Literacy and Numeracy: Final Report.* Canberra: AGPS.

18  Coleman, J. S. (Chairman) (1974). *Youth: Transition to Adulthood. Report of the Panel on Youth of the President's Science Advisory Committee.* Chicago: University of Chicago Press.

19  Sheehan, P. J. 'Economic Aspects of Youth Unemployment'. In R. F. Henderson (Ed.) (1977). *Proceedings of Second Symposium of the Academy of the Social Sciences in Australia on Youth Unemployment. November 7 and 8, 1977 — Canberra.* Canberra: Academy of the Social Sciences.

20  Bulcock, J. W. op. cit.: 9.

21  Sheehan, P. J. op. cit.

22  ibid. See also Stricher, P. and Sheehan, P. J. 'Youth Unemployment in Australia: A Survey', *Australian Economic Review*, **9** (1).

23  Keeves, J. P. and Bourke, S. F. op. cit.

24  Wright, A. F. and Headlam, F. (1976). *Youth Needs and Public Policies.* Melbourne: Department of Youth, Sport and Recreation, Victoria. p.18.

25  OECD. Education Committee. op. cit., p.55, para. 164.

26  ibid., p.57, para. 170.

27  Wright, A. F. and Headlam, F. op. cit.:59.

28  OECD. Education Committee. op. cit., p.46, para. 137.

29  Coleman, J. S. (Chairman), op. cit.

30  Australia. Commission of Inquiry into Poverty. op. cit.:113.

31  Wright, A. F. and Headlam, F. op. cit.:18.

32  Further details of these programs are given by the Hon. T. Street in 'Commonwealth Policy on Youth Unemployment'. In R. F. Henderson (Ed.) (1977). *Proceedings of the Second Symposium of the Academy of the Social Sciences in Australia on Youth Unemployment. November 7 and 8, 1977 — Canberra.* Canberra: Academy of the Social Sciences.

33 Australia. Department of Education. (1977). op. cit.:98.
34 Smith, B. O. and Orlosky, D. E. (1975). *Socialization and Schooling. The Basics of Reform.* Bloomington, Indiana: Phi Delta Kappan.
35 Coleman, J. S. (Chairman). op. cit.

# III. The Renewal Program: An Overview

# 16. Some Key Issues for the Future of Australian Schools

## J. V. D'Cruz and P. J. Sheehan

By the end of 1978 the renewal program for Australian schools, as defined by the Karmel report, will be five years old and indeed may be regarded as having come to an end in many of its aspects. This volume constitutes an attempt to analyse and assess the various features and phases of this renewal program. There can be little doubt that, in spite of the humanity and freshness of the Karmel report's discussion, in spite also of the dedication of the Schools Commission and of the vast sums of money provided by the Commonwealth Government, the prevailing tone of this assessment is a critical one. The renewal program is perceived, both by the authors represented in this volume and by the community at large, as having been less productive of *educational* improvements than might have been reasonably expected. Although problems always remain, a number of unresolved matters seem to us to have particular urgency after the educational and other developments of the past five years. This concluding article surveys three of the issues which we regard as especially important for future educational debate in Australia:

1 The question of resources and the improvement in the quality of Australian education, particularly as concerns educational goals and curriculum development.
2 The question of the means of funding non-government schools in Australia and of the principles by which access to resources by all groups within Australian education should be secured.
3 The nest of the questions surrounding the relationship between work and education and the implications for educational theory and practice of a rapidly deteriorating labour market.

Aspects of these issues, as well as the important matter of the future role of the Australian Schools Commission, are also taken up in our introduction to this volume.

## RESOURCES AND QUALITY IN EDUCATION

### Resource targets and renewal goals

Reflecting the state of public debate at that time, the terms of reference given to the Interim Committee for the Australian Schools Commission were couched almost entirely in terms of resource inputs, their major task being 'to make recommendations ... as to the immediate financial needs of schools, priorities within these needs and appropriate measures to assist in meeting these needs'.[1] The Schools Commission Act has a very similar orientation, but a clause is included which allows the Commission to inquire into 'any other matter relating to primary or secondary education in Australia . . . which the Commission considers to be a matter that should be inquired into by the Commission'.[2] With the exception of some matters recently emerging, the Commission has made little use of this very wide clause and its major thrust has been the attempt to achieve the resource targets laid down by the Karmel report.

The Karmel report was commendably explicit about the targets which lay behind its recommendations for recurrent grants. Leaving aside special assistance for the disadvantaged and the handicapped, the Committee's recommendations were based on an attempt to increase the volume of recurrent resources per pupil employed in government primary schools by 40 per cent, and in government secondary schools by 35 per cent, by 1979. For Catholic systemic schools, the target appears to have been to bring recurrent resource use up from some 80 per cent of the current levels in government primary schools (in 1973) to the government target figure by 1979 (an increase of some 75 per cent in six years), while the Karmel programs are also aimed at bringing those non-systemic non-government schools currently below the 1979 target up to that target resource use by 1979.

The April 1978 Report of the Schools Commission declared in relation to government systems that

> only New South Wales and Western Australia at the primary level and Queensland at the secondary level are likely to be short of the targets by the end of 1978

and that 'the original targets may be reached by almost all government systems by the originally scheduled year of 1979'.[3] Table 1 shows the composition of the increase in recurrent resource use in government schools systems between 1972 and 1976 and indicates that even by 1976 the targets of 40 per cent and 35 per cent increases for primary and secondary systems respectively were almost achieved for government systems in aggregate. Even so, the composition of the increase in recurrent resources per pupil may give rise to some questions, for in both types of school more than half of the improvement in recurrent resources has been accounted for by categories other than teachers. In keeping with its emphasis on broad resource aggregates, the Commission has not provided any analysis of the efficiency of the pattern of increased resource use which has taken place, but at first glance it is disturbing that nearly half (primary) and over half (secondary) of the increase in resource use has been accounted for by increases in general ancillary staff (janitor or caretaker), superannuation and pensions, and goods and services.

The Commission is much less sanguine about resource trends in the non-government school sector in recent years. Full figures are available only for 1976, but between 1972 and 1976 per pupil resource use increased by 27 per cent in non-government primary schools and by 26 per cent in secondary schools in this sector. In spite of an annual rate of growth of real resource use

**Table 1. Components of Total Recurrent Resources Per Pupil, Government Systems, 1972 and 1976.**
(Base of total index, 1972 = 100 for both primary and secondary)

| | Primary | | Secondary | |
|---|---|---|---|---|
| | 1972 | 1976 | 1972 | 1976 |
| Teachers | 81 | 98 | 78 | 87 |
| Professional staff | 1 | 4 | 2 | 4 |
| Ancillary staff | | | | |
| Instructional | — | 4 | — | 4 |
| Clerical | 4 | 2 | 7 | 3 |
| General | — | 8 | — | 10 |
| Superannuation & | | | | |
| pensions | 3 | 5 | 3 | 5 |
| Goods & services | 11 | 16 | 10 | 16 |
| | 100 | 137 | 100 | 129 |

Source: Schools Commission. (1978). *Report for 1979-81 Triennium*, Table 3.1, p.26.

per pupil of over six per cent during these four years, non-government schools fell further behind government schools — resources per pupil in non-government primary schools were 77 per cent of those for government primary schools in 1972 and 72 per cent in 1976, while for secondary schools the corresponding figures were 81 per cent and 85 per cent.[4] This lower resource use in non-government schools is mainly due to the Catholic system — in all Catholic systemic schools in 1976, 67 per cent of students were enrolled in schools which had only 70 per cent or less of the average recurrent resource use of government schools in 1975–76.[5]

Thus it seems that by 1979 the Karmel report resource targets will have been achieved in government schools systems, although one may query some aspects of the composition of that increase, and per pupil resource use in non-government schools will have increased very rapidly but not to an extent to make any progress towards the Karmel report goal of closing the gap between resources used in government and non-government schools. Faithful to the spirit of the resources-based renewal program, the Commission in its April 1978 Report sees the main need for the immediate future as the provision of additional resources to non-government schools, from both government and private sources, so that the resource use gap with government schools can begin to be closed. This diagnosis, together with the fact that the resource targets are being attained for the government systems, in our view raises again the fundamental issues about the renewal program: Is the main *educational* need of Australian schools increased resource use in the non-government school sector? Indeed, is there evidence that the achievement of the resource targets in government schools has been associated with a corresponding increase in the *quality* of education in these schools? Are there not serious educational

267

deficiencies requiring attention in many government schools, particularly among those in poorer socio-economic areas? In general, does it make sense to approach an educational renewal program primarily through financial and resource targets?

These fundamental questions raise philosophical and value as well as empirical issues and simple answers could not be given even if much more empirical evidence was available, but we will cite three considerations which seem to us to be relevant. Firstly, our subjective judgment would be that, in spite of the achievement by the government school systems of the Karmel report resource targets, community concern about the adequacy of the education provided in these schools has increased rather than declined over the past five years. Of course, there could be many explanations of this fact, if it is such: rising community expectations about schools, the focusing of community concern about economic or other developments on the schools and so on. But it is at least consistent with the view that the basic problems in the schools lie elsewhere than in the amount of resources available.

Secondly, on the basis of the existing empirical information, which inevitably makes use of truncated measures of educational quality, it would appear that Catholic schools are achieving higher levels of educational outcomes than government schools in spite of lower resource inputs. Several relevant pieces of evidence concerning this question can be gleaned from the results of the IEA study of an Australia-wide sample of schools reported by Keeves in this volume.[6] Students in Catholic schools are shown by the IEA data to be performing appreciably better on word knowledge and science tests at the 14-year-old level than students in government schools, in spite of the fact that the resources employed in government schools per' pupil are considerably greater. Keeves also studied the distribution by state and school system of the low-performing schools in the IEA sample; the striking thing from the current point of view is that, in spite of the very low resource use levels in many Catholic schools, no Catholic school was included in the 29 lowest schools on the word knowledge test, and only 2 Catholic schools were in the 28 lowest-performing schools on the science test. It is also worth noting, in view of the correlation between socio-economic disadvantage and low educational performance, that, as the Karmel report puts it, 'generally, the patterns of disadvantage (of school neighbourhoods) described for the government schools are replicated in the Catholic systems'.[7] Similar results were reported in the Education Research and Development Committee report, *Australian Studies in School Performance*. Table 2 reports the survey results of that study in terms of the percentage of the sample from each type of school who achieved mastery of simple reading and numeration tests. For all four cases the performance of students from Catholic schools was superior in 1976 to that of students from government schools in spite of the fact that in that year the average resource use in Catholic primary schools, for example, was only 70 per cent of that in government primary schools.

Thirdly, analysis of the IEA samples by Rosier[8] (see Keeves[9]) presents

**Table 2: Literacy and Numeracy by School Type, 1976.**
(Percentage of sample achieving mastery; %)

| School type | Government | Catholic | Independent |
|---|---|---|---|
| Reading | | | |
| 10-yr.-olds | 51 | 58 | 62 |
| 14-yr.-olds | 69 | 80 | 89 |
| Numeration | | | |
| 10-yr.-olds | 74 | 80 | 77 |
| 14-yr.-olds | 72 | 79 | 90 |

Source: Bourke, S.F. and J.P. Keeves (Eds) (1977). *Australian Studies in School Performance*, Volume III. Canberra: AGPS. Tables 6.4 and 6.5, pp.92-95.

somewhat more direct evidence. Studying variations between schools in their level of achievement in science, Rosier found that, of the many variables concerned with the resources available to schools, the only one which had significance in explaining variations between schools in student achievement in science was the availability of laboratory assistants and other ancillary staff. Although there are many qualifications to be made to any such analysis, Rosier found that the important variables were ones concerned with the dedication of teachers, the form of organization of the school and the intellectual orientation of the courses. Such Australian studies are in line with the majority of overseas studies in finding little or no correlation between the obvious measures of resource availability and student achievement. For example, after re-analysing the data from three of the largest and most comprehensive surveys ever undertaken, viz. the Equality of Educational Opportunity and Project Talent surveys in the USA and the Plowden survey in the UK, Jencks concludes that 'no measurable school resource or policy shows a consistent relationship to schools' effectiveness in boosting student achievement' and when in any particular survey a given resource is significant 'the gains associated are almost always small'.[10]

These pieces of evidence inevitably employ only partial measures of quality in education, but they do to our mind cast very serious doubt on the wisdom of placing the central focus in educational renewal on increased provision of resources. In particular, there is no reason for thinking that in *educational* terms (as opposed, perhaps, to terms of equity or justice) the major national need for 1979 is to increase the resources available to Catholic schools. More generally, the evidence surely suggests that the primary deficiency lies in the quality of the educational activities which are carried on within the schools (and within homes) rather than in the amount of resources available to facilitate these activities. Issues of quality are of course more difficult to pin down than the hard facts of finance and resource use, but they are not for that reason any less real. In the remainder of this section we make some comments on two matters which we regard as central to a quality-oriented renewal program, namely

269

clarity about aims and goals of education and schools and the development of new approaches to curriculum.

## Education in schools: aims and priorities

As Professor Crittenden points out, the authors of the Karmel report try to find a place within the ample folds of their document for most of the conflicting interpretations of the role of the school in circulation at the present time.[11] The school is to be an instrument of socialization[12]; it 'provides a practical point for the attack on poverty' and is to be an agent for promoting social and economic equality[13]; schools, by building within themselves a caring community in which both people and education are valued, can be a regenerating force in society[14]; schools, however, have certain special functions, such as the acquisition of skills and knowledge and initiation into the cultural heritage[15]; at the same time, they should respond both to the needs of the individual and to the demands of both the local communities and wider groups. Such an all-embracing approach is disturbing, not because schools may not perhaps be validly called upon to fulfil each of these functions nor because the Interim Committee overlooked vital distinctions, but simply because the Committee's approach to educational renewal did not seem to be founded on a firm conceptual base setting order and priorities among these disparate goals. The Schools Commission has done little to attempt to impose priorities on these goals and seems to have operated with a similarly wide range of conceptions.

For our part, we would seek to insist on two fundamental distinctions. The first is the distinction between education and schooling. While there may be many disputes about what education is, to educate a person is clearly conceptually distinct from putting him through school. In other times and places and perhaps even in our own, men have been educated without, or perhaps even in spite of, attending school, and clearly a school can offer other things (such as socialization, religious instruction or physical development) than education. The Interim Committee rightly stressed the importance of education as a life-time process, not to be terminated at the date of leaving school[16], and hence acknowledged the distinction being pointed to here. This simple and obvious distinction raises two matters on which any school renewal program must declare itself — what it conceives the nature of education to be and what priority it gives to education among the many goals which a school may seek.

These are clearly matters on which the community must reach a decision. The decision can be reached as a result of a conscious process of deliberation, in which case what we value has some chance of determining what we do in education, or else simply emerge as the *de facto* result of a multitude of educational policies and decisions. Our own approach would be to regard education as a process which attempts to initiate a person, by a range of morally acceptable methods, into the patterns of thought, feeling and action characteristic of the culture in which he is being educated. This involves, *inter alia*, bringing him to some familiarity with and competence within various areas of human knowledge and understanding, to some commitment to the values implicit in those areas of knowledge and in that culture, and to the ability to distance himself from that culture and re-assess any given aspect of it. This approach would stress the central place of knowledge and understanding in the life of any person, be it the understanding of those areas in which his income is earned, the understanding of other people necessary to live in human society, or the understanding of artistic and cultural matters necessary for a fulfilling recreation. We would argue that in the current organization of society, it is essential that the schools be thought of above all as agencies for providing education in this sense and that this primary function of schools should be jealously guarded against the many forces which work to dilute it.

The second fundamental distinction is between outcomes which are thought of as being achieved by educating a person and those other outcomes which a school may seek to attain, but by other means than by providing an education. For example, most migrants coming into Australia share a common European culture with the local community, even though they differ in the manifestations and artefacts of culture. A school may seek to integrate these migrants into the community either by providing them with the best possible education it can (and thus, for example, teaching where necessary in migrant languages and making use of migrant cultural influences as well as local material to initiate them into the common culture) or by a variety of non-educative assimilation programs. While the point cannot be adequately developed here, we would believe that many of the apparently non-educative goals which schools are asked to achieve can be reached only by providing adequate education and that schools should only undertake non-educative programs after serious consideration.

Because of its primary concentration on resource targets, the Schools Commission seems to have given little serious attention to specification of the educational goals towards which its programs are directed. This has in turn resulted in a tendency for funds being used to support a wide range of activities, many of which, while undoubtedly worthwhile, have little or no direct relevance to improving education in the sense outlined above. (One example is the massive increase in janitor/caretaker staff in schools referred to above, which accounted for almost one-third of the increased resource use in government schools between 1972 and 1976.) We would argue strongly that an essential feature of any educational renewal program is an attempt to seek some community consensus about the aims and goals of education and of schools; our own view would be that renewal should centre on an attempt to improve the ability of the schools to educate in the sense we have given and that other factors should be given a secondary role. Only in the context of some explicitly formulated aims can activities be structured and attention centred on the central issues pertaining to quality, one of which is curriculum development.

It should be noted that the Schools Commission is strongly resistant to this view. In the April 1978 Report, the Commission indicates that it

> accepts the developmental model of school change which begins from looking at what is being done, not from debate about aims. Such debates are inevitably conducted at such a high level of generality as to have little significance for practice. What is being done, not the rhetoric, is what is significant.[17]

This is a remarkable statement, for there is of course no significance inherent in facts or actions themselves, independently of human purposes, aims and values. Only in relation to a given aim or value will a particular development be significant or irrelevant, and one can judge whether what is being done is or is not significant only in relation to some specified aim or value.

## Curriculum and culture

As noted in the introduction to this volume, recent Schools Commission reports have given some hints that the dominance of resource targets is being broken and one of these hints is the indication that curriculum development will be increasingly important in the years to come. Although we would have some doubts about the direction in which the Commission appears to be moving on curriculum, this is a welcome initiative, for curriculum issues directly affect the quality of educational activities in the classroom.

References to curriculum are scattered throughout the Schools Commission documents, from which the following points may be culled as expressing the Commission's views. Firstly, there is a heavy stress on the autonomy of the teachers, the schools and the school systems and on the right of all pupils to equality of opportunity both in provision and outcomes. Secondly, there is the shift of emphasis from the old divisions of the talented and untalented to the notion of advantaged and disadvantaged. Thirdly, notions of autonomy and individuality are bedded in the context of agreement that all pupils will learn habits of thought and of communication as well as necessary functional skills. Fourthly, there is a somewhat pious and undeveloped thought that schooling ought to be meaningful.

These positions occasionally leave the Schools Commission in contradictory stances. Because the Schools Commission has not, as it could not have, ignored a functioning society with well-established divisions of labour and of opportunity, the stress on autonomy does not easily produce any practical outcomes. There are, however, more serious problems. For example, there is the problem of arriving at forms of education and of meaningfulness in which autonomy and individuality are a basis for structures and practices, while at the same time those structures provide a workable context for education without necessarily limiting autonomy and individuality. If the idea of autonomy were pushed to its logical extreme, it would be a recipe for anarchy. If the Schools Commission's thinking on the curriculum, with its stress on autonomy, is to be workable and become practically applied in schools, it needs a context with constraints such as we now have with divisions of labour.

For various and perhaps understandable reasons, the Schools Commission has not yet been able to consciously and systematically develop an adequate basis for its thinking on curriculum. It has responded, perhaps for political reasons, to certain values which have become widespread in the community in recent years. The ideas of autonomy and of independence of thought, and of a meaningfulness which attaches to personal activities and which renders the individual person an active agent in a more general context, are old ideas in education. What is new about these ideas is that they are now apparently valued far beyond their old confines of special intellectual groups and leisured classes. These are ideas which have been inherent in intellectual culture and in Christian traditions of universal brotherhood. In the past, these ideas were held but they were not universal practices. Their practice was limited in various ways. In the Catholic tradition, the universality of equality and personal responsibility were constrained by transcendental considerations. In the Protestant tradition, although a more earthly one, equality and personal responsibility were part of a project which combined transcendentalism, scientific understanding and control of the world, which effectively led to capitalism, class society and the theoretical domination by scientific elites. Such restrictions or constraints are now increasingly rejected, and for our part we do not wish to see the re-establishment of the type of elitism that once prevailed. However, some restriction on personal autonomy is necessary if social meaningfulness and an actual existence is to continue. While there may be little left in Matthew Arnold's particular ideas on the manner in which cultural processes would restrain the anarchy of individual enterprise, it is still true that a culture must provide both the basis of, and the restrictions on, the development of individuality.

In moving beyond the autonomy of schools and of school systems to the content of curriculum and to the possibility of a common core curriculum, two approaches have surfaced in recent discussion. One approach sees the common core of curriculum development as founded on the need to provide students with a basic grid of skills necessary for life in modern society, while the other argues for a mapping of our culture and a synthesis of the results as the foundations of the common core curriculum. Neither of these approaches seems to us entirely appropriate to the present situation.

Our objection to the skill specification of the content of curriculum is that it seriously devalues the content of the culture to which education provides an initiation. This content involves a whole pattern of knowledge, values, attitudes, experiences and ways of acting, and while there are conflicts and disagreements within society about many of these aspects the attempt to reach a common program through concentration on content-neutral skills empties the curriculum of essential elements. Our concern about the program to generate a common core curriculum by firstly producing a map of the features of our culture and by secondly generating some synthesis and reconciliation of conflicting elements, turns on the criteria on which, and the process by which, the synthesis or reconciliation is achieved. A map of Australian or Western culture will be very extensive and will include many conflicting elements, so that any core curriculum project will need to impose priorities and structures, and what criteria are appropriate here will be disputed within the society. Further, if, as seems to be intended by the proponents of this view, the mapping and the synthesis and reconciliation are to be carried out by a group of academics or bureaucrats, it is very doubtful whether the results of this intellectual exercise will generate a practical response from those involved in the actual teaching situation.

The suggestion we would make is that the movement towards a common curriculum should start with the promotion of a wide-ranging discussion among teachers and within the community at large about what features of our present culture are necessary for life in Australian society at the present time.[18] Such grass-roots *discussion* would reduce the chances that any results were purely intellectual creations which did not impinge on the classroom situation, while the focus on *necessities* would both embody a view about the appropriate criteria to employ and provide the basis on which different groups might agree on the types of content which were appropriate for a common curriculum, while taking different views about central issues within each area. This approach would also provide the appropriate basis for discussion of values in education, for any culture must possess an underlying value framework, and coming to understand what values are necessary for life in one's society is a crucial aspect of both learning and living.

## FINANCING INDEPENDENT SCHOOLS

### Recent developments

The Karmel report cannot be said to have a fully developed theoretical position about the role of independent schools in the Australian education system, but its remarks on this topic are at once puzzling and intriguing. The authors of the report made various suggestive remarks about the long-term situation, but envisaged a quite different position in the short term. The Interim Committee placed strong emphasis on diversity in approaches to schooling and, partly as a result, 'values the right of parents to educate their children outside government schools' and asserted that when all schools are raised to the present high standard of many private schools even such private schools 'would be equally eligible for public support along with all other schools of comparable standard'.[19] At one point, the Interim Committee looked to 'the eventual development of a school system itself diverse, where all schools supported by public money can operate without charging fees'[20] and elsewhere it suggested that, in a context of a

> price for choice, . . . parental contributions might be expected to cover a fair share of the costs of running non-government schools and thus some matching of fees to Commonwealth contributions could be required.[21]

In the long run, then, the Interim Committee envisaged a diversity of types of schools (government schools, existing religious and non-religious independent schools and new kinds of independent schools)[22], all eligible for government support, so that 'the level of resources in all schools having access to public funds would be determined on essentially common criteria'[23], while a special contribution would be required from those sending their children to non-government schools. In historical perspective, one of the major aspects of the Karmel report may prove to be this commitment to a unified approach to all Australian schools.

This striking new perspective on the role of independent schools could not be implemented, however, because 'priorities must be established'.[24] For the immediate future, then, the Committee's position was that, because of gross differences in standards between schools and because of limited availability of funds, priority must be given to those schools with standards below desired levels, 'thereby deferring the eligibility for extensive support of schools presently having very high standards until others have been raised nearer to them'.[25] Thus, while there are many schools below target standards, the Committee argued that parents are free to send their students to schools with resources above target levels but it 'does not accept their right to public assistance to facilitate this choice'.[26] The result was the well-known classification of independent schools (apart from Catholic systemic primary schools) by resources employed, aid being scaled down as resource use increases and being phased out entirely for those schools in the highest category. Aid to systemic schools was to be provided as a block grant determined in terms of the average resource use level of the schools in the system. Many other aspects of the Interim Committee's funding methods are illuminatingly discussed in the article by Mortensen in this volume.[27]

This general approach has been adopted by the Schools Commission and, after some variations, has resulted in 1977 and 1978 in commonwealth recurrent grants per student to non-government schools equal to a given percentage of the per student recurrent expenditure in government schools. The percentage recommended by the Commission for 1978 varied according to resource use in the schools, from 12 per cent for the highest level schools to 32 per cent for those at the lowest level. These percentages were struck after having regard to state contributions, with the intention that the total public recurrent expenditure contribution to independent schools should range between 30 per cent and 50 per cent of per student recurrent expenditure in government schools. However, in the 1978 and 1979 guidelines to the Commission, the Federal Government indicated that it wished to see the federal per capita payment to all schools phased up to a minimum of 20 per cent, so that the percentage of standard costs being provided to the top two levels of schools is being phased up to this figure. For 1979, grants will range between 16 per cent and 33 per cent of standard costs for primary schools and between 15 per cent and 31 per cent for secondary schools. Nevertheless, the levels of resource use are so defined that, for independent schools in 1976, 88 per cent of all primary enrolments and 59 per cent of all secondary enrolments

(76 per cent overall) were in the lowest level and were in receipt of the maximum subsidy figure.

## Problems in current approaches

In spite of its adoption of this general approach deriving from the Interim Committee report, the Schools Commission continues to express doubts about its adequacy and equity. One reflection of these doubts was the proposal in the 1976–78 Triennium Report to establish a category of 'supported' independent schools, which would be fully supported by government funds on the condition that enrolments are open to all students and that a minority of public nominees are accepted on the governing board.[28] While reduced in scale in subsequent reports, this potentially revolutionary proposal has continued to be supported by the Commission, which sees it as a way of meeting the needs of low fee, low standard schools which cannot be met within the existing subsidy arrangements. In its 1977–79 Triennium Report the Commission also raises but does not attempt to resolve the issue of 'whether the level of public subsidies can continue to relate only to resource levels in schools without regard to parental effort and capacity'[29], but this becomes a dominant issue in the 1979–81 Triennium Report.

It does seem clear that the current theory and practice of funding independent schools is unsatisfactory and in justification of this claim we will offer three specific and two general points. The three specific points are:

1 As Professor Crittenden has pointed out[30], there are in Australia some high standard government schools which are above the target standards. Indeed, the Commission's own data indicate that in 1976 some government systems in aggregate were above the target standards. If what disqualifies certain parents 'public assistance to facilitate their choice' is that the school chosen is above target standards, it would seem to follow that parents sending children to those government schools should be deprived of assistance also. In general, it does seem highly anomalous that there can be wealthy parents who happily send their children to a high quality government school at public expense while parents on average incomes who choose an independent school of comparable quality have in principle no rights to public assistance.

2 Consider now two sets of parents on equal incomes, one of which sends their children to a high quality independent school while the other chooses an independent school of low standards. The implication of the Karmel report's short-term principles is that only the parent who chooses the lower standard institution is entitled to public assistance and the poorer the institution he chooses the more assistance he receives. The only difference posited between the two sets of parents is that one chooses to devote a higher proportion of their income to the education of their children and this disqualifies them from public assistance. Such a situation is manifestly inequitable and will also have the effect of reducing the

incentive for parents to invest in education. This in turn relates to an issue which is a major concern in the 1979–81 Triennium Report, namely the relation of government funding to personal effort.

3 One problem which both the Interim Committee and the Schools Commission recognize in the present pattern of funding is as follows.[31] Consider a Category 2 school which currently has resources at about the 1979 target standards as a result of charging high fees and receives only a little federal assistance and consider a Category 6 school with low fees (suppose 10 per cent of those for the previous school) and large federal funding grants. The Karmel report assumes that fees etc. will rise in line with average incomes so that fees in the Category 6 school will remain 10 per cent of those in the Category 2 school. If the Karmel grants had their planned effect and raised the Category 6 school to the same resource use standard as the Category 2 school by 1979, then in 1979 we would have two independent schools operating at similar levels, one primarily as a result of fees and the other primarily as the result of government grants. This would be grossly inequitable between parents on similar incomes sending their children to these schools. The Karmel report recognizes the problem of which the above is a dramatic example and says that it 'should be considered as a matter of urgency by the Commission'.[32] One possibility the Karmel report suggests, however, is that

> parental contributions might be expected to cover a fair share of the costs of running non-government schools and thus some matching of fees to Commonwealth contributions might be required.[33]

The Interim Committee then acknowledged that a radically different pattern of funding of independent schools to the one proposed would soon be needed.

The two general comments we would offer on the Karmel report's short-term funding programs are these. Firstly, each of the three specific problems discussed above arises because the Committee chooses to decide the level of support by reference to the resources of schools rather than of parents. It is children who get well or poorly educated and, in the independent school sector, it is primarily parents who combine with governments to finance the cost of educational services provided for their children, and hence it is primarily parents and their children who are the beneficiaries of government assistance. This being so, the only way we can see of developing an equitable system of funding independent schools is for the government to take account of the circumstances of individual parents. Secondly, given the way social programs develop a momentum and strength of their own, it does seem unrealistic of the Committee to propound one view as a long-term goal and yet implement programs for the short-term based on quite different principles. Unless changes are made, the short-term policy will become so entrenched that it will be impossible to implement quite different principles, and this is certainly one interpretation of the generally hostile reaction given to the new proposals made in the Commission's 1979–81 Triennium Report. If the

Interim Committee really did desire implementation of its long-term position, it would have been necessary to establish priorities within a framework consistent with that position.

## The Schools Commission's new proposals for financing non-government schools

Responding to these and other difficulties seen as inherent in the existing financial arrangements, the Schools Commission proposed in its April 1978 Report a quite new approach to financing non-government schools. The new scheme envisages three levels of commonwealth support, corresponding to three levels of resource use in schools and of commitment of private and state resources. The three levels are as follows:

Group 1. Schools operating at or above target resource standards. Resources contributed by various groups as a percentage of target resource standards:

| | |
|---|---|
| School community | 60 per cent (+) |
| State Government | 20 per cent |
| Federal Government | 20 per cent |

Group 2. Schools operating at 89–99 per cent of target resource standards:

| | |
|---|---|
| School community | 39–49 per cent |
| State Government | 20 per cent |
| Federal Government | 30 per cent |

Group 3. Schools operating at 85–88 per cent of target resource standards:

| | |
|---|---|
| School community | 25–28 per cent |
| State Government | 20 per cent |
| Federal Government | 40 per cent |

Schools which are unwilling or unable to provide from their own resources at least 25 per cent of target resource levels will continue to receive federal subsidies based on existing percentages of *target resource levels* (33 per cent for primary and 31 per cent for secondary schools), provided that they continue private effort at present levels in real terms. If this proposal was acceptable to the government, the Commission planned to phase it in over the three years 1979–81, but the government did not accept it in the guidelines for 1979 and both the Commission and the government are to publish discussion papers on the issue towards the end of 1978.

Among the main features of this new scheme are the change to expressing federal government contributions to non-government schools as a proportion of target resource standards rather than of standard government school costs and the partial freedom which it gives to schools or school systems to *opt* for a given level of government support provided they can meet the requirements about private effort.

One of the main reasons which led the Commission to propose this scheme was its concern over trends in low resource non-government schools. As indicated in the first section of this article, between 1972 and 1976 resource

**Table 3. Income per Student from Private Sources — Catholic Systemic Schools.**
(Constant December 1977 prices)

|  | 1974 | | | 1976 | | |
|---|---|---|---|---|---|---|
|  | Primary schools | Mixed schools | Secondary schools | Primary schools | Mixed schools | Secondary schools |
| Fees | 56 | 63 | 132 | 62 | 155 | 176 |
| Other cash income | 51 | 27 | 70 | 57 | 50 | 51 |
| Contributed services | 182 | 234 | 369 | 134 | 157 | 167 |
| Total | 289 | 324 | 571 | 253 | 362 | 394 |

Source: Schools Commission. (1978). *Report for the Triennium 1979-81.* Table 6.4, p.70.

use in these schools fell further behind that in corresponding government schools, in spite of increasing quite strongly in actual terms. This was partly due to a decline in the relative contribution of what the Commission refers to as 'private effort' in these schools. Some data on income from private sources for Catholic systemic schools in 1974 and 1976 is shown in Table 3. It is evident that for both primary and secondary schools, but not for mixed schools, in these systems the total real value of income per student fell sharply between 1974 and 1976, the fall being 12.5 per cent in the case of primary schools and 31 per cent in the case of secondary schools. These falls are almost entirely due to a fall in contributed services — services provided at little or no cost by religious and at less than full Commission salary rates by lay staff. Contributed services have declined in all types of Catholic systemic schools because of falls in the number of religious working in the schools and as a result of the increase in the salaries of lay staff in Catholic schools towards those paid in government schools. Nevertheless other income (from fees and other cash income) has increased in real terms in each type of school shown in Table 3.

This decline in income from private sources has meant that the Catholic systemic schools have not met the requirement that 'private effort be maintained', which the Commission interprets as implying that income from private sources increase in line with average weekly earnings. At the same time, Catholic systemic schools have continued to experience low relative resource use and high government funding ratios — for Catholic systemic primary schools in 1977, some 67 per cent of enrolments were in schools with resource use less than 70 per cent of that in government primary schools and which were over 70 per cent government funded. These facts all imply a dilemma for a Commission committed to using government funds to bring all schools up to the target level, and the new scheme involves an attempt to induce all schools and school systems to move up to 85 per cent of target resource use. For a primary school system operating at 70 per cent of target resources in 1978, resulting say from grants of 33 per cent and 17 per cent of

279

target resources from Federal and State Governments respectively and 20 per cent from private sources, the scheme would involve a move to at least 85 per cent of resource targets, the federal and state contributions increasing to 40 per cent and 20 per cent respectively and private contributions rising to at least 25 per cent of target resource use. The increase in the federal contribution would, of course, be contingent on the appropriate increase in private contributions.

In our view it is clear that this is not an adequate system for the financing of non-government schools in Australia and in support of this view we will outline four objections to the scheme:

1  The new proposal still uses the characteristics of the school as the basis for determining grants, and so does not avoid most of the problems outlined in the section 'Problems in current approaches'. For example, for two sets of parents with equal incomes, the federal government grant will amount to 40 per cent of target resource use if they choose a Category 3 school but to only 20 per cent if they choose to devote a higher proportion of their income and send their children to a Category 1 school. It is true that this effect has been muted a little in the current version, but only as a result of what we regard as another adverse development, namely a reduction of the progressivity of federal grants in favour of lower resource schools.

2  One major reason for the new scheme is said to be the need to induce greater private contributions so that these, together with higher government grants, will lead to higher resource use in these schools. But there are many disincentives to higher private effort — indeed incentives are provided only for schools to move up to Category 3 (85–88 per cent of target resource use) and above that the inducements are all in the direction of disincentives. For schools near the top of Categories 2 or 3 there is a positive incentive *not* to move into a higher group, while for schools near the bottom of Categories 1 or 2 there is a strong incentive to move *down* into a lower group. Table 4 gives an example of a primary school currently on 88 per cent target resource use, with 38 per cent of the target provided from private sources. When the proposed scheme was fully in operation, this school would be much better off provided it remained on 88 per cent, requiring only 28 per cent of target resources to be derived from private sources. But it would have a strong incentive not to increase resource use, for if it moved to 90 per cent (and to Category 2) its federal grant would drop to 30 per cent and it would have to raise an additional 12 per cent of target resources but only obtain a two per cent increase in school resources in return. This point also applies in the reverse direction — if a school moved from 90 per cent to 88 per cent resource use it would save 12 per cent of target resources on private contributions while giving up only two per cent on school resource usage.

3  We know that many schools and some school systems are operating below 70 per cent of target resource standards and an important aim of

**Table 4. Funding Proposals, at 88-90 per cent Resource Use.**
(Percentage of target resource use; non-government primary school)

| Funding source | Existing | Proposed (Category 3) | Proposed (Category 2) |
|---|---|---|---|
| State | 17 | 20 | 20 |
| Federal | 33 | 40 | 30 |
| Private | 38 | 28 | 40 |
| Total | 88 | 88 | 90 |

the scheme is to induce these schools to move up to at least 85 per cent of target resource use. The Commission calculates that, assuming a continued decline in contributed services and that all additional real private income is derived by way of fees, average fees in Catholic systemic primary schools would need to increase in *real* terms by 66 per cent between 1976 and 1981 while for secondary schools the increase would be 34 per cent. Obviously for some of the poor school systems the increase would be greater than this, and some schools and school systems will not be able or willing to meet the requirement of 25 per cent of target resources being provided from private sources. For these schools and systems, presumably the poorest in Australia, federal grants will be held at 33 per cent of target resources (primary) and will fall as a proportion of actual government school costs if these rise further. Thus the scheme implies that for the poorest schools all levels of government in Australia should provide 53 per cent of target resources while for the richest schools the provision would be 40 per cent and for schools reaching Category 3 the provision would be 60 per cent. In terms of increases in federal funds over the next few years, these would flow, firstly, into the richest schools as their federal grant moves up to 20 per cent and secondly, into those schools who are in or can opt for Category 3, as their federal grant moves up to 40 per cent of target resource use. Thus the Karmel report principle of a special commitment to the poorest schools would now be completely abandoned.

4 But our most fundamental objection to this scheme is that it seeks to impose the obsession with resource use levels which has characterized the renewal program so far on schools, and indeed to make acceptance of this view a condition of obtaining the highest level of federal assistance. We have presented evidence above that many low-resource Catholic schools seem to be performing better in educational terms than some of their high resource counterparts in the government sector, and one could also find examples of such schools outside the Catholic system. Given this we can readily imagine a poor community or diocese which has schools of low resource use but fairly high quality taking the view that further additions to school resources constituted a low priority in terms of the uses of funds of the local community. They may believe that such additional funds

which could be obtained should be devoted to community development or welfare projects (or that such funds should not be sought, given the typical low family income) and that improvements in educational quality are most likely to be achieved through curriculum developments or other changes which do not involve additional resources per pupil. We can see no reason why such a community should receive a lower federal grant than a wealthier community which devotes more income to its school or than a community of similar financial standing which has a different set of priorities or different views about quality in education. In particular, given that funds are limited and that there are different views about what contributes to improved quality in education, it seems to us quite wrong to penalize schools which either do not or cannot place the same overwhelming priority on increased resource use as does the Schools Commission.

## An alternative approach

In considering issues surrounding parents' choice in education, three conflicting matters need to be kept in mind, namely:
1 the goal of equality of opportunity in education;
2 the right of parents to choose the type of education they require for their children; and
3 the right of parents to use their resources to improve their children's education.

The Interim Committee, and the present authors, accept these three principles, but it is clear that they tend to work in opposing directions. The principle *raison d'etre* of the state school system has been the need to make reasonably high standard education equally available to all sectors of the population, but single-minded improvement of the government sector, when combined with escalating educational costs, can emasculate parents' choice. On the other hand, government support for independent schools, together with use of financial resources by parents, risks a continuing situation in which such children of wealthy parents obtain a much better education than those of poor parents. Space precludes a thorough discussion of ways of reconciling these goals in an Australian context and of taking account of the necessity to direct resources to those in greatest need. We wish to suggest, however, that the following pattern of funding of independent schools appears to provide a viable solution.

The suggestion would be that the government make available to all parents choosing non-government schools a basic recurrent grant equal to some proportion of the average recurrent costs of educating a child in a government school. This grant would be taxable, would replace both present direct payments to schools and taxation concessions and would be paid partly direct to the school and partly by tax credit to the parent. By agreement between government and school authorities, the grants payable to parents would be divided between payment to the school and tax credit to parents. This division might take place in line with a roughly estimated average amount of tax that would be paid on the grant by the parents in a given school, subject to official constraints. If the grants were $1000 per pupil, a school with parents on 60 per cent effective marginal tax rate would receive $400 and the parents a tax credit of $600, while if for a school in a poor area the marginal tax rate was 20 per cent, the school would receive $800 per pupil and the parents a tax credit of $200. This would allow parents whose marginal tax rate was below the school average to attain a net reduction in tax (or net tax credit) and parents above the school average would have a net addition to tax. Of course, what proportions any school opted for would not affect the total flow of funds from the government. The proportions chosen only influence the distribution of that flow between direct payments to the school and tax credits or payments.

This basic approach, of a grant to the school which is subject to tax for the parents, could be varied in several ways. Given the recent lowering of marginal tax rates, it would probably be desirable to make the scheme more progressive (in the fiscal sense) than is implied by the use of normal marginal tax rates, and a new set of tax rates tied to taxable income could be laid out for this grant. Obviously many variants are possible here; for example, it might be ruled that no tax is paid if the income of the family head is $5000 per annum but one per cent of the grant would be paid in tax for every additional $200 dollars taxable income, so that the grant was fully recalled in tax at an income of $25 000 per annum. This would mean that for parents on $5000 per annum the school-parent partnership would receive the full $1000 grant, while there would be no net benefit for parent incomes of $25 000 per annum or over. An approach to funding independent schools of this type would have numerous advantages, including the following:

1 By comparison with both the existing and proposed Schools Commission scheme, parents would not be penalized, relative to either parents on similar or higher incomes, for seeking high standard education for their children.

2 While parents would still have to pay a 'price for choice' this price would be tied to parents' income and would not need to be crippling for any individual.

3 Because of clustering of low standard schools in low income areas, federal funds would flow in greater degree to the school-parent partnership in low standard schools. At the same time, all schools would receive some federal funds, the extent of these being determined by the division decided upon between payment to the school and tax credit to the parent.

4 The anomalies which the Karmel Committee expected would arise on its proposed funding pattern would not be a problem in this scheme, for schools of similar standards would be in receipt of different government grants only to the extent to which the average incomes of parents

attending the schools differed, and schools of different standards would receive equal grants only if the difference in standards was due to differences in parental efforts rather than parental incomes.

5 Above all, a scheme such as this would be compatible with the Committee's desire to aid first those most in need and yet also with the long-term aim of a stable and equitable scheme in which many types of independent schools are funded on a non-controversial basis. The scheme could be introduced initially with a grant of say 50 per cent of average government costs per pupil and a highly progressive tax take associated with the grants (so that the 'clawback' of funds is high), but as initial inequalities are overcome the size of the grant could be increased and perhaps the progressivity of the clawback eased. The scheme need not be more costly than current schemes, and the parameters could be set to provide any given level of support to schools and to parents in the non-government sector.

## Some reactions to this suggestion

Since the initial publication of this proposal in the first edition of this book there have been a number of discussions of the underlying issues. In paragraph 3.34 of its Report for the 1976–78 Triennium, the Schools Commission comments on the question of whether funding should be focused on the school or the individual. While indicating that the Commission's concern is with students and their needs, it is argued that the school should be the focus of funding, for two reasons. Firstly, unless the schools are the focus, the Australian Government cannot be sure that its grants will be directly translated into benefits to students. Secondly, as the Commission cannot assess the individual parental resources of children at any particular school, a practical response is to assess the school's resources in relation to student needs, and this leaves it up to the individual school to allocate resources and make calls on individuals. It is important to note that neither of these points touch the proposal made here. The first point is only an argument for ensuring that funds are paid to the school rather than to individuals, who might indeed spend them on non-educational goods or services. The second point simply avoids all the issues about equity between parents: the whole problem here is that the situations of the parents of children attending a given school vary enormously. As noted earlier, and in spite of this insistence on the advantages of funding on a school basis, the Commission is still deeply concerned in its 1977–79 Triennium Report about the relationship between public support of non-government schools and parental effort and capacity. We would hold that this problem can only be resolved in terms of some scheme such as the above, in which the level of government support varies with the level of parental income.

In their survey 'The Economics of Education in Australia', forthcoming in the Academy of the Social Sciences series, Blandy, Woodfield and Hayles discuss this proposal and argue that the scheme would not be feasible because it required that schools must have access to, and process, information on parental incomes.[34] This is a misunderstanding of our general point, although one facilitated by the original exposition of the proposal. All that is necessary is that the responsible school authorities (e.g. the school board) determine, in conjunction with the parents, the proportion of the per capita grant which is to be payable to the school, within the limits laid down by the authorities. If the school had an estimate of the relevant average marginal tax rate of the parents whose children attend the school, it could determine the school grant component in such a way that on average the parents would receive no change in tax payable. But this would only hold on average — some parents would pay more tax and others would pay less, depending on income — and clearly it would not matter if the proportion was struck in a way which did not precisely reflect the average marginal tax rate. Thus it is not required that the school have access to parental incomes.

## SCHOOL, WORK AND THE REASSESSMENT OF AUSTRALIAN EDUCATION

One of the beneficial effects of a crisis in a human society is the way in which it can prompt a fundamental reassessment of the aims and values of particular activities within that society or of the society itself. Recent developments and research results have clearly indicated that Australian education is facing severe problems arising out of the school/work relationship and it is to be hoped that this crisis leads to a fruitful re-evaluation of the values and attitudes prevalent in Australian education. Many of the issues here have been illuminatingly discussed by Keeves and Matthews in this volume, but they are of such importance that further discussion is warranted. These problems have not been *caused* by the high level of youth unemployment but the unemployment levels have brought them to the surface and will intensify their effects. In 1977 and in the first half of 1978, the rate of unemployment among persons 15–19 years averaged about 16 per cent, and in June 1978 the average duration of unemployment for persons 15—19 years was 22 weeks. During 1978–79 the unemployment rate among these young people is likely to rise to over 20 per cent, and during the foreseeable future labour market conditions will continue to highlight inadequacies in the school/work relationship. It is useful to start by considering the following facts which have been demonstrated or confirmed in recent years:

1 Among persons aged 15–19 years unemployment rates are much higher for persons who left school early (at 14 or 15 years) than those who left later. As shown in Table 5, for persons who left school between 1971 and May 1976, 24 per cent of those who left school at 14 and entered the labour force were unemployed at May 1976 and 13.1 per cent of those leaving at age 15 in that period were unemployed, while the unemployment rate among persons leaving school at 16–18 years in this

**Table 5.  Unemployment Rates, May 1976, by Age and Year of Leaving School**
(Percentage of relevant labour force)

| Year of leaving school | Age of leaving school (years) | | | | | |
|---|---|---|---|---|---|---|
| | 14 | 15 | 16 | 17 | 18+ | Total persons 15-19 |
| Before 1967 | 2.6 | 2.3 | 2.0 | 2.1 | 1.7 | 2.4 |
| 1967-68 | 9.2* | 6.5 | 4.1* | 3.0* | 2.4 | 4.4 |
| 1969-70 | 11.1* | 8.1 | 6.6 | 1.8* | 2.5* | 5.2 |
| 1971 to May 1976 | 24.0 | 13.1 | 8.1 | 9.1 | 6.2 | 10.1 |

* Based on estimate of less than 4000 persons, and hence having a high standard error.

Source: Australian Bureau of Statistics, Persons aged 15 to 64 years, Employment Status and Period since leaving School, May 1976, Table 4.

period was 8.0 per cent. A similar pattern is evident for persons leaving school in the years 1967–1970, the May 1976 unemployment rates by age of leaving school being 9.3 per cent (14 years), 7.4 per cent (15 years) and 3.6 per cent (16–18 years).

It thus seems to be a basic, if not altogether unexpected, feature of the Australian labour market that persons who leave school early are much more likely to experience unemployment than those who stay longer at school. One person in four of those leaving at 14 years between 1971 and May 1976 were unemployed at May 1976 and, in view of the subsequent deterioration in the labour market, this figure is likely to have worsened in the last two years.

2 In the important survey of literacy and numeracy among Australian school-children referred to above (see Table 2) the authors found that a substantial proportion of 14-year-olds were lacking in these fundamental skills. For example, they found that 25–30 per cent of the 14-year-olds in their sample were unable to pass simple tests in exercises involving reading comprehension of continuous prose such as would be found in normal school texts and reference books; only 50 per cent of the 14-year-olds were able to satisfactorily prepare a letter of application of employment; they estimated from their results that about 25 per cent of the 14-year-olds did not possess mastery of the basic skills in numeration. We have no way of knowing whether this constitutes an improvement or a deterioration of the situation prevailing in earlier years. But it does seem clear that these students lack the basic skills necessary for further learning at school, that consequently they will tend to leave school at the earliest possible time and that they are likely to have severe difficulties in developing a meaningful life in a world which places so much stress on literacy and numeracy skills.

3 At the other end of the educational spectrum it has become clear recently

286

that the expansion of tertiary education over the past decade is leading to dramatic increases in the stock of tertiary graduates in the labour force. In the 1970s, the total number of graduates in the labour force has been increasing at a rate of 10–12 per cent per annum and this is likely to continue over the next five years or so as the recent increase in enrolments at Colleges of Advanced Education is reflected in graduations. Although precise estimates are impossible because of data limitations it now seems likely that the stock of university and CAE graduates either working or seeking work will have approximately doubled between 1972 and 1978 while the total number of persons in civilian employment will have increased by only about five per cent over this period. Over the next five years at least this trend for the number of graduates seeking employment to grow very much faster than total employment will continue and, on the current stance of educational policy, may well continue for the remainder of this century. As it is not possible that the structure of labour demand is changing so rapidly in favour of graduates, it follows that to the extent that many graduates find work this will be as a result of their accepting positions of lower income, status or responsibility than they anticipated when they began their studies. This will have two effects. Firstly, for those who approached education primarily as a means towards achieving higher level employment there is likely to be some adverse reaction towards education generally, as it has not proved efficacious in achieving this goal. Secondly, as graduates and others move down the occupational ladder in search of work a more general re-adjustment will ensue, with the consequence that those with fewest educational and skill qualifications will be further displaced from the labour market. Increasing 'credentialism' will thus eventually most heavily affect those whose credentials are fewest.

4 There is now considerable evidence that Australian schools are not adequately educating those with lower levels of academic ability, and that frustration with and hostility towards schools are strong among this group. At the same time the deteriorating labour market situation is leading to increasing numbers of young people using schools as a refuge from unemployment, so that schools have to cater for large numbers of pupils who are attending school only under sufferance or as a second best option.

In their study for the Poverty Inquiry, Wright, Headlam, Ozolins and Fitzgerald examined in 1974 and 1975 the experience of school of a representative cross-section of 150 eighteen-year-olds.[35] In respect of the failings of the schools, they found that a high proportion of students (59 per cent) felt that they were not treated as individuals up to Form IV and that most students felt that personal attention from teachers was forthcoming only when (or if) they reached the top two years of secondary school; a high proportion of students, especially those with less academic ability, found the curriculum irrelevant to their interests and

287

**Table 6. School Participation Rates: Australia.**
(Proportion of the relevant population attending school; per cent)

| Age | Year | | | | |
|---|---|---|---|---|---|
| | 1973 | 1974 | 1975 | 1976 | 1977 |
| 15 years | 82.3 | 81.6 | 85.7 | 84.5 | 86.6 |
| 16 years | 54.4 | 53.8 | 56.1 | 57.5 | 59.2 |
| 17 years | 30.0 | 29.7 | 30.5 | 31.1 | 32.4 |
| 18 years | 7.7 | 6.7 | 6.8 | 6.8 | 6.9 |

Source: Australian Bureau of Statistics, Schools 1977, Cat. No. 4202.

needs and regarded school as providing an inadequate preparation for life; only 11 per cent of the students in the sample who left after Form IV (or earlier) found the career advice they received at school fairly or very helpful, and the authors argue that in very many cases the streaming system was one of various factors contributing to a situation in which 'the failures at school are left to make their way in the world' with little in the way of a constructive legacy from their school years.

Table 6 provides some data on the proportion of the population of four single year age-groups who were attending school in the years 1973–1977. It is clear that there has been a substantial jump in school participation rates as so defined, the upward movement being from 1974 and coinciding with the increase in unemployment. For both 15- and 16-year-olds about five per cent more of the relevant population were attending school in 1977 than in 1974, while an additional 2.7 per cent of 17-year-olds were in school. For these three age groups, total school attendance in 1977 was about 35 000 persons higher than it would have been if the 1974 participation rates had continued to obtain. Thus current economic conditions are generating increased return to school in the 15–17 years age-groups and this means that on top of their current inadequacies in educating those of less academic orientation schools are having to cope with increased numbers of unwilling learners.

In our view, these facts point indubitably to a crisis of major proportions in the Australian education system surrounding the inter-relationships between schools, education and work. Many of those with lesser academic ability are not being adequately initiated into our common culture, in that they are not developing at school those basic skills and understandings necessary to take an active and fulfilling place in the community and in that they are not being prepared to enter into one central aspect of the culture, work. At the other extreme, many of those with higher academic ability are being led deeper into the educational system in the expectation of levels of employment which will not materialize for the majority of them.

This emerging crisis cannot be discussed in any detail here. We are sure, however, that it is most unsatisfactory to respond, as the Schools Commission has responded, by saying that 'what useful response the schools might make to this situation or indeed its relevance for education in general is by no means clear' and leaving it at that.[36] Nor is it appropriate to respond by focusing on the symptoms of the underlying malaise and producing stop-gap programs to increase the supply of the particular skills in demand in the labour market at present. We cannot avoid a fundamental re-thinking of our basic purposes in education and their relation to work and of the relative roles of the various institutions involved in preparing youth for life in society. We conclude by making two points which we regard as important within this re-thinking.

In any local community the school is the obvious institution which groups young people together and through which they are accessible to training or other schemes. This being so, when any new problem concerning youth arises there is a temptation to impose either the responsibility, or the mechanisms, for solving it on the school, so that over time the school becomes loaded with a wide range of functions in addition to its primary educative one. In the issue presently under discussion, for example, we would regard it as crucial that a distinction be made between responses to the problem which imply better education (e.g. better basic literacy and numeracy programs in schools, teaching of basic material in ways which touch the world and the imagination of less academically gifted students) and those which involve other programs, such community service experience schemes or the development of specific skills relevant to the labour market at a particular time. We would argue that initiatives of both types are probably necessary but that neither will be satisfactorily achieved if both types are loaded onto the schools. Improving the *education* available to the less academically gifted is a vital need in Australian society at the present time; this will require the schools to co-operate with institutions carrying out programs more directly related to the labour market and to rising unemployment, but it will also require that the schools resist too broad a diversification of their role.

In post-war Australia a vast expansion of education has been 'sold' to individual parents and students as a means of access to increased income and status within society. Such an implicit promise — that more education will lead to more rewarding and better paid employment with higher social status — can only be delivered for a short time and only in circumstances in which rapid economic growth provides a continued up-grading of work opportunities. Indeed it is evident from the foregoing that even in the post-war decades in Australia this promise was not being met for those at the lower end of the educational spectrum, either in terms of basic skills necessary for life in society or in terms of position within the labour market. Economic and demographic developments over the past five years have brought to the surface the contradiction between what the individual can achieve in terms of improved job prospects through higher education and what is possible for the community as a whole. It is perhaps too much to hope that the current crisis might lead to a reassertion within society of the value of education as an initiation of all students to the various facets of our culture, as a process which prepares them to lead a richer and more meaningful life in society and thus is of value independently of any accidental spin-off in terms of increased access to income and status. But it is only through a re-assertion of this basic value that we will find a lasting resolution of the issues about education, schools and work.

## Notes

1 Australia. (1973). *Schools in Australia. Report of the Interim Committee for the Australian Schools Commission.* (Chairman, P. Karmel). Canberra: AGPS. para. 1.1.
2 Australia. Schools Commission. (1978). *Report for the Triennium 1979–81.* (Chairman, K. McKinnon). Canberra: AGPS. p. 2.
3 ibid., para. 3.32.
4 Australia. Schools Commission. (1977). *Report for the Rolling Triennium 1978–80.* (Chairman, K. McKinnon). Canberra: AGPS. Table B. 8.
5 Australia. Schools Commission. (1978). op. cit., Table A.22.
6 Keeves, J. P. 'The Needs of Education in Australian Schools', Chapter 4 in this volume.
7 Australia. (1973). op. cit., para. 9.33.
8 Rosier, M. J. 'Factors Associated with Learning Science in Australian Secondary Schools', *Comparative Education Review*, **18**(2): 180–187.
9 Keeves, J. P. 'Approaches to the Goal of Educational Equality: Will the Karmel Report Work?', Chapter 6 in this volume.
10 Jencks, C. (1972). *Inequality.* New York: Basic Books. p. 96.
11 Crittenden, B. S. 'Arguments and Assumptions of the Karmel Report: A Critique', Chapter 1 in this volume.
12 Australia. (1973). op. cit., para. 2.21.
13 ibid., para. 9.10.
14 ibid., para. 2.22.
15 ibid., para. 2.21.
16 ibid., paras 2.23–2.25.
17 Australia. Schools Commission. (1978). op. cit., para. 9.28.
18 This section ('Curriculum and culture') draws upon an early draft of notes made by Doug. White and J. V. D'Cruz on the Schools Commission and the development of a common core curriculum.
19 Australia. (1973). op. cit., para. 2.12.
20 ibid., para. 2.14.
21 ibid., para. 6.56.
22 ibid., para. 2.11.
23 ibid., para. 2.13.
24 ibid., para. 2.12.
25 loc. cit.
26 loc. cit.
27 Mortensen, K. G. 'Finance for Independent Schooling', Chapter 10 in this volume.
28 Australia. Schools Commission. (1975). *Summary Report for the Triennium 1976–78.* (Chairman, K. McKinnon). Canberra: AGPS. paras 13.76–13.79.
29 Australia. Schools Commission. (1976). *Report: Rolling Triennium 1977–79.* (Chairman, K. McKinnon). Canberra: AGPS. para. 3.22.
30 Crittenden, B. S. 'Arguments and Assumptions of the Karmel Report: A Critique', Chapter 1 in this volume.
31 Australia. (1973). op. cit., paras 6.55–6.56; see also Australia. Schools Commission. (1976). op. cit., para. 3.22.
32 Australia. (1973). op. cit., para. 6.55.
33 loc. cit.
34 Blandy, R., R. Woodfield and A. Hayles, 'The Economics of Education in Australia'. In F. R. Gruen (Ed.) (1978). *Economics in Australia*, Vol. II. Canberra: Academy of the Social Sciences.
35 Wright. A., F. Headlam, U. Ozolins and R. T. Fitzgerald, 'Poverty, education and adolescents'. In Australia. Commission of Inquiry into Poverty. (1978). *Outcomes of Schooling: Aspects of Success and Failure.* Canberra: AGPS.
36 Australia. Schools Commission. (1978). op. cit., para. 1.2.

# IV. Bibliography

# 17. The Australian Schools Commission: a Bibliography

Denise Jepson

This bibliography includes all major publications of or relating to the Australian Schools Commission and many journal articles and newspaper reports discussing aspects of its programs.

The bibliography is divided in the following ways:

**A. Primary sources**
    1 Parliamentary material (Acts, Debates)
    2 Reports
    3 Material published by the Schools Commission
      (Progress reports, periodicals, bibliographies)

**B. Secondary sources**
    1 Material concerning the Schools Commission in general
      (a) Books and chapters in books
      (b) Journal articles
      (c) Newspaper articles
      (d) Reports, conference papers, submissions
    2 Material concerning specific programs funded by the Schools Commission.

The sources for the bibliography were as follows:
    1 *Australian Education Index*
    2 Australian Government Publications
    3 *Australian National Bibliography*
    4 Australian Public Affairs Information Service
    5 *A Bibliography of Radical and Progressive Writings in Victorian Education 1964–1976.* (Innovation Centre, La Trobe University, 1976)
    6 *Catalogue of Critical Australian Education Writings* (Education Subscription Service, 1976)

## A. PRIMARY SOURCES

**1. Parliamentary material and ministerial material**
AUSTRALIA. PARLIAMENT. (1975). *Schools Commission Act* 1973 (No. 213). *Acts of the Australian Parliament 1901–1973*, Vol. 10, pp. 667–675. Canberra: Australian Government Publishing Service.
AUSTRALIA. PARLIAMENT. HOUSE OF REPRESENTATIVES. (1974). *Schools Commission Bill* 1973 (Act No. 213 of 1973). *Parliamentary*

*Debates* [*Hansard*] Vol. H of R 85, 86, 87, 21 August 1973 to 13 December 1973. Canberra: Australian Government Printer. Sections beginning are: pp. 1635, 1982, 1999, 2018, 2026, 2069, 2072, 3705, 3934, 3947, 4332, 4337, 4647, 4649, 4758.

AUSTRALIA. PARLIAMENT. SENATE. (1974). *Schools Commission Bill 1973. Parliamentary Debates* [*Hansard*]. Vol. S 57 and 58, 21 August to 13 December 1973. Canberra: Australian Government Printer. Sections beginning are: pp. 1204, 1607, 1718, 1727, 1807, 1911, 1979, 2013, 2217, 2462, 2474, 2560, 2710, 2718, 2791.

AUSTRALIA. SCHOOLS COMMISSION. (1973). Correspondence from the Prime Minister and the Minister for Education to the Chairman of the Interim Committee for the Australian Schools Commission and address by the Minister for Education at the initial meeting of the Interim Committee for the Australian Schools Commission, Department of Education. 24pp.

## 2. Major reports

AUSTRALIA. SCHOOLS COMMISSION. (1973). *Schools in Australia. Report of the Interim Committee for the Australian Schools Commission.* (Chairman, P. Karmel). Canberra: Australian Government Publishing Service. 167pp.

AUSTRALIA. SCHOOLS COMMISSION. (1975). *Report for the Triennium 1976–78.* (Chairman, K. McKinnon). Canberra: Australian Government Publishing Service. 401pp.

AUSTRALIA. SCHOOLS COMMISSION. (1975). *Summary Report for the Triennium, 1976–78.* (Chairman, K. McKinnon). Canberra: Australian Government Publishing Service.

AUSTRALIA. SCHOOLS COMMISSION. (1975). *Report for 1976.* (Chairman, K. McKinnon). Canberra: Australian Government Publishing Service.

AUSTRALIA. SCHOOLS COMMISSION. (1976). *Report: Rolling Triennium 1977–79.* (Chairman, K. McKinnon). Canberra: Australian Government Publishing Service.

AUSTRALIA. SCHOOLS COMMISSION. (1977). *Report for Rolling Triennium 1978—80.* (Chairman, K. McKinnon). Canberra: Australian Government Publishing Service.

AUSTRALIA. SCHOOLS COMMISSION. (1978). *Report for the Triennium 1979–81.* (Chairman, K. McKinnon). Canberra: Australian Government Publishing Service.

## 3. Material published by the Schools Commission or under its auspices — including periodicals, newsletters, bibliographies, progress reports and directories.

AUSTRALIA. SCHOOLS COMMISSION. (1975). *Disadvantaged newsletter*, 1. Woden, ACT: Schools Commission. ISSN 0312–1976.

AUSTRALIA. SCHOOLS COMMISSION. *Formation of Area Review*

*Committees, new procedures for the Supplementary Grants Committee.* 6pp. (Available from the Education Subscription Service, document no. 04/46—6.)

AUSTRALIA. SCHOOLS COMMISSION. *Guidelines for evaluating innovations projects.* (Available from the Education Subscription Service, document no. 10/43.)

AUSTRALIA. SCHOOLS COMMISSION. (1975). Innovations News Exchange. *Innovation program: directory of Victorian projects.* Collingwood, Vic. ISSN 0312-8091.

AUSTRALIA. SCHOOLS COMMISSION. (1975). Innovations News Exchange. *Newsletter,* 1(1). Collingwood, Vic. ISSN 0312-8083.

AUSTRALIA. SCHOOLS COMMISSION. (1974). Media release. C. Brammall, *Social change and the education of women.* 2pp. (Background to forthcoming report on sexism in education.) (Available from the Education Subscription Service, document no. 05/33-2.)

AUSTRALIA. SCHOOLS COMMISSION. (1976). *National directory of innovations projects funded by the Schools Commission.* Canberra: Schools Commission. 166pp.

AUSTRALIA. SCHOOLS COMMISSION. (1974) *Newsletter,* 1. (Nos 3-5 available from the Education Subscription Service, document nos. 02/33, 04/41, 04/42.)

AUSTRALIA. SCHOOLS COMMISSION. (1975). *Non-Government Schools: statistics 1974.* Canberra: Schools Commission. 51pp.

AUSTRALIA. SCHOOLS COMMISSION. (1974-.). *Progress report on disadvantaged schools program.* Canberra: Schools Commission. 67pp.

AUSTRALIA. SCHOOLS COMMISSION. (1974-.). *Progress report on general building grants program.* Canberra: Schools Commission. 35pp.

AUSTRALIA. SCHOOLS COMMISSION. (1974-.). *Progress report on program administration.* Canberra: Schools Commission. 35pp.

AUSTRALIA. SCHOOLS COMMISSION. (1974-.). *Progress report on special education programme.* Canberra: Schools Commission. 28pp.

AUSTRALIA. SCHOOLS COMMISSION. (1975). *Residential accommodation for secondary school students.* (Project team, K. White et al.). Adelaide: South Australia Council for Educational Planning and Research. 94pp., 12 leaves, plans. Project sponsored and funded by the Australian Schools Commission.

AUSTRALIA. SCHOOLS COMMISSION. (1975). *State Grants [Schools] Act 1972-1974. Funds available and expenditure.* Canberra: Schools Commission. ISSN 0312-3960.

AUSTRALIA. SCHOOLS COMMISSION. (1975). *State Grants [Schools] Act 1972-1974. Annual report, 1974.* Canberra: Australian Government Publishing Service. ISSN 0312-780X.

AUSTRALIA. SCHOOLS COMMISSION. (1974). *Supplementary funds for programs administered by the Schools Commission: report to the Hon. K. E.*

*Beazley, M.P. Minister for Education.* Phillip, ACT: Schools Commission. 5pp., 3 leaves.

AUSTRALIA. SCHOOLS COMMISSION. (1976). Aboriginal Consultative Group. 'Aborigines and technical and further education: Aboriginal and islander views'. (Report by Aboriginal Consultative Group). In *Aboriginal Child at School*, 4: 3–19.

AUSTRALIA. SCHOOLS COMMISSION. (1975). Aboriginal Consultative Group. 'The Consultative Group's report', *Aboriginal News*, 2(1): 6–9.

AUSTRALIA. SCHOOLS COMMISSION. (1975). Aboriginal Consultative Group. *Education for Aborigines; report to the Schools Commission.* Canberra: Schools Commission. 34pp.

AUSTRALIA. SCHOOLS COMMISSION. Disadvantaged Schools Committee. *List of Grants.* (Available from the Education Subscription Service, document no. 02/37.)

AUSTRALIA. SCHOOLS COMMISSION. Innovation Programme. *Grants Lists A – L.* (Available from the Education Subscription Service.)

AUSTRALIA. SCHOOLS COMMISSION. (1976). Innovation Programme. *The Innovations Assembly Book.* Funded by the Schools Commission, P.O. Box 596, Haymarket, NSW. 1000 printed only. (Descriptions of about 70 innovations programs in NSW.)

AUSTRALIA. SCHOOLS COMMISSION. (1975). Innovation Programme. National Broadsheet. *Wallpaper 1.* (Available from the Education Subscription Service, document no. OP14.)

AUSTRALIA. SCHOOLS COMMISSION. (1974). National Innovations Committee. 'Schools Commission News', (summary of progress), *The magazine of education subscription service and the open book*, 3:6–7.

AUSTRALIA. SCHOOLS COMMISSION. (1974). Primary Schools' Libraries Committee. *Guidelines for library services in primary schools.* Canberra: Schools Commission. 29pp.

AUSTRALIA. SCHOOLS COMMISSION. Supplementary Grants Committee. *Newsletter and List of Grants*, (and further list of grants). (Available from the Education Subscription Service, document nos. 04/43 04/44.)

RANDELL, SHIRLEY K. and JENNIFER M. TURNBULL. (comps) (1976). *The school and the community: a bibliography.* Canberra: Schools Commission. 105pp.

TORSH, DANY, ROBYN DRYEN and MARTHA KAY. (comps) (1974). *A bibliography of social change and the education of women.* Woden, ACT: Schools Commission. 86pp.

## B. SECONDARY SOURCES

### 1. Material concerning the Schools Commission in general

### (a) Books and chapters in books

ALLWOOD, L.M. (Ed.) (1975). *Australian schools: the impact of the*

*Australian Schools Commission.* Melbourne: International Press and Publications. 161pp.

BASSETT, G.W. 'Innovation Programs'. In D'Cruz and Sheehan. (1978). *Renewal of Australian Schools.* (Second Edition). Hawthorn, Vic.: ACER, Ch. 13.

CHIPPENDALE, P.R. and PAULA V. WILKES. (Eds) (1977). *Accountability in education.* St. Lucia, Queensland: University of Queensland Press.

CRITTENDEN, B.S. (1974). 'Arguments and assumptions of the Karmel Report: a critique'. In D'Cruz and Sheehan. (1975 and 1978). op. cit. (First and Second Editions), Ch. 1. Also published in *20th Century,* **29**: 3–20.

CRITTENDEN, B.S. (1977). 'Equality and education'. In D'Cruz and Sheehan. (1978). op. cit. Ch. 14. Originally published in *Australian Journal of Education,* **21**(2): 113ff.

D'CRUZ, J.V. and P.J. SHEEHAN. (Eds) (1975). *The renewal of Australian schools: essays on educational planning in Australia after the Karmel Report.* Richmond, Victoria: Primary Education. 180pp. Also published as *20th Century,* **29**: 1–180.

D'CRUZ, J.V. and P.J. SHEEHAN (Eds) (1978). *The renewal of Australian schools: a changing perspective in educational planning.* Second and enlarged edition. Hawthorn, Vic.: ACER.

D'CRUZ, J.V. 'Accountability in education: the concept and its implications'. In D'Cruz and Sheehan. (Eds) (1975 and 1978). op. cit., Chapters 6 and 8 respectively. Also published in *20th Century,* **29**: 97–173.

D'CRUZ, J.V. and P.J. SHEEHAN. 'Culture and the Schools Commission in educational renewal'. In D'Cruz and Sheehan. (Eds) (1978). op. cit. Introduction.

D'CRUZ, J.V. 'Towards an inclusive notion of accountability'. In Chippendale, P.R. and Paula V. Wilkes (Eds) (1977). *Accountability in education.* St. Lucia, Queensland: University of Queensland Press, Ch. 15.

KEEVES, J.P. 'Approaches to the goal of educational opportunity: will the Karmel Report work?'. In D'Cruz and Sheehan. (Eds) (1975 and 1978). op. cit., Chapters 4 and 6 respectively. Also published in *20th Century,* **29**: 59–76.

KEEVES, J.P. 'The needs of education in Australian schools'. In D'Cruz and Sheehan. (Eds) (1975 and 1978). op. cit., Chapters 2 and 4 respectively. Also published in *20th Century,* **29**: 38–58.

KEEVES, J.P. and J.K. MATTHEWS. 'Youth: Transition from school to work — an emerging problem'. In D'Cruz and Sheehan. (Eds) (1978). op. cit., Chapter 15.

MATTHEWS, J.K. and J.P. KEEVES. 'Renewal in Australian education: a changing prospect'. In D'Cruz and Sheehan. (Eds) (1978). op. cit., Chapter 11.

MORTENSEN, K.G. 'Finance for independent schooling'. In D'Cruz and Sheehan. (Eds) (1975 and 1978). op. cit., Chapters 8 and 10 respectively. Also published in *20th Century*, **29**: 135–159.

MUSGRAVE, P.W. 'Changing society: some underlying assumptions of the Karmel Report'. In D'Cruz and Sheehan. (Eds) (1978). op. cit., Chapter 2. Originally published in *Australian Journal of Education*, **19**: 1–14.

MUSGRAVE, P.W. 'Teachers, the public and educational change'. In D'Cruz and Sheehan. (Eds) (1975 and 1978). op. cit., Chapters 2 and 5 respectively. Also published in *20th Century*, **29**: 23–37.

SELBY SMITH, C. 'The macro-economics of educational renewal'. In D'Cruz and Sheehan. (Eds) (1975 and 1978). op. cit., Chapters 7 and 9 respectively. Also published in *20th Century*, **29**: 117–132.

SHEEHAN, P.J. 'The renewal programme after the Karmel Report'. In D'Cruz and Sheehan. (Eds) (1975). op. cit., Chapter 9. Also published in *20th Century*, **29**: 163–80.

SHEEHAN, P.J. and J.V. D'CRUZ. 'Some key issues for the future in Australian schools'. In D'Cruz and Sheehan (Eds) (1978). op. cit., Chapter 16.

TOWNSEND, H.E.R. 'Towards a multicultural society'. Paper given at the Fink Memorial Seminar, University of Melbourne, 1975. In Stephen Murray-Smith. (Ed.) (1976). *Melbourne Studies in Education 1976*. Melbourne: Melbourne University Press, pp. 28–40.

TURNER, MERV. 'The McKinnon prescription'. In D'Cruz and Sheehan. (1978). op. cit., Chapter 12. Originally published in *Arena*, **40**: 101–11.

WALKER, W.G. 'Autonomy and control in educational renewal'. In D'Cruz and Sheehan. (1975 and 1978). op. cit., Chapters 5 and 7 respectively.

WHITE, DOUG. 'Create your own compliance: the Karmel prospect'. In D'Cruz and Sheehan. (1978). op. cit., Chapter 3. Originally published in *Arena*, **32/33**: 35–48.

## (b) Journal articles

'Aboriginal education: the Schools Commission's views', *Aboriginal News*, **2**(1): 5.

'Activating the Karmel plan', *Parents & Citizen*, **25**(5): 8.

'An analysis of the progress of the Schools Commission', *Associate News*, **8**(9): 3–4.

ANDREWS, R.J. (1973). 'The Karmel Report and special education in Australia', *Slow Learning Child*, **20**(3): 154–159.

'APC submission to the Schools Commission', *APC Review*, **11**: 6–7.

BARCAN, A. (1975). 'Equality and funding', *ACES Review*, **2**(7): 7–8.

BASSETT, G.W. (1975). (Review) *The renewal of Australian schools: essays on educational planning in Australia after the Karmel report*, J.V. D'Cruz and

P.J. Sheehan (Eds). In *The Journal of Educational Administration* **13**(2): 108–109.

BLACKBURN, JEAN. (1975). Australian Government policies to schools (ATF Convention paper). *Teacher Feedback*, **3**: 27–34.

BLAZELY, L.D. 'The innovations programme: a system view'. (Paper presented at MTMA Evaluating Educational Innovation Conference, Melbourne, May 1975). *Modern Teaching*, **32**.

BLOCH, C. (1975). 'Schools Commission looks at sexism', *Quest*, **17**: 48–9.

BROWN, L.M. (1975). 'Politics of education: the Schools Commission Report', *Independent Education*, **5**(2): 1–9.

BROWN, W.L. (1973). Editorial. *Australian Library Journal*, **22**: 289–290.

CATCHLOVE, J.E. (1975). 'Schools Commission Innovation Project: report on film-making for primary schools', *Society for Mass Media and Resource Technology Journal*, **5**(1): 13–17.

CHADBOURNE, ROD. (1975). 'Social justice and the Australian Schools Commission', *Graylands Educational News*, **10**: 75–80.

CLARK, E.P. (1974). Editorial. 'The Schools Commission', *Queensland Teachers Journal*, **79**: 2–3.

CONNORS, L. (1976). (Review) *National directory of innovations funded by the Schools Commission*. In *Education News*, **15**(10): 60–61.

'Department acts on Karmel recommendation', *Western Teacher*, **3**(7): 1.

DYER, DAVID and JAMES LITTLETON. (1973). 'The Karmel Report. Parts 1 and 2', illus., *Annals '73*, **84**: 25–28, 30–32.

EDWARDS, E.F. (1973). 'Karmel Report brings change to Association', *Welfare News*, November 1973, pp. 1, 7.

EVANS, N.R. (1975). 'The procrustean obsession', *ACES Review*, **2**(8): 6–7, 10, 16.

EVANS, R. (1973). 'In the wake of Karmel', *Western Teacher*, **2**(12):2.

FEE, RICHARD W. (1976). 'Parental involvement and participation: a follow up study of disadvantaged schools', *Innovations News Exchange Newsletter*, **5**: 8–9, 16.

GILDING, JACK. (1974). 'The advantages of being disadvantaged', *The magazine of the education subscription service and the open book*, **4**: 10–11.

GILDING, JACK. (1975). (Review) *Schools Commission Report for the triennium 1976–78*. In *The magazine of the educational subscription service and the open book*, **9**:8.

GILDING, JACK. (1975). 'Supported schools (Report for the triennium 1976–1978)', *The magazine of the educational subscription service and the open book*,**10**; 8.

HERBISON, J.M. (1976). (Review) *Girls, school and society: report by a study group*. In *Journal of Educational Administration*, **14**(2): 282–283.

HINKSON, JOHN. (1974). 'Community, and confinement: new directions in educational planning', *Arena*, **35**: 15–22.

HOLDAWAY, E.A. (1976). 'Federal initiatives in education in Australia: Have they implications for Canada?', *Education Canada*, **16**(3): 4–13.

HUGHES, G. (1975). 'The curate's egg', *ACES Review*, **2**(7): 10–16.

JENNINGS, R. (1973). 'Reflections on the Karmel Report', *Educational Magazine*, **31**(2): 40–46.

JEPSON, DENISE. (1976). 'Women's education and feminism', *Arena*, **44/45**: 8–13.

JOHNSTON, G.L. (1973). 'Planning for educational equality', *Education News*, **14**(3–4): 29–32.

JONES, A.W. (1974). 'Schools in Australia. An analysis of the Report of the Interim Committee for the Australian Schools Commission (Chairman: P. Karmel)', *Developing Education*, **2**(1): 1–10.

'The Karmel Committee Report. A synopsis', *Independent Education*, **3**(3): 5–20.

KING, R.B. (1974). 'An inquiry into the Karmel Report's perspective on equality and education', *Education Research and Perspectives*, **1**(1): 38–48.

KIRKALDY, J. (1976). 'Planners come under strong attack', *Times Educational Supplement* no. 3193 (13 August 1976) p. 8.

KIRKALDY, J. (1975). 'Schools Commission urges major spending', *Times Educational Supplement* no. 3133 (13 June 1975) p. 13.

LENAHAN, R. (1973). 'Implications of the Karmel report for Queensland education', Australian College of Education. Queensland Chapter. Newsletter, **12** (August 1973): 7–8.

McAULEY, J. (1975). 'A blueprint for ockers', *ACES Review*, **2**(7): 3–4, 8.

McCULLOCH, RAY. W. (1975) 'The Karmel Report, the School resource centre and the librarian's role', *Australian School Librarian*, **12**(2): 5–11.

McDONALD, E.M.A. (1976). (Review). *Girls, school and society: report by a study group*. In *South Pacific Journal of Teacher Education*, **4**(3): 272–275.

MacDONALD, MARION. 'Suspense for the private schools', *Bulletin*, 28 July 1973, pp. 14, 17.

McKINLAY, BRIAN. (1973). 'The Karmel Report', *Primary Education*, **4**(8): 5.

McKINLAY, BRIAN. (1975). (Review). *The renewal of Australian schools; essays on educational planning after the Karmel report*, J.V. D'Cruz and P.J. Sheehan (Eds). In (Victorian) *Teachers' Journal*, **1**(5): 11.

McKINNON, K.R. (1974) A.T.F. Annual Meeting, Brisbane, 8 January 1974. 'Prospects for the Schools Commission', *Queensland Teachers' Journal*, **79**(1): 6–10. Also in *Western Teacher*, **3**(1): 10.

McKINNON, K.R. (1976). 'The innovations and teacher development programs of the Schools Commission', *South Pacific Journal of Teacher Education*, **4**(3): 213–219.

McLEAN-WILLIAMS, IAIN. (1973). 'New name wanted?', *Welfare News*, November 1973, p.2.

'A major breakthrough by Federation', *Education* (NSW), **54**(11): 165, 175.

MARTIN, F.M. (1975). (Review). *The renewal of Australian schools: essays on educational planning in Australia after the Karmel report*, J.V. D'Cruz and P.J. Sheehan (Eds). In *Victorian Catholic Education Bulletin*, **8**(4): 7–9.

MATTHEWS, J.K. and R.T. FITZGERALD. (1975). 'Educational policy and political platform: the Australian Labor Government', *Australian Education Review*, **7**(4): 1–70.

MOORE, SUSAN. (1976). 'Anti-intellectualism in the Schools Commission Report', *Forum of Education*, **35**(1): 48–51.

MORTENSEN, K.G. (1973). 'Education and family economics', *News-Weekly*, no. 1527 (8 August 1973) pp. 8–9.

MORTENSEN, K.G. (1973). 'Implications. Karmel Report', *The Advocate*, 30 August 1973, pp. 13–14.

MUSGRAVE, P.W. (1974). 'Education as an active agent in changing society'. In *Australian College of Education. Western Australian Chapter. Conference.* Bunbury, W.A., 22–24 March, 1974. Reprinted *Unicorn*, **1**(1) 17–27.

NOVICK, D. (1975). 'Innovations projects, why evaluate?', *Pivot*, **2**(2): 20–21.

'Progress report on program administration: Schools Commission 1974–75 programs', *Developing Education*, **2**(6): 2–22, 31–35.

'Progress report on program administration: Schools Commission 1974–75 programs, Canberra, December 1974', *Teacher Librarian*, **39**: 30–35.

PUSEY, M. (1976). 'Innovating: a profile of the Schools Commission Innovations Program', *Education News*, **15**(10): 4–13.

REID, G. (1974). 'Karmel ignored', *Secondary Teacher*, **195**: 21–28.

ROPER, TOM. (1973). 'The Karmel Report: Australia's education priority areas', *Brotherhood Action*, **201**: 6–7.

SAMPSON, S.N. and LYNDSAY CONNORS. (1977). (Review article). *Girls, school and society.* 'Part 1: An overview', by S.N. Sampson. 'Part 2: The teacher's responsibility', by Lyndsay Connors. In *Education News*, **16**(1): 30–33.

SAMUEL, PETER. (1974). 'Education: new thoughts on school aid', *Bulletin*, 10 May 1974, pp. 20, 23.

SAMUEL, PETER. (1975). 'The great schools fiasco', *Bulletin*, 20 September 1975, pp. 14, 17.

SAMUEL, PETER. (1976). 'The "slow learners" aren't dunces', *Bulletin*, 30 October 1976, pp. 19–20.

SAMUEL, PETER. (1975). 'Vouchers and the ASC', *ACES Review*, **2**(7): 5–6.

'Schools Commission innovations program', *Western Teacher*, **3**(3): 10.

'Schools Commission members named', *Parent & Citizen*, **25**(1): 1.

'The Schools Commission report and its implications for Victorian

Schools'. Comments from the Director General, *News Exchange*, **12**, (1975).

SCHOOLS COMMISSION STUDY GROUP. (1974). 'The school in the community', *The magazine of the education subscription service and the open book*, 5:1–15. Special Issue. Contents: Background — p.2; Press release — p.3; Working papers — 1. Jack Gilding, 'Schools Commission study on school and community', pp.3–6, 2. Marion D. Tenezakis, 'Some thoughts on "Options for funding"', pp.6–7. 3. Gerry Tickell, 'The community in the curriculum', pp.7–9, 4. Evan Walker, 'Architectural implications of community use of schools', pp.9–15.

'Schools Commission TAFE reports: covering 1976–78 triennium', *Western Teacher*, 4(6): 2–3.

SEGALL, PATSY and R.T. FITZGERALD. (1974). *Finance for education in Australia: an analysis*. In *Australian Education Review* (formerly *Quarterly Review of Australian Education*), 6(4): 1–77.

SHARP, RACHEL. (1976). 'Girls, school and society — a review', *Refractory Girl*, **11**: 38–40.

'Specific ideas presented to the Schools Commission', *Panorama* (Tasmanian Education Department) 1(2): 18–20.

SMITH, THOMAS. (1977). 'The Aboriginal Consultative Group; a new development in aboriginal education', *Identity*, 3(1): 24–25.

STREAT, W.L. (1974). 'New wine, old bottles' (Address at Australian Teachers Federation, National Convention of Teachers, Sydney, 16 January 1975), *Western Teacher*, 4(2): 10–11.

STREAT, W.L. (1975). 'The Schools Commission Innovations Programme', *Modern Teaching*, **32**. 13pp. Paper presented at the Modern Teaching Methods Association Evaluating Educational Innovations Conference, 1975.

TRAVERS, B.H. (1976). 'Government interference in education' (Paper given to the Seminar on Educational Justice, Sydney, 1976), *APC Review*, **11** (August 1976) pp. 10–12.

WARD, JOHN. (1973). 'The Australian Schools Commission Interim Report', *School Libraries in Australia*, 2(3): 3–4.

WATT, A.J. (1976). 'Freedom of choice: for whom? A point of view', *Journal of Educational Administration*, 14(2): 261–269.

WAUGH, PAM. (1976). 'Girls, school and society', *Education* (NSW), 57(9): 161.

'[W.A. Teachers] Union discusses Karmel Report', *Western Teacher*, 2(13): 1,3.

WYNHAUSEN, ELISABETH. (1973). 'Anomalies in grant system', *Bulletin*, 18 August 1973, pp.18, 20.

ZLOTNIK, MIKE. (1974). '35 in a kindergarten class? Well, I think it's criminal', *Teachers' Journal*, 1(1): 641–644.

**(c) Newspaper articles**

ANWYL, J. (1973). 'Has Karmel Report enemies in those hidden corridors?', *Age*, 28 August 1973, p.14.

BESSANT, BOB. (1974). 'Education report "for elite"', *Age*, 28 March 1974, p.13.

CHARLESWORTH, MAX. (1975). 'Karmel — revolution or flop?' (Review of D'Cruz and Sheehan (1975) op. cit.), *Catholic Worker*, **461**: 16.

CLARK, ANDREW. (1975). 'Beazley: even if Labor loses, his education programme will continue', *National Times*, 7–12 July 1975, p.12.

CLARK, ANDREW. (1975). 'Schools are getting too much too fast: doubts on education plans', *National Times*, 28 April—3 May 1975.

'Concern on Karmel funds', *Canberra Times*, 15 July 1974, p.6.

CONNORS, LYNDSAY. (1976). 'Education still needs big money or the tiny gains will be lost', *National Times*, 26 April–1 May 1976, p.19.

DALE, DAVID. (1975). 'What progressive education aims to do for your child', *National Times*, 22–27 September 1975, pp.24–25.

DOYLE, JOHN. (1975). 'Evaluating the Karmel report' (Review of *Twentieth Century* **29**, later published as D'Cruz and Sheehan (Eds) (1975). op. cit.), *Catholic Leader*, 13–19 April 1975.

DUFFY, D. (1974). 'Critical needs in schools (Karmel Report's inadequate consideration of curriculum development)', *Courier-Mail*, 21 May 1974, p.8.

GILDING, JACK. (1974). 'Funding from the Schools Commission', *Learning Exchange*, **13**: 4.

GOLD, R. (1975). 'Ectoplasm after the Karamel' (Review of D'Cruz and Sheehan (Eds) (1975) op. cit.), *Nation Review*, 23–29 May 1975, p.840.

GOLDMAN, RONALD. (1973). 'It's a great leap forward for Australian schools', *Age*, 5 June 1973, p.21.

HAYDEN, CHRISTOPHER. (1973). 'Report seeks $660 m. for schools', *Canberra Times*, 31 May 1973, pp.1, 29.

HILL, BARRY. (1975). 'High and low marks for schools report', *Age*, 12 June 1975, p.8.

HILL, BARRY. (1973). 'Karmel — Federal Fabian of schools', *Age*, 12 June 1973, p.19.

HILL, BARRY. (1975). 'Realities of financing our school system' (Review of D'Cruz and Sheehan (Eds) (1975) op. cit.), *Age*, 31 May 1975, p.15.

HILL, BARRY. 'Schools Commission in flight meets pressure from ground', *Age*, 20 February 1973, p.15.

HILL, TONY. (1973). 'How St. Paul's Frankston, got into the same class as Geelong Grammar' *Herald* (Melbourne) 10 August 1973, p.4.

HOLMES, JEAN. (1975). 'Karmel report: are we getting value for money?' (Review of D'Cruz and Sheehan (Eds) (1975) op. cit.), *The Advocate*, June 5 1975.

HUGHES, G.E.F. (1973). 'The great leveller: education — Labor style. A

Liberal look at the Karmel report', *Australian Financial Review*, 5 July 1973, pp.2–4.

HUGHES, G.E.F. (1974). 'Karmel report a hollow triumph', *Australian Financial Review*, 14 June 1974, pp.12, 14.

HURLEY, TOM. (1975). 'School as education?', *Catalyst*, 27 October 1975, p.5.

JOHNS, BRIAN. (1973). 'State aid: setting the battle line', *Sydney Morning Herald*, 30 November 1973, p.6.

JONES, K.D. (1974). 'Autonomy for ACT government schools', *Canberra Times*, 7 August 1974, p.2.

JUDDERY, BRUCE. (1975). 'New schools policy taking shape', *Canberra Times*, 15 March 1973, p.2.

'Karmel made 73 Australia's "most significant year" ', *Australian Financial Review*, 9 January 1974, p.5.

KELLY, PAUL. (1976). 'The crisis in Catholic education', *National Times*, 23–28 August 1976, p.15.

KELLY, PAUL. (1973). 'School heads fail the Karmel test', *Australian*, 6 September 1973, p.11.

KELLY, PAUL. (1973). 'Tough delivery for Kim Beazley's baby; friends fall out over the Schools Commission', *Australian*, 28 November 1973, p.11.

KNIGHT, T. (1975). 'Our schools must change to give all a real choice', *Age*, 18 June 1975, p.22.

KOVACS, Z. (1974). 'Quality in education' (Interview with Professor P. Tannock), *West Australian*, 27 May 1974, p.12.

KRAMER, LEONIE. (1975). 'A recipe for lower school standards', *Sydney Morning Herald*, 25 August 1975, p.6.

McKINNON, K.R. (1975). 'Seeking quality and equality in education and opposing the doctrine of inherited privilege', *Sydney Morning Herald*, 21 August 1975, p.6.

McLEAN, DONALD. (1973). 'The other side of the Karmel report', *Sydney Morning Herald*, 23 August 1973, p.7

MATHEWS, IOLA. (1973). 'Two problems sitting on Kim Beazley's lap', *Age*, 14 August 1973, p.12.

'Report urges more say for schools', *Sydney Morning Herald*, 4 June 1975, p.8.

ROPER, TOM. (1973). 'Big disparity in private schools', *Nation Review*, 10–16 August 1973, p.1334.

ROPER, TOM. (1973). 'Karmel report: what's in it for schools', ibid., p.1354.

SCHOENHEIMER, HENRY. (1974). 'Do you want $20,000?' (Australian Schools Commission's Innovations Programme), *Australian*, 18 February 1974, p.8.

SCHOENHEIMER, HENRY. (1973). 'Keeping the Karmel study in perspective', *Australian*, 21 August 1973, p.10.

SCHOENHEIMER, HENRY. (1973). Review (of Karmel Report), *Australian*, 5 June 1973, p.8.

SHEARS, L. and A. SCOTT. (1973). Review (of Karmel Report), *Age*, 19 June 1973, p.13.

SIMSON, STUART. (1975). 'Education chews up the $$$$$', *Australian Financial Review*, 9 May 1975, pp.2–3.

SMITH, GEORGE T. (1973). 'The great upraiser: a teacher's look at the Karmel Report, education — Labor style', *Australian Financial Review*, 24 July 1973, pp.2–3, 6.

TRANTER, B.C. (1975). 'Education and the Karmel Committee' (Review of D'Cruz and Sheehan (Eds) (1975) op. cit.), *Newsweekly*, 14 May 1975, p.10.

TRENGOVE, ALAN. (1975). 'Money is not the answer' (Review of D'Cruz and Sheehan (Eds) (1975) op. cit.), *Sun*, 26 March 1975.

WARNEKE, ROSS. (1975). 'Education spending boom under question as another report goes to Parliament: the school stocktaking', *Age*, 3 June 1975, p.9.

WARNEKE, ROSS. (1975). 'Exciting project for neglected Richmond', *Age*, 28 April 1975, p.9.

WARNEKE, ROSS. (1974). 'School aid scheme backfires (Karmel money to private schools)', *Age*, 12 December 1974, p.9.

WARNEKE, ROSS. (1975). 'What the Schools Commission report said: massive state aid proposed', *Age*, 4 June 1975, p.12.

WATSON, PETER. (1975). 'A commission's credo', *Australian*, 9 September 1975, p.18.

WILLIAMS, GRAHAM. (1973). 'Pity the poor little rich school', *Australian*, 29 November 1973, p.13.

WILLIAMS, GRAHAM. (1973). 'Questions go a-begging in Karmel report', *Australian*, 3 July 1973, p.9.

**(d) Reports, conference papers, submissions**

BLACKBURN, J. (1974). The role of the Schools Commission in developing a contemporary strategy for Australian education. (Paper presented at the Australian Unesco Seminar, 'Learning to be', Canberra, 1974).

EDGAR, DON. (1975). *The Schools Commission and rural disadvantage*. (La Trobe Sociology Paper no. 33). Bundoora, Vic.: La Trobe University, School of Social Sciences, Department of Sociology.

GOODMAN, DOREEN. (1976). 'Policy of the Schools Commission on school library development'. In Library Association of Australia. 18th Biennial Conference, August 1975, Melbourne. *Proceedings*. Melbourne: Conference Committee. pp.133–143.

NEW SOUTH WALES TEACHER'S FEDERATION. (1974). *Submission to the Australian Schools Commission for the 1976–78 triennium* (compiled by C.M. Adams). Sydney: NSW Teachers Federation. 42pp.

NORTH EASTERN COMMUNITY SCHOOL. (1975). *Submission to the Schools Commission [Supported Schools]*. (Available from the Education Subscription Service, document no. 10/41.)

PARENTS AND FRIENDS' FEDERATION OF VICTORIA. (1973). *Karmel Report recomendations: a comment on some of the financial aspects of the Report, especially as they affect non-government schools*. Fitzroy, Vic. (various pagings).

VICTORIA. COMMITTEE OF INQUIRY INTO SPECIAL EDUCATION IN VICTORIA. (1973). *Special education in Victoria. The implications for the Education Department, Victoria, of the Report of the Interim Committee for the Australian Schools Commission, May 1973*. Interim Report of the Ministerial Committee of Inquiry into Special Education in Victoria. (Chairman: R.L. Senior). Melbourne: Education Department. 84pp.

VICTORIAN FEDERATION OF STATE SCHOOL MOTHERS' CLUBS. (1974). *Submission to the Australian Schools Commission for the 1976–78 report from Victorian Federation of State School Mothers' Clubs and Victorian Council of School Organizations*. Melbourne. 35pp.

## 2. Program descriptions

**A select list of journal articles describing innovative schools in general or particular innovative programs in schools that have been wholly or in part funded by the Schools Commission.**

BRICKEN, BILL. (1973). 'Coonara children's community: some information', *The Open Book*, **2**.

Brunswick Girls High School cross age tutoring program. *Report to the Myer Foundation*, 5 May 1974, by Roger Holdsworth. (Available from the Education Subscription Service, document no. 03/34.)

CLAYDON, L.F. (Ed) (1974). *Open schooling: parents in limbo. B.Ed. Task Force Report No. 2*. Prepared by the Task Force Team at Collingwood High School. Bundoora: La Trobe University, School of Education. 110pp.

DUNSTAN, A.F. (1973). 'Wagaman Open School (Northern Territory)', *Developing Education*, **1**(2): 15–16.

FITZROY VOCATIONAL EDUCATION CENTRE. Getting close — Part 1, F.V.E.C. at F.C.Y., 1974. Melbourne State College, Team 9. 8pp. (Available from the Education Subscription Service, document no. 06/46–8. Also Part 2, (document no. 06/47–8.) )

GILDING, JACK. (1975). 'Education Centres (NSW)', *The magazine of the education subscription service and the open book*, **8**: 16.

GILL, PRUE. (1973). 'Involving parents at Brunswick Girls' High', *Secondary Teacher*, **190**: 15–16.

'Glebe Primary School, NSW', *Current Affairs Bulletin*, **50**(4) 8–9.

HAMEL-GREEN, F. (1975). 'Innovations — on the way out?', *Associate News*, **9**(20): 12–13.

HILL, B. 'Brunswick Girls High School, Victoria', *Current Affairs Bulletin*, 50(4): 7–8.

HORTLE, R.E. and G.H. PAGE. (1972). 'Open planning (at Geilston Bay High School, Tasmania)', *Tasmanian Journal of Education*, 6(4): 97–100.

JAGGS, WILLIAM. (1975). 'English is not enough: the bilingual program at Brunswick Girls High School, Melbourne', *Education News*, 15(2/3): 42–43.

MILNE, C. (1974). 'Community will be classroom (Elizabeth High School)', *Advertiser*, 23 May 1974. p.6.

MORELAND HIGH SCHOOL. (1974). Papers relating to the workout program, 1971–1974. Coburg, Vic. 6pp. (Available from the Education Subscription Service, document no. 05/42–6.)

NATHAN, PAM. (1976). *The Diamond Valley Learning Centre*. Occasional Paper. Bundoora, Vic.: Innovation Centre, School of Education, La Trobe University.

NOYCE, PHIL. (1975). 'A sub-school? It can be done (Fawkner High School)', *Secondary Teacher*, 14: 9–10.

PARA HILLS HIGH SCHOOL. (1975). *Para Hills '75: a continuing development in open-space education*. Para Hills, South Australia. 64pp.

PENNANT HILLS COMMUNITY RESOURCE CENTRE COMMITTEE. (1974). *Proposal for a community resource centre at Pennant Hills, NSW*. Beecroft.

PETTIT, DAVID. (1974). *Huntingdale Technical School — an introduction*. Hawthorn, Vic.: Australian Council for Educational Research.

RUSSELL, N. (1974). 'School without walls. Out of the classroom and into the workplace', *Canberra Times*, 1 April 1974. p.2.

SEALEY, BOB, BARRIE FENBY and ANNE KORAB. (1975). 'A study of examples of curriculum innovations', *Curriculum and Research Bulletin*, 10(2): 42–52. (Ballam Park Tech., Geelong College, Fish Creek Primary, Clifton Hill Primary, Williamstown Tech.)

SMYTH, G. (1973). 'New look schools (a report); Neill Street Primary School, Sydney Road Community School, South Yarra Annexe, Nathalia High School, Thomastown High School, Ferntree Gully High School, Shepparton South Technical School, Swinburne Community School', *Educational Magazine*, 30(4): 2–16.

'Special grant for school project' ($15,000 for School Without Walls), *Canberra Times*, 24 August 1974. p.3.

TRUEMAN, P. and J. AMBRENS. (1974). *Report on 'PLART': a school holiday activity programme held at Richmond Technical College*. Richmond, Vic. (Available from the Education Subscription Service, document no. 02-46.)

*'Victoria: An alternative community school in Fitzroy? A draft proposal'*, *The Open Book* 5: 6–10.

VICTORIA. EDUCATION DEPARTMENT. Curriculum and Research Branch. (1973). *Multi-purpose workshop programme. Ballam Park Technical*

*School, Term 3, 1973*, by I. Gordon. (Curriculum evaluation case study no. 1). Melbourne: Education Department. 14pp.

WILLIAMS, G. (1975). 'School's out and working. (Marist Brothers High School, Kogarah)', *Australian*, 13 November 1975, p.11.

WRIGHT, BRUCE. (1973). 'Democratic practice at Monterey Technical School', *Secondary Teacher*, **187**: 22–23.

YOUNG, J. (1973). 'Living in the community: Kibbutz life at Huntingdale Technical School', *Study of Society*, **4**(3): 6–7.

ZOË COMMUNITY SCHOOL, HOBART. (1975). 'Zoë: an experiment in education', *University of Tasmania Newsletter*, **17**: 6–7.